THE LUTHERAN CHURCH
IN COLONIAL AMERICA

THE
LUTHERAN CHURCH
IN
COLONIAL AMERICA

By

LARS P. QUALBEN, Ph.D., Th.D.
St. Olaf College
Author of *A History of the Christian Church*

WIPF & STOCK · Eugene, Oregon

Wipf and Stock Publishers
199 W 8th Ave, Suite 3
Eugene, OR 97401

The Lutheran Church in Colonial America
By Qualben, Lars P.
ISBN 13: 978-1-60608-135-8
Publication date 01/31/2009
Previously published by Thomas Nelson, 1940

PREFACE

These chapters have been prepared as a part of a more extensive treatise to be published, it is hoped, in the near future, but the author has yielded to requests that this material be published now. A study of these pages should help the reader to a better knowledge of his spiritual ancestry and to a fuller appreciation of the Lutheran Church in America. This again should make for better and more intelligent church membership.

Lutherans are not late arrivals here in America. They played a relatively important role in the development of Colonial America, and they took their share in the fight for independence. The Lutheran Church is deeply rooted in the past, and yet inspired by an ardent idealism for the future. As the third largest Protestant body in America, the Lutheran Church should play an important part in the affairs of this land of destiny. The best contribution the Lutheran Church can make is to develop along the lines of inherent and latent characteristics and possibilities.

May the study of these chapters help the student into midstream, as it were, of the great life and thought of this historic Church.

THE AUTHOR

CONTENTS

PREFACE v

MAPS AND DIAGRAMS .... ix-x

INTRODUCTION 1
    1. Definition. Scope and Divisions. 2. Value of This Study.

CHAPTER I. THE AMERICAN LUTHERAN ANCESTRY 7
    I. Roots in the Old Testament. II. Firmly Grounded in the New Testament. III. Relation to Subsequent Church Development. IV. The Lutheran Reformation. V. Lutheranism according to Luther. VI. Later Lutheran Developments: 1. Tradition. 2. The Concord Movement. 3. Orthodoxy. 4. Mysticism. 5. Pietism. 6. Rationalism. 7. Schleiermacher. 8. Ritschl. 9. Summary.

CHAPTER II. LUTHERANS IN COLONIAL DAYS, 1492-1763   111
    I. The Significance of American Colonization. II. The Spanish Settlements: 1. Lutherans in Venezuela, 1528. 2. French Lutherans (Huguenots) in Brazil, 1555. 3. French Lutherans (Huguenots) in Florida, 1562-65. III. The French in North America. IV. English, Dutch and Swedish Colonization of North America: 1. Episcopalianism Transplanted to Virginia, 1607. 2. Congregationalism Established at New Plymouth, 1620. 3. Arrival of the Dutch Reformed, 1623. 4. Lutheranism Transplanted to New Netherland, 1623. 5. Swedish Settlement on the Delaware, 1638. 6. Establishment of other Protestant Groups in America in Colonial Times. V. Lutheranism in America, 1664-1700: 1. James Island, South Carolina, 1674. 2. New York. 3. New Jersey. 4. New Sweden. 5. German Lutherans in Pennsylvania before 1700. 6. Other Lutheran Settlements before 1700. 7. Retrospect. VI. Lutheranism in America, 1700-1742: 1. Eclipse of the Swedish-Finnish Churches. 2. The Falckner Brothers. 3. Early Palatine Immigration: a. The Small Palatine Immigration of 1708. b. The Large Palatine Immigration of 1709. 4. Later German Immigration: a. Pennsylvania. b. New York and New Jersey. c. New England. d. Maryland and

Virginia. e. North and South Carolina. f. Georgia. 5. Palatine Contributions. 6. The First Lutheran Synod in America, 1735. 7. The Great Awakening, 1734-44. 8. Forerunners of Muhlenberg. VII. From the Coming of Muhlenberg to the American Revolution, 1742-63: 1. Muhlenberg's Years of Preparation. 2. Early Pastoral Work in Pennsylvania. 3. Organization of the Second Lutheran Synod in America, 1748. 4. Constitution for St. Michael's Lutheran Church, 1762. 5. A Native Lutheran Clergy. 6. Muhlenberg's Views and Contributions. VIII. Early Lutheran Education. IX. Lutherans in Canada. X. Retrospect. XI. Appendices: 1. Constitution of the First Lutheran Synod in America, 1735. 2. Zinzendorf versus Muhlenberg, 1742. 3. The Liturgy of 1748. 4. Constitution for St. Michael's Lutheran Church, 1762. 5. Constitution of the Second Lutheran Synod in America, 1781.

CHAPTER III. LUTHERANS AND THE ESTABLISHMENT OF THE AMERICAN NATION, 1763-89 237

I. General Development in England. II. Developments in the Thirteen Colonies. III. Conditions Leading to Revolution: 1. General Trends. 2. The Religious Problem. 3. The Economic Problem. 4. The Political Problem. 5. The Problem of Unification. IV. The American Churches and the War: 1. The Established Church. 2. The Congregational Church. 3. The Presbyterian Church. 4. The Roman Catholic Church. 5. The Baptist Church. 6. The Wesleyans or Methodists. 7. Quakers, Mennonites and Moravians. 8. The Lutheran Church. V. Two Prominent Lutheran Leaders: 1. Henry Melchior Muhlenberg. 2. John Hanson, First President of the United States in Congress Assembled. VI. Other Lutheran Contributors. VII. Conclusion.

MAPS AND DIAGRAMS

	PAGE
1. Branches of Church History	3
2. Resources of the *homo sapiens*	10
3. How Jewish and Pagan People Met and Separated in Christ	11
4. Psyche-Soma: Personality	15
5. Divine and Human Elements in Christ and the Bible	15
6. Diagram of Resurrection Theories	21
7. Development of the Myth	22
8. The "Hot Spot" of the Myth	23
9. Spiritual Levels for the Disciples	30
10. The Growth of Christianity, A.D. 30-68 and 68-100	34
11. The Spread of Christianity Eastward	35
12. The Great Christian Centers in the Apostolic Age	37
13. Early Catechetical School Centers	38
14. The Relation between Apostolic Council, Galatians, Romans and the Protestant Reformation	39
15. The Official Relation between Apostles, Deacons and Elders	40
16. The Chief Offices in the Apostolic Church	42
17. The Roman Empire, A.D. 100	44
18. Where is the Church?	47
19. Periods in Church History	48
20. Location of the Five Patriarchs	50
21. Parallel Organization of State and Church	51
22. The Three General Ancient Symbols	52
23. European Monasteries about A.D. 1300	55
24. Apostolic and Catholic Christianity Compared	56
25. Map Illustrating the Life of Luther	59

MAPS AND DIAGRAMS

26. Location of Chief European Universities Founded before A.D. 1500 61
27. The Essence of Morality as Luther Understood It .. 65
28. Europe on the Accession of Emperor Charles V, A.D. 1519 67
29. General Course Followed by Main Church Bodies .. 69
30. The Religion of Luther and Loyola Compared 73
31. Relation of Lutheranism to Roman Catholicism 76
32. Luther's Church Government in Theory and Practice 79
33. Calvin's Church Government in Theory and Practice 80
34. Communion between God and Man as Understood by the Reformers and by the Radicals 82
35. The Church Visible and Invisible 86
36. The Conflict of Rationalism and Faith 102
37. Microcosm and Macrocosm 104
38. The Known World in A.D. 800 and the Known World Today 112
39. Various Civilizations 113
40. Political Map of Present South America 114
41. European and American Movements Compared 116
42. North America in 1783 119
43. Location of Lutheran Church in Old New York 134
44. Swedish-Finnish Settlements in New Sweden 140
45. The Homeland of the Palatines 167
46. Early Palatine Settlements in New York 180
47. Frontier Line of the English Colonies in 1740 199

INTRODUCTION

Ever since the dawn of history, there has been a mighty life stream flowing to man through the channel of revealed religion, as disclosed in the canonical Scriptures. Since the founding of the Christian Church nearly two thousand years ago, this life stream has been called Christianity, after Christ.

The student of history will know how Christianity came to touch human life in all its phases. Note the influence of Christianity upon the religious, intellectual, social, cultural, economic and political life of the people with whom it came in contact. Note its influence upon the world of art, letters and science, as well as the reaction of these upon Christianity.

Lutheranism represents the mid-stream of this mighty influence of Christianity. Lutheranism is not Christianity plus or minus certain ideas of Luther. Lutheranism is simply consistent Christianity, neither more nor less. And Lutheranism in America is not a specific brand of Lutheranism, but simply the Lutheran faith transplanted to America.

The Lutheran Church, therefore, is not a new growth but a restoration of the original Christian Church, or what Luther called the Apostolic Evangelical Church. However, the Lutheran Church is more than a mere restoration. Being firmly rooted in the great historic past, the Lutheran Church moves forward with the very life of the nations; and in so doing, it is an ever growing organism, in vital touch with every phase of human life. This is also true of the Lutheran Church in America.

1. **Definition, Scope, and Divisions.**

(a) *Lutheran*. The term "Lutheran" was first used on July 4, 1519 by Luther's opponent, Dr. John Eck, at the famous Leipzig

2   THE LUTHERAN CHURCH IN AMERICA

Disputation.[1] Other Catholic leaders quickly adopted the word as a nickname for the supposed *heresy* of Luther and his followers.[2] Luther and his associates preferred to designate themselves as members of the "ecclesia apostolica catholica," the Apostolic Catholic or Evangelical Church. Shortly after 1580, however, the Lutherans adopted "Lutheran" as a name of honor, at the initiative of Jacob Andreae. The term designates all who adhere to the confessional standards of the Lutheran Church.[3]

Today there are over 82,000,000 baptized Lutherans in the world. The Lutheran Church is the Mother Church of Protestantism; it is the largest Protestant communion in the world; and it is the third largest Protestant communion in America.

(b) *Church.* This word is evidently formed from the Greek "kyriakon" which means "the Lord's," and may refer to one of two things, (1) the Lord's "body" or congregation of believers, and (2) the Lord's "house" or consecrated building.[4] The New Testament also designates the congregation of believers as the "ecclesia," a Greek word meaning "those called together"

---

[1] Eck's intention was to secure a papal bull of excommunication against Luther because of the reformation movement Luther had started. The old leaden seals of the official papal documents resembled bubbles; hence the name *bull* from the Latin word for *bubble* or *knob*. Excommunication was directed against individuals belonging to the Catholic Church. The lesser excommunication deprived a person of the sacraments; the greater cut him off from all rights.

[2] Up to around 1560 the French Protestants were usually nicknamed "Lutherans" or "Heretics of Meaux," although after 1536 the real leadership of this group was supplied by John Calvin.

[3] These confessional standards include the three Ecumenical Creeds, namely, the Apostle's Creed, the Nicene Creed, and the Athanasian Creed; the Unaltered Augsburg Confession; the Apology of the Augsburg Confession; the Schmalkald Articles; the Small Catechism of Luther; the Large Catechism of Luther; and the Formula of Concord. Though some of these symbols are not formally recognized by all Lutheran bodies, none of them are expressly rejected.

[4] Luther did not like the word *church* because of its double and rather vague meaning. He preferred the term *ecclesia*. Nevertheless, the term *church* was adopted.

or "those called out" or simply "assembly." The corresponding Old Testament terms are "edhah" and "kahal," both meaning "assembly."

(c) *America.* This is, of course, a purely geographic term designating the "New World," the North and South American countries and their possessions. A history of the Lutheran Church in America must consequently set forth in orderly arrangement the rise and progress of the Lutheran Church in these countries, and also the history of the American Lutheran mission work in American possessions and in foreign lands.

(d) *Divisions.* Various aspects or branches of this history, as of church history in general, may easily be distinguished, depend-

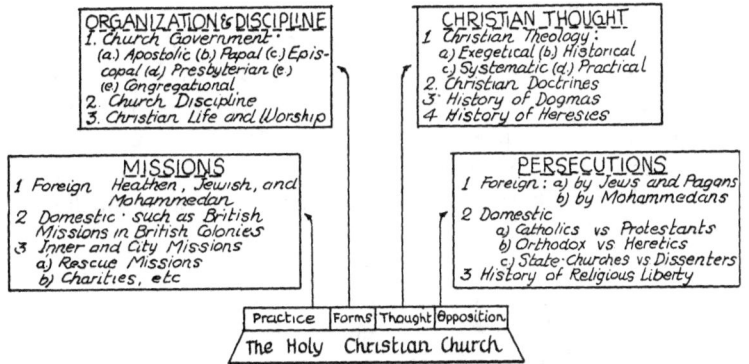

BRANCHES OF CHURCH HISTORY

ing on whether the emphasis is upon practice, forms, thought, or opposition. Lutheranism as expressed in *practical life* naturally deals with the history of Lutheran Home and Foreign Missions and their subordinate activities such as charities, hospitals, rescue missions. Special consideration of the *forms* of Christian life involves a History of Church Polity (organization and discipline) and a History of Worship. Special study of Christian *thought* leads to a History of Creeds and Confessions, and a

History of Lutheran Theology or Learning. Similar attention to the *opposing forces* involves a History of Religious Liberty.

It is convenient and practical to divide the history of the Lutheran Church in America into larger divisions or periods because they serve as landmarks along the route the student is to travel. The following chronological outline is suggested: I. The Lutheran Ancestry. II. Lutherans in Colonial Days, 1492-1763. III. Lutherans and the Establishment of the American Nation, 1763-1789. IV. Characteristics of American Christianity. V. Nationalization of the Lutheran Church in America, 1789-1830. VI. The Age of Sectionalism, 1830-1870. VII. The Age of Industrialism, 1870-1918. VIII. The Age of Lutheran Solidarity, 1918-Present. IX. American Lutheran Missions. X. Lutheran Unity.

2. The Value of a Study of Church History.

(a) Lutheran Church history brings the student in touch with his spiritual ancestry. A patriotic citizen should know the history of his country, because such knowledge makes for more intelligent citizenship. A corresponding knowledge of the history of the Lutheran Church makes for better and more intelligent church membership.

(b) A knowledge of church backgrounds broadens the perspective, and gives a more correct evaluation of Jesus Christ. He is the central figure in both universal and church history. In the pre-Christian systems of religion, philosophy, and government, mankind was prepared—positively and negatively—for his coming. The full significance of Christ for the Christian world is revealed, not merely in the New Testament, but also in the twenty centuries of Christian history. Church history helps to portray the fullness of the stature of Christ.

(c) It promotes highmindedness and toleration. It reveals the comprehensiveness of the Kingdom of God upon earth. It leads to a study of Christianity in all its phases. The study of the great religious controversies of the past should cultivate proper respect for the opinion of others. A general and widely diffused knowledge of the Church is also a most powerful factor in eliminating disconnected, isolated group movements.

(d) A knowledge of the Church of the past serves as a basis for understanding the present. History does not merely repeat itself; yet, the past has many parallels to the present. Adequate knowledge is the best preventive for the repetition of mistakes of the past; it generally helps in the solution of problems of the present.

(e) It has a stabilizing influence. Christianity has a stabilizing influence upon society. But we live in an age of scepticism. The very foundations of Christianity are challenged and shaken. The older order of things must, as it seems, give room to new customs, modes, and ideas. Are these things simply old errors exploded long ago, or are we witnessing the birthpangs of a new order? Shall we display the red signal at every attempt to change things? Will these changes lead to defeat, or to ultimate victory for the Church? The records of the Church will shed much light on these problems, and Church History will furnish one of the strongest proofs of the continuous presence of the Lord with his people.

(f) Many think it strange that the Christian Church is broken up into so many denominations or sections. Why the many doctrinal systems and variegated forms of organization, life, and worship? Church History will answer the *why*. It will reveal the larger unity that exists between these groups.

(g) It has a special value for church leaders. Church History is a veritable storehouse of information on successful religious leadership. Christian leaders cannot preserve the historic continuity of their groups without a knowledge of the past. Furthermore, this history presents a wealth of material that may be used in sermons and addresses.

(h) Finally, it has intellectual, cultural, and stimulating values. The constant search for the relation between cause and effect develops the intellect. Furthermore, the Christian Church has always succeeded in establishing itself in the great centers of culture and civilisation. Christianity and true culture go hand in hand. The influence of Christianity upon society has produced some of the choicest fruits of modern culture. Knowledge of Church History leads to a better appreciation of this culture. Lastly, the study of the noble lives and the great ideals of apostles, evangelists, martyrs, reformers and other saints of God, is pregnant with inspiration and vitalising enthusiasm.

1. REVIEW QUESTIONS

1. What is the origin and meaning of the term "Lutheran"?
2. How is the Lutheran Church related to other Protestant bodies (a) organically? (b) in size?
3. Explain the word "church" and its Old and New Testament equivalents. Why did not Luther like this term?
4. How extensive should the scope of a history of the Lutheran Church in America be? Why?
5. What advantages do you see in presenting or studying this history by larger divisions or periods?
6. Which are the generally recognised divisions and sub-divisions of church history?
7. Why may a study of church history make for better and more intelligent church membership?
8. Why does a knowledge of church history help us to a better appreciation of the person and work of Jesus Christ?
9. In what ways may a study of church history promote high-mindedness and toleration?
10. How do you explain the stabilising influence of Christianity?
11. What special values has a study of church history for church leaders?
12. What relation is there between Christianity and culture and intellectual achievement?

TOPICS FOR SPECIAL STUDY

1. Discuss the secular meaning of the Greek *ecclesia* and the Roman *curia*.
2. Christianity and Culture.
3. The Mother Church of Protestantism.

CHAPTER I

THE AMERICAN LUTHERAN ANCESTRY

All history must take account of *origins*. To know a river in such a way as to account for its size, its currents, its color, its tributaries and the nature of the land through which it flows, you must do more than merely stand upon its bank at a given point. You must investigate the very sources of that river and track it onwards to the ocean. This principle also applies to American Lutheran history. To know American Lutheranism you must know its European background and Luther; to know Luther you must know and appreciate his historical antecedents; to know these antecedents you must know and appreciate the person and work of Jesus Christ and the writings of the New Testament; and to know the New Testament you must know and appreciate its antecedent, the Old Testament.[1]

History must also take account of *interpretation*. Undue emphasis on origins leaves history sterile. After the critical problems of a document have been settled, the who? when? where? and for whom? the interpreter must try to detect, express and release the spiritual message of that document.[2] He must carry the student into the life stream out of which the document has come. He must appropriate the values within the

---

[1] St. Augustine said, "The New Testament is concealed in the Old, and the Old is revealed in the New." Rudolf Otto in his *Idea of the Holy* has shown that the *Numinous* element is present in the Old Testament as well as in the New, and that both Testaments must be reckoned with as religious resources.

[2] The interpreter plays an important part. Consider Arturo Toscanini's interpretation of music to the common man. Toscanini has in himself complete control, complete possession and complete self-offering. These are the essentials of a good interpreter.

document to present needs. After all, do people in general care so much where a train comes from so long as they know it takes them to their station?

History must also take account of *personalities*. This is especially true of religious history. Historic Christian experience is salvation through Jesus Christ. Man is a personality and God is a personality. These personalities cannot come together as a mere chemical process. It must be done on the basis of *personal* relationships through the channel of personality. Entering into a personal relationship with God through Jesus Christ, certain men of history have laid hold of a divine power that has been irresistible. This is true of such men as Martin Luther and the Apostle Paul. The origin and genius of the Reformation must be sought, not in a favorable environment, but in the *personal experiences* of Martin Luther. The unique influence of the Apostle Paul must likewise be sought, not in his environment, but in his rather unique relationship to Jesus Christ. Lutheran history cannot be properly understood apart from such personalities.

I. Roots in the Old Testament.—American Lutheranism is firmly and deeply rooted in the Old Testament Scriptures. Five of the most pronounced beliefs recorded in these Scriptures, namely belief in God, sin, salvation, selection and evangelization, are also the beliefs of the Lutheran Church. The personal God who calls Abraham, who delivers Israel, who inspires the prophets, is the God of the Lutheran confession. The problems of sin and salvation in the Old Testament are essentially the problems recognized by the Lutheran Church. Being thoroughly convinced of the divine authority of the Old and New Testaments, Martin Luther took as the first cardinal principle of the Reformation, the absolute *supremacy of the Bible* as the norm for life and doctrine.

The second cardinal principle of the Reformation, *justification by faith alone,* finds its first classic expression in Abraham, the

THE AMERICAN LUTHERAN ANCESTRY 9

father of all who believe.[3] Abraham was not saved by faith and good works, or by divine grace and human merit, but by faith alone. He believed in God and God reckoned it to him for righteousness.[4] This covenant of faith which God made with Abraham was not disannulled by the law which was given several hundred years later.[5] Salvation by faith apart from works is also the keynote of David and of the Prophets.[6]

Luther's third cardinal principle that salvation is accessible to every believer without the mediation of a priest, or, *the priesthood of all believers,* is latent in the Old Testament, though not so clearly expressed. The Old Testament believer was a member of "an elect race, a royal priesthood, a holy nation, a people of God's own possession."[7] Though the service of God in Tabernacle or Temple was performed by priests and Levites, yet the first-born son of every household in Israel was the property of Jehovah,[8] destined to the temple service originally and before the institution of the Levites. Hence the first-born sons had to be presented to God as His special property, but were redeemed from Him for five shekels.[9] By this ordinance every household in Israel was reminded of its precious right. Furthermore, the Old Testament does not assert that outside the priest there is no salvation. The activity of the prophet is practically as prominent as that of the priest.

Considering the Bible as the norm for faith and doctrine, what does the Old Testament say about God and man? From Genesis to Malachi it is clearly expressed that the believer bows before a God whom he longed for, but could not find because of his sin. God, therefore, came to man and revealed His plan of salvation and also provided the means for this salvation. Man was to be saved, not by his own efforts, works, or merits, but alone by the pure and unmerited grace of God through faith

---

[3] Cf. Rom. 4:16. [4] Gen. 15:6; Rom. 4:1-22; Gal. 3:6.
[5] Gal. 3:17-18; Cf. Exod. 12:40-41.
[6] Psalm 32:1-2; Isa. 55:1f.; etc.
[7] I Pet. 2:9; Exod. 19:6.
[8] Numb. 8:14f. [9] Numb. 18:16.

10 THE LUTHERAN CHURCH IN AMERICA

in the Savior. Old Testament revelation centers, therefore, in *God's activity*, in salvation which man could never get alone by himself. This Old Testament revelation is diametrically opposite to the view of Naturalism and Humanism.

Naturalism and Humanism deny the existence of an unseen supernatural power, the necessity of obedience to such power, and the subsequently divinely conditioned morality.[10] Humanism claims that man has exhausted all emotional and intellectual energy in reaching upward, trying to support a fictional God or Deity. Hence man must cut off from the top, and then he will find that all resident forces are inherent in human nature.[11] Naturalism goes one step further to include the cosmic resources.[12]

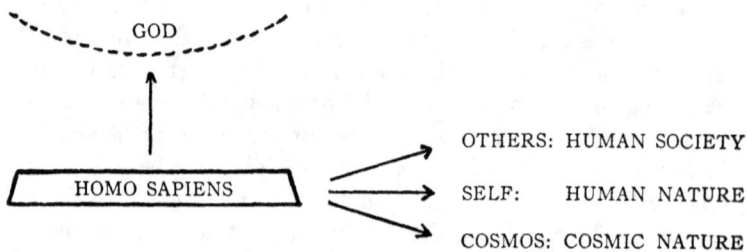

RESOURCES OF THE HOMO SAPIENS

If this threefold area—nature, self and society—were a sufficient realm and had room for all experiences needed for human life, why was not the original *homo* satisfied with these re-

[10] See Leuba, *Psychological Study of Religion,* and *The Beliefs in God and Immortality*; also Dewey, *A Common Faith,* and Cameron, *The Passing of God.* Leuba is the Humanist *par excellence.* Cameron presents the communistic outlook.

[11] John Dewey, *A Common Faith.*

[12] One difference between a Naturalist and a Humanist is that the Humanist stops with the human resources while the Naturalist goes back to cosmic resources. Naturalism and Humanism spring from the same source.

sources? Everything was there before man arrived; yet when he did arrive, he almost immediately turned upward to invisible resources for assistance.[13] This indicates, as Schleiermacher, Otto, Hacking and others have pointed out, that religion is present in the lowest structure of man's experience. If you could drive out religion you would change human nature.[14]

Luther accepted the view of Genesis that God is the Creator of the universe; that man was created in His image; that this

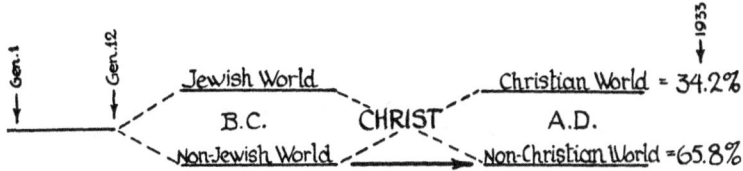

How Jewish and Pagan People Met and Separated in Christ

image was distorted by man's fall in sin; that God promised a Savior; that in preparing mankind for this Savior, God selected Abraham; and that through Abraham and his descendants God promoted an evangelizing influence on the rest of mankind. From Abraham until Christ the preparation of mankind for redemption had a twofold aspect. In Israel man developed under the influence of a direct, divine revelation. In paganism man developed *apart* from the influence of a direct, divine revelation. "When the fullness of time came, God sent forth his Son, born of a woman."[15]

[13] Whether you accept the Genesis account or adhere to the evolutionary theory, you must admit that there was a time when the *homo sapiens* appeared. Why did not this *homo* develop the way the evolutionist would have him develop? If man could have been satisfied with the cosmic and human resources at hand, why did he almost immediately turn to an invisible God for assistance?

[14] Contrary to views expressed by William James in *Varieties of Religious Experience* and by John Dewey in *A Common Faith*, Rudolf Otto has shown in his *Idea of the Holy* that religious experience is different, not only in degree but also in kind, from all other experience.

[15] Gal. 4:4.

2. REVIEW QUESTIONS

1. Why study the American Lutheran ancestry?
2. What part should the interpreter play in the study of history?
3. Why must history take account of personalities?
4. What pronounced beliefs of the Old Testament are also the beliefs of the Lutheran Church?
5. What is the keynote in the religious experiences of Abraham, David and the Prophets?
6. How do you account for the fact that the activity of the prophet in the Old Testament is practically as prominent as that of the priest?
7. What is the essence of Old Testament revelation?
8. What claims do Naturalism and Humanism make as to the resources of man?
9. What evidences contradict these claims?
10. How fundamental is religious experience to human nature?
11. What relationship do you see between the process of selection in the Old Testament and the preparation of mankind for redemption?
12. Through what means did Old Testament Israel exert an evangelizing influence on mankind?

TOPICS FOR SPECIAL STUDY

1. God and man in Old Testament revelation.
2. Evidences that man is essentially religious.
3. The nature of religious experience.
4. The problem of selection in Old Testament times.
5. The fact of sin, the "missing of the mark."
6. The way of salvation in the Old Testament times.
7. Faith lives by its object.

II. Firmly Grounded in the New Testament.—The Lutheran Church believes in the *Incarnate* Jesus Christ of the New Testament. The great *concept* of the Incarnation is that God became man. "The Word became flesh, and dwelt among us."[16] The *purpose* of the Incarnation is expressed in John 3:16, "For God so loved the world, that he gave his only begotten Son, that whosoever believeth on him should not perish, but have eternal life."

Old Testament history holds nothing more pathetic than the frequent lapses of Israel into idolatry. Israel was forbidden to make any material image of God, but the insatiable desire for

[16] John 1:14.

THE AMERICAN LUTHERAN ANCESTRY

something the people could grasp through the material senses led to the worship of gods presented in material form. The desire for an adequate revelation of God had been met in some measure in Old Testament times as when God clothed Himself in the burning bush, in the fiery cloud and in natural figures. But personality can not be satisfactorily expressed in impersonal things. If God was to adequately reveal Himself to man, He must come out of the vast universe and clothe Himself in human form.[17]

In Jesus Christ God laid aside His incomprehensible attributes and stretched out His loving arms to mankind.[18] What Jesus Christ was for mankind for thirty-three years, God is for all time.[19] The *Incarnate* revealed God by applying to Him a new name "Father," and He put into that name a higher than human content. He made the *"Father" concept* the center of the divine nature. The name "Father" for God occurs nearly one hundred times in the New Testament. Jesus gathered all of God's attributes into one short precious sentence, John 3:16.

[17] Socrates (460-399 B.C.), the Athenian philosopher, also concluded that God can reveal Himself intelligently to man only in terms of human nature.

[18] Homer tells in *The Iliad*, Book VI, lines 601-607, about the parting of Hector and his little son before the fatal battle outside the walls of Troy. The great warrior, clad in armor from head to foot, stood ready to enter his chariot. He stretched out his arms to take the boy, but the little fellow, frightened by the giant form clothed in armor, and with a special fear of the glittering brass helmet and the horse-hair plume, screamed in terror and clung to his nurse. Quickly the father removed the helmet with the plume and the child, recognizing his father, bounced into his arms. In similar manner man stood trembling and frightened before an Infinite and Omnipotent God. But in Jesus Christ He laid aside His incomprehensible attributes, and man, recognizing Him as the Father in Christ Jesus, threw himself into the outstretched arms without fear.

[19] To the ageless question, "Does God care for man?" Jesus answered by saying, "Are not two sparrows sold for a penny? And not one of them shall fall to the ground without your Father: but the very hairs on your head are numbered." Matth. 10:29-30; cf. 5:25-34. To another ageless question, "Will God who is holy and perfect forgive sins?" Jesus gave a most assuring answer, of which the threefold parable in Luke 15 is an illustration.

The act of redeeming man stands as a unit among the works of God's omnipotence. The entire act of redemption, from beginning to end, is really a single act, just as a boy's education, extending for a period of years, may be considered one single act. Every act is made up of a purpose, a method and a power. The *purpose* of redemption is that man may have access to the Father.[20] The *method* of redemption is Jesus Christ.[21] The *power* is the Holy Spirit.[22] It is a salvation to the Father through the Son and by the Holy Spirit. Hence the divine nature is three persons but one God.[23] Make either person unworthy of the others and salvation is not complete. If it be not for the Father, the Son's redemption is vain. If it be not for the Son, the Father waits and the Holy Spirit moves for naught. If it be not for the Holy Spirit, the Father's arms are open, and the method of grace is perfect, yet the unmoved soul stands inactive and unsaved.

Revelation by Incarnation has another aspect. It throws light on the relationship between mind and matter. Kant[24] has clearly shown that philosophy has never been able to settle the dualism between mind and matter, body and soul. The solution lies in incarnation. The mind or *psyche* unites with the body or *soma* to form a body-mind or psyche-soma relationship which is expressed through personality. There is no other known way of uniting the psyche and the soma, the spiritual and the material except through the body. This union is expressed through human personality. Furthermore, there is no other way of rationalizing the divine and the human in Jesus except through personality.[25]

Revelation by Incarnation also throws a clear light on the

---

[20] Eph. 2:18; cf. 1 Tim. 2:4.
[21] Acts 4:12; Matth. 1:21; etc.
[22] 1 Cor. 12:3; Acts 1:8; John 16:7-15; etc.
[23] This does not describe or define God. It is merely a history of man's salvation to God through Jesus Christ by the Holy Spirit.
[24] Immanuel Kant in *Critique of Pure Reason.*
[25] This is the solution of the divine-human problem of Jesus Christ in the Chalcedonian Creed of A.D. 451.

THE AMERICAN LUTHERAN ANCESTRY 15

nature of the Christian Church. There are some who insist that the Church is altogether *invisible* because, they say, it is a spiritual association only. There are others who make the Church essentially *visible* by identifying it with the external ecclesiastical organization. This apparent dualism between the *invisible* and

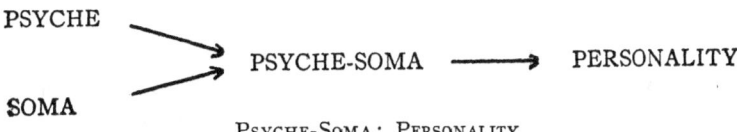

PSYCHE-SOMA: PERSONALITY

the *visible* finds its clear solution in the Incarnation. Christ as the Head of the Church was not merely *psyche* but also *soma*. The historic Christ, the Christ of the Gospels, comprised both the *invisible* and the *visible*, both the *psyche* and the *soma*, both the *spiritual* and the *material*. For, "the Word became flesh." What is true of the Head of the Church is also true of the Body. Hence the Christian Church on earth is both *invisible* and *visible*. Consult the diagram on page 86.

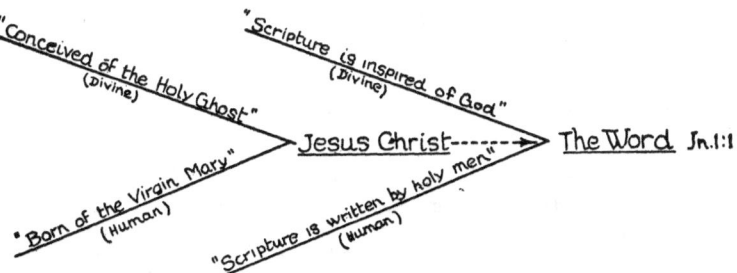

THE DIVINE AND THE HUMAN RELATION IN JESUS CHRIST AND IN THE BIBLE

Revelation by Incarnation also throws a clear light on the *nature* of the Word of God. "In the beginning was the Word, and the Word was God." This *Word* of John 1:1 is, of course, the Incarnate Jesus Christ of the Gospels. Furthermore, the

Bible is the written *Word* about this Incarnate Word. In both you see a perfect union of the divine and the human elements. In the Apostle's Creed the Incarnate Christ is confessed to be "conceived by the Holy Ghost, born of the Virgin Mary." And of the Bible, the Word about the Word, the statement in 2 Peter 1:21 is true that "no prophecy ever came by the will of men; but men spake from God, being moved by the Holy Spirit."

The Lutheran Church believes that *the Jesus Christ of the Gospels* is *the Jesus Christ of history*. In answer to critics who want to distinguish between the Jesus of the Gospels and the Jesus of history,[26] the Lutheran Church refers to the Messianic consciousness of Jesus Christ as disclosed in the accepted and authentic source material of the written Gospels.

Critics refer to *Document Q* (Quelle) as a common source material for the canonical Gospels.[27] This document is supposed to have been written about twenty years before Mark. If, upon careful investigation, *Document Q* should disclose the same Messianic consciousness of Jesus as is found in the four Gospels, there is no longer any need for staying with *Document Q* only, nor is there any reason for making an essential distinction between the Jesus of the Gospels and the Jesus Christ of history.

Document Q starts with the baptism of Jesus. When Jesus was baptized heaven opened and a voice was heard, "Thou art my beloved Son." This is a subjective, direct statement to Jesus himself.

[26] Some interesting experiments are carried on at present by exponents of *Form Criticism*. This term was coined by Prof. Martin Dibelius of Heidelberg University in a document published in 1921 called *Form Criticism of the Gospel*. It involves a technique by which they seek to get back to the oral tradition which underlies the written documents. Dr. Burton Scott Eastman of General Seminary has published a book on the subject called *The Gospel Before the Gospels*. Dr. F. C. Grant, newly elected Professor to Union Theological Seminary, has translated a work with the English title *Form Criticism*. Dr. Donald Riddle of the University of Chicago has published a book called *The Early Christian Life*. Dr. Robert Henry Lightfoot in his *Bampton Lectures, 1934*, dealt with the topic of *History and Interpretation of the Gospels*. See Chapter II.

[27] See Adolf Harnack in *Hibbert Journal*, 1912.

Immediately after that Jesus was "led by the Spirit into the wilderness." Critics deny that Jesus got the Spirit, and yet here it is stated in their accepted *Document Q*. Then for forty days Jesus had time to think things over. Was he really the Messiah? And if so, how was he to meet life in carrying out his Messianic mission?

At the end of forty days he was tempted, and during the temptation and ever since, there was never any shadow of doubt in his mind that he was the Son of God. Jesus must have related this temptation experience to his disciples and to the people because he was alone at the time. Hence in this record we are dealing with the direct consciousness of Jesus himself.

The first temptation was to change stone into bread. "If thou art the Son of God," then demonstrate it. Jesus could have done this but he sought no special favors for himself. When he did use this power, as in the feeding of the 5000, it was for the use of others. To him the religious problem was primary and the economic problem was secondary.

Document Q also relates the second temptation experience, Jesus on the pinnacle of the Temple. "If thou art the Son of God," if this is your decision, then demonstrate it. Again there was a test of his Messianic consciousness. Jesus did not yield to temptation but later he did demonstrate his mastery over the law of gravitation as when he walked on the sea.

The third temptation, Jesus on the mountain, is also related in *Document Q*. Again there was a test of his unique relationship to God and again he refused to yield to temptation. He wanted to win the world, but he did not want a kingdom of this world. When the people later tried to make him king, he turned away.

In the temptation scene as depicted in *Document Q* you meet a tremendous personality with a tremendous power. There was in the mind of Jesus an unshaken conviction that he was the Messiah, the Son of God, and that he was determined to carry out his Messianic mission on earth in accordance with the will of his Father.

After the temptation experience, Jesus did not go back to Nazareth to live. A change had taken place which could be seen in his outward conduct. He was led by the Spirit.

Next in *Document Q* comes the calling of the twelve apostles. Jesus was teaching, preaching and healing all manner of disease. Then he called the twelve. If Jesus did not have a special consciousness, he would never have asked these men to give up their business for his mission. This Messianic consciousness of Jesus never seems to have waned. In unexpected crises he was able to cope with every situation because of this consciousness.

All critics are willing to accept the Beatitudes as genuine. Consider the closing words of the Beatitudes, "Persecuted for *my* sake . . . for so they persecuted the prophets that were before you." Jesus here claims to be to his followers what God was to the prophets. Jesus is placing himself beside God. And any one who asks people to suffer for one has a strange consciousness.

Still using *Document Q*, let us consider Jesus in relation to the Law. You could not in Hebrew or Jewish consciousness expect to find any one who would dare to speak against or change the Law. Yet, what do we find in the Sermon on the Mount? What did Jesus say? "Moses said . . . but I say." In every case where Jesus differs from Moses he lifts the matter to a higher level than Moses.

Next is his relation to the sabbath. Jesus said, "The Son of man is lord even over the sabbath." This is all from *Document Q*. Next we consider the statement that Jesus rejoiced in the Holy Spirit and said, "I thank thee, O Father, Lord of heaven and earth. . . . All things have been delivered unto me of my Father." Here we find in *Document Q* the unique Father-Son relationship, the highest Messianic consciousness ever expressed in any of the four canonical Gospels.[28]

[28] There are various theories as to when this Messianic self-consciousness of Jesus came into existence. (1) The prenatal theory, "conceived by

THE AMERICAN LUTHERAN ANCESTRY 19

This brief examination of *Document Q* may be sufficient to indicate that in this commonly accepted source material you find all the marks of the self-consciousness of Jesus that you find in the written Gospels. His entire public ministry was dominated by this Messianic self-consciousness. Hence the Jesus Christ of the Gospels is essentially the same as the Jesus Christ of history. Statements to the contrary are not founded on fact.[29]

The Lutheran Church believes in *the crucified and risen Lord Jesus Christ of the New Testament*. Modernism stops the Gospel at Calvary and makes it subjective. But there is nothing *numinous* in that. It was from the resurrection experience the disciples believed that Jesus was the Christ. By the resurrection from the dead, God had made Jesus "both Lord and Christ."[30]

It is self-evident that the question of the resurrection of Jesus Christ not only directly affects the credibility of the Gospel narratives, but it involves the very existence of Christianity. It is the "burning question" as to the divine or the merely human conception of Jesus Christ. The Old Testament foretold that the Messiah would rise from the dead. Jesus Christ presented Himself as the Messiah and said repeatedly that He would be put to death, and that He would rise again from the dead. His biographers Matthew, Mark, Luke and John affirm that He did

---

the Holy Ghost." The Apostle's Creed starts here. (2) At His birth. (3) At the age of eight days when He was dedicated in the Temple. (4) At the age of twelve when He visited the Temple. (5) At the age of thirty years when He was baptised. (6) At Caesarea Philippi. This is the famous theory. (7) Jesus never had such self-consciousness. It is something that the Church has read back into His life. (8) Jesus had this self-consciousness but He was of an unsound mind. (9) Jesus was conscious of His Messiahship and attempted to reveal His secret to the people but found it quite impossible to do so.

[29] A certain group within the historical critical school still maintains that the real Jesus was not the Jesus of the Gospels.

[30] If the Christian Church had kept the crucifixion and the resurrection together, we would never have had the history of the atonement we now have. By separating the crucifixion and the resurrection the Christian Church cut off one half of the picture. The emphasis should be on the two together. The Church historically has neglected the resurrection.

rise on the third day; and in Acts and the New Testament Epistles the doctrine of His resurrection became interwoven in all the preaching and writing as the very foundation of the Church, as the connecting link of every hope of the human race.

If it can be shown beyond a reasonable doubt that Jesus Christ actually rose from the dead, no other proof of His divine mission on earth need be asked for. If it can be proved that He actually came forth from the grave after a real death, it must be admitted that all other miracles sink into insignificance in the presence of this stupendous display of God's presence and power. Harnack said concerning the resurrection, "We will never come to the true cause until psychology has been heard."

The following theories have been suggested or used[31] to solve the problem of the resurrection of Jesus Christ from the dead, namely the Fact theory, the Fraud theory, the Phantom theory, the Fancy theory, the Vision theory and the Phantasy or Myth theory. Each of these may be briefly examined and tested in the light of science and the Scriptures.

Fact theory states that the resurrection of Jesus simply could not happen. This theory is unscientific because the explanation of any phenomenon must include every fact and factor known concerning that phenomenon. If it explains all but *one* fact or factor which can not be explained, then the theory is not sound.

Fraud theory[32] involves the honesty and integrity of the disciples who are supposed to have stolen the body of Jesus. It even involves the veracity of the Master Himself. We are asked to believe that He deceived His disciples with His promise of resurrection and that He deceived them in the failure to fulfil this promise. This theory seems psychologically impossible and

---

[31] These theories have been advocated by men who seek to give a purely natural account of the origin of Christianity. At the bottom of it all is the admissibility of the supernatural in the form of a miracle.

[32] The Fraud theory, which was first set forth by Jewish religious leaders, Matth. 28:11-15, has been seconded by more recent writers such as Reimarius, Réville and Oskar Holtzman. At present it is relegated into oblivion.

THE AMERICAN LUTHERAN ANCESTRY

it certainly has no basis in Scriptures. Would the Jews, with their horror for touching a dead body, have any desire to defile themselves with the dead body of Jesus? The Fraud theory is a minor theory which very few have ever taken seriously.

Fancy theory[33] asserts that Jesus did not really die on the cross but that His body was taken down and buried during a swoon; that He was revived again and was actually seen by some of His disciples; that He lived long enough to be seen by Paul; that He finally died a natural death; and that all His disciples looked upon this temporal revival as an actual resurrection. The difficulty with this theory is that it eliminates the very foundation of the incident itself. It is unscientific because it does not explain the facts or factors involved.

Vision theory[34] asserts that the supposed appearances of the

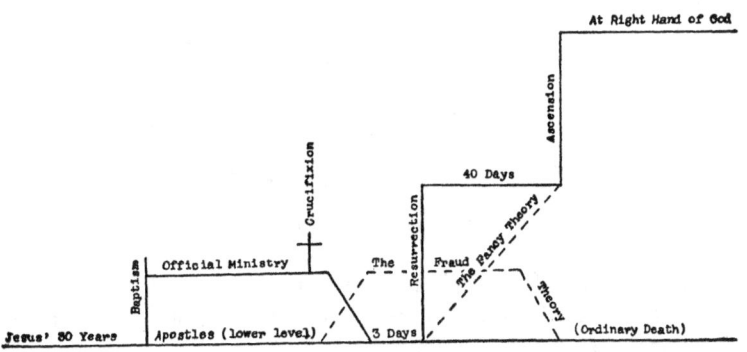

DIAGRAM OF RESURRECTION THEORIES[35]

[33] The Fancy or Swoon theory was proposed by Dr. Paulus and partly upheld by Schleiermacher, and Huxley. It was adopted by Herder and Hase but was effectively rejected by Strauss. It has little support among recent writers.

[34] The Vision theory has been upheld by Renan, Pfleiderer, Schmiedel, Harnack, Weizsacker and Loisy.

[35] This diagram illustrates the resurrection narratives and the Fraud and the Fancy or Myth theories. The other theories can not very well be illustrated by a diagram. This diagram has been suggested in part by Dr. Albert Clarke Wyckoff.

risen Christ were purely subjective. In their great religious excitement the disciples longed to see the Lord once more. They thought they saw Him several times but it was, nevertheless, a hallucination. Renan began with the experience of Mary Magdalene. Strauss and Pfleiderer began with the experience of Saul outside Damascus. Keim has shown in his *Life of Jesus of Nazareth* how the Vision theory is altogether untenable.

Phantom theory[36] allows for appearances of Jesus which were not purely subjective but had an objective cause. These appearances, however, were not of the real body of Jesus Christ risen from the grave, but only of the glorified spirit of Christ pro-

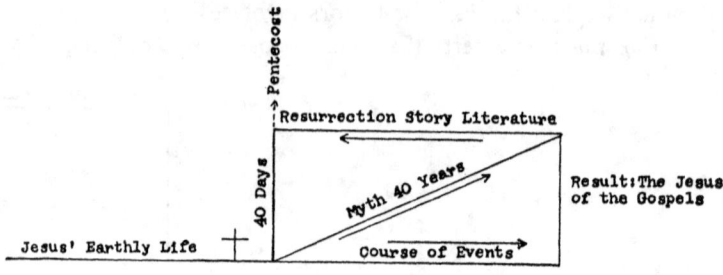

DEVELOPMENT OF THE MYTH

ducing visions of Himself for the comfort of His faithful ones. This theory is also unscientific because it does not explain every fact or factor recorded in the resurrection accounts.

Phantasy or Myth theory[37] claims that there were no appearances to be accounted for, but that the belief in the literal resur-

---

[36] The Phantom or Telegram theory, proposed by Keim, not only tampers with the resurrection narratives, but it makes God responsible for a deception of the disciples. It does not explain the facts of the resurrection accounts.

[37] Advocates of the Myth or Phantasy theory differ as to how this myth may have started. According to the Chicago theory the myth started with the apostle Peter. Dr. Beacon of Yale claims it started with the apostle Paul. Others have claimed the apostle John as the originator of this supposed myth.

THE AMERICAN LUTHERAN ANCESTRY 23

rection of Jesus Christ grew, like the myths gather around various celebrities. This theory asserts, furthermore, that the disciples spoke convincingly of the continued life of the Crucified One, and that this gave rise to misunderstanding in the Apostolic Church, and that this misunderstanding embodied itself in the traditions of Christophanies recorded in the Gospels. The Myth theory is the only one that has been widely accepted. Hence some attention should be given to this theory.

Time is essential in the development of the myth. Not in the first or second generation but in the third can the myth be produced. At least forty years must be allowed for this process. The

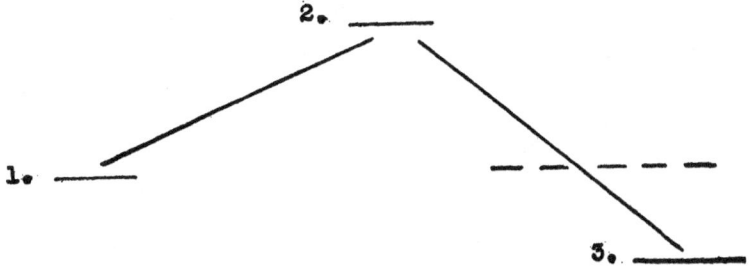

THE "HOT SPOT" OF THE MYTH

ideal proceeds over something real. Space also counts. For example, in other lands there may be myths about America. The diagrams may prove useful in the study of the development of the myth.

In the development of the myth you first have some historical event as indicated by 1 in diagram above. Then that event or experience is idealized by the folk mind and raised up, as in 2 in diagram above, until you have a "hot spot" after a period of about forty years. Then the myth begins to cool; the emphasis goes down until it sinks below the original level. According to this myth theory, the hot spot of interest in the resurrection of Jesus Christ should be about forty years after the event took place. Whether or not this position is well taken will be seen in the subsequent investigation.

Applying the Myth theory to the resurrection of Jesus Christ, the advocates of this theory start with the "supposed" historical event of the resurrection. Following this event is the Pentecost; and out of this grew the Church. A little group came out of seclusion and began to proclaim certain definite convictions as to Jesus Christ. Some say the nucleus of this group was the *koinonia* or fellowship. Others claim it was the *atonement* which helped the disciples come out in the open. Others again say it was the idea of the *Second Coming* of Christ which stimulated them to proclaim their convictions. The New Testament, however, states that the disciples got their courage and inspiration at Pentecost.

Advocates of the Myth theory say that the *koinonia* promoted new ideas not found in the Old Testament, such as the resurrection. This original idea had to be accepted by the group; and before it could be made a folk faith, it had to be rounded out in all its details. This took time—about forty years. The Gospels were written after this myth was produced. Hence this myth is incorporated in the Gospel accounts, they say. But this brings us face to face with two obstinate difficulties; *first,* according to this theory, the hot spot of interest in the resurrection of Jesus Christ should be about forty years after the event took place, while the New Testament indicates clearly that the hot spot was three days after the crucifixion and during the days immediately following; *secondly,* this theory assumes that the *Book of Acts* is a late product and can not really be relied upon as to its account of the resurrection.

Historical criticism places the *Book of Acts* late. It is maintained that several addresses in the *Book of Acts* were not actually made at the time claimed, but that they are homilies found so helpful that they are fitted back into that period by late writers. Paul's conversion was not so late, but the writing about it was late, it is claimed. The trouble with historical criticism is

THE AMERICAN LUTHERAN ANCESTRY 25

that it has not taken time to hear what the psychologist has to say, and it is not wise to draw any conclusions until all the facts in the case are in.[38]

No one denies the existence of the Church, but how did it come about? In making any scientific explanation of any phenomenon, every fact and factor known concerning that phenomenon must be explained. If a theory explains all but one fact or factor, that theory is not sound. Apparently it seems easy to say that the resurrection of Jesus Christ is a myth, but the theory falls to pieces when it seeks to explain how the myth could create the story of the early Church and its consequent power. Psychologists find that the resurrection story does not fit any of the above named theories. Who then created this "fiction" of the resurrection that the human mind is not capable of conceiving?

A brief examination of the *Book of Acts* may be in place. Conclusions will be drawn after the facts are registered.

Acts 1:3 states that Jesus Christ showed himself alive after his passion by many infallible proofs (tekmeriois) or by evidence which proved conclusive. His appearance was not in the realm of vision but he was physically present. The twentieth chapter of John indicates how satisfying this evidence was and how it was complete in every detail.

Acts 1:21f. gives a vivid picture of the significance attached to the resurrection of Jesus. "Of the men therefore that have companied with us all the time that the Lord Jesus went in and went out among us, beginning from the baptism of John, unto the day that he was received up from us, of these must one become a witness with us of his resurrection." No one could be an apostle unless he had witnessed the resurrection.

---

[38] The trained psychologist, like the trained jurist, can soon discover whether or not he is dealing with the testimony of an eyewitness. In the myth, for instance, there are three fundamental elements that you can not find in material produced by an eyewitness, namely, 1) A small amount of historical reality; 2) A large amount of imagination; 3) A story or a testimony motivated by a felt need.

Acts 1:24f. states that the apostles prayed to Jesus. "And they prayed, and said, Thou, Lord, who knowest the hearts of all men, show of these two the one whom thou hast chosen." Here is the beginning, the germ, of the New Testament Christological idea. They prayed to the risen and ascended Lord. According to this, was Christology produced or germinated in Paul's mind, or did it grow immediately after Pentecost?

Acts 2:14f. pictures the twelve, all of them standing before the large audience and bearing testimony to the risen Lord, while Peter speaks on their behalf. Would these twelve act that way unless they had very definite convictions based on "infallible" proofs of the resurrection?

Acts 2:22f. speaks of "Jesus of Nazareth, a man approved of by God." This expression certainly indicates that the *Book of Acts* was written early, because when the Christological idea had developed, Christ was never referred to as "a man approved of by God." Note how Peter is talking directly to people among whom these things had happened. He did not make any effort to prove these events because such proofs were not necessary. Later in Acts Peter is found talking to people among which these things had not happened, and then he talks quite differently from what he does here.

Acts 2:23 refers to the trial of Jesus as "unlawful." Every single step in the trial of Jesus was unlawful. In the first place it was held early in the morning. In the second place there was too little time between the first and the second trials.

Acts 2:24 states that God raised Jesus from the dead. This again indicates the early writing of the *Book of Acts*. Peter would not have used this expression after the Christological idea had been developed and formulated.

Acts 2:27 makes reference to Hades. The myth theory leaves the body in the grave. The early Christians did not bother with the grave. Peter shows how Christ's body could not see corruption. This is a Hebraic idea expressed before you later get into the Greek atmosphere.

THE AMERICAN LUTHERAN ANCESTRY 27

Acts 2:29 states that David saw corruption. Two things are insisted on by the myth theory; *one* is that the soul remains in Hades; the *other* is that the body remains in the grave. See how Peter refutes these ideas in verse 31 where he insists that Christ "neither was left in Hades, nor did his flesh see corruption."

Acts 2:32 maintains that all twelve apostles were witnesses to the actual and resurrected Jesus. We have it from Peter's own mouth how these twelve twice in the short speech of Peter testified to this fact. These men all knew Jesus and could not be fooled by substitutes. Note also how the Holy Spirit is poured out upon these witnesses. Should they then immediately afterward stand up and tell a deliberate lie?

Acts 2:36 refers to Jesus as "Lord and Christ." Previously it had been difficult even for the apostles to believe that Jesus was the Christ. This is also the first testimony as to what the resurrection did. "Let all of the house of Israel therefore know assuredly, that God hath made him both Lord and Christ, this Jesus whom ye crucified."

Acts 2:38 indicates how the people reacted to this statement of Peter. They did not speak to Peter alone, but to "the rest of the apostles" also. They were terrified that they had become fighters against God. You could never have gotten this reaction unless there had been in the apostolic group an accepted belief in the resurrection of Jesus Christ. They realized that God had set His seal upon Him as the Messiah.

The baptism was to be in the name of Jesus. In Matthew 28:20 the baptism was to be in the name of the Father, and of the Son, and of the Holy Spirit. Previously in this chapter the apostles had asserted their faith in the Father. The Holy Spirit had just been given. Hence the stress on baptism here in the name of Jesus only indicates that we are dealing with early material.

Acts 3:4f. tells of Peter and John going up to the temple. Note the numinous consciousness throughout this story. The story also has the vividness of an eyewitness. Peter "fastening his eyes upon him" verse 4; and the healed man "held Peter and John" verse 11.

Acts 3:12 tells how Peter spoke to the people in the temple. In verse 13 the term "paida" is used of Jesus as the Son of God. This is a Hebraism, and we do not find this term used later of the risen Lord except in Acts 4:27, 30. Hence this material must be early.

Acts 2:13, "whom ye delivered up," brings a direct accusation against the audience which is different from that to which Peter spoke in chapter 2. If you did not have the Gospel accounts, you could rewrite the Gospel story quite well from these early chapters in the *Book of Acts*. Who was responsible for the crucifixion of Jesus? Here is an accusation by one who himself was a Jew.

Acts 3:14-15, you "asked for a murderer" to be granted you. In verse 15 the expression "Prince of Life" is a Hebraism which is not used later. God raised Him from the dead, whereof Peter and John were witnesses.

Acts 3:16f., "by faith in his name," salvation would come to the people. The people had acted in ignorance, verse 17, but Peter admonished them to "repent," verse 19. Here is the material out of which the Gospels were built. The emphasis is on the fact of the resurrection. It is entirely contrary to the myth theory. Here the interest is hot immediately after the event, while in the myth it requires some forty years to arouse such interest. And there it does not become hot until it is generally accepted by the group.

Acts 4:2 calls attention to the conflict with the Sadducees. Why did the apostles suddenly walk out of their hiding place? Here they speak boldly in public to the annoyance of the Sadducees who denied the resurrection of the dead. Something has happened that the psychologist must account for.

Acts 4:6 introduces Peter and John face to face with the actual religious leaders of the people. This is the first time they are in court. When Jesus was in court they ran away. Here we find them "filled with the Holy Spirit" verse 8. It is the power

THE AMERICAN LUTHERAN ANCESTRY   29

of the risen Lord which makes it possible for Peter and John to face these leaders.

Acts 4:11 has a keen thrust. "He is the stone which was set at nought of you builders." And in verse 12 Peter states that "in none other is there salvation." If Israel had accepted this second chance, the history of Israel would have been quite different, even in present day.

Acts 4:13 the religious authorities took knowledge of the apostles that they had been with Jesus. They related this unusual power and influence directly to their contact with Jesus.

Acts 10:36 presents Jesus as "Lord of all." Peter speaks to a Gentile audience, Cornelius and his household at Caesarea. In verse 38 Peter says of Jesus that "God anointed him." This is clearly an early form or expression used before the people had grown sensitive to the divinity of Jesus Christ. Twenty years later you do not find this expression. Hence the *Book of Acts* deals with early material.

In all this early material the main point is that God raised Jesus from the dead. Secondly, the resurrection is a fact. Later the *function* of the resurrection enters in. That is just the way things develop in literature.

The conversion experience of Paul is an important factor in the resurrection study. Conversion is not a sudden thing. A conflict goes on for quite some time from within and then the final issue is a triumph on one side or the other.

What were the big issues in Paul's conversion experience? The two things that aroused Paul against the Christians were, *first,* their insistence that Jesus was the Messiah; *secondly,* that God had raised him from the dead. In the three accounts of Paul's conversion, Acts 9 by Luke who was not an eyewitness, and Acts 22 and 26 as told by Paul himself, there is an insistence upon the fact that Paul saw and spoke with the risen Lord. After this appearance of the risen Lord, there was a change of mind in Paul. He believed that Jesus was the Christ and that God had raised him from the dead. This is abundantly evidenced by three documents which all skeptics who have any pretension to scholarship concede were written by Paul, namely, Romans, First Corinthians and Galatians.[39]

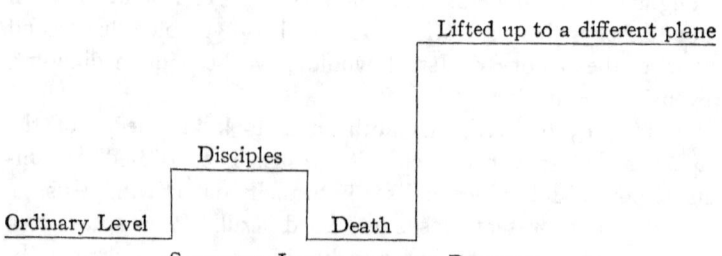

SPIRITUAL LEVELS FOR THE DISCIPLES.

This brief examination certainly indicates that the *Book of Acts* deals with early material, and that the resurrection fact raised the interest to its greatest height in the early days immediately following the event itself. Later the interest cools a little. In all the New Testament writings you find the resurrection and the ascension settled and accepted facts. Hebrews has only one statement concerning the resurrection. In First Peter the "living hope" is in the resurrection of Jesus Christ from the dead. In Second Peter the interest has cooled down. In Revelation the resurrection of Jesus is dramatized, but here you have an entirely different emotional quality. In Post-Apostolic literature the interest in the resurrection has cooled down a little more. It gets so cool, in fact, that the interest in the atonement steps in and the interest in the resurrection slips out.

[39] The Gospel accounts agree precisely in all their leading characteristics and features of the resurrection of Jesus Christ from the dead. They all affirm that he actually died upon the cross; that his body was given by Pilate to Joseph of Arimathea; that his body was laid in a new sepulchre; and that he rose again on the third day. In reading the four Gospel accounts of the death, burial and resurrection of Jesus Christ, it is impossible for an honest mind to escape these impressions, (1) The Gospels give four independent accounts which differ in some details, but which agree in all essentials; (2) Each account bears striking indications of having been given by an eyewitness; (3) These narratives are characterized by natu-

THE AMERICAN LUTHERAN ANCESTRY 31

Do these facts fit the Myth theory of the resurrection of Jesus? Do they fit in with the other resurrection theories? If not, the Lutheran Church can continue to believe in the actual resurrection of Jesus Christ from the dead, and still maintain its intellectual integrity.

3. REVIEW QUESTIONS

1. Why revelation by Incarnation?
2. Why a Trinity in redemption?
3. How does Incarnation clarify our conception of personality?
4. What problems center around the Messianic consciousness of Jesus?
5. What contribution does a psychological analysis of *Document Q* make to our conception of the historic Jesus Christ?
6. Why will we "never come to the true cause until psychology has been heard" with reference to the resurrection of Jesus?
7. Why does the Church stress the crucifixion and the resurrection of Jesus Christ?
8. How do you evaluate the various resurrection theories? Why?
9. How does the Myth theory explain the resurrection and the beginning of the Church?
10. How is the Myth theory refuted by science and by the Scriptures?
11. What evidences do you have that the material in the *Book of Acts* is early?
12. What contribution does a psychological analysis of the *Book of Acts* make to the study of the resurrection of Jesus?

TOPICS FOR SPECIAL STUDY

1. Revelation and incarnation.
2. Trinity and redemption.
3. Incarnation and personality.
4. The Messianic consciousness of Jesus.
5. Apostolic and prophetic consciousness.
6. Crucifixion and resurrection as a unity.
7. Resurrection power, Rom. 1:1-4; Eph. 1:19; etc.
8. Lutheran faith and intellectual integrity.

Jesus Christ is, of course, the founder of the Christian Church. That he intended to organize a Church is clearly seen from the essentials he left for a church organization. Notice that the

---

ralness, straightforwardness, artlessness and simplicity; (4) Unintentional evidence of words, phrases and accidental details clearly indicates that here we have to do with early, first-hand material.

Augsburg Confession[40] defines the Church as "the congregation of saints, in which the Gospel is rightly taught and the sacraments rightly administered." Christ gave to his Church the following essentials, 1) The preaching of the Word of God. Christ is himself the Word.[41] 2) The Sacrament of Baptism and the Sacrament of the Altar. Christ himself instituted these two sacraments, and these two only. 3) Church leaders, or Apostles, with a special call and a special training.[42] 4) The special guidance of the Holy Spirit.[43] 6) The Power to exercise the necessary church discipline.[44]

Pentecost, Acts 2:1-4, is usually taken as the real birthday of the Christian Church. On that day the Holy Spirit was given as promised by the Lord. A great change came over the disciples. They came out of their hiding places and witnessed boldly and with power as to the crucified and risen Lord. In response, 3000 were baptized.[45] Soon the number grew to 5000.[46] A little later Luke states that believers were the more added to the Lord, multitudes of both men and women.[47] The next chapter states that "the word of God increased; and the number of the disciples multiplied in Jerusalem exceedingly; and a great company of priests were obedient to the faith."[48]

As the Church in the Apostolic Age was to be a faithful prototype of the Christian Church of later centuries, careful attention should be given to the distinctive features of this early Church as to life, worship, doctrine and organization.

---

[40] Article VII.
[41] See diagram illustrating this fact.
[42] Through this selection Christ originated the "apostolate," the first office of the Christian Church, Luke 6:13; Matth. 28:16-20. These apostles came to have a special authority in the early Church, 1) because of their special call by the Lord; 2) because of their special training by the Lord; 3) because of the special revelations given to them by the Lord after his resurrection.
[43] See John 16:13; Acts 1:8; Acts 2:1-4.
[44] Matth. 18:15-20; 16:16-19.
[45] Acts 2:41.
[46] Acts 4:4.
[47] Acts 5:14
[48] Acts 6:7.

THE AMERICAN LUTHERAN ANCESTRY 33

a. *Life.*—Luke gives a brief, quadrilateral description of the life of the early Church in Acts 2:42. They continued steadfastly in the apostle's teaching, that is, the Word of God was their standard for faith and life. This is their *first* characteristic. They continued steadfastly in "fellowship." Luther calls this the "priesthood of believers." Fellowship with one another in brotherly love; and free access to God through Jesus Christ without the mediation of a priest or an ecclesiastical institution. This is the *second* characteristic. They continued "in the breaking of bread," that is, for some time they took Holy Communion every day, usually after the common supper meal. "This do in remembrance of me," had the Lord said. This was their *third* characteristic. They also continued steadfastly in "prayers." Diligent use was made, not only of the Means of Grace, the Word of God and the Sacraments, but much time was spent in prayer. This was their *fourth* chief characteristic.

In consequence of these qualities, the Church had a tremendous power. "Many signs and wonders were done through the apostles." Those who did not belong to the youthful Church were prevented from making premature attacks upon the Christians. "Fear came upon every soul."[49]

Steadfastness, unity, gladness, praise and thanksgiving and popular favor characterized these early Christians.[50] They were not *separatists*, but continued "steadfastly and with one accord in the temple," where they tried to put new life and meaning into the existing religious order of things.

Well chosen and sanctified leadership also marked the early Church. Though Peter was the recognised leader on the Day of Pentecost and immediately after, the leadership of the early Jerusalem Church soon passed into the hands of James "the Just," a half-brother of the Lord. He was particularly well qualified to stand in the breach between the old and the new order of things. Under his tactful leadership, every effort was made to win the disciples of Moses for Jesus Christ. Later in

[49] Acts 2:43.   [50] Acts 2:46-47.

the Apostolic Church, Paul comes to the front as the great church leader. He is the great representative of Gentile Christianity. The development of Christianity during the life time of Peter, James and Paul, may be likened to two massive pillars, one representing the Jewish and the other representing the Gentile sections. During the leadership of the apostle John,

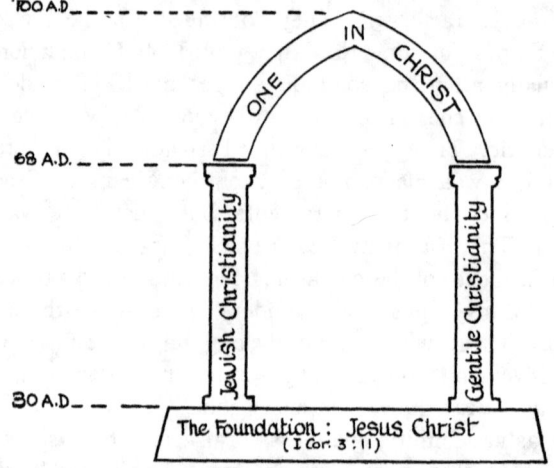

THE GROWTH OF CHRISTIANITY FROM 30 TO 68, AND FROM 68 TO 100 A.D.

about 66-98 A.D., these two massive pillars were connected by a beautiful arch. Thus, each leader was particularly well suited to the period in which he served.

The Lord and his apostles had a community of all goods, that is, they had a common treasury. The apostles naturally extended this relation to the whole Christian community in Jerusalem. In this manner they tried to follow an exhortation given by the Lord.[51] They had "all things in common; and they sold their possessions and goods, and parted them to all, accord-

[51] Luke 12:33.

ing as any man had need."[52] But they did not make this a legal ordinance. This experiment of having all goods in common was evidently never repeated in any other congregation. Read, for instance, about the rich and the poor in the Epistle of James.

THE SPREAD OF CHRISTIANITY EASTWARD

The Jerusalem experiment served as an illustration, not of what the Church should do, but of what the Church should *not* do in such matters.

Tabitha or Dorcas illustrates the charitable activities of the Church in some localities.[53] Inter-church relations are described in chapter 11 of the *Book of Acts*, where Christians in Antioch sent relief to the famine stricken Christians in Jerusalem. In chapter 15 we are told how various churches sent delegates to the Jerusalem Council.

The early Church was essentially a missionary church, and it

[52] Acts 2:45.
[53] Acts 9:36-43.

soon became a persecuted Church. But in spite of opposition, the early Christians were faithful to their calling of preaching, baptising and teaching, starting in Jerusalem and continuing toward the ends of the earth. Thus the grain of mustard seed soon developed into a tree of considerable proportions, with branches reaching out to Jewish and Gentile communities in many parts of the world.

b. *Worship.*—The worship as described in the second chapter of the *Book of Acts* had the following distinctive features: (1) Peter read from the Scriptures, Joel 3:1f., before he began to preach and based his sermon on the text he read. (2) The essential part of this impressive worship was not ceremony but the preaching of the Word of God. Peter was the preacher on the Day of Pentecost, and he preached a revival sermon in the purest sense of the word, with special emphasis on sin and grace. (3) The Sacraments were used diligently. The 3000 were not taken into membership of the Church until they had been baptised. And those who had become members continued steadfastly "in the breaking of bread," that is, they took Holy Communion. (4) They made use of public prayers,[54] some from Old Testament Israel, and some from contemporary Christians. (5) They had a regular place for worship, namely the Temple.[55] Hence these early Christian services must have been marked, not only by stirring interest and remarkable power, but also by dignity. Outside Jerusalem the synagogue was frequently used.[56] (6) They had regular time for worship, invariably on Sunday.[57] (7) There was naturally no formal confession of Faith on the Day of Pentecost. The Apostle's Creed was formulated later. But the essentials of this Creed are stated by Peter in his sermon. (8) There is no specific mention of singing on the Day of Pentecost; but the Lord had used a hymn when he instituted the Lord's Supper, and it would be strange if the apostles left

---

[54] Acts 2:42. [55] Acts 2:46. [56] James 2:2.
[57] Acts 20:7; 1 Cor. 16:2; Rev. 1:10. Sunday was hallowed by "sunrise" service and evening "love-feast" or agape.

THE AMERICAN LUTHERAN ANCESTRY 37

out this part of the original ceremony in their services. Singing became an attractive feature of the early Christian worship, and the Apostolic Church had the richest material for sacred poetry and music.

c. *Doctrine.*—Two of the cardinal doctrines of the early Christian Church, namely the Word of God as the standard for faith and life and the "priesthood of believers," have already

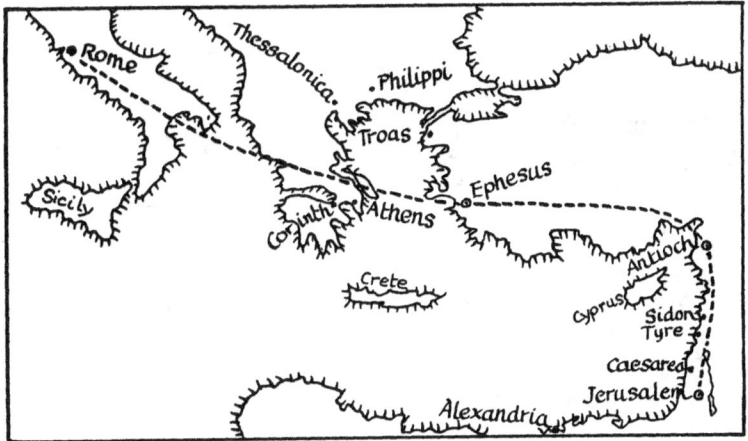

MAP INDICATING THE GREAT CHRISTIAN CENTERS IN THE APOSTOLIC AGE

been referred to in a previous paragraph under *Life*. The third cardinal doctrine, justification by faith alone, became the focus of attention at the Apostolic Council in Jerusalem. A door of faith had been opened unto the Gentiles through the preaching of the apostle Paul. On what terms should these Gentile Christians be admitted to membership in the Church? Was not the transition to be made by way of Jewish Christianity, that is, by way of circumcision and the observance of the Ceremonial Law? Or, was justification by faith in Jesus Christ alone, without circumcision and Mosaism, sufficient qualification for Church membership?

The issue was settled at the Apostolic Council in Jerusalem as recorded in *Acts* chapter 15. James the Just, authoritative head of the Jerusalem Church, settled the problem in favor of the Gentiles, according to the witness of prophecy. His verdict was sanctioned by the apostles and the elders and by the entire Church. Gentile Christianity was emancipated from circumcision and the bondage of Jewish Ceremonial Law, and Paul was officially recognized as an apostle to the Gentiles. It was a great

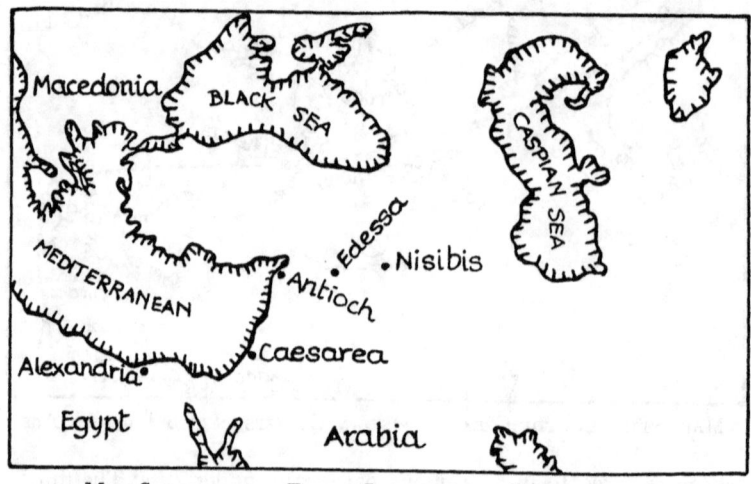

MAP SHOWING THE EARLY CATECHETICAL SCHOOL CENTERS

and far-reaching decision. Justification by faith alone without human merit had been recognized as a universal law in the Kingdom of God on earth. It was this principle Paul re-asserted in his epistles to the Galatians and to the Romans. It was this same basic law which was re-emphasized by Luther in the Reformation. These four, the Apostolic Council in Jerusalem, the Epistle to the Galatians, the Epistle to the Romans, and the Lutheran Reformation, constitute a four leaf clover because they all deal with the same fundamental problem, namely, that man is

THE AMERICAN LUTHERAN ANCESTRY 39

justified and saved by faith alone, and not by faith and human merit.

d. *Organization.*—On the Day of Pentecost, Acts 2:1-4, the Holy Spirit was sent as the divine guide of the Church in all matters. Extraordinary importance was attached by the early Church to the direct guidance of the Holy Spirit. In the first

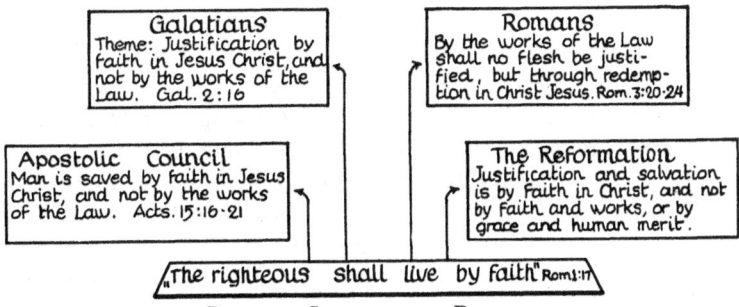

DIAGRAM SHOWING THE RELATION
BETWEEN
THE APOSTOLIC COUNCIL, GALATIANS, ROMANS, AND THE PROTESTANT REFORMATION

recorded case of church discipline, the sin of Ananias was considered a "lie to the Holy Spirit," and not to Peter or to the other apostles.[58]

Christ had also arranged for the guidance of the Church through the office of the *Apostolate*.[59] The apostles became the recognized leaders of the Church because (1) of their special call from the Lord, (2) of their special training by the Lord, (3) of their miraculous endowments and their God-given authority from which there was no appeal, and (4) of their special revelations from the Lord after his resurrection. Hence the apostles differed from other early Christians who also possessed special or extraordinary gifts of the Holy Spirit. The *Apostolate* embraced all the various orders or functions which the Church

[58] Acts 5:3.
[59] Luke 6:13; Matth. 28:16-20.

40   THE LUTHERAN CHURCH IN AMERICA

transmitted to later times. The functions which were later assigned to bishops, presbyters, deacons, pastors, prophets, evangelists and charismatic persons did all originally center in the apostles.

As the Church grew rapidly and the work soon became too extensive for the apostles, the congregation in Jerusalem elected a committee of seven to assist them. The duties of the Seven are implied in Acts 6:1-3. From this it appears that the *Deaconate* was the second office to be instituted in the Church. The Seven in Acts 6:1-6 are not called deacons, however, and consequently some have claimed that the Presbyterate and not the Deaconate was the continuation of the Seven. But it should be remembered that the office and the function of the presbyters were at that time still vested in the apostles themselves. The Seven were the assistants to the apostles, as the deacons later were the assistants to the elders or presbyters. The apostles, and later the elders or presbyters, retained the supervision and guidance of the deacons.[60]

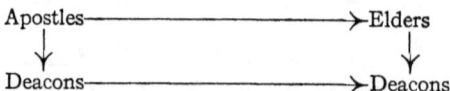

THE OFFICIAL RELATION BETWEEN APOSTLES, DEACONS AND ELDERS

The *Presbyterate* or the office of elders was probably the third office to be instituted in the Church. Nothing is said of the origin of this office, but it very likely shaped itself after the synagogue. Christian presbyters are mentioned for the first time in Acts 11:30. In the New Testament there are two names used interchangeably for these officials, namely "presbyteroi" or presbyters and "episcopoi" or bishops (cf. pastor, minister, elder). Some believe that "presbyter" was a title of dignity, and that "bishop" was a corresponding title of function; but the facts presented in 1 Tim. 3:1-7 and 5:17-22 do not warrant such conclusion. The

---

[60] Acts 14:23; Phil. 1:1; 1 Thess. 5:12; cf. Acts 20:17.

THE AMERICAN LUTHERAN ANCESTRY 41

only difference between presbyters and bishops seems to have been a difference in name. From Acts 14:23 it is clear that Paul and Barnabas, on their First Missionary Journey, entrusted the general leadership of the various local churches they had founded to local elders. These succeeded the apostles as the spiritual leaders and the general directors of the local congregations.

Paul made it a practice to organize all the churches he founded, or came in contact with, according to a definite system. He selected from each local congregation a group of elders who should function as spiritual leaders and general directors, each group for its own local church. This he did on his First and Second Missionary Journeys, as also during the last years of his life.[61] Local elders, or presbyters, succeeded the apostles as the leaders of the churches, and the deacons assisted the elders.[62] This was the prevailing church organization, at least in the regions of Asia Minor and Europe, during the time of the apostle Paul.

The monarchical episcopate, of which there was no trace in the Pastoral Epistles, or in the time of Paul, first gained a foothold in the provinces of Asia toward the close of the Apostolic Age. This is evidenced in the epistles of John and in Revelation. The monarchical episcopate had become the highest office in the local church, that is, the leadership of each congregation centered in one single official who was superior to the other elders and to the deacons. This is clear from the messages of the Lord to the Seven Churches.[63] At the time these messages were given, around 94-96 A.D., the name "episcopos" or bishop had evidently not as yet become the regular title of individual bishops, as was the case in the epistles of Ignatius, written around 110 A.D. The authorized leaders of the Seven Churches are designated by two symbols, "The seven stars are the angels of the

---

[61] Tit. 1:5; 1 Tim. 3:1-13; etc.
[62] Phil. 1:1; 1 Tim. 3:1-13; etc.
[63] Rev. chapt. 2-3.

seven churches."[64] Stars in Scriptural language frequently designated those who govern or rule; and the name "angel" is used in the Old Testament to designate prophets and priests whom God had sent to the people to proclaim the will and the word of God. The officials of the Seven Churches are called "stars" because of leadership; and angels because of their exalted position and their great responsibility. Notice how the Lord placed the entire responsibility for the congregation on a single official, and not on a group of elders.

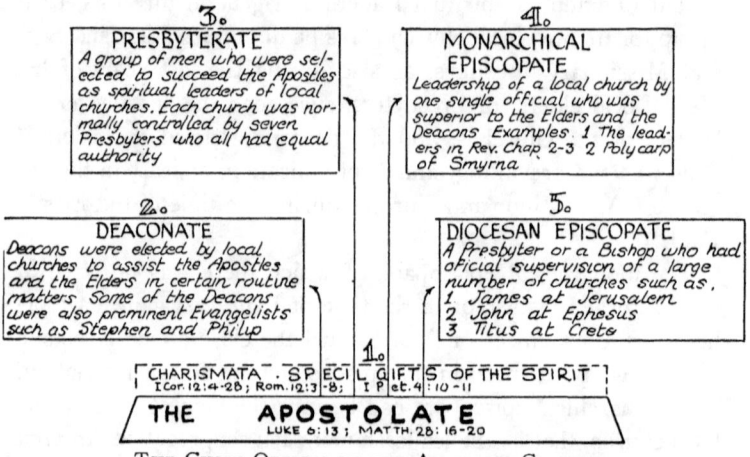

THE CHIEF OFFICES IN THE APOSTOLIC CHURCH

Timothy and Titus were not ordinary elders or presbyters, but above them. Both acted as temporary representatives of Paul in his apostolic capacity, Timothy in Ephesus and vicinity, and Titus on the island of Crete. Paul felt responsible for the development of the churches in these two districts, especially with reference to doctrine and organization. In the temporary functions of Timothy and Titus one may see, perhaps, the rudiments of the Diocesan episcopacy, although this office was not formally instituted until the second century. But the position of the apostle

[64] Rev. 1:20.

THE AMERICAN LUTHERAN ANCESTRY 43

John in Ephesus, at the time he wrote the epistles and Revelation, had nearly all the characteristics of a later diocesan bishop. Compare also the earlier relation of James the Just to the Jewish churches, as reflected in the Epistle of James.

There were also Christians who had received special and extraordinary gifts of the Holy Spirit. These special endowments belonged to no special order or office in the Church, but were given as the Spirit willed.[65] These gifted or charismatic persons, with the exception of women,[66] were allowed to teach and to preach in the congregation. Some of them were employed as special evangelists.[67] The office of the deaconesses is referred to in Rom. 16:1. From 1 Tim. 5:9 it appears that only widows above the age of sixty were admitted to this office. They took care of the poor, the sick, and the strange women in the congregation.

Careful instructions were given as to the qualifications of candidates for church office.[68] A brief study of the first recorded election in the Apostolic Church[69] leaves the following impressions: (1) the qualifications of those to be elected were defined by the apostles; (2) the right to elect the candidates was regarded by the apostles as vested in the Church; (3) the election itself was performed by the congregation, but the appointment and the consecration were completed by the apostles; (4) the final act was the imposition of hands, signifying the divine communication of power and grace. This procedure evidently became the accepted order in the early Church.

Brotherly love[70] was the guiding principle in the life of the Christians. "By this shall all men know that ye are my disciples, if ye have love one to another." This love expressed itself in tender care for sick and needy, and in a remarkable hospitality. Their pure and unselfish living soon aroused the admiration of the non-Christians. The Christians acted as a wholesome

---

[65] 1 Cor. 12:11.
[66] 1 Cor. 14:34; 1 Tim. 2:12.
[67] Acts 21:8; Ephes. 4:11.
[68] 1 Tim. 3:1-13; Acts 6:3.
[69] Acts 6:1-6.
[70] John 13:34-35.

leaven in a decaying society. Christianity checked and gradually removed three great evils of antiquity, namely, contempt for foreign nationalities, slavery and the degradation of womanhood.[71]

Church discipline was quite severe. Heretics, apostates and those who had committed gross sins, were excluded from communion with the Church. The idea was also current that certain sins committed after baptism admitted of no pardon, but involved

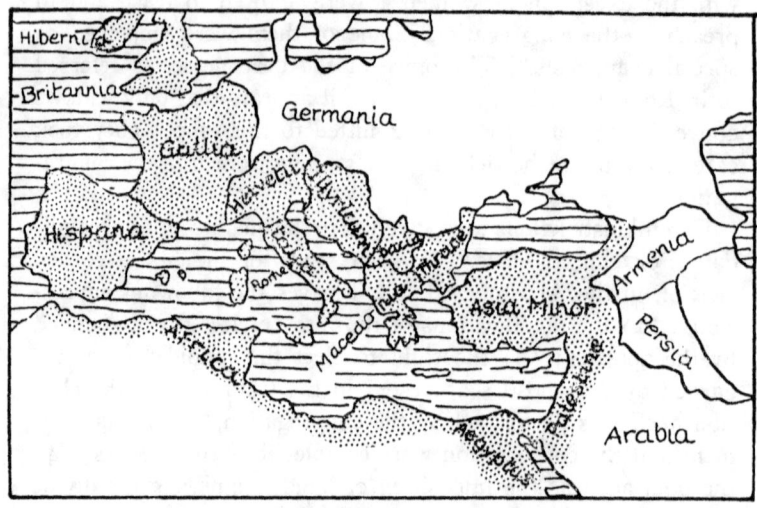

THE ROMAN EMPIRE, 100 A.D.

permanent exclusion from the Church. For this reason baptism was preceded by careful instruction, not only in doctrine, but also in the things Christians were to seek and shun.

e. *Summary.*—Since the life and development of the Church in the Apostolic Age became the basis for all future developments of Christianity, an attempt to summarize the characteristics of this early Church may prove useful. Note the following, (1) the apostles and the other Christians preached the crucified and risen

[71] Gal. 3:28.

THE AMERICAN LUTHERAN ANCESTRY

Lord; (2) they believed that the Triune God asserted His actual and full presence in the Holy Spirit; (3) the Word of God and the Sacrament of Baptism and the Sacrament of the Altar were the only Means of Grace; (4) man is justified and saved by faith in Christ alone, without any merit of good works; (5) the Word of God is the only standard for faith and life; (6) every Christian has direct access to God through faith in Jesus Christ; personal communion with God and the forgiveness of sins are not conditioned by the mediation of a priest, but by faith in Jesus Christ only; (7) it is the blessed privilege of every Christian to have full certainty of salvation; (8) the Church as a living organism took on its own characteristic forms of organization, life and worship; (9) like a grain of mustard seed planted, the Church soon grew into a mighty tree whose branches reached out to many parts of the world.

4. REVIEW QUESTIONS

1. Why is Jesus Christ the founder of the Christian Church?
2. Why is Pentecost, Acts 2:1-4, taken as the birthday of the Church?
3. What characterized the life of the early Christians?
4. How did God provide for leadership?
5. What do we know about the early Christian worship?
6. Which were the cardinal doctrines of the Apostolic Church?
7. How did the Lord provide for organization of his Church?
8. What place did the Holy Spirit have in the government of the Church?
9. Why the apostolate, the deaconate and the presbyterate?
10. What is meant by monarchical episcopate and diocesan episcopacy?
11. What place did the specially gifted (charismatic) persons have in the general work of the congregation?
12. What general procedure was followed in the election of church officials?
13. What was the guiding principle in the life of the Christians? Why?
14. How was church discipline practiced?
15. How would you state the essential characteristics of the early Christian Church?

TOPICS FOR SPECIAL STUDY

1. The Word of God as Standard for Faith and Life.
2. The Relation between Faith and Merit.

3. Compare the Spiritual Priesthood of Believers with the Special Priesthood (1) of the Old Testament; (2) of the Roman Catholic Church; (3) of the Protestant churches.
4. Cardinal Principles in the Apostolic Church.
5. The Conception of the Church in the Apostolic Age.
6. The Place of Woman in the Apostolic Church.
7. The Place of Charismatic Persons in the Early Church.

III. Relation to Subsequent Church Developments.—The Church in the next few centuries may be likened to a great smeltery where the ore is reduced by fusion in a furnace. The liquid metal is poured into set forms where it cools, taking on a permanent shape. The Church at this time was subjected to fiery trials, severe persecutions from without and besetting heresies from within. As Christianity spread westward—like the ore reduced by fusion—the organized life of the Church was gradually and permanently moulded by the Roman genius for government, law and order. This process resulted in Catholicism and paved the way for the adoption of Christianity as the official state religion after 325 A.D.

What is meant by Catholicism? Viewed in the light of apostolic and post-apostolic Christianity, Catholicism involved two distinct changes, a change of *church government* and a change of *faith*.

In the Apostolic Era the universal, spiritual priesthood of all believers was generally recognized by the Church. There was no special priesthood; hence there was no division of the Christians into "clergy" and "laity," nor was there any distinction between a higher and a lower spiritual order of believers. So far as spiritual position and privileges were concerned, ordinary church members were on the same level as church officials. Apostles, prophets, teachers, and other "gifted men," as well as the ordinary church members—all alike had *immediate* access to God through *faith*. A mediating priest or bishop was not necessary to salvation. A sinner received forgiveness by confessing his sins directly to God, as revealed in Jesus Christ through the Bible. Assurance of forgiveness of sins and of salvation came to

THE AMERICAN LUTHERAN ANCESTRY 47

the believer through the Word of God, not by the mouth of a mediating priest. There was no special priesthood which could bar or excommunicate the individual or a community from direct access to God and His grace, the Word and the Sacraments. The Church was not identified with any specific office, but rather with the assembly of believers, the "congregation of saints." Christ said, "Where two or three are gathered in my name, there I am in the midst of them."[72] A direct, personal

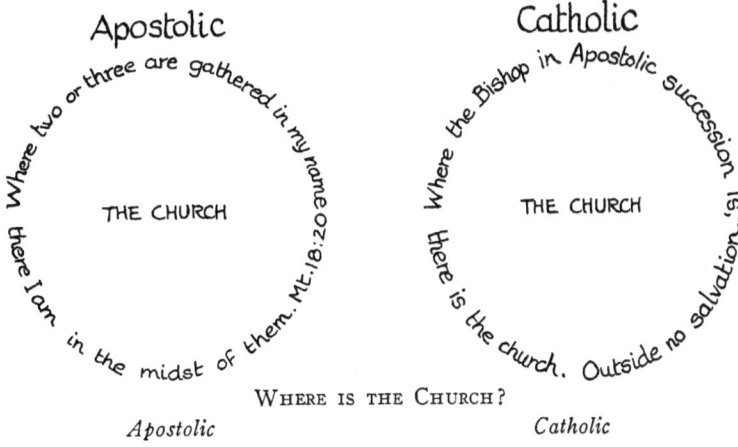

WHERE IS THE CHURCH?
Apostolic   *Catholic*

communion with God through *faith* in Jesus Christ was the *essence* and the *power* of the early Christian life.

God gave "some to be apostles; and some, prophets; and some, evangelists; and some, pastors and teachers."[73] The local churches had elders and deacons who supervised and directed the work of the congregation, administered its charity, took care of the sick, and saw to it that its regular services were held. But the early church organization was not centered in *office* and in *law*, but in the *special gifts* of the Spirit. The preaching, the teaching and the administration of the Sacraments were conducted

[72] Matth. 18:20.   [73] Eph. 4:11.

by the "gifted men" of the congregation. An elder might also preach or teach or administer the Sacraments, but he did not do so because he was an elder, but because he was known to have the "gift." None of these "gifted men" held church office in a legal or judicial sense. The preaching and the teaching and the administration of the Sacraments were not *legally* confined to any specific office. The Gospel could be preached and the Sacraments could be administered in the presence of any assembly of believers who were gathered in the name of the Lord.

Toward the close of the first Christian century a change took place. A general lack of confidence in the special gifts of the Spirit, a desire for more specific order, and a pressing demand

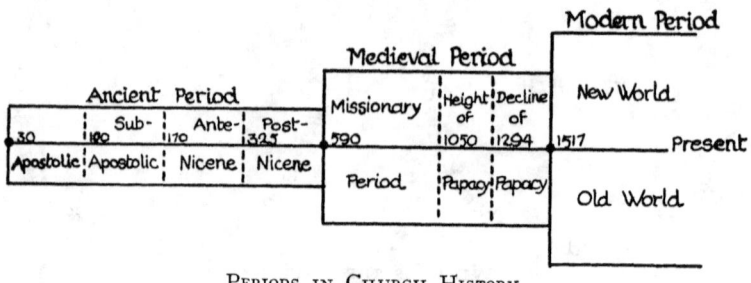

PERIODS IN CHURCH HISTORY

for proper safeguard against heresy resulted in a gradual transfer of the preaching, the teaching and the administration of the Sacraments from the "gifted men" to the local elders. These elders again were elected because they possessed some of the special "gifts," especially the gift of teaching. The official functions were now performed by elders only. The ministry of the Word and the Sacraments became official, and this marked the beginning of the division of the Christians into "clergy" (chosen ones) and "laity" (the masses).

During the second and third centuries another important change took place. Instead of government by a group of elders, the local churches were headed by single officials for whom the

THE AMERICAN LUTHERAN ANCESTRY 49

name "bishop" was exclusively reserved. This change took place in certain regions of Asia Minor even toward the close of the first Christian century, although the name bishop was not used to designate these officials. The election of the bishop became a *legal* ordinance, and the bishop alone had a right to teach and to preach and to administer the Sacraments, because he alone, it was believed, had been endowed and appointed by God to be the leader of the congregation. The presence of the bishop or his representative was now essential to every valid act of the congregation. In fact, without the bishop there could be no congregation. Any society, to be a church, must have a bishop; and any person desiring to be a Christian, must be subject to a bishop. Outside of this Church, the Church of the bishops in apostolic succession, there was no salvation. The Church was no longer understood to be the holy people of God believing on Jesus Christ, but rather a group of persons belonging to the churches of these bishops.[74] The personal communion with God, and the assurance of the presence of Christ, was now definitely conditioned on strict adherence to certain outward forms. *This is the essence of Catholicism.*

This momentous transformation in the conception of the Church did not merely involve a change of church organization, but also a change of faith. Communion with God was now possible only by a communion with the bishop. The original spiritual priesthood of believers yielded to a special priesthood, the clergy, and the evangelical conception of the Church as a "congregation of saints" yielded to the Catholic conception of the Church as a group of believers belonging to the episcopate.

Several reasons may be given for this rapid rise of the historic episcopate. (1) The extraordinary spiritual gifts of miracle working and prophecy, as exercised by the early Church, were gradually replaced by formalism in teaching and in worship.

---

[74] For the formative influence of Clement of Rome (95 A.D.) and Ignatius of Antioch (110-17 A.D.) see Qualben, *A History of the Christian Church,* Third Edition, pp. 90-91.

(2) As Christianity spread westward, the Roman genius for law and order created a more specific organization, and also introduced a *legalistic* relationship between God and the believer, like a legal contract between two parties. (3) The conflict with heresies made it expedient to transfer the responsibility to a single office. False teachers claimed to possess the truth as delivered to the Church through the apostles. The Church answered by investing the office of the bishop, the only direct succession from the apostles, with the power to determine and

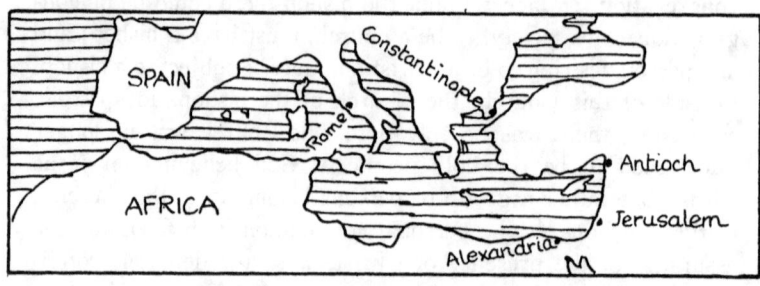

The Location of the Five Patriarchs

interpret true doctrine and saving faith. (4) As the Church came into increasingly intimate contact with the cultural and intellectual life in the Empire, the educational standards of the church leaders had to be raised. Economically, it seemed easier to educate one rather than several leaders for a single congregation. (5) Several churches became large organizations which were difficult to manage, especially as to discipline, charity and finance. Disagreement among the presbyters would often prevent a desirable unity in the Church. Hence the need of episcopal authority was strongly felt, and the vindication of such authority was sure to follow. (6) The heroic martyrdom of a number of the bishops added to the prestige of the office. (7) The specially "gifted" became fewer and their prophecies perhaps less reliable; the expectation of the speedy return of the Lord was no longer so general; a new generation had grown up that had not been

THE AMERICAN LUTHERAN ANCESTRY 51

won directly for the Church from paganism, but had been born and educated in Christian homes; and, instead of the immediate gifts of the Spirit, Christians relied on organization and outward religious authority.

Uniform adoption of the episcopal form prepared the Church for a successful encounter with certain difficulties. What the Christian Church lost in purity it gained in strength of organization. The Church, in preparing for the conquest of the world, developed a strong hierarchy of officers, headed by a single

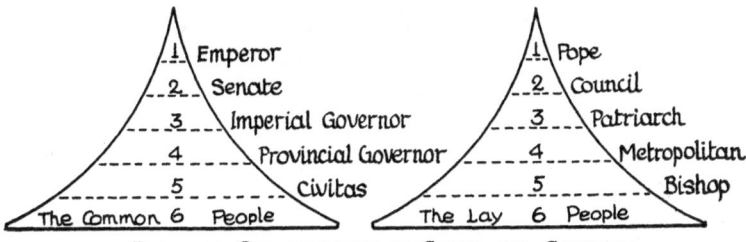

PARALLEL ORGANIZATION OF STATE AND CHURCH

governing official, to lead the believers and guard against the dangers of unsteady mass movements. When the Roman Empire crumbled in 476 A.D., the Church had developed a strong organization which made it possible for her to withstand and partly to transform the flood of barbarism which swept over Europe. On the other hand, the misuse of this organization ultimately demanded drastic adjustments.

Christianity, like a leaven, gradually permeated Graeco-Roman life, but paganism in turn reacted decidedly upon Christianity. As the masses began to join the Church, pagan ideas and practices gained undue popularity. Many nominal Christians sought compensation for their heathen beliefs and their heathen deities in veneration of angels, martyrs, saints, images and relics. The meritoriousness of good works was advocated by prominent church leaders. Pilgrimages to sacred places such as Palestine, Mount Sinai, the tombs of Peter and Paul, became general because of the excessive merit or work-righteousness attached to such acts of devotion.

The simple rites of Baptism and the Lord's Supper were greatly elaborated, and new sacraments were added. Confirmation became a sacrament toward the close of the fourth century. The idea of the Christian priesthood as a divine institution led to the establishment of Ordination as a sacrament. Augustine regarded Marriage as a sacrament. The sacrament of Extreme Unction began to be recognized during the pontificate of Innocent I (401-417). But the Catholic system of seven sacraments was not definitely fixed until the year 1215, the seven sacraments being Baptism, Confirmation, Lord's Supper, Penance, Extreme Unction, Ordination and Marriage.[75]

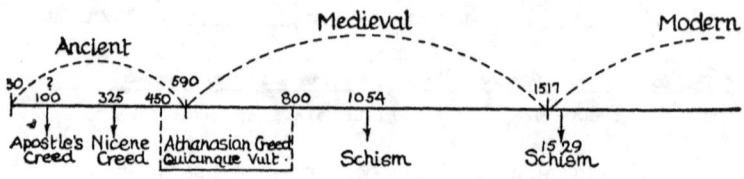

THE THREE GENERAL ANCIENT SYMBOLS

Since Christianity was considered a chief unifying force in the Empire, great efforts were made to unify the doctrine of the Church. But where was the true Church? The criterion was formulated and defined by the Five General or Ecumenical Councils, namely (1) Nicea, 325; (2) Constantinople I, 381; (3) Ephesus, 431; (4) Chalcedon, 451; and (5) Constantinople II, 553. The doctrinal definitions of these Councils, especially those of the Nicene and the Athanasian Creeds, have always since been accepted by the main body of the Church.

Efforts to unify the Church in organization and practice centered increasingly in the clergy. In the course of the fourth and the fifth centuries an ever-widening chasm developed between

[75] Rudolf Sohm claims that the real Roman Catholic Church started around 1200 A.D. as a corporation.

THE AMERICAN LUTHERAN ANCESTRY 53

clergy and laity, until the view prevailed that only the clergy constituted the Church proper. Several causes contributed to this strange development.

First, the clergy became an economically independent order. Many new privileges were gradually added. The privilege of receiving legacies and donations made the Church wealthy. This property was generally divided so that the bishop received one fourth; the priests in his territory received one fourth; one fourth was used for the maintenance of the congregations; and one fourth was given to charity. These donations added to the income of the clergy and promoted their interests in secular affairs. The income of the country churches was also under the supervision of the bishop and his clergy.

Secondly, the Church became a legal tribunal with a very extensive jurisdiction. Constantine gave the episcopal tribunals right to settle all legal disputes within the Church, and also civil matters which did not involve criminal cases. The clergy could henceforth avoid altogether the secular courts. Through the peculiar privilege of intercession, which formerly also had belonged to heathen priests, the clergy could often obstruct the course of justice in the civil courts.

Thirdly, the clergy became a special order with special customs and a distinct career. The clergy was separated from the laity not only by their official capacity, but also, it was believed, by higher religious and moral gifts and an *indelible character* imparted through ordination. Once a priest, always a priest. Enforced celibacy belongs to a later period. Official penance was abolished in favor of private penance before the clergy, and later also before the monks. In dress, in shaving the crown of the head, and in other external ways, the clergy manifested their distinction.

Fourthly, codification of church (canon) laws and traditions began. Some of the doctrines and practices of the Church did not have any support in Scripture, so officials sought support, like the Pharisees of old, in Tradition.

In the infancy and youth of the new Latin-Teutonic civilization which developed during the Middle Ages, the Church through the popes became more and more involved in secular affairs. Pope Gregory VII (1073-85) states his view of the papal office in these words, "The Roman Church was founded by God alone; the Roman pope alone can with right be called universal; he alone may use the imperial insignia; his feet alone shall be kissed by all princes; he may depose emperors; he himself may be judged by no one; the Roman Church has never erred, nor will it err in all eternity."

The Roman Catholic Church promoted a world view which was decidedly false. Superstition and fear dominated the religion of the common man. Fear of the Devil and his world, God's awful Judgement Day, hell and purgatory exerted a tremendous influence upon him. How could he protect himself against Satan? And how could he obtain salvation, thereby escaping the torments of hell? He looked to the Church, and the Church gave the following answer.

(1) Protection against the forces of evil and salvation reside in the Church, and in the Church only. It had been asserted for many centuries that "there is no salvation outside the Church." Communion with God and the forgiveness of sins were possible only through a communion with the Church, represented by the clergy.

(2) The Church had a great number of means whereby man could protect himself against Satan and the evil spirits. Charms and amulets were sold to the people for such purposes. Prayers to the Saints and to the Virgin Mary were particularly effective.

(3) The Sacraments were necessary to salvation. They were in the pope's power, and could be withheld if the organization of the Church did not approve. The pope had the power of excommunication and of placing cities, provinces, or kingdoms under interdict.

(a) Excommunication was directed against individuals. The lesser excommunication deprived a person of the Sacraments;

THE AMERICAN LUTHERAN ANCESTRY 55

the greater cut him off from all rights. If a king, his subjects were released from their oath of allegiance. Mass could not be celebrated in the presence of the excommunicate. He could not hold a benefice, exercise jurisdiction, or take part in an election pertaining to the Church. Any one who provided him with food or shelter, incurred the penalties of the Church. Christian burial was denied him.

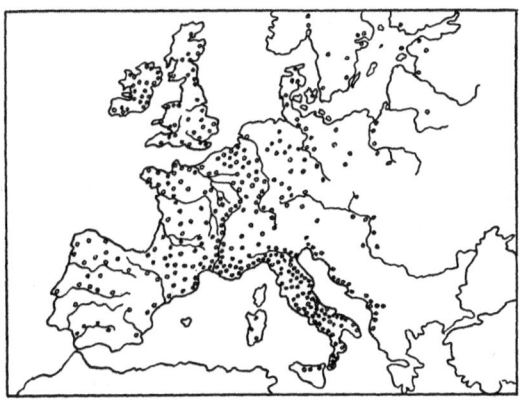

EUROPEAN MONASTERIES ABOUT 1300 A.D.

(b) The Interdict was directed against a city, province or kingdom. The total interdict forbade public worship, the administration of the Sacraments and Christian burial. The churches were closed; no bell could be rung; no marriage could be celebrated; no burial ceremony could be performed. The Sacraments of Baptism and Extreme Unction alone could be administered.

(c) The ban of the Empire was a secular punishment, a declaration of outlawry, upon any excommunicated person or community.

(4) Penance consisted of the contrition of the heart, confession, and satisfaction. Auricular confession was necessary before

absolution could be received. All known sins had to be enumerated before the confessor. Satisfaction and release from punishment could usually be secured by means of good works, such as prayers, alms, pilgrimages and the like.

(5) All arrears of temporal punishment were inflicted in Purgatory, a place of punishment before the resurrection. Souls in Purgatory might be delivered by masses, intercessions, alms, and good works. No one needed to fear hell if he rightly used the Sacrament of Penance.

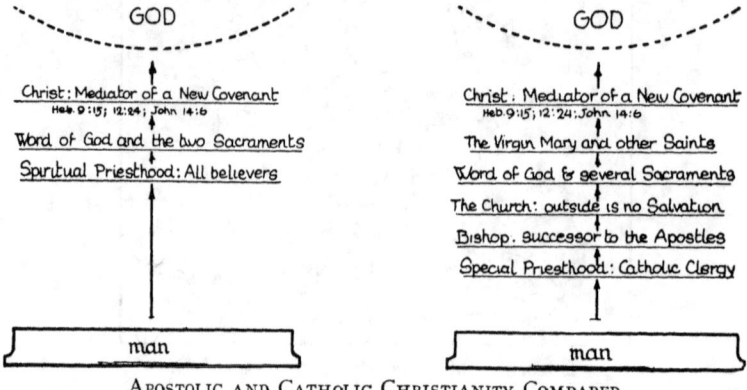

APOSTOLIC AND CATHOLIC CHRISTIANITY COMPARED

(6) Punishment for sins of the living and for those in Purgatory could be lightened or remitted altogether by securing indulgence from the Church. These indulgences were sold for money. The practice of indulgence rested on the theory that Christ and the Saints had performed more good works than were needed. These surplus merits were at the disposal of the Church and could be given or sold to less fortunate people.

(7) The merits of good works were greatly extolled. This work-righteousness had its roots in Pharisaic legalism and in the legalistic religious conceptions inherited from the ancient Romans.

For centuries the Church insisted on being a kingdom of this world in distinct opposition to Jesus Christ, the founder, who

THE AMERICAN LUTHERAN ANCESTRY 57

emphatically had stated, "My kingdom is not of this world." The accumulative effects of this sinful state of affairs were bound to be keenly felt. Many pagan and worldly elements had come to exert an undue influence. While the simple Gospel was obscured, the pope and other church officials set their faces like flint against any reforms.[76] Meanwhile the new Latin-Teutonic civilization was slowly emerging from the chaos of the early Middle Ages. The dawn of a new day had come. The Latin element in the new civilization reached its majority in the Renaissance or Revival of Learning. The Teutonic element reached its maturity in the Protestant Reformation.

5. REVIEW QUESTIONS

1. How do you account for the change from Apostolic to Catholic Christianity?
2. What is the essence of Catholicism as seen in the light of the early Church?
3. How do you explain the rapid rise of the historic episcopate?
4. Why did the Church organize parallel to the State?
5. Was it a good thing that Christianity became a state religion?
6. What efforts were made to unify the doctrine of the Church?
7. Why the increasing cleavage between clergy and laity?
8. What views did pope Gregory VII hold as to the papal office?
9. What was the Catholic world view toward the close of the Middle Ages?
10. How did the Church seek to meet the religious needs of the average man?
11. What is meant by excommunication, interdict, ban?
12. Why was a reformation bound to come?

TOPICS FOR SPECIAL STUDY

1. Roman influence on church organization.
2. Significance of the Apostolic Succession.
3. Apostolic and Catholic conception of the Church.
4. Penance, its history and significance.
5. Lutheranism and the Ecumenical Councils.
6. Work-righteousness as reflected in church life.
7. The Catholic world view.

[76] For a discussion of these reform movements, see Qualben, *A History of the Christian Church,* Third Edition, pp. 191-195.

IV. The Lutheran Reformation.

—When Martin Luther appeared as a reformer,[77] there had been for two centuries an increasing criticism of the Church. The demand for reform was general and of long standing. The Protestant Reformation was peculiarly favored by a timely convergence of forces as to time, place, persons, circumstances, and religious and political relations. Yet this favorable environment did not produce the Reformation. Luther worked out his own position by himself, regardless of previous rebellions and repeated refusals of reform. The origin and genius of the Reformation must be sought, not in a favorable environment, but in the *personal experiences* of Martin Luther of the truth of the Gospel, and in the growth of his religious convictions as based upon the Word of God.

From his parents Martin Luther received hereditary traits that were of great value to him in his work. The vigorous peasant nature, the powerful physical and mental energies, helped him to survive the abuses of monastic life and the titanic work connected with the Reformation. He also inherited that fearless, fighting spirit, that vigorous humor, and that rustic rudeness which marked his ancestors. He possessed a love for hard work, a determination of will and a peculiar common sense conservatism. His intimate knowledge of the language of the common people, his close contact with nature and with the people of the lower classes, his knowledge of the popular religious life and his thorough education, made him a man of the people in the best sense. The German people recognized him as one of their own; they listened to him and loved him as few Germans have ever been loved.

Luther's childhood home was one of medieval Catholic piety. There were no reformatory tendencies in the religious family life. His father was a pious Catholic on very friendly terms

---

[77] Luther started his reform movement in 1517; Zwingli started his in 1519; Calvin started his in 1536. Zwingli owed much of his reform ideas to Luther, and Calvin always regarded Luther as the great founder of Protestantism.

THE AMERICAN LUTHERAN ANCESTRY 59

with two of the priests of Mansfeld. In 1497 when two new altars in Mansfeld were dedicated, promise of indulgence for sixty days was given to all who heard the first mass, and Luther's father was among the first to receive an indulgence. Luther was taught the Creed, the Ten Commandments, the Lord's Prayer,

MAP ILLUSTRATING THE LIFE OF LUTHER

and some simple hymns and chants. He also learned that the Emperor was God's ruler on earth, and that the Church was the House of the Pope. Christ was pictured to him as a severe Judge, "sitting on a rainbow with his Mother and John the Baptist on either side as intercessors against his frightful wrath." He heard terrible stories about the devil and about evil spirits which filled the air and the water, the forests and the meadows, the mountains and the valleys, and did a lot of harm to the people and the cattle. Even more dangerous were the witches whose secret power over the people could accomplish terrible things.

The magistracy of Mansfeld demanded that all school children should go to church and that the choirmaster should teach them to sing. All boys had to attend the church festivals where the impressive ceremonies and especially the singing made lasting impressions upon the young minds. The people of Mansfeld were good Catholics who honored the pope, attended the church services, believed in saints and relics and bought indulgences. Luther grew up in this pious environment.

Severe discipline at home and in school and strict legalism of the Catholic religion as taught and implanted in Luther, promoted in him a feeling of religious *uncertainty* and *fear*. God was not presented to him as a loving Father but as a terrifying, unapproachable Being. Christ was not presented as a merciful Savior but as a threatening and severe Judge. Salvation was to be gained through the mediation of Saints and the Church and by good works. But Luther could not rest in these things. His deeply religious and somewhat introspective nature, his passion for the absolute, and his invincible urge to examine the very essence of his own religious life, separated him from his contemporaries and gradually led him to work out his own position. He was painfully conscious of his personal responsibility to God and wanted to know presently if he would be saved or condemned.

While studying at Magdeburg, 1497-98, Luther was strongly influenced by the stress of his teachers on practical Christianity coupled with mystical piety. At Magdeburg he also made his first acquaintance with the Bible. Magdeburg was the seat of the archbishopric of that region, and the city had many beautiful churches and impressive religious processions and ceremonies. Young Luther was strongly impressed by these surroundings. He also remembered seeing on the streets a young nobleman, the Prince of Anhalt, who had joined the local Franciscan

THE AMERICAN LUTHERAN ANCESTRY 61

monastery and walked the streets in penitent garb, begging. Luther wondered if this did not constitute the perfect Christian life.

At St. George's School in Eisenach, 1498-1501, Luther was for some time a ward in the home of Frau Ursula Cotta, born Schalbe. In this pious home he came under the influence of the Renaissance in culture and refinement of manners. His

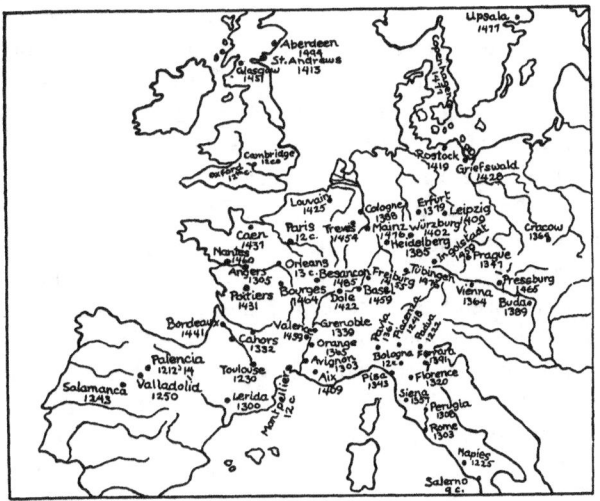

LOCATION OF THE CHIEF EUROPEAN UNIVERSITIES FOUNDED BEFORE 1500

connection with the Cotta home also gained him many friends among the Franciscan monks of the Schalbian Monastery, located at the foot of Wartburg, near Eisenach. This intimate contact with people who devoted their whole lives to religious interests no doubt strengthened Luther's impression from Magdeburg that the monastic life was, perhaps, the ideal Christian life.

Luther studied at the University of Erfurt from 1501 till 1505, receiving his Bachelor of Arts degree in 1502, and his

Master of Arts degree in 1505. His fellow students referred to him as the "learned philosopher," and Melanchthon says that "the extraordinary talents of the young man were at that time the admiration of the whole University." As a university student Luther was a good, pious Catholic. He began every day with prayer and by going to early mass. He took an active part in the religious life of the city, and he listened often to Sebastian Weinman, a powerful preacher who sharply rebuked the prevailing vices. Luther also listened to other preachers but said later that he had never heard one truly evangelical sermon from any pulpit in that city. Consequently, the general religious environment in Erfurt did not bring Luther in contact with any reformatory tendencies.

Any specific reformatory tendencies were also conspicuously lacking in the University of Erfurt. This institution of learning had been among the foremost in Germany to introduce the new learning, and the Humanistic influence had created a general desire for a more liberal intellectual culture, as well as an aspiration for the improvement of the affairs of the Church. But there existed a close and strict alliance between Church and University, and each professor had to swear to teach nothing contrary to the doctrines of the Roman Church. No one dared to depart from tradition, and no one ventured to strike out into any independent course. There was, as in all Humanistic circles, much severe criticism of prevailing vices and corruptions, but this criticism did not lead any one to the Gospel way to God and to salvation.

While Luther applied himself with characteristic energy to his studies, his deeply pious nature would frequently turn his thoughts from the abstract, speculative realm to the practical and the religious. He was conscious, not only of the austere requirements of God, but also of his own small offences in thought, word, and deed. One of his fellow students relates that Luther would frequently say as he washed his hands, "the more we wash ourselves, the more unclean we become." Luther was not guilty

THE AMERICAN LUTHERAN ANCESTRY 63

of any peculiar sins, but as he took inventory of his own religious life, his conscience told him that many seemingly unimportant things were really transgressions against God's holy law. How could he get a clean heart?

Luther's religious problem became more and more acute. His friend, Melanchthon, relates that Luther's agony and fear at times left him almost physically and mentally exhausted. All his efforts to find peace with God were seemingly of no avail. Several external events seem to have increased his religious tension. (1) His casual acquaintance with the Bible at the university library may have helped him to see some of the differences between the Word of the New Testament and the practices of the contemporary Church. (2) During his early student days at Erfurt, he accidentally cut one of his arteries and was in grave danger of bleeding to death twice in 24 hours. This event awakened in him thoughts of dying. (3) Similar thoughts came to him during a serious attack of sickness somewhat later. (4) A friend of Luther named Lang became a monk. (5) The sudden death of another friend, Hieronymous Buntz, made a profound impression upon him. (6) A pestilence which raged at that time in and around Erfurt turned his thoughts toward the future life and the destiny of man. (7) The study of law did not appeal to him, and he is quoted as saying, "show me a lawyer who loves the truth." (8) His Damascus hour came on July 2, 1505, as he returned alone from Mansfeld to Erfurt. Near the village of Stotterheim Luther was caught in a terrible thunder storm, and he became so frightened by a sudden crash of lightning that he fell to the earth and tremblingly exclaimed, "Help me, holy Saint Anna, I will become a monk." Saint Anna, the supposed mother of the Virgin Mary, was the patron saint of the miners.

There is no record that Luther had for some time previous to this event thought seriously of becoming a monk. A timely convergence of forces had prepared him for this great decision, but he later declared that his monastic vow was made involuntarily and unexpectedly and partly because of terror of death. His many friends had the impression that he had been subject to a sudden catastrophe. A university friend named Crotus Rubeanus said in 1519 about Luther's experience that "a heavenly light had thrown him to the ground like a second Paul." Another friend, Justus Jonas, expressed himself in similar terms. When the remark was made to Hans Luther at the banquet after Luther's first mass, that he had become a monk admonished by a heavenly vision, the father replied, "Just so it was not a trick of the devil." It seems evident, therefore, that "a revelation from heaven," (Erscheinung vom Himmel), "a heavenly call," was the deciding factor for Luther. Many years later he stated that he had become a monk "by compulsion." His friends advised him against going to the monastery, since his vow had not been made after due and sober consideration, and for a very brief period Luther himself regretted his vow. But on July 16, 1505, he said good-bye to his friends, and on the following day they accompanied him to the gates of the Augustinian monastery at Erfurt. Luther became a monk and "was entirely dead to the world, as long as it seemed good to God."

The future Reformer had had his Damascus hour. Like Paul of old he had seen a heavenly light and had heard a heavenly call; and as the Apostle had been "three days without sight, and did neither eat nor drink," Acts 9:9, but "prayed fervently," Acts 9:11, so Luther had to spend three years, 1505-1508, in the monastery at Erfurt before he saw the first rays of spiritual light and experienced the dawn of a new day.

In the gigantic spiritual struggles of Luther, 1505-1508, five factors are easily distinguished. (1) He had entered the monastery in order that he might live a life that was pleasing to God. Hence Luther's main concern was to gain divine approval. (2) This led to the problem of sin which became the central concern in the spiritual struggles of Luther. He came to the conclusion that his essential sin was a lack of love toward God and toward his fellow men, and he also discovered that even his "good works" were tainted with this sin. Like Paul of old he

THE AMERICAN LUTHERAN ANCESTRY

exclaimed, "Wretched man that I am! who shall deliver me out of the body of this death?"[78] (3) But according to the theology of Occam and of Gabriel Biel, and even of Bernhard of Clairvaux (cf. the Pharisaic view of the apostle Paul before his conversion), man was capable of giving to God what man *willed* to give. Luther had been trained in the doctrines of Occam and of Biel, and consequently he thought that his particular trouble was that he did not *want* to give up sin. He painfully realized that he was utterly incapable of proper repentance, and

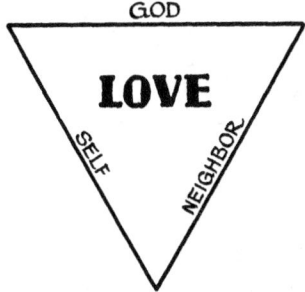

THE ESSENCE OF MORALITY
(As Luther understood it)

that he could not of himself produce the unselfish love which God required of every righteous person. (4) Seeing that he utterly failed to attain a valid righteousness, he turned to another phase of Occam's theology, the doctrine of predestination. Why did not God do His part and give him the due reward, namely love?[79] He came to believe that the motive for the divine redemption of mankind must be sought in God's *will*, and not in God's *love*. He believed, during these years of struggle, that God had selected some to be lost and some to be saved, and that those who were saved *must* fulfill God's law and the ordinances

---

[78] Rom. 7:24.
[79] Man must, according to Occam's view, first do his part (meritum congrui), then God will reward him by "grace" (divine power) and later by "infused love."

of the Church in every detail. It was this view of God and religion, coupled with a painful consciousness of his own shortcomings, which almost drove Luther to despair. He himself described these experiences, in contrast to 2 Corinthians 12:2, by saying that at times he suffered such violent hellish tortures, that if they had lasted even for ten minutes, he would have perished and his limbs would have turned into ashes. (5) The dawn of a new day came to Luther through several channels. (a) His novice-master reminded him of the words of the Creed, "I believe in the forgiveness of sins." (b) John Staupitz, the Vicar-General of the Augustinian order in Germany, intensely encouraged Luther to read the Bible, and he gradually turned Luther's attention away from the works of the law to a gracious Savior.[80] (c) In 1508 he began to study the writings of St. Augustine and paid special attention to Augustine's views on *sin* and *grace*. Faint rays of the Gospel light began to penetrate his troubled soul. For three years, 1505-1508, he had groped about in spiritual darkness, while at the same time he had lived the monastic life with more thoroughness than any other person of his time.[81] His experimental knowledge of divine truth told him that man *can not* be justified by good works, but he did not as yet see the full meaning of the statement in Romans 1:17, "the righteous shall live by faith."

Luther was consecrated priest on April 3, 1507. In 1508 he was called to teach at the University of Wittenberg where Staupitz was Dean. In the fall of 1509 he was recalled to teach at the University of Erfurt, and he remained there for three semesters. In the winter of 1510-1511 he was sent on an important mission to Rome. This visit was highly instructive. "No one," he said, "can believe the scandalous acts which are openly done, unless you have seen or heard them." Upon his return he

---

[80] His advice was, "first find yourself in the wounds of Christ, and God's predestination will give you the greatest comfort."

[81] Luther was at this time recognized as one of the most talented monks among the Augustinians in Germany.

THE AMERICAN LUTHERAN ANCESTRY 67

completed his studies and received the Doctor biblicus degree in October, 1512. Three weeks after his graduation he succeeded Staupitz as Professor of Theology in the University of Wittenberg, a position he held until his death in 1546.

EUROPE ON THE ACCESSION OF THE EMPEROR, CHARLES V, 1519 A.D.

It was the duty of Luther as a Doctor biblicus to lecture at the university on books of the Bible. He lectured on the Psalms in 1513-15, on Romans in 1515-16, on Galatians in 1516-17, and on Hebrews in 1517-18. Besides, he had many other duties.[82] He soon became very popular both as a preacher and as a teacher. Students from all parts of Germany came to hear him,

[82] In 1512 he was appointed Sub-Prior of the Augustinian monastery at Wittenberg; he was already the appointed preacher for that monastery. In 1515 he was made District Vicar over the eleven Augustinian monasteries in Meissen and Thuringia, a position which involved considerable correspondence and travel. That same year he was also requested by the city council to assist the sickly priest, Simon Heinz at the city church, in preaching and hearing confessions. By 1516 he had become so popular as a preacher that the people demanded to hear him once every day.

and even grave burghers of Wittenberg matriculated as students in order to hear his lectures.

When did Luther first clearly understand the Biblical doctrine of *justification by faith* as set forth in Romans and Galatians? Luther himself declares that he did not know the light at the time he became a Doctor of Theology in 1512. But it is evident from his lectures on the Psalms, that he had experienced this new revelation by the time he started these lectures. In his preparation for these lectures on the Psalms, he constantly turned to Romans for help and, illumined by the Holy Spirit, he saw the prophetic word in Romans 1:17 in the same light as Paul himself had seen it,[83] and like Paul he made justification by faith the fundamental principle of the Christian life.[84] Luther had for many years tried to take the Kingdom of Heaven "by force."[85] Like Jacob of old he had "striven with God,"[86] and now a word from Scripture brought him the solution. The Bible had done for him what St. Augustine, Bernhard of Clairvaux, Staupitz and others could not do. No wonder, therefore, that Luther came to consider the Bible as the only source and standard for life and faith. In this momentous revelation which Luther experienced in the monastery at Wittenberg during the winter of 1512-13, the birth of the Lutheran Reformation took place.

Luther's discovery of the Biblical doctrine of salvation did not immediately cause him to break with Rome. He was still a good, pious Catholic who did not feel himself in opposition to the system of doctrine of the Church, and he attacked as yet only the evils and the abuses which were not sanctioned by the Roman Catholic Church herself. Four additional years, 1513-17, were required before Luther had matured as a reformer, and

---

[83] Rom. 3:25.

[84] Luther realized that "justification" did not mean (a) the righteousness which God has; (b) nor the righteousness of life by God's aid, i.e., sanctification; but (c) the righteousness which God gives us in Christ and which we grasp by faith.

[85] Matt. 11:13.   [86] Gen. 32:28.

THE AMERICAN LUTHERAN ANCESTRY 69

during these years he adjusted himself to the evangelical system of salvation by ridding himself of certain strong traditional influences, including (1) the papal authority in so far as this was contrary to Scripture, (2) the theology of Occam, especially the doctrine of predestination unto damnation, and (3) the idea that monastic piety and good life gained special favor with God.

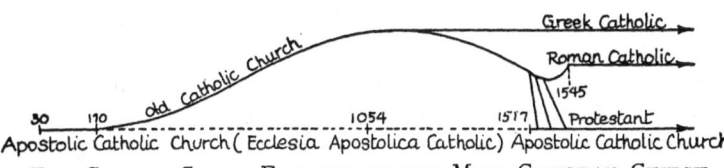

THE GENERAL COURSE FOLLOWED BY THE MAIN CHRISTIAN CHURCH BODIES

Four main factors influenced Luther's theological development during the years 1513-17. *Firstly,* Occam's theology helped him to build his faith upon positive facts of revelation and to mistrust reason. But this same theology caused him much trouble by its strong accentuation of the will of God and the resulting doctrine of absolute predestination. In Luther's lectures on Romans in 1515-16, it may be observed how the thoughts connected with this doctrine at times overwhelmed him and seemed to crush him to the ground; but these same lectures also reveal how he in the midst of such struggles invariably threw himself over on God's saving grace in Christ Jesus and rested there. His legalistic religion was replaced by a religion of grace, and he re-established that direct, personal relationship with God which had characterized the original Christian faith and life. *Secondly,* his diligent study of the writings of St. Augustine and of St. Paul helped him to comprehend fully the Scriptural doctrines of human sin, and of the righteousness of the law, and of the true righteousness which is of God. *Thirdly,* Luther was painfully conscious of the fact that the Humanists did not fully comprehend Paul's doctrine of sin and salvation. By working out his own position and on the basis of his personal experiences, Luther was able to discover how Paul had felt and thought, something the Church of the Middle Ages had not been able to do. He based everything on the promises of God in the Gospel, that is, on the Word and the two Sacraments. *Fourthly,* the last important factor in Luther's long personal development was his ability to acquire *full certainty of God's grace and his own salvation.* The Roman Church of the Middle Ages, and even later,[87] had not been able to give its adherents that certainty. The believers could only *hope* to be saved. Luther himself had up to this time thought that certainty of his own salvation would lead to abominable pride or to false assurance, but through the study of the apostle Paul[88] and through the influence of the German mystics, he came to realize that it was the privilege of every Christian to have the blessed assurance of salvation in the Gospel message. What a happy discovery! Without this assurance Paul could never have become the great Apostle to the Gentiles, and without this assurance Luther could never have become the great Reformer and the giant of faith.

Luther had been led, step by step, to an experimental knowledge of the basic Christian principles. The Renaissance appeal to the sources had led him to re-discover Apostolic Christianity in all its purity and effervescence. No wonder he held the attention of most of Germany even in 1517. But Luther had as yet no thought of separating himself from the Church of Rome. He called the Bohemians who had renounced the Church "wretched heretics." He still believed in the divine origin and the divine right of papacy, the episcopacy, the priesthood, and the infallibility of the Church. He was "loaded" with reformation ideas, but he attacked as yet only the abuses which the Church herself did not sanction.

[87] The Council of Trent, Canon 13.
[88] The Pauline Epistles contain numerous references to such assurance. See 2 Tim. 1:12; etc.

THE AMERICAN LUTHERAN ANCESTRY 71

6. REVIEW QUESTIONS

1. Why must the origin and the genius of the Reformation be sought in the personal experiences of Luther rather than in favorable circumstances?
2. How did heredity help Luther in his great work as a Reformer?
3. How would you describe Luther's childhood and early youth? How did he differ religiously from his contemporaries?
4. Why did not Luther during his academic training come in more direct contact with reformatory or revolutionary tendencies?
5. Why did Luther suddenly become a monk?
6. In what ways were the religious experiences of Luther similar to those of the apostle Paul?
7. How did Luther's visit to Rome influence his future work?
8. Which were the outstanding events in Luther's life in 1512?
9. Why did Luther assume so many official duties?
10. When did Luther fully understand the Biblical doctrine of justification by faith?
11. What factors influenced Luther's religious development, 1512-17?
12. How would you summarize or describe the religious convictions Luther had in 1517?

TOPICS FOR SPECIAL STUDY

1. What makes a great man, (1) is it primarily native ability, or (2) is it primarily favorable environment, or (3) is it a specific combination of native ability and environment, or (4) is it something else?
2. Luther's childhood and early youth.
3. Luther as a university student.
4. Luther's spiritual struggles, (a) from 1505-12; (b) from 1512-17.
5. Luther, the teacher and the preacher.
6. "Justification" as defined by Luther and by the Roman Catholic Church.
7. Luther's idea of predestination in his former and latter years.
8. Luther's experience as to certainty of salvation.

V. Lutheranism according to Luther.—It is not the purpose here to trace, even in summary fashion, the historic events of the Reformation.[89] Since the origin and the genius of the Reformation must be sought, not in outward events, but in the personal experiences of Martin Luther, an attempt has been made in the previous section to trace these experiences up to

---

[89] For a detailed discussion of the Lutheran Reformation, see Qualben, *A History of the Christian Church,* Third Edition, pp. 203-306.

the year 1517. At that time he was fully equipped to step forward as the great Reformer. An attempt will be made in the present section to point out how these religious convictions of Luther, when announced to the world, met with favor or with determined opposition. Luther's convictions had to stand the test of time and circumstances. In this testing process and its outcome, one must seek the essence of Lutheranism according to Luther.

Two major principles of the Reformation are generally stressed, each with its attending corollary. *First,* the recovery of the Bible as the standard for faith and life. Then its corollary, the right of private judgment in its interpretation. *Secondly,* the recovery of the New Testament way of salvation, justification by faith. Then its corollary, the universal priesthood of believers. The experience of liberation resulting from these ideas made Protestantism the parent of civil and religious freedom, and had far reaching effects upon the political, social, literary, artistic and economic life of the nations concerned. Luther's main convictions and decisions will now be briefly considered.

1. The Scripture was recognized as the absolute standard for faith and life. This is sometimes called the *formal* principle. In Luther's gigantic spiritual struggles it was the Bible that brought him light and assurance of salvation. The Bible did for him what no person or agency had been able to do.[90] Luther, like Zwingli and Calvin, rejected the Roman Catholic coordination of the Bible and Tradition as joint rules of faith and conduct. Luther accepted the Scripture as the Word of God, inspired by the Holy Spirit. Through the revealed Word of the Scripture the Holy Spirit comes to men, and not through the church organization or the Church. All the Church can do is to bring the Gospel through preaching and the administration of the two Sacraments. The teaching of the Church has no

[90] Luther regarded the Bible as a living organism rather than as one equally divine Book. He made a distinction between author and author, and set one book above another in spiritual value.

THE AMERICAN LUTHERAN ANCESTRY 73

authority except insofar as it is grounded in the Scripture. Since the Bible is of such vital importance to the people, it must be made available in a language which the people can read. Hence the monumental Bible translations which made the Bible a book of the common people.

2. Man is justified or saved by a living faith in Jesus Christ alone, without human merit. This is sometimes called the *material* principle. Luther tried as sincerely as any man in all history to gain salvation or divine favor by good works, but the more

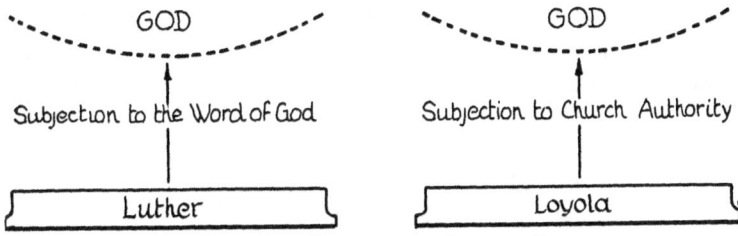

THE RELIGION OF LUTHER AND LOYOLA COMPARED

he tried, the more he failed. It was, perhaps, the greatest day in his earthly life when he was able to understand Romans 1:17, "the righteous shall live by faith," in the same light as the apostle Paul had understood it. From that time on he firmly rejected the Roman Catholic doctrine of salvation by faith and good works, or salvation by divine grace and human merit. Justification by faith was made the very soul of Lutheranism and Protestantism. Faith was not merely a form of knowledge, or a cold intellectual assent to religious truth, but a personal experience in which man throws himself over upon the mercy of God and surrenders his life and will. Man can not do certain good works in order to *become* a child of God. On the other hand, after a person has a living faith, he will show definite evidences of good works because he *is* a child of God. Through this doctrine Luther set men free, not only from their anxious dependence upon their own works and merit, but from their dependence upon the Roman Catholic Church which claimed to dispense salvation through the Sacraments and a storehouse of merits. Man could come directly to God through Jesus Christ through the mediation of Scripture.

3. Luther's third cardinal principle is commonly called the priesthood of all believers. This is sometimes called the *polity-principle*. God, as revealed in Jesus Christ, is accessible to every believer without the mediation of a priest. God Himself gives the believer the power to throw himself directly on the mercy of God. The believer is a member of "an elect race, a royal priesthood, a holy nation, a people of God's own possession."[91] But this was directly against the Roman Catholic doctrine that a mediating priest was essential to salvation. In the Roman Church a gulf separated the clergy and the laity. The Roman clergy held the keys to heaven and hell, it was believed. The clergy could refuse to communicate the grace of God to the laity, yes, even bar lay people from all access to God. By a stroke of the pen the pope could excommunicate the individual, and he could place a city, or province, or kingdom under interdict. In the Medieval Church the layman had no voice in spiritual matters, and he could not even read the Bible without the permission of the priest. Luther struck directly against a special, mediating priesthood by proclaiming the spiritual priesthood of all believers. This made for a spiritual democracy and for civil and religious liberty. Lay people were again given a voice in spiritual matters and in the government and the administration of the Church, as in the days of the Apostles.

4. The fourth cardinal principle was the absolute indefeasible *right of private judgment*. Luther emphasized this principle almost for the first time in history. Under Luther this principle represented a revolt against a fixed and binding interpretation of Scripture by the Roman Church. The Word of God was not a word merely to the clergy and for the sole interpretation of the clergy; it was a word to all. Among Christians there is a

[91] I Pet. 2:9; Exod. 19:6.

THE AMERICAN LUTHERAN ANCESTRY 75

difference of *office*, but no difference in spiritual rights. Henceforth there is no such thing as a priest in the sacrificial sense except Christ alone. It is a defiance of the letter and the spirit of the New Testament to use the word "priest" except in the sense of presbyter to describe the functions of the clerical order, and it is wrong to identify the "priest" with the Christian minister. The Holy Spirit is given to *all* Christians. Hence it is at once the duty and the privilege of every Christian to test his faith by the Scriptures. "To ascertain and judge about doctrine pertains to all and every Christian; and in such a way that let him be an anathema who injures their right by a single hair."[92] Luther gave the following rules for the interpretation of Scripture. He insisted (1) on the necessity for grammatical knowledge; (2) on the importance of taking into consideration times, circumstances, and conditions; (3) on the observance of the context; (4) on the need of faith and spiritual illumination; (5) on keeping what he called "the proportion of faith," that is, avoiding to isolate and distort any one passage into authoritative contradiction to the whole tenor of Scripture teaching; and (6) on the reference of all Scripture to Christ.[93]

5. Luther's religion was a *revelation* religion. Revelation to him meant God's activity, something man could never get alone by himself. This meant something more than reducing Christianity to a system of ethics, as the rationalists did; or, relegating it to the realm of metaphysics, as the orthodox did; or, making it a system of psychology, as Schleiermacher did. The Gospel was to Luther the gracious *revelation* of God through

[92] *Werke*, Erlangen Edition, XXVIII, 339.
[93] It was not easy for Luther to maintain this right of private judgment. In his controversy with the Zwickau prophets, and with Zwingli, Erasmus, Carlstadt, Campanus, Emser and the Anabaptists, all appealed to Scripture as constantly and—apparently—as sincerely as Luther did. Melanchthon suggested getting over the difficulty by "a consensus of pious men." Calvin talked with futility about a "synod of true Bishops." As these methods would restore external dictation of the sense of Scripture, Luther decidedly rejected them. He preferred the storm of controversy to the stagnation of enforced uniformity.

Jesus Christ. In this Gospel message God calls man to acknowledge his sin and to accept the consolation and the forgiveness in Jesus Christ. The essence of Lutheranism according to Luther is, perhaps, this, that *man accepts what God gives.* In other words, the essence of Lutheranism is *grace.*

6. Luther's theology was Christ-centered. It has been said that his explanation of the Second Article in the Creed in his *Small Catechism* is the most comprehensive sentence in all literature. This sentence explains the person and work of Jesus Christ. To Luther the historical Jesus Christ was the *only* Revealer of the Father. Hence, to know the Father was to know

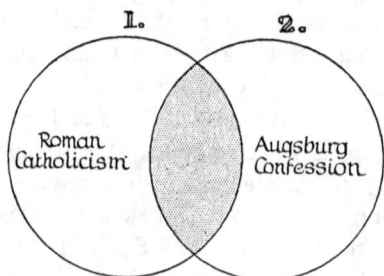

RELATION OF LUTHERANISM AND ROMAN CATHOLICISM

Him through the Jesus Christ of history. "He that hath seen me hath seen the Father."[94] In his *Large Catechism* Luther declares, "We would never recognize the Father's grace and mercy were it not for our Lord Jesus Christ, Who is the mirror of the Father's heart." Luther, like Paul and Athanasius, found his salvation in the Deity of Christ.

7. Luther brought a portion of the Christian Church back to the three great original principles of Christianity. The Augsburg Confession[95] is based on these principles which are in full harmony with the Old Christian Church. Luther said concern-

[94] John 14:9.
[95] For a discussion as to origin and nature of the Augsburg Confession, see Qualben, *A History of the Christian Church,* Third Edition, pp. 248-50.

THE AMERICAN LUTHERAN ANCESTRY 77

ing the Augsburg Confession, "This is the sum of doctrine among us, in which can be seen nothing which is discrepant with Scripture, nor with the Catholic or even with the Roman Church, so far as that Church is known from the writings of the Fathers." Luther had simply demanded that the Roman Catholic Church should eliminate certain unscriptural doctrines and practices in order that he and his adherents might remain in the Romish Church and worship God according to the dictates of a conscience which was bound by the Word of God.[96] But the Romish Church not only refused to be reformed, but even threatened to suppress Lutheranism by force. Consequently, the Catholics forced the schism as much as the Lutherans did. The Lutherans did not form a new Church after the schism with Rome. They merely formed a continuation of the early Christian Church as it is known in the New Testament and the early Church Fathers. The Augsburg Confession still remains the fundamental position of Lutherans in all lands.

8. In arranging for a form of worship which could adequately express the genius of the new Evangelical movement, Luther preserved historic continuity by retaining those ceremonies in the Catholic worship which he did not consider contrary to Scripture; but certain elements such as the sacrifice in the mass and the meritoriousness of church attendance, were definitely removed. Emphasis was shifted from the things which may be *seen* to the things that may be *heard,* and from elaborate pompous ceremonies which appealed to the eye, to the emotions of Evangelical preaching which appealed to the intellect and to personal faith.

The Roman Catholic Church centered the worship in the altar service, while Luther centered it in the pulpit, or rather, in the preaching of the Word of God. The reason is obvious. Because Jesus Christ "entered in once for all into the holy place, having obtained eternal redemption," Hebr. 9:12, the completeness and finality of Christ's sacrifice made the altar of the Old Testa-

[96] See page 1, and diagram on page 69.

ment worship *superfluous*. The New Testament had no altar save the one on which the Savior died, and that was a cross. The Christian Church in the New Testament times had no altar at its services, and for the Lord's Supper a table was used. The Christians had no sacrifice to bring that required a visible altar. The sacrifices of prayer, praise and thanksgiving were to be offered everywhere and at all times; and the gifts for the poor and for the support of the church work needed no altar.

In the course of time, however, the donations to the love feasts and other gifts brought to the congregation came to be looked upon as *sacrifices* or gifts to God. Furthermore, the Lord's Supper came to be regarded, not only as a sacrament (divine assurance to man), but also as a sacrifice (act of worship toward God), and this led to the Graeco-Roman doctrine of the sacrifice of the mass. The Lord's Supper came finally to be regarded as "an unbloody repetition of the atoning sacrifice of Christ by the priesthood for the salvation of the living and the dead." The consecrated elements of bread and wine were literally changed, it was believed, into the body and blood of Christ, and this body of Christ was literally offered every day and hour upon the many altars of Christendom. Several altars were erected in the same church at which specially designated priests would say mass, or offer intercessory prayers for the living and for the dead. To order a mass came to be regarded as a meritorious deed. Finally, the idea of the *sacrifice* in the Lord's Supper completely overshadowed that of the *sacrament*.

Luther and the other Reformers rejected the sacrifice of the mass; but Luther retained the altar, nevertheless, as a *symbol* of Christ's sacrifice for our sins. But the proclamation of the Gospel, or rather the *sermon*, became the center of Lutheran worship. The vernacular language was substituted for Latin. The service throughout reflected a dignified, yet joyful character. Congregational singing of German church-hymns was made the second main factor because singing led the congregation to more active participation in the service. Luther published a German

THE AMERICAN LUTHERAN ANCESTRY 79

hymnary. He also revised the Order of Baptism and the Solemnization of Marriage. The private Confessional was retained as an important means for doing pastoral work. The cup was given to the laity in the Lord's Supper. Catechetical instruction was made a necessary part of the evangelical service. Luther maintained that it was not necessary "that human traditions, rites, or ceremonies, instituted by men, should be everywhere alike."[97]

9. Luther drew a sharp distinction between secular and spiritual power. The Church must recognize the supremacy of the State in temporal affairs; the State must acknowledge the sovereignty of the Church in spiritual matters. But Luther's

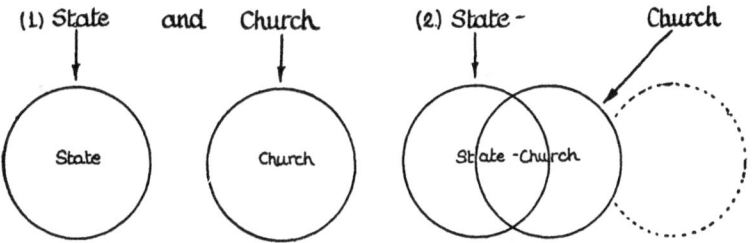

LUTHER'S CHURCH GOVERNMENT IN THEORY AND PRACTICE

idea of the separation of Church and State was entirely too advanced for the time. The people were not capable of governing their own church affairs, and Luther's faith in the "common man" was somewhat shaken after the Peasants' War. Hence Luther saw no other way but to place the Church under the general supervision of the State. As the central government in Germany was very weak, the control of the Church was actually placed in the hands of the evangelical princes and the evangelically disposed city-councils. State control over the Lutheran Church in Germany was continued until the revolution in 1918. In Scandinavia, State control is still maintained.

[97] *Augsburg Confession,* Art. VII.

80   THE LUTHERAN CHURCH IN AMERICA

Calvin, like Luther, made a clear distinction between the spiritual and the secular powers, between the church and the state. Theoretically, each was independent and sovereign in its own sphere, but since all power was ordained of God, both state and church were to be governed by the will of God, and all their activities were to reflect the glory of God. Consequently, the two theoretically independent powers had to work in such intimate cooperation, that Calvin thought of the Christian community as a *unit* where the church and the state were *one*. In this cooperation of church and state, the pastors were best qualified to know the will of God as revealed in Scripture. Calvin urged, therefore, that the secular government seek the

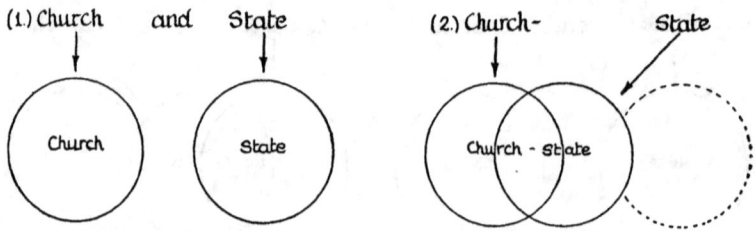

CALVIN'S CHURCH GOVERNMENT IN THEORY AND PRACTICE

advice of the pastors and actually submit to their decisions. This resulted in a Church-State, as contrasted to Luther's State-Church.

10. Luther's new theory of individual judgment and individual responsibility called for a general education of all citizens. In his great reformation program he had substituted the religious authority of the Bible for the religious authority of the Church; he had substituted individual judgment in the interpretation of Scripture and in formulating decisions for the collective judgment of the Church; and instead of collective or institutional responsibility for salvation through a personal faith in Jesus Christ. According to the older theory only a few needed to be educated, but according to Luther's theory, edu-

THE AMERICAN LUTHERAN ANCESTRY 81

cation was necessary for all. Each person should be able to read the Bible, participate intelligently in the church services, and take an intelligent part in the affairs of the State. The ideal of supplying an education for all could not be generally realized, however, until the nineteenth and the twentieth centuries.

11. Luther's attitude toward radical reform movements was remarkably broad, but firm and positive. When Carlstadt and the Zwickau prophets stirred up excitement which bred fanaticism in Wittenberg, and the city experienced daily disorders and riots which spread to other districts, Luther left his hiding place at Wartburg and came to Wittenberg. After a brief but careful study of the situation he preached in the city church for eight successive days and thereby made himself master of the situation. He made no personal references; he blamed no individuals for the disorders; but he made it clear that the Evangelical faith must be promoted and accepted without force or compulsion. "The Word created heaven and earth and all things; the same Word will also create now," said Luther.

He took an even more determined stand against the Anabaptists.[98] Anabaptism was a collective name for a wide variety of religious opinions held by various groups. The promoters were representatives of the mystical piety of the closing Middle Ages, with which they frequently combined socialistic principles and sometimes apocalyptic visions. While the groups differed widely from one another in many respects, they had at least three things in common: (1) they all rejected infant baptism and re-baptised members who had been baptised as children; (2) they would have nothing to do with state churches or national

[98] There were two types of Anabaptists. (1) The *Quietists*, who believed in passive resistance and who advocated the strictest segregation from the world. Balthasar Hubmaier and Caspar Schwenkfeld represented this group. (2) The *Revolutionaries*, who advocated forceful abolition of all existing authorities in Church and State, even the killing off of all the ungodly, in order that a visible kingdom of God might be established on earth, controlled by true saints and believers. Exponents of this group were the Zwickau prophets, and Thomas Munzer, Melchoir Hoffmann, Jan Matthys and John of Leyden.

82   THE LUTHERAN CHURCH IN AMERICA

churches because these, they claimed, numbered many nominal Christians, while the true Church should be an association of true believers only; (3) they subordinated the written Word of God and the Sacraments to the *subjective* experience of the "inner light" of the Spirit. The Spirit was everything and had no need of infant baptism or the "bodily" Word. But how could they recognize the voice of the Spirit? Here the adherents followed two opposite directions. Some listened to the voice of the Spirit through their reason, paving the way for rationalism. Others identified the voice of the Spirit with *feeling* or with an

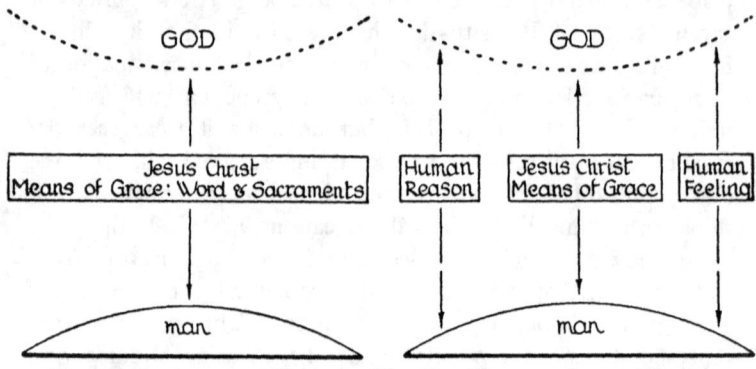

Communion between God and Man as Understood by (1) the Reformers, (2) the Radicals

extreme mysticism, paving the way for later mysticism. Luther answered these radicals by affirming that externally "the Church is the congregation of saints, in which the Gospel is rightly taught and the Sacraments rightly administered. And to the true unity of the Church, it is enough to agree concerning the doctrine of the Gospel and the administration of the Sacraments."[99] Internally "the Church is not only the fellowship of outward objects and rites, as other governments, but it is in principle a fellowship of faith and the Holy Ghost in hearts."[100]

[99] *Augsburg Confession*, Art. VII.
[100] *Apology of the Augsburg Confession*, IV, 5.

THE AMERICAN LUTHERAN ANCESTRY 83

12. Luther's doctrinal conference with Zwingli from October 30 to November 5, 1529 resulted in agreements as to the first fourteen points to be discussed and frank disagreement of the fifteenth point regarding the Real Presence of Christ in the Lord's Supper. Zwingli taught that the words, "This *is* my body," must mean "This *signifies* my body," and that the same is essentially a token by which Christians may be known; while Luther held to the literal interpretation and maintained that the Sacrament is essentially an assurance of God to man that life and salvation have been prepared for him. Zwingli maintained that the Lord's Supper was a memorial feast only, and that the bread and wine in the Supper were purely emblematic and symbolical. Luther insisted that God does not mock believers with empty signs. The communicants truly ate the body of Christ and drank his blood in the Lord's Supper.[101] He found Zwingli's theory unspiritual, unchurchly and unscriptural. The conference between the two reformers failed. Luther parted with Zwingli saying, "You have a different spirit from us."[102]

13. Luther's attitude toward contemporary Humanists is clearly seen in his conflict with Erasmus. In their study of the ancient classics, the Humanists also gained knowledge of the earliest sources of Christian truth and history. This knowledge led them to see the great contrast between the early and the contemporary Church. They openly criticized the prevailing religious corruption and tried to bring about reform. But the Humanists had a *man-centered* rather than a *God-centered* em-

---

[101] Luther wrote in his book, *Of the Supper of Christ*, published in 1528, "Similarly I also speak and confess of the Sacrament of the Altar, that therein the body and the blood in the bread and wine are truly eaten and drunk orally, even if the priest who administers it or those who receive it, do not believe or otherwise misuse it; for it does not stand upon the belief or unbelief of men, but upon the Word and Ordinance of God."

[102] This was true to a higher degree than Luther realized at that time. But he declared himself willing to continue the negotiations in the hope of reaching a full agreement in the future. He also offered an armistice. Zwingli on his part repudiated the agreement after his return to Switzerland and thereby made the division permanent.

phasis. This may be seen, at its best, in Erasmus who represents the best religious thought the Humanists produced. Despite many common ideas, Erasmus and Luther differed radically in their emphasis and interpretation of Christianity. In his *Freedom of the Will*, Erasmus attacked Luther most severely. Luther's reply, *On the Will in Bondage,* provoked a second attack by Erasmus in his *Hyperaspistes*. This led to a complete breach between the two men and it also alienated Luther from the majority of the Humanists.[103]

14. After the Diet of Augsburg in 1530, when the Catholic princes threatened the Lutherans with open warfare, the Evangelical princes and cities formed a defensive league at Schmalkald in February, 1531. This forced Luther to state *his view on war*. After much deliberation he finally gave his consent to the formation of the Schmalkald League on the ground that the princes and the free cities constituted the government to which the Christians concerned owed their allegiance. The emperor was elected by the princes and not by God; and the princes had a right to oppose the emperor if he violated their rights. The relation between the princes and the emperor was a political question which the jurists, not the theologians, should decide. The Christians were in duty bound to take up arms in defense of their princes when these were unlawfully assaulted.

15. In his tract, *Von dem Papsttum zu Rom,* written in 1520, Luther developed in some detail his conception of the nature of the Church. To him the Church is "the assembly (Versammlung) of all Christian believers on earth," also "the regenerated," or "the new creation of God," or "an assemblage of hearts in

---

[103] The Renaissance affected Italy and Northern Europe differently because the Italian got his main inspiration from ancient Rome and Greece, while the North European got his main inspiration from Palestine, the birth-place of Christianity. But while the Humanists interested themselves in the original languages of the Bible and also in church reforms, they failed to lead into the Gospel of Jesus Christ—the true source and comfort of the human soul. Hence Humanism at its best was merely preparatory for the Gospel.

THE AMERICAN LUTHERAN ANCESTRY 85

one faith." The Church as a spiritual association of those who believe on Christ is therefore in essence *invisible* and perceptible only by faith. But since the Word and the Sacraments are necessary to the existence of the Church; and since the Word and the Sacraments, as externally and sensibly set forth, call into existence the inner spiritual Church; the Church is in one aspect an external, *visible* association.[104] For wherever the Means of Grace are, there faith assumes the presence of a community of saints. Hence some outward ecclesiastical association is necessary. While this *visible* association must be carefully distinguished from the "inner spiritual church," the two are, nevertheless, related to one another as body and soul in man. The external association includes or may include hypocritical members. Hence the *visible* Church is not identical with the true spiritual Church.[105] The purpose of every divine service is the preaching of the Word. Though the preaching and the teaching in reality belong to all Christians, the public exercise of these duties should be restricted to regularly called officials. The office of preaching is the highest office in the Church.[106] No ecclesiastical government has authority to impose laws without the consent of the congregation. As the inner unity of the Church is established through Christ as the Head, so the external unity is established through the pure doctrine of the Gospel,[107] and not through any particular type of church organization. Luther recognized in no form of church government any divine right beyond that of the sovereignty of the individual congregation,

---

[104] Luther says, "Where baptism and the gospel are, there let no one doubt that there are also saints, even though it should be only children in their cradles."

[105] A tragic mistake of the Roman Catholic Church is the identification of the visible Church, i.e., the external organization, with the true spiritual Church.

[106] The office of the pastor can not be outranked by any supposedly higher ecclesiastical office, such as bishop or a hierarchy.

[107] Luther's emphasis on pure doctrine had a practical aim. Pure doctrine meant the teaching and the preaching of the Gospel in conformity with the "word of Christ." He placed spiritual life before pure theory.

86 THE LUTHERAN CHURCH IN AMERICA

which included the office of preaching the Gospel and the administering of the Sacraments.[108]

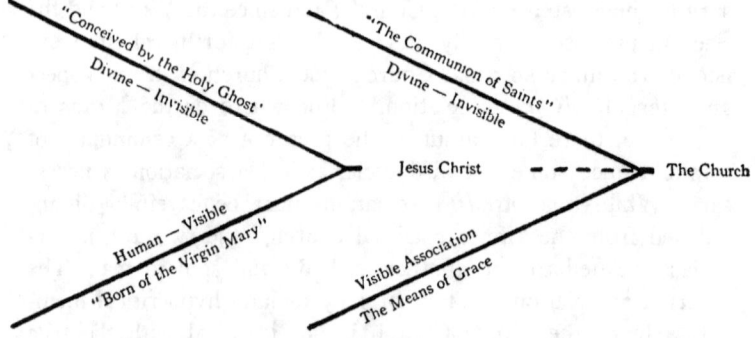

THE CHURCH VISIBLE AND INVISIBLE[109]

16. Luther dealt a death blow to the double standard of medieval piety by reconstructing the domestic life, including the home life of the evangelical clergy. This was a new chapter in the history of civilization. In the Catholic communion there

---

[108] Luther did not establish an Evangelical episcopate. In 1535 he introduced the Rite or Order of Evangelical Ordination at Wittenberg. Candidates for the Evangelical ministry were to be examined and ordained by the "learned men of Holy Scriptures." The Theological Faculty at Wittenberg elected Bugenhagen as Ordinator, but the ordination was often performed by Luther himself. Luther had requested the princes to protect the Church against Catholic aggression. This *aid* was gradually turned into *dominion*. The prince became the recognized head of the church in his territory, a position similar to that which he had held previously in the Roman Catholic Church. He controlled all activities of the church, even doctrine and form of worship, although decisions on doctrinal matters were usually left in the hands of the clergy. In 1539 a special ecclesiastical court was established at Wittenberg for the purpose of deciding such matters as church discipline, divorce and the like. The members of this court, or "Consistorium" as it was called, consisted of theologians and jurists selected by the Elector. After the death of Luther this Consistorium was changed from a court to a governing body which functioned much like the former Catholic episcopacy. The majority of Lutheran churches in Germany copied this form of church government.

[109] Consult diagrams on page 15.

THE AMERICAN LUTHERAN ANCESTRY 87

existed an unscriptural distinction between a lower morality for the common people and a higher morality for priests and monks who formed a spiritual nobility. Marriage was considered inconsistent with this special priesthood because married life, they thought, was of an inferior order. Luther pointed out that perpetual celibacy was unscriptural and unnatural. It was unscriptural because the Jewish priesthood, including the high priests, married; and the apostles and other church leaders of the early period married, even the apostle Peter whom the Catholics claimed as the first pope. Perpetual celibacy was unnatural because God had created man for marriage, and He had sanctified and blessed the family life. Hence Luther and the other reformers married, and they urged the Protestant clergy to do likewise.

17. Luther's reformatory work was the watershed of many divergent influences. The rise of democratic governments, a powerful impetus to progress of all sorts, an active participation in industrial and commercial undertakings, a growing emancipation of thought, the rise of a spirit of criticism and free inquiry, were natural and ultimate consequences. In the realm of literature Luther's name stands pre-eminent. Through his Bible translation he gave Germany her national language. In the realm of hymnody Luther's name will live as long as song and music endure, especially in connection with the great battle hymn of the Reformation, "A Mighty Fortress Is Our God."

7. REVIEW QUESTIONS

1. Which are the two major Reformation principles and their corollaries?
2. What is meant by the *formal* principle of the Reformation?
3. How do you explain the *material* principle of the Reformation?
4. What is meant by the *polity-principle* of the Reformation?
5. Why did Luther assert the right of private judgment?
6. Why is *grace* the essence of Lutheranism?
7. Why was Luther's theology a Christ-centered theology?
8. How is Lutheranism related to (a) the Church Fathers? (b) the Roman Catholic Church?

88   THE LUTHERAN CHURCH IN AMERICA

9. What characterized Luther's arrangement of the Evangelical worship? Why?
10. How did Luther define the relation between State and Church?
11. Why a Lutheran state-church?
12. What were some of the consequences of Luther's new theory of individual judgment and individual responsibility?
13. What attitude did Luther take toward radical reform movements? Explain.
14. Why did Luther part with Zwingli?
15. Why was Luther alienated from the majority of the Humanists?
16. What did Luther say about war?
17. How did he explain the nature of the Church?
18. How did he affect the double standard of morality?
19. What were some of the other natural and ultimate consequences of the Reformation?

TOPICS FOR SPECIAL STUDY

1. What is Lutheranism according to Luther?
2. Luther's ability to seize essentials.
3. Luther and Melanchthon.
4. Select any of the review questions for special study.

VI. Later Lutheran Developments.—The creative work and inspired leadership of Martin Luther is related to Protestant posterity much the same as the Church in the age of the Apostles is related to the Christian development in all succeeding centuries. The early Church was a faithful prototype of the Christian Church of later generations. Like the grain of mustard seed it contained the sole authentic germ of the living organism known as the Holy Christian Church. Luther, because he brought a portion of the Church back to the great original principles of Christianity, likewise exerts a formative and lasting influence upon the great historic Church which bears his name.[110]

But vital religion is never static because it is an essential part of human life. The Church believes in "a changeless Christ in a changing generation." Ever since its origin, Christianity has

[110] Luther, because of his creative instinct, did more than simply to reproduce the thought of the Apostolic Age. He made use of many ideas and elements which he derived from the entire historical development which intervened. In this sense, the pre-Reformation period may be said to have started with St. Augustine.

THE AMERICAN LUTHERAN ANCESTRY 89

witnessed far-reaching changes. With the possible exception of a relatively barren period during the Middle Ages, each era has been fertile of new ideas, some of which have deeply affected Christian life and thought. The Church, because it is deeply rooted in the past, yet inspired by an ardent idealism for the future, is at once the most conservative and the most progressive of all societies. Happy is the Church in which changes come with a minimum of conflict and without violating the law of Christian continuity.

It frequently happens that movements get beyond the control of those who set them in motion, and their momentum carries them further than it was intended they should go. This, however, was not the case of the Lutheran movement. As Lutheranism gradually became a world force, winding its course through many lands, it reminds us of a river whose water may be variously colored by the soil through which it flows, yet it is the same river, the same stream.

1. *Tradition.*—However, Lutheranism did pass through certain modifications, even in the life-time of Luther, especially with regard to *tradition*.[111] After 1530 Philip Melanchthon, the "Preceptor of Germany," exerted an ever increasing influence among Lutherans. At heart Melanchthon was essentially a Humanist, although he always tried to agree with Luther.[112] Melanchthon's interest in classic philosophy and literature caused

[111] Some of the doctrines and practices of the Roman Church—such as celibacy, saint worship, the Seven Sacraments, sale of indulgences and papal authority—had no support in Scripture. Church officials accordingly sought support, like the Pharisees of old, in Tradition. Like the Pharisees, the Roman Church not only made Tradition a joint rule with Scripture for doctrine and life, but in some cases Tradition was placed above Scripture.

[112] There were two doctrines upon which Melanchthon consciously differed from Luther, namely, on free will and on the Lord's Supper. As a Christian Humanist Melanchthon tried to arrange all human knowledge of God and the world into a definite system, with data secured partly from Scripture, partly from the dogma of the Church, and partly from Greek philosophy, especially from Aristotle. The Greek primacy of intellect was asserted.

him to make new inroads on the Lutheran world for Aristotle whom Luther called "a condemned heathen,"[113] and for a new Lutheran scholasticism.[114] His love for the classics led him to entertain an increasingly high regard for church *tradition*.[115] This, coupled with pressure from without from Radicals and Catholics alike, led to the acceptance of the Augsburg Confession, the Apology and Luther's two Catechisms as standards of the Lutheran doctrine. The Schmalkald Articles of 1537 enjoyed a similar recognition in Germany, and after 1535 the members of the Schmalkald League were required to subscribe to the Augsburg Confession. In 1543 Melanchthon practically gave *tradition* an independent position, in coordination with Scripture. He influenced the Lutherans to accept the three oldest symbols, the Apostle's Creed, the Nicene Creed and the Athanasian Creed as binding. His fear of the religious ideas of the Radicals caused him to place additional emphasis on tradition and the office of the church. He influenced the Lutherans to follow a course of development which reminds the student of the early stages in change from Apostolicity to Catholicity.

2. *Concord Movement.*—The great creative and prophetic age of Luther was followed by a didactic age, much as the period of Old Testament prophets was followed by the age of the Great Synagogue. Doctrine threatened to swallow up life, while

[113] The Schoolmen of the Middle Ages not only copied the dialectic method of Aristotle, but they studied his metaphysics, physics, psychology and ethics and wrote commentaries upon them. The result was a secularized theology. Luther called Aristotle "the constructor of words, the deluder of minds." Melanchthon said, "Just as in these modern times of the church we have embraced Aristotle instead of Christ, so, immediately after the beginning of the church, Christian doctrine was weakened through Platonic philosophy."

[114] What Luther mainly objected to in Scholasticism was this that "with its doctrine of free will, merit, righteousness, and works, it directed to a false view of salvation, which led only to doubt and despair."

[115] Luther, with his keen sense for the historical development, did not entirely reject Tradition. He accepted that portion of it which was in harmony with Scripture, but he would never tolerate anything but the Scripture as the norm for faith and life.

THE AMERICAN LUTHERAN ANCESTRY 91

the followers of Luther fought for his spiritual heritage.[116] Most of the controversies centered around points of doctrine on which Luther and Melanchthon had partly disagreed. Hence one party was called Gnesio-Lutherans or Genuine Lutherans and the other party was called Philippists or Melanchthonians. But Flacius, leader of the Genuine Lutherans, went to such extremes that many left him and formed a third or Middle Party which finally settled the controversies with the help of the princes.

The *Antinomistic* (*anti*: against + *nomos*: law) Controversy concerned the place of the Decalogue in the plan of salvation. Luther had maintained that both the Law and the Gospel should be preached because "through the law cometh the knowledge of sin."[117] But how is it possible to preach about the forgiveness of sins where there is no consciousness of sin, or where sin is not present? John Agricola and others held that the Decalogue belonged to the hall of justice and not in the pulpit. The Gospel only should be preached because this alone was capable of producing a real change of heart and life.

The *Adiaphoristic* (*adiaphoron*: matter of indifference) Controversy was caused by Melanchthon's attitude toward Roman ceremonies in the Leipzig or Small Interim. Melanchthon had introduced almost all of the Roman ceremonies for the sake of compromise under the pretext that these rites were neither commanded nor forbidden in God's Word, and hence were nonessentials, *adiaphora,* or matters of indifference. He also compromised with Rome on the doctrine of justification and the Seven Sacraments. The Peace of Augsburg in 1555 removed the cause for this controversy, but no agreement on the principle had been reached.

The *Majoristic* Controversy started with the contention of George Major, a disciple of Melanchthon, that good works were

---

[116] Luther had a remarkable ability to seize essentials without being troubled by minor details. Of him the saying is true, "The eagle that soars near the sun does not worry itself about how to cross the rivers."

[117] Rom. 3:20; cf. *Schmalkald Articles*, Part III, Art. 2.

necessary to salvation. Forgiveness of sins was obtained by faith alone, but no one would be saved without good works. The Gnesio-Lutherans raised a vigorous opposition on the ground that this was a return to the Roman doctrine of salvation by faith and good works. Old Amsdorf, for one, even went so far as to say that reliance on good works was injurious to salvation.

The *Eucharistic* or Crypto-Calvinistic Controversy concerned the doctrine of the Lord's Supper. The Philippists held views similar to those of Calvin. The Gnesio-Lutherans stirred up such violent opposition that many of the Philippists were driven over to the ranks of the Calvinists.

The *Synergistic* (*syn*: together + *ergon*: work) Controversy centered around whether or not the human will or effort co-operated with divine grace in conversion and salvation. Some contended that the sinner was completely dead to good impulses, and even "contrary, resisting, or hostile toward the work of God." Man could contribute nothing whatever toward his conversion. Others maintained that the human will was a co-agent with the Word and the Spirit of God in man's conversion and salvation. Sinful nature had the freedom either to resist or to accept the grace of God. Consequently, man was responsible for his own salvation or damnation.

The *Osiandrian* Controversy centered around a theory of justification proclaimed by Andrew Osiander of Nuremberg. According to the accepted Protestant view, justification is a single, forensic act of God, definitely distinguished from sanctification which follows as a gradual process. In the Catholic system justification is *merged* with sanctification as a gradual process, conditioned by faith and good works. Osiander identified the two. He taught that Christ, "the Personified righteousness of God," received by faith into the heart, overcomes all unrighteousness and impels man to all kinds of good works, and thus man is justified by the indwelling, living Christ. Osiander's view differed from the Catholic mainly in this respect, that he did

THE AMERICAN LUTHERAN ANCESTRY 93

not take any account of human merit[118] or good works, but only of the merit and power of Christ.[119]

The *Christological* Controversy arose in connection with the Lord's Supper. The real question was whether or not Christ could give his body and blood in the sacrament. Some said with the Reformed that he could not, since his body was a real body and was confined to space in heaven; others taught that he could, because his body, by the personal union with the divine nature, was a glorified body and on account of the *communicatio idiomatum* could be made present.

Such disputes filled the years 1548 to 1577. So pernicious was the spirit of conflict that the Gnesio-Lutherans denied the Philippists, after 1557, the right to claim adherence to the Augsburg Confession, thereby excluding them from the benefits of the Religious Peace of Augsburg, secured in 1555. As this made for political as well as for religious disunity, the Lutheran princes felt themselves compelled to use every legitimate means of restraining these theological conflicts and, if possible, bring about a German Lutheran Concord.[120]

The resulting concord movement, which went through three successive stages, finally led to the preparation of a formula of concord which was intended to settle the disputed religious questions of the preceding decade. This document, which was ready in its final form in 1577, became known as the *Formula*

[118] Rom. 4:6.
[119] Rom. 10:4; cf. 1 Cor. 1:30.
[120] At the Diet of Augsburg in 1555, the Lutheran Reformation finally received legal recognition. Some of the principles agreed on may be stated as follows: (1) Two religions were permitted to exist within the empire, namely Roman Catholicism and the religion of the Augsburg Confession; while Zwinglianism, Calvinism and Radicalism were excluded from toleration. (2) Each prince had a right to decide which of the two religions he and his state should have, in accordance with the principle, "one local government, one religion." (3) A Catholic government was not required to tolerate Lutherans, nor was a Lutheran government required to tolerate Catholics, but the dissenting minority should have a right to emigrate.

of Concord. Immediately it assumed a position among the regulative symbols of Lutheranism in Germany. But the Lutherans also felt the need of a Body of Doctrine which would not only be accepted by all Lutherans in all lands, but which would also define Lutheranism as over against Calvinism and Roman Catholicism. With this in mind they prepared the *Book of Concord*, which included the Apostle's Creed, the Nicene Creed, the Athanasian Creed, the Augsburg Confession of 1530, the Apology, the Schmalkald Articles, Luther's two Catechisms, and the Formula of Concord. The *Book of Concord* was published in 1580 on the fiftieth anniversary day of the presentation of the Augsburg Confession to the Diet of Augsburg in 1530. This collection of confessions was signed by fifty-one princes, thirty-five cities, and about nine thousand theologians. The publication and the signing of the Book of Concord marked the doctrinal completion of German Lutheranism.

3. *Orthodoxy.*—The Concord movement, which marked the close of the Reformation period for the Lutheran world, consolidated Lutheranism and gave it a definite standing as over against Calvinism, Roman Catholicism and other religious bodies. But the peace and internal harmony thus secured were dearly bought. Doctrinal unity, as given to Lutheranism through the *Book of Concord* and retained for centuries, tended by an *undue emphasis* on the part of its adherents to stifle vital Christian life and spiritual productivity.[121] The central spiritual values in Luther passed somewhat out of focus and in their place came an undue stress on pure doctrine.[122] Pure doctrine was in turn to be interpreted and regulated by qualified theologians[123]

---

[121] This stifling tendency diffused the entire realm of German Lutheran culture. It even choked Humanistic culture.

[122] Flacius proposed the theory of verbal inspiration of the Bible. He was ably seconded by the Danish professor and later bishop, Jesper Brochmand (d. 1652).

[123] These were the duly elected theological professors who trained pastors at the universities.

THE AMERICAN LUTHERAN ANCESTRY 95

and by the Lutheran princes.[124] This development came as a distinct blow to Luther's principle of a general priesthood of believers. Furthermore, the sharp lines drawn doctrinally by the orthodox Lutherans drove many of the Philippists of Western Germany over to the ranks of the moderate Calvinists.[125]

The orthodox movement caused another shift away from Luther. Theoretically the orthodox exponents considered the accepted confessional symbols merely as a correct expression of the teachings of the Bible, but in practice the Bible was really interpreted in terms of these confessional books, especially the Formula of Concord. This led to a distinct tendency to place the confessional element above the Bible as a sort of Protestant pope. Christianity became a matter of intellect rather than of heart. While Luther centered assurance in a personal relationship with God through Jesus Christ, the tendency of orthodoxy was to center assurance in Truth as expressed in pure doctrine and grasped by the intellect. In consequence correct exposition and knowledge of pure doctrine came to overshadow Luther's demand or emphasis on personal repentance and assurance of the forgiveness of sins. Faith was more an intellectual acceptance of a certain body of doctrine than a heart which relied entirely on the grace of our Lord Jesus Christ.[126]

Wittenberg became the great stronghold of Lutheran ortho-

[124] The Peace of Augsburg of 1555 practically made each Lutheran prince the highest religious authority or "jus episcopale" of his state. The prince exercised this authority through designated officials and boards: ordination through the appointed Superintendent, and legal and administrative control through the Consistorium.

[125] These Philippists, especially those of the Palatinate, seem to have formed the nucleus of that middle group between extreme Calvinists and extreme Lutherans, which came to be known about 1580 as the Reformed Church. Later, of course, the name Reformed was applied to all adherents of Calvinism. (Cf. Holmquist, "Kirkehistorie," II, p. 206).

[126] The orthodox movement retarded efforts toward a ministry of mercy, and it even denied the obligation of the Church to carry on foreign mission work. The missionary command of the Lord, the orthodox asserted, was for the apostles only; and through the original apostles, it was claimed, the Gospel had been preached once to the entire world.

doxy, and Abraham Calovius (1612-86), who held Luther's former chair of theology at Wittenberg University, became the most dominant exponent of orthodoxy. He was ably supported by his colleague, Andreas Quenstedt (1617-88). The greatest Lutheran theological work of the seventeenth century came, however, from Johann Gerhard (1582-1637), professor at the University of Jena.[127] His *Loci theologici* in nine volumes is generally considered the most important Lutheran theological production in the period between Melanchthon and Schleiermacher.[128] Doctrinally, the most lasting contribution of orthodoxy was the dogma on *Satisfaction* with its twofold content: *obedientia activa* or Christ's vicarious fulfillment of the Law, and *obedientia passiva* or his vicarious suffering for sin.

While the orthodox movement had its decided defects it also had its strong merits. In the stormy and distressing seventeenth century, orthodoxy formed a hard but necessary bulwark or shell within which Lutheranism could preserve its best heritage. Orthodoxy produced strong Christian personalities. Much stress was laid on the religious instruction of the young. The movement also produced a Christian morality which was able to hold its own against demoralizing tendencies which followed the Thirty Years' War.

4. *Mysticism.*—Besides the strong orthodox movement, several lesser movements exerted their influence on seventeenth century Lutheranism, and one of these was mysticism. The mystic believes that man, by nature, is capable of holding direct communion with God.[129]

Johann Kepler (d. 1630), the great astronomer who clari-

[127] The twelve volume work of Calovius, *Systema Locorum theologicorum*, ranks second. His *Biblia illustrata* runs a close third.

[128] He combined the best in orthodoxy with the evangelical piety of Johann Arnd (1555-1621).

[129] See diagram on page 82. The opposite concept of mysticism is enthusiasm. Plato said that poetry must be God-possessed. Enthusiasm means something that is God-possessed or divinely inspired. Mystics and enthusiasts are great enemies. Luther and Calvin fought the mystics, and John Wesley fought George Fox and other mystics of his day.

THE AMERICAN LUTHERAN ANCESTRY 97

fied and explained the theory of Copernicus, belonged to the Lutheran fold and wished to be a man "taught of God." He sought his spiritual inspiration and nourishment in a study of Nature and of the Universe. His naturalistic mysticism as set forth in his immortal work *Harmonice mundi,* pointed toward new ways of thinking and toward a new conception of the universe.

Valentine Weigel (1533-88) was a Lutheran pastor who during his lifetime adhered to the Formula of Concord; but manuscripts published after his death disclosed him as a pantheistic mystic who adhered to the doctrine of the "inner word" or "inner light." He exerted a considerable influence through his writings.

Jacob Bohme (1576-1624), known as "the German Gnostic," is one of the greatest, most profound and most ingenious mystics of all time. Outwardly he adhered to the Lutheran Church, but his speculations were anything but churchly. His mystic views appealed to the cultured classes as well as to a number of theologians. But his strongest following was from among the great masses of ordinary lay people.

Johann Valentine Andreae (1586-1654), a Lutheran court preacher, also belongs to the group of mystics. He founded the secret brotherhood known as the "Rosicrucians," a name which signifies the union of science and Christianity, as symbolized by the rose and the cross (*rosa*: rose + *crux*: cross). Rosicrucian organizations are found today in various parts of Europe and America.[130]

It is easy to see how the mystics deviated from Luther and the Bible. The mystics subordinated the Word of God and the Sacraments to the subjective experiences of the "inner light" of the Spirit. Their immediate divine revelations, visions and dreams were generally placed above the authority of the Bible.

---

[130] Besides nourishing certain mystical speculations, the Rosicrucians aimed to combat alchemy and Roman Catholicism. The movement has since undergone a recrudescence in connection with Freemasonry.

Church organization was generally repudiated as inimical to the Spirit. Freedom of the Spirit was the essential thing. But how could they recognize the divine voice? Some recognized the Voice through human reason, and this paved the way for a religious rationalism. Others listened to the Voice through their inner, emotional experiences, and this paved the way for a dwarfed and distorted religious life.[131]

5. *Pietism.*—Pietism is the name given to a great religious awakening within the Protestant churches of the seventeenth and eighteenth centuries in behalf of practical religion. From religious gatherings called *collegia pietatis* the movement was nicknamed "Pietism." This movement, combining the mystical and the practical tendencies within the Lutheran and the Reformed churches, came as a reaction against the inordinate stress of orthodoxy on pure doctrine and formalism. The movement started almost simultaneously in Holland, Germany and Switzerland.

Philip Jacob Spener (1635-1705), a Lutheran clergyman, was the founder of German pietism. His main emphasis was on personal conversion followed by a true Christian conduct in everyday life. The essentials of his program may be stated as follows: (1) The Word of God should be more widely diffused through religious gatherings (*collegia pietatis*) of lay people where the Bible is read and discussed under the guidance of the pastor. (2) In accordance with the principle of a general priesthood of believers, the Christian lay people should be encouraged to take a more active part in practical church work, such as religious instruction, mutual edification and care for the salvation of others. Due attention should be given to the fact that Christianity is far more a life than an intellectual attitude.

---

[131] There is also a normal Christian mysticism which, like the Lord and his Apostles, lays stress on a personal living faith in God. This primacy of a personal communion with God and the resulting assurance of the forgiveness of sins, were also emphasized by Luther and the other Reformers. But this mysticism was always subjected to and regulated by the Word of God.

THE AMERICAN LUTHERAN ANCESTRY 99

(3) More gentleness and love between denominations should be manifested, and all theological controversies should be purged of personal, selfish polemic. (4) The theological training schools should be thoroughly revised so they become the work-shops of the Holy Spirit. An experimental knowledge of salvation should be required of all theological students. (5) A complete change in the current method of preaching should be effected. Sermons should be prepared for the purpose of building up the Christian life of the hearers. Undue rhetorical art and the controversial and argumentative elements should be eliminated from the sermon.

Spener also promoted interest in the Sunday School, in catechetical instruction and in Protestant confirmation. He quickened interest in prayer meetings and Bible study and fought for the privilege of private devotional meetings. He opposed dances, card playing and the theater and inculcated moderation in food, drink and dress. He stirred up much interest in missions among Jews and heathen. But the formation of *ecclesiolae in ecclesia* or a "congregation within the congregation"[132] soon gave cause for friction by magnifying the contrast between "converted" and "unconverted." General contempt for the Sacraments on the part of the pietists and stress on visions and ecstatic experiences, even by Spener himself, brought the movement into discredit, especially among the orthodox.[133]

August Herman Francke (1663-1727) brought the pietistic movement in Germany to its climax. In 1687 he experienced a very sudden conversion, preceded by a great spiritual struggle

[132] Pietism was not an organized movement. Spener and Francke did not want their adherents to form a new church. They should form groups within the constituted church and serve as a spiritual leaven for the larger group by promoting a "living Christianity."

[133] Pietists were harsh in their judgment of the "unconverted," and if the pastor did not adhere to their views, they would at times nourish a conscious opposition of a spiritual priesthood of lay people to a special priesthood of the clergy. In 1682 some of the most extreme followers of Spener even advocated a separation from the constituted church, a move which Spener succeeded in checking.

and a conviction of sin. His conversion was so real and so vivid that he could state accurately its time and place. His followers soon insisted that Francke's experience furnished the standard whereby all real conversions should be tested. This insistence on a methodical form of conversion frequently led to a narrow, severe and unjust judgment of the "unconverted."

While Francke promoted the general program of Spener, he also added features of his own. He made the work of Inner Missions a central factor in Lutheranism. A special feature of his Inner Mission work was his famous "Institutions" at Halle. Under his direction the Canstein Bible Institute was established at Halle in 1704. The University of Halle became the great pietistic center which supplied Europe with teachers, pastors, foreign missionaries and influential laymen.

The pietistic movement deviated from historic Lutheranism on these essential points: (1) The pietists claimed that regeneration of man took place, not in baptism, but in a specific conversion modelled after the conversion of Francke. After conversion the pietists were to follow a code of conduct which bordered on Pharisaism. Their Christianity was gloomy, austere and legalistic. (2) Justification was not conceived of as a forensic act, but as sanctification which might lead to relative perfection in this life. (3) The pietists paid inordinate attention to the study of the Second Coming of Christ and the Millennium; and their reliance on visions and dreams led, at times, to an unbridled subjectivism.

But these glaring defects should not lead the student to underestimate the central values of the pietistic movement. Pietism came as a one-sided reaction against the one-sidedness of the orthodox movement. The gradual fusion of these two movements produced a healthy, vigorous type of Christianity.[134]

---

[134] One of the best known representatives of pietism was Johann Albrecht Bengel (1687-1752), famous for his work in New Testament exegesis. His *Gnomon Novi Testamenti*, published in 1742, found a wide

6. *Rationalism.*—The eighteenth century marked a turning-point in human thinking and progress, culminating in a new world-view and in a new outlook on life. This new attitude found expression in an undue emphasis on human reason, in the formation of modern constitutional governments including the United States of America, and in the French Revolution. These changes prepared for the remarkable religious, intellectual, political and social activities of the nineteenth century.

Three specific lines of thought combined to form a new philosophy of life which, to begin with, was rather critical of the traditional religion. (1) The humanistic idea of the dignity of man, the freedom of the human will and the ability of man to do the will of God, came as a revival of the ancient Greek philosophy of man. Human reason was made the final test of all things. (2) Bacon's inductive method and Descartes' "hypothetical doubt" gave rise to a general demand that all things received as true must be capable of proof. (3) The revolutionary discoveries in science, especially by Copernicus, Galileo and Sir Isaac Newton, cautioned men to discover new truth by observance of known facts.

The thrill of the new discoveries gave rise to a spirit which was less conscious of God and more conscious of man and his inherent powers and possibilities. Man became the measure of all things, and human reason, *ratio*, was enthroned as the only religious authority. This gave rise to rationalism. A system of "natural religion" replaced the traditional religion. In England this system ran out into Naturalism or Deism. In France it led to the actual worship of the Goddess of Reason. In Germany it produced the "Illumination" or Aufklärung, a movement which started about 1720. As far as evangelical Germany was concerned, the movement ran through four successive stages:

---

circulation both in the Lutheran and in the Anglican world. Bengel wanted to have the Bible in place of orthodoxy, although he interpreted the Bible in an orthodox manner.

102 THE LUTHERAN CHURCH IN AMERICA

(1) in popular philosophy as introduced by Christian Wolff;[135] (2) in a new theology known as neology, whose best known representative was Johann Salomo Semler;[136] (3) in rationalism *per se*, as typified by Samuel Reimarius and H. E. G. Paulus; and (4) in supranaturalism as seen in Gottlob Christian Storr, founder of the Older Tübingen School.[137]

Reason	Faith	Reason	Faith	Reason	Faith	Reason
Renaissance	Reformation	Orthodoxy	Pietism	Rationalism	Confessionalism	Scientism
Classicism	Melanch-thonian	Syncretism	Latitudinarianism	Unitarianism	Unionism	Liberalism
Mysticism	Humanism	Quietism	Formalism	Supernaturalism	Criticism	Fundamentalism
Faith	Reason	Faith	Reason	Faith	Reason	Faith

THE CONFLICT OF RATIONALISM AND FAITH

This diagram, suggested by Dr. O. M. Norlie, should not convey the impression that the historical movements are mechanical. The intention is merely to show that faith and reason are frequently at odds, and that each new appearance of faith and reason has a new complexion. Within these epochs are, of course, many other conflicting currents.

Rationalism exerted a paralyzing influence upon Protestant and Roman Catholic church life during the latter half of the eighteenth century. The movement ran its course in all countries. Its climax was marked by Kant's philosophy. Kant took his followers, as it were, to the very summit of pure reason to

---

[135] Wolff gave to the German "Enlightenment" its scientific independence. Next to Philip Melanchthon he was considered the great evangelical teacher of Germany.

[136] Johann Ernesti, Johann Michaelis and Johann Salomo Semler constituted a famous triumvirate of Bible critics. Semler felt a close spiritual kinship to Pelagius and to Erasmus.

[137] Gotthold Ephraim Lessing, Jean Jacques Rousseau and Immanuel Kant marked the culmination of rationalism as well as the beginning of its defeat. Storr represented a union of pietism and orthodoxy for the purpose of resisting rationalism. He vigorously defended the inspiration of the Bible and the deity of Christ.

THE AMERICAN LUTHERAN ANCESTRY 103

point out its marvellous possibilities as well as its distinct limitations. He actually pointed reason back to its own limited territory by showing that pure reason could neither demonstrate nor overthrow the objects of belief. He even rose to the support of Christianity by emphasizing the validity of Christian experience.

It is easy to see how rationalism deviated from historic Lutheranism. (1) Reason, and not the Bible, became the authority for faith and life. (2) Luther's conception of man and of Jesus Christ was rejected. (3) For Luther's revealed religion they substituted a natural religion. (4) In method they followed a neo-Aristotelian scholasticism which Luther had strongly condemned.

Rationalism also produced some good, practical results. Its emphasis on intellectual freedom and individual liberty paved way for political democracy. People trained to think independently demanded to govern themselves, as demonstrated by the French Revolution and by the establishment of the United States of America. It also promoted religious toleration, and affected the temporary abolishment of the Society of Jesus.

7. *Schleiermacher.*—Next to Luther and Calvin, the most outstanding Protestant theologian is doubtless Friedrich Daniel Ernst Schleiermacher (1768-1834), German pastor and university professor. He has been called the Origen of the nineteenth century because his reinterpretation of Christianity had such far-reaching and lasting influence on religious life and thought. The older rationalists had made religion a matter of *knowledge*; Kant had made it a matter of *will*; Schleiermacher defined religion as "the *feeling* of absolute dependence," as the immediate consciousness of absolute dependence on God. This Christian *consciousness* was alone the true interpreter of religion and the standard for testing truth. Religion was thereby removed from the realm of reason and placed in the realm of life or experience. He became the founder of what may be called the

psychological school of exegesis and also aided in the creation of the science of comparative religion.[138]

Schleiermacher wrested the scepter of theological learning from rationalism, but failed to restore Protestantism to Biblical Christianity. He became, in fact, the founder of a new rationalism which has largely dominated the religious thought of the nineteenth and twentieth centuries. The human intellect, as compared with a lit candle or lamp, has two distinct qualities: it gives *light* and it gives *warmth*. Eighteenth century rationalism

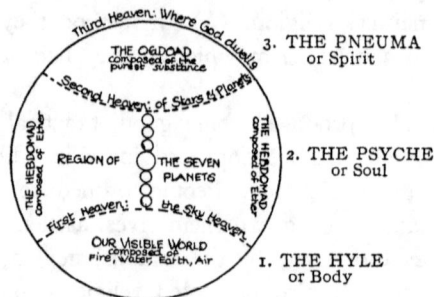

MICROCOSM AND MACROCOSM

stressed the first of these qualities, while nineteenth century rationalism stressed the second; which accounts for the peculiar emphasis on *feeling* as the seat of all religion. Feeling in this sense is not merely sense and taste for the Divine, but the immediate *consciousness* of absolute dependence on God.

The God revealed in the *feeling* of Schleiermacher was not a personal Being, but rather according to the pantheistic view, an impersonal force which was immanent in the world. God was to him the "absolute unity," the permanency, the universal, the absolute, the eternal principle indwelling in the world. The life of this universe was mirrored in each individual. Man was a *microcosm*, a reflection of the universe. In his relation to God

[138] Schleiermacher was professor of Lutheran theology at the University of Halle. Later he became professor at the University of Berlin.

as the eternal, man felt himself finite, limited, temporary and dependent. This feeling of dependency was the true basis of religion. Christianity was not the final form of religion, but it was the best religion known to men because it produced the best God-consciousness and brought man into harmony with God.

Jesus Christ was not conceived of as "God revealed in the flesh," but only as an ideal, sinless man, unique in his God-consciousness. Christ redeemed man, not so much from sin as from ignorance of God. Atonement in the traditional Christian sense was not admitted of in Schleiermacher's system. Christ realized in himself the ideal of humanity, and in his consciousness he realized the perfection of fellowship with God. The Christian consciousness of God was created and sustained by Christ through the Church. Schleiermacher's theology was strongly Christo-centered, though not in the orthodox sense. He gave a new recognition to the importance of the person of Christ and the Church, and stirred up much discussion regarding the Christ of history as compared with the Christ of experience.

Schleiermacher held that the whole human life was an educational process under the tutelage of the Divine Instructor. In this world process Christianity was conceived of as the primary factor of redemption. But other religions were also related to this process because they, like ancient Greek philosophy, were preparing the way for Christ.

While Schleiermacher did not become the founder of a school, yet he inspired many who were more or less his followers, and among these were men of at least three different schools: the extremely conservative *Confessional* School with its renewed emphasis on the historic creeds of Lutheranism, and consequently opposed to the union of Lutheran and Reformed churches; the *Mediating* School which tried to smooth out the differences between the conservatives and the older radicals without surrendering to either group;[139] and the *Ritschlian* School which stressed religious pragmatism and the use of historical or "higher" criticism. The influence of these schools soon extended to other lands, especially to Scandinavia, England and America.

Among the most serious defects of Schleiermacher's system may be noticed his extreme subjectivism, his inadequate views on God, of the historic Jesus and of immortality. There is, undoubtedly, a great distance between Schleiermacher on the one hand, and Paul and Luther on the other. Recently there has been much intense discussion as to whether or not Schleiermacher led to retrogression, rather than to a forward movement in the thinking of the evangelical world.[140]

8. *Ritschl.*—The outstanding theologian of the latter half of the nineteenth century, and second only to Schleiermacher in point of influence, was Albrecht Ritschl (1822-89). Before the end of the century he had a large following in Germany, Scandinavia, England and America. Ritschlianism became the great competitor of orthodoxy in evangelical Germany.

The secret of success of the Ritschlian movement was evidently this that in a time of much confusion and uncertainty of opinion, members of this School claimed that there is a ground of *certainty* in religion which is independent of, and unassailable by, all scientific and metaphysical theories. Faith has a certainty which antecedes, and is not derived from criticism; hence criticism can permanently establish nothing to the real disadvantage of faith. This certainty of faith springs immediately out of the experience of the revelation of God in Christ, as Christ meets

[139] Representatives of the Mediating School, such as Rothe, Mueller, Dorner and Neander, affirmed the personality of God, the supernatural revelation and the miracles of the Scriptures. They believed in the true inspiration, but not in the verbal inerrancy of the Bible. Their conception of true piety combined Kant's emphasis upon the will, Hegel's upon thought, and Schleiermacher's upon emotions.

[140] The so-called dialectic theology as represented by Karl Barth and Fr. Gogarten refutes Schleiermacher's idea of religion as feeling and experience. They have been ably seconded by Emil Brunner.

THE AMERICAN LUTHERAN ANCESTRY 107

you in the Gospel page.[141] The impression Christ irresistibly makes on you in the Gospel is that in Christ God draws near to you, and as God is present and acting before you, the natural distrust of your heart toward Him is banished, and you receive power to fulfill your moral destiny. This irresistible compulsion which Christ produces in those brought spiritually in contact with him seems, according to Ritschlians, to consist of the believer's impression of Christ's spiritual greatness and superiority to everything else in the world. Since Christ brings God to the believer, he has the value of God to the believer.

Christianity must begin, then, with the living, historical Christ who mediates to the believer faith in God. But the Ritschlians definitely rejected the orthodox Christology which they regarded as the result of a fusion of Christian ideas with Greek and Alexandrian metaphysics. Ritschl himself tried to remove all theoretical speculations concerning metaphysics, and sought to limit religion to an excessive religious pragmatism, that is, to the actual, *here and now,* needs of man. In religion, said Ritschl, we have to do only with "judgments of value," that is, not with the objective or scientific aspects of truth, but solely with their relation to our practical ends. The primary questions of faith are what the life and teaching of Christ have meant to us, and not what Christ is in his innermost nature. Hence there was no place in the Ritschlian system for such problems as Christ's pre-existence, the Virgin birth, Christ's bodily resurrection, his miracles, and the like.

A third focal point in Ritschlianism, and possibly the main one, was the central position given to the idea of the kingdom of God. To Ritschl this was the key to the understanding of the whole of God's revelation. In God's purpose to found such kingdom, Ritschl saw the explanation of creation and of the government of the world. His conception of the kingdom of God

---

[141] Ritschl tried to build the Christian religion on the New Testament revelation in its totality. The state of mind of God and of Christ, as revealed in these Scriptures, is genuine, authentic Christianity.

was simply that of the *ideal moral society*, an organization of humanity, in which all members act from the motive of love. Hence the goal of redemption is the creation of a holy society, the kingdom of God. To that end Christ came to the world to mediate in the believer faith in God. Christ had such perfect identity of mind and will with God that God's end was his end. In this perfect solidarity with God is the meaning of the predicate "Godhead" as applied to Christ.

Ritschl made Jesus Christ basic in the Christian religion; he stressed the social element in the doctrine of God; he emphasized the validity of Christian experience as the proof of Christianity; he served as a check upon a proud intellectualism and an extravagant emotional mysticism; and he gave history and experience prime consideration in the study of Christianity. But in his emphasis on the ethical element in religion, he overlooked the problem of sin as a radical evil. He denied original sin, and actual sin was so largely due to ignorance that it was a proper subject of pardon. Hence no atonement in the traditional or orthodox sense was needed; only a subjective reconciliation was mediated by Christ's life and death. Ritschl was also a pronounced anti-mystic who would hear nothing of a direct spiritual communion of the soul with God. He regarded the Scriptures as sources from which to learn the state of mind of the writers, rather than as records of permanent truth. His watchword, *theology without metaphysics,* and his attempt to create a divorce of faith and theoretic knowledge, opened up a wide door to subjectivity.[142]

Members of the Ritschlian School, such as Wilhelm Herrmann, Julius Kaftan, Julius Wellhausen, Adolf Harnack, Heinrich Holtzmann, A. Jülicher, Fr. Kattenbusch, Fr. Loofs and

---

[142] While Ritschl and his followers agreed in their absolute separation of theology from philosophy and theoretical knowledge, they did not agree in their theories of knowledge. Hence the movement held within it from the first, opposing tendencies. (Consider the theories of *knowledge* in the history of European philosophy, as set forth by Plato, Kant and Lotze).

THE AMERICAN LUTHERAN ANCESTRY

others, have carried the Ritschlian movement a long way beyond Ritschl.

9. *Summary.*—Just as it is true that Luther did more than merely to reproduce the religious thoughts and principles of the Apostolic Age, by making use of many ideas and elements which he derived from the entire historic development which intervened; so it is also true that present day Lutheranism is more than a mere reproduction of the thoughts and ideals of Luther. While modern Lutheranism goes back to Luther because he had such perfect identity of mind and will with the Tri-Une God as revealed in Scriptures, due recognition is also given to certain ideas and elements which have affected Christian life and thought in a positive way in intervening four hundred years between our time and Luther's.

8. REVIEW QUESTIONS

1. What attitude should one take toward the entire historic development from Luther to the present?
2. How is Lutheranism related to Tradition? Why?
3. Why the Lutheran Concord Movement?
4. How do you evaluate the historic movement known as Orthodoxy?
5. What relation, if any, has Mysticism to Lutheranism?
6. In what ways did Pietism influence Lutheranism?
7. How do you explain causes and effects of historic Rationalism?
8. In what ways did Schleiermacher influence the Christian world?
9. How do you evaluate Ritschl and his School?
10. In view of these historic developments, how would you re-state the position of Luther?
11. What is Lutheranism?
12. Why are you a Lutheran?

TOPICS FOR SPECIAL STUDY

1. Lutheran Conservatism and Progressivism.
2. Tradition and the Lutheran Symbols.
3. A Re-evaluation of Orthodoxy.
4. Christian and Non-Christian Mysticism.
5. Present Day Influences of Pietism.
6. Present Day Influences of Rationalism.
7. Schleiermacher in Modern Thought.
8. Ritschl in Modern Thought.

9. Theories of Knowledge as Set Forth by Plato, Kant, Lotze and the Ritschlians.

A SELECTED BIBLIOGRAPHY FOR CHAPTER I

1. Otto, Rudolf, *The Prophetic Imagination*.
2. Orr, James, *The Resurrection of Jesus*.
3. Hayes, *The Resurrection Fact*.
4. Westcott, *The Revelation of the Risen Lord*.
5. Simpson, *The Resurrection and Modern Thought*.
6. Ayer, *A Source Book for Ancient Church History*.
7. Lightfoot, *Dissertation on the Apostolic Age*.
8. Gilson, Etienne, *The Spirit of Medieval Philosophy*.
9. McGiffert, *Martin Luther*.
10. Scheel, O., *Dokumente zu Luthers Entwicklung*.
11. Scheel, T., *Martin Luther: Vom Katolizmus zur Reformation*.
12. Muller, *Luthers Werdegang bis zum Turmerlebnis*.
13. Meissinger, *Luthers Exegesis in der Fruhzeit*.
14. Gottschick, *Luthers Theologie*.
15. Tschackert, *Die Entstehung der Lutherischen und der Reformierten Kirchenlehre*.
16. Ihmels, *Das Christentum Luthers in seiner Eigenart*.
17. Ihmels, *Das Dogma in der Predigt Luthers*.
18. Bohmer, *Luther im Lichte der neueren Forschung*. 5th ed.
19. Reu, *Thirty Years of Luther Research*.
20. Berger, *Luther in kulturgeschichtlicher Darstellung*.
21. Wentz, *Martin Luther in the Changing Light of Four Centuries*.
22. Smith, P., *The Personal Side of Luther*. (Homiletic Review, October, 1917).
23. Smith, P., *A Decade of Luther Study*. (Harvard Theol. Review, April, 1921).
24. Kutzke, *Aus Luther Heimat*.
25. Richard, *The Confessional History of the Lutheran Church*.
26. Neve, *The Augsburg Confession*.
27. Voigt, *Distinctive Doctrines of Lutheranism*.
28. Gerberding, *Lutheran Fundamentals*.
29. Hunton, *Facts of Our Faith*.
30. Jacobs, *The Way*.

CHAPTER II

LUTHERANS IN COLONIAL DAYS, 1492-1763

Considerable space was devoted in the first chapter to the American Lutheran ancestry because this ancestry must be recognized and appreciated before the student can properly understand and evaluate present day Lutheranism in America. Furthermore, if Lutherans should lose their sense of their traditional background, they would soon lose their anchor and begin to drift on a sea of change. In the present chapter an attempt will be made to study Lutherans in colonial America, not as an isolated group, but rather as an integral part of the general colonial life and development.

I. The Significance of American Colonization.—The heroic discovery of the "new" world leads to interesting considerations. First, there was the extension of man's geographical knowledge; next, there was the significance of the discovery and the settlement of the new world for mankind in general and for the Christian Church in particular.

Man's geographical knowledge was very limited about 800 A.D. The early civilization which had centered so much around the great river valleys had shifted to the Mediterranean and to a small part of the Atlantic. Few ships dared to enter the forbidden waters beyond the Pillars of Hercules (the Strait of Gibraltar). But a world movement of geographical discovery and European expansion soon made the Atlantic and the Pacific highways of the world's intercourse and commerce.

It was no mere accident that the modern world was to be controlled by Western or Teutonic-Latin civilization. Oriental civilization had made repeated attempts to gain world supremacy, but Western civilization had always proved its superiority. From the first serious clash of the Persian Wars to the Battle of Vienna in 1529, Western civilization always turned back the Orient.

The amazing possibilities of the new world were hidden for many millenniums until the "fullness of time" had come. Civilized

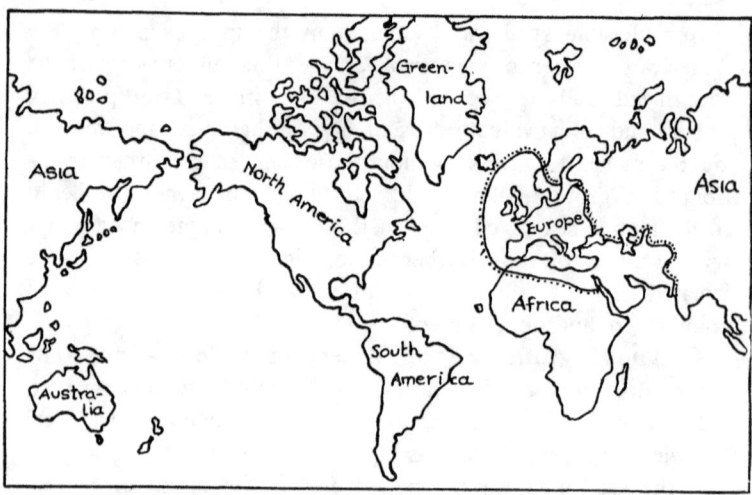

THE KNOWN WORLD IN 800 AND THE KNOWN WORLD OF TODAY
(The Known World in 800 is limited by a heavy line accompanied by dots)

man was not permitted to enter into the new world before he was prepared to control it. The Norse discovery of North America ("Vinland") about the year 1000 A.D. and the later missions from Greenland and Iceland did not eventuate in permanent settlements. If they had, North America might well have duplicated the history of South America. As it was, all attempts to begin a Christian civilization in America proved futile until a revived Christianity could be transplanted. The beginning of Protestantism and the beginning of American colonization were contemporaneous events.

LUTHERANS IN COLONIAL DAYS, 1492-1763

The discovery and colonization of America was, perhaps, as significant as the development of the Roman Empire.[1] The transplanting of European culture and religion resulted in unique contributions to world progress. The colonies established independent democratic governments which embraced peoples of diverse nationalities and different religious faiths. Thirteen independent and autonomous States united into a single federated nation without destroying the independence of the States. The Federal Constitution declared for religious freedom and refused to give preference to any special creed. All religions were per-

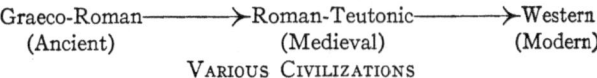

Graeco-Roman ───→ Roman-Teutonic ───→ Western
(Ancient)   (Medieval)   (Modern)
VARIOUS CIVILIZATIONS

mitted and none was favored by law. No religious test was necessary as a prerequisite to holding any office. Complete separation of Church and State threw the American churches upon their own resources and left them free to develop according to inherent tendencies. Religious liberty laid the foundation upon which the American system of free, public schools have been built up.

II. The Spanish Settlements.—The first modern colonial empires were founded by Spain and Portugal. France and the Netherlands came in for a fair share of colonial expansion, while England was more than a century behind Spain in getting started.

Early Portuguese explorations had led to the establishment of a great Portuguese commercial empire including the coasts of Africa and Asia, the Moluccas and other islands of the Pacific archipelago. These regions were dotted with fortresses, factories and Roman Catholic missions.

Upon the return of Columbus, King Ferdinand at once requested pope Alexander VI to confirm his title to the land discovered. The pontiff accordingly issued a bull wherein he drew

[1] Qualben, *A History of the Christian Church,* Third Edition, pp. 8-14.

114   THE LUTHERAN CHURCH IN AMERICA

from pole to pole a line of demarkation through the Atlantic, one hundred leagues west from the Azores or Cape Verde. All unclaimed heathen lands lying east of this line were confirmed to Portugal, while Spain was entitled to the lands lying west. This line was later moved two hundred and seventy leagues farther west. The Portuguese were prohibited from sailing any of the seas under the dominion of Spain, or from visiting as traders any of her lands, and the Spaniards were barred from

POLITICAL MAP OF PRESENT SOUTH AMERICA

waters or lands granted to the Portuguese. This arrangement did not hinder Spain, however, from gaining possession of the Philippine Islands; furthermore, the Portuguese established a colony in Brazil.

This papal bull contemplated conquests for Christianity and gains for the Church, as well as territory and revenues for the kings. Every Spanish expedition of discovery, invasion and colonization, was accompanied by priests who acted as chaplains to the Spaniards and as missionaries to the natives. Spanish missions were first established on the West Indies and in Mexico. A bishopric was established at Santo Domingo in 1512;

LUTHERANS IN COLONIAL DAYS, 1492-1763

another at Santiago de Cuba in 1522; and another in the city of Mexico in 1530. The University of Mexico was established in 1551, almost eighty years before the founding of Harvard; and the University of Lima was founded in 1557. From Mexico and the West Indies Spanish missionaries found their way to South America. In 1535 Peru was conquered, and by 1553 the Spaniards had extended their empire to Chile. Argentine was the next field of invasion, and in 1580 the first Spanish settlement was made at Buenos Aires. Brazil was settled by the Portuguese, beginning in 1510. All of South America was gradually conquered, and Roman Catholicism was established as the official religion.

1. *Lutherans in Venezuela, 1528*

Venezuela, however, formed an interesting exception. Venezuela or "Little Venice" was discovered by Columbus on August 1, 1498 on his third voyage. In consideration of a loan, Charles V permitted the Welsers, famous bankers and traders of Augsburg, Germany, to occupy Venezuela from 1526 to 1556, and the region was renamed Welserland. German Lutherans arrived in Venezuela in 1528,[2] and by 1532 the entire colony is said to have accepted the Lutheran faith.[3] At present there are about 1000 Lutherans in Venezuela, with congregations in Caracas, Valencia, Puerto Cabello and Maracaibo, with a colony at Taroa.[4]

2. *French Lutherans (Huguenots) in Brazil, 1555*

Less fortunate was the Huguenot colony established in 1555 near the present city of Rio de Janeiro, Brazil, through the instrumentality of the great Huguenot leader, Duke de Coligny. Since French Protestants up to about 1560 were usually called "Lutherans" or "Heretics of Meaux," there may be some justi-

[2] See diagram on page 116.
[3] Karl von Kloden in *Zeitschrift für Allgemeine Erkunde*, Vol. V, 1855.
[4] *Lutheran World Almanac*, Vol. VIII, p. 13.

116 THE LUTHERAN CHURCH IN AMERICA

fication for calling these Protestant settlers in Brazil Lutherans, though they are more properly designated Huguenots. In 1566 the Duke of Coligny sent two pastors, Pierre Richer and Guillaume Chartier, to the colony. They were the first Protestant preachers to cross the Atlantic ocean. In the course of a few years, the governor of the colony, Villegagnon, renounced Protestantism. With the sanction of the home government, which was Roman Catholic, he soon destroyed the Protestant character of the colony, partly by deporting the

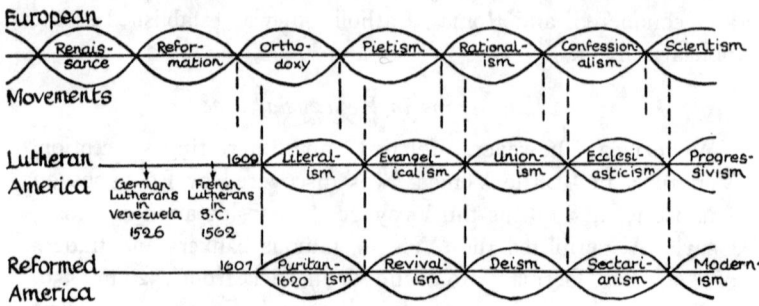

EUROPEAN AND AMERICAN MOVEMENTS COMPARED
(Suggested in part by Dr. O. M. Norlie)

Huguenot pastors and the chief men, and also by putting others to death. In 1558 he caused the death by drowning of Pierre Bourdon, Jean du Bordel and Mathieu Verneuil. These became the first martyrs to the Protestant cause in the New World.

Within the United States, Spanish missions were first established in Florida. Ponce de Leon, Governor of Porto Rico, had been told by Indians that to the north lay an island where gold was abundant, and where there was a river whose waters would restore youth to the aged. He set out in search of this island in 1513 and discovered Florida (Flowerland), which he took possession of. All attempts to colonize Florida failed until September, 1565, when the foundations of St. Augustine, the oldest city in the United States, were laid. During the one hundred and fifteen years Spain had exclusive possession of Florida, the Spanish missionaries made some imposing gains in that region, but their mission work was sustained by Spanish arms and by subsidies from the Spanish treasury. When Florida was transferred to the British crown in 1763, the Spanish missions in that territory collapsed.

3. *French Lutherans (Huguenots) in Florida, 1562-65*

Three early attempts to settle French Lutherans (Huguenots) in Florida failed. These settlers were not exclusively French, however, but also numbered some Alsatian and Hessian Protestants who likely were Lutherans.[5] The first expedition of two vessels, sent by Admiral Coligny in 1562, and commanded by Jean Ribault, settled at Port Royal, only about twenty miles east of the region where the Lutheran Salzburgers settled in 1734. When the provisions had given out, these settlers left Port Royal. A second expedition came in 1564, headed by Rene de Laudonniere, and built Fort Carolina on the May River. This settlement was about to be abandoned when Jean Ribault arrived in 1565 with seven vessels carrying six hundred persons. They came in August, but less than a month after their arrival a Spanish expedition of thirty-four vessels and two thousand six hundred men, commanded by Pedro Menendez, came "with commission to destroy all the Lutheran French that had dared to settle on soil claimed by his country." The massacre at Fort Carolina occurred on September 20, 1565, and the Protestant colony was soon destroyed.

Several other Huguenot settlements in the present United States and Canada could be mentioned, but these later colonists had more in common with the Reformed than with the Lutherans. Hence they do not come in under the scope of the present treatise.

Spanish missions were established in New Mexico and in California. In New Mexico the missions prospered until a dis-

[5] F. H. Henoch, *Handbuch des Deutschtums in Auslande*, p. 113.

astrous native revolt destroyed all churches and convents and killed all Spaniards north of El Paso. Spanish rule was restored in 1700, but the missions never recovered from this stunning blow. In California the beginnings of Spanish settlements and missions date from 1769. The three most northern missions, San Juan Capistrano, Santa Clara and San Francisco, were founded between 1775 and 1777. But Spanish missions were dependent on military protection, and conversion was in too many instances by coercion. When California was annexed to the United States, the Spanish missions in the province deteriorated.

III. The French in North America.—French explorers, traders and missionaries opened up the northern part of North America. The first permanent French colony was established in Quebec in 1608.

With the founding of Quebec the French began to evolve their plan to found a splendid French empire. Men like LaSalle and Champlain, inspired by French royalty, planned a gradual spiritual and secular conquest of the entire continent. The French government sent shiploads of emigrants every year at the expense of the crown. French colonies enjoyed royal patronage, endowment and protection. The French claims in North America included Canada, Louisiana, half of New York, half of Maine, and half of Vermont. Everywhere the French colonists were accompanied by Jesuit priests who established Roman Catholic missionary stations and built churches, convents and schools. It appeared that North America was to have a uniform Roman Catholic population.

But the dream vanished as in a mist. Many causes contributed to this sudden collapse. The king subordinated colonial interests to his ambitious European policies. Strict governmental control from distant France smothered all worthy individual aspiration and enterprise. French colonies were closed against all save Catholic immigrants. New France was too much concerned with trade and too little concerned with settlement and self-supporting agriculture. The French could not, like the British, found colonies basically European in stock. They lacked French men and women. French colonists, like the Spanish, frequently intermarried with native tribes people, tending to lower rather than to elevate the standard of living. The close friendship of the French with the Hurons aroused the opposition of the fierce Iroquois. This tribe not only annihilated the Hurons but also checked the French advance southward. At the close of the Seven Years' War, 1756-63, Canada and all French possessions

NORTH AMERICA IN 1783
(The dotted region indicates U. S. territory)

in North America east of the Mississippi, save New Orleans and a little adjoining land, were ceded to England; and Louisiana west of the Mississippi River was ceded to Spain. France, accordingly, lost every foot of land she had in North America, excepting only two little islands, Miquelon and St. Pierre, in the Gulf of St. Lawrence, upon which she retained fishing rights. The French Catholic Church was almost completely removed from North America, save in eastern Canada, in parts of Maine and in certain western regions.

IV. English, Dutch and Swedish Colonization of North America.—The attempts of Spain and France to establish magnificent colonial empires in America ended in dismal failure. Would England fare any better in her empire building and colonization? The disconnected colonies along the Atlantic seaboard, with different languages and divers creeds, unsustained by governmental arms or treasuries, did not offer much promise of success; and yet these very colonies became the nucleus of a new English state.

Various reasons may be given for English colonial success. The destruction of the Spanish Armada in 1588 left England the mistress of the seas. The English colonies in America were able to supply settlers of their own stock. The settlers were concerned, not merely with trade and search for gold, but also with the development of industry and self-supporting agriculture. Huguenots and English colonists—women as well as men—were particularly skilled. English representative institutions, Lords and Commons, trained the colonists in selecting their own rulers and in successfully governing themselves. Practically all early settlers were Protestants who came to America in search of religious freedom or material gain.

Some attention will now be given to the chronological order in which some of the more representative religious groups arrived and settled in the American colonies. On this general background the place and contribution of the Lutherans may be better evaluated.

1. *Episcopalianism transplanted to Virginia, 1607.*—Henry VII of England had asked John Cabot and sons to make explorations in western and northern seas. In 1497 the Cabots sighted land in the vicinity of Newfoundland and took possession of it in the name of the King of England. A later expedition explored the coast from Labrador to the capes off North Carolina. On the basis of these and other alleged discoveries, the English based their claim to the American coast from Labrador to Florida.

Sir Walter Raleigh explored the central coast of North America and named it Virginia in honor of the virgin queen, Elizabeth. His glowing account of the beauty and riches of this land led to the establishment of the first permanent colony at Jamestown, Virginia, in 1607. The settlement, named in honor of James I of England, was largely a commercial venture, although not lacking in religious character. The settlers were English cavaliers, all members of the Established Church of England. This Church remained established by law in Virginia till 1776, and clerical appointments were made by the Bishop of London. The William and Mary College was founded in 1693 for the purpose of training a native ministry. However, the influence of plantation life, the failure to provide an adequate supply of native clergy, and the lack of direct episcopal oversight, reacted against the growth of a vigorous church life.

The history of the Church of England in other southern colonies is parallel to that of Virginia. North and South Carolina established the Church of England by law. Maryland, established as a Roman Catholic colony, was transferred to the crown of England in 1691, and the following year the Anglical Church was established by law. Many Anglican congregations were also founded among early settlers in Georgia, New York and New Jersey.

2. *Congregationalism established at New Plymouth in 1620.*—The history of the Plymouth colony goes back to England and to Holland. John Robinson (d. 1625), a Fellow at Cambridge, had been suspended because of his separatist tendencies. He joined a separatist congregation at Gainsboro and followed this group to the Netherlands. At Leyden he organized a congregation of several hundred English refugees, mostly industrial workers and farmers, in 1609. Two years later Henry Jacob (d. 1624), the founder of the English Independents (Congregationalists), joined the group. Jacob's Congregational theory may be stated as follows: (1) The Church shall be a national church, consisting of the old, established congregations which shall be supported by the State. All separatist tendencies are to be op-

posed. (2) Each local congregation shall be independent in its external and internal affairs. Bishops, presbyters and synods have no authority over the local churches. Resolutions and decisions of the synods are merely advisory. (3) Within the local church, the predestined shall by a "Covenant" create its own organization. The official pastor shall perform all ministerial acts, but this special organization has a right to call its own evangelists, to hold special divine services and to have communion for the elect only. Jacob organized a congregation in London according to these principles in 1606. Robert Browne had organized a congregation at Norwich in 1580 much according to the same principles. For this reason the early Independents (Congregationalists) were frequently called Brownists.

A large constituency of the Robinson congregation at Leyden desired to return to English soil; yet the group did not wish to conform to the laws of the Anglican Church. Finally some land was secured in Virginia, and the group embarked in two vessels, the *Mayflower* and the *Speedwell*, to sail for America by way of England. The *Speedwell* was found unseaworthy and did not cross the Atlantic. The "Pilgrim Fathers" crowded into the *Mayflower* and from Plymouth, England, the ship set sail in 1620. Storms drove the ship far off its course and it finally landed, not in Virginia, but at Cape Cod, on November 9, 1620. The following month the Pilgrims moved to the western side of the Massachusetts Bay where they founded a town, calling it Plymouth from the last place they had seen in the old world.

Between 1620 and 1638 the Congregational colonies of Plymouth, Massachusetts, Connecticut and New Haven established Congregationalism by law. In Connecticut this law remained effective till 1818, and in Massachusetts till 1833. Harvard College was founded in 1636, and Yale College was founded in 1701. John Eliot (1604-90), "Apostle to the Indians," started the mission work which led to the formation of the Society for the Propagation of the Gospel in New England in 1649.

LUTHERANS IN COLONIAL DAYS, 1492-1763   123

3. *Arrival of the Dutch Reformed in 1623.*—Though the Bay of New York was visited by a European navigator in 1524,[6] the history of New Netherland starts with the year 1609 when Henry Hudson, an Englishman in the service of the Dutch India Company, explored the Hudson River from Manhattan to Albany, and took possession of the explored region in the name of the Dutch Republic.[7] Two years later Henrich Christiansen (Hendrick Cortiansen) arrived and began to chart the region concerned. To him goes the credit of having built the first dwellings for white people on the Island of Manhattan.[8] The northern limit of New Netherland[9] was the forty-fifth parallel; the southern limit was the South River, later called Delaware River; the eastern limit lay between the Hudson and the Connecticut rivers; and the western never extended many miles west of the Hudson River.

A few straggling traders established their posts along the Hudson. They gave the Indians glass beads, strips of cotton and divers other articles in exchange for skins of beaver, otter and mink. In 1614 they organized the United New Netherland Company, and obtained a charter from the States General which granted them the right of trading in New Netherland. This charter expired in 1618, but the company continued its trade until the Dutch West India Company was formed in 1621. The charter vested in the Dutch West India Company both mercantile and political power, with authority to found colonies and to govern them under the supervision of the States General.

New Netherland became a political entity in 1623. Its govern-

[6] Giovanni da Verrazzano, an Italian employed by Francis I of France to discover a short cut to the East Indies, anchored in New York Bay in April, 1524. His report is published in New York Historical Society's Collections, new series, vol. I, p. 45.

[7] Henry Hudson's intention was to discover a north-west water-way to seas beyond.

[8] Henrich Christiansen came from the German town of Cleve on the Rhine. Investigation shows that he was a Lutheran.

[9] New Netherland always occurs in the singular, while the Netherlands of Europe are plural because they are an aggregation of small states.

THE LUTHERAN CHURCH IN AMERICA

ment was vested in the Dutch West India Company. In colonial matters New Netherland possessed all legislative, executive and judicial powers, but the States General should confirm the appointment of the highest officials and the instructions given them. The Roman-Dutch law of the fatherland was to prevail when special laws did not meet all needs.

DIRECTOR-GENERALS OF NEW NETHERLAND[10]

Cornelius Jacobsen May	1624-25
William Verhulst	1625-26
Peter Minuit	1626-32
Sebastian Jansen Krol	1632-33
Wouter van Twiller	1633-38
William Kieft	1638-47
Peter Stuyvesant	1647-64

In 1623 New Netherland received its first genuine settlers,[11] about thirty Dutch and Walloon[12] families, who were concerned, not merely with trade, but also with settlement and self-supporting agriculture and industry. About eighteen of these families settled at Fort Orange, near where Albany now stands. Others settled on Manhattan, while others went as far south as to the Delaware River, near what was later named New Sweden. Another large group of settlers arrived from Holland in 1625 and settled on Manhattan, which they named New Amsterdam.

Manhattan, an island twenty-two square miles in extent, on which New Amsterdam (New York) was built, was bought in 1626 for sixty guilders in beads and ribbons, or the equivalent of twenty-four gold dollars.[13] The purchasing value of gold

---

[10] Peter Minuit was the first to enjoy the title of Director-General, though his predecessors acted in similar capacity.

[11] The earliest white traders along the Hudson were too much concerned with trade, and too little concerned with settlement and self-supporting industry and agriculture. They were mere transients. The majority of the immigrants of 1623 and 1625 came for real settlement.

[12] The Walloons were for the most part Protestant exiles from the southern provinces of the Spanish Netherlands.

[13] Later there was some uncertainty as to whether or not the white settlers had bought Manhattan from the right party. It seemed as though the Indians, and not the Palefaces, got the better end of the deal.

LUTHERANS IN COLONIAL DAYS, 1492-1763   125

being considered, this sum would at present be about $120.00. In 1629 the system of patroons was established for the purpose of encouraging immigration.[14] A patroon's grant of land was given on condition that each patroon would bring fifty adult persons to New Netherland and settle them in the colony. This system of colonization increased the immigration somewhat, and yet the population in New Amsterdam as well as in New Netherland remained surprisingly small. New Amsterdam (New York) was incorporated in February, 1653. In that same year

ESTIMATED POPULATION IN NEW AMSTERDAM

In 1628	270 people
In 1642	1,000 "
In 1653	800[15] "
In 1660	1,800 "
In 1664	2,400 "

ESTIMATED POPULATION IN NEW NETHERLAND

In 1647	1,500 people
In 1653	2,000 "
In 1664	10,000 "

the city was enclosed by palisades or a wall, from which the present Wall Street bears its name. A "burgher-recht" or citizenship was established in 1657. The first public Latin and Greek school in the "New World" was established in New Amsterdam (New York) in 1652.[16]

The *public* religious life of New Netherland apparently began in 1626 with the arrival of two Comforters of the Sick, Sebastian Jansz Crol and Jan Huyck. They also conducted some simple divine services. The first Dutch minister to the colony was Jonas Michaelius who arrived in the spring of 1628. On August 11, 1628, he organized the first Dutch Reformed congregation in New Netherland, in New Amsterdam on Manhattan. This congregation, whose charter members comprised Dutch, Wal-

---

[14] Most famous was Kiliaon Van Rensselaer, who was the patroon of the region around Albany.
[15] The population was reduced on account of Indian wars.
[16] Cubberley, *History of Education*, p. 369.

loons and French, became the earliest representative of the Presbyterian policy in America. In 1629 the Dutch Reformed Church obtained legal recognition of its establishment in the colony. In a new charter of July 19, 1640, the Dutch West India Company became even more explicit by stating in part, "And no other religion shall be publicly admitted in New Netherland, except the Reformed, as it is at present preached and practiced by public authority in the United Netherlands."

New Amsterdam, however, soon developed a cosmopolitan character. Huguenots, Lutherans, English Puritans, Mennonites, Quakers, Jews and others found their way to the new settlement. The colonial authorities imposed penalties and fines on Lutherans, Quakers and Jews for alleged violations of the official religious decrees. It appears that the Lutherans did not secure the right of public exercise of their religion till after the conquest of New Netherland by the British in 1664.[17]

4. *Lutheranism transplanted to New Netherland in 1623.*—The first permanent group of Lutherans came with other immigrants from Holland in 1623 and in 1625 and settled in New Netherland. Lutherans were numerous and influential in Holland in the seventeenth century,[18] and wealthy Dutch Lutherans of Amsterdam, Holland, cooperated with their countrymen in the establishment of Dutch American colonies.[19] Some of these thrifty Lutherans came with the early settlers. Furthermore, there was much reciprocity in the seventeenth century between the

---

[17] This is not surprising in view of the fact that as late as in 1604, the Dutch Reformed in Amsterdam, Holland, tried to deny the numerous and wealthy Lutherans of that city the right of private worship.

[18] At Amsterdam, Holland—at that time *the* emporium of the world—the Lutherans had at that time the largest congregation in the world, consisting of about thirty thousand souls, with two churches and six ministers. There was a Lutheran congregation at Leyden, Holland, with seven hundred members and two ministers. Powerful Lutheran congregations existed also in Rotterdam, Woerden and other Dutch centers.

[19] Lutherans in Amsterdam were among the wealthiest and most enterprising in the city.

LUTHERANS IN COLONIAL DAYS, 1492-1763

Dutch and the Scandinavians.[20] Many Scandinavians lived in Holland, and a considerable number of Hollanders lived in Norway and in Denmark.[21] A surprisingly large number of Scandinavians soon found their way to the New Netherland colony. It is the merit of Dr. John O. Evjen to have collected 188 authentic biographies of Scandinavians who lived in New Netherland during the years 1630-74.[22] In that same work he also gives an annotated list of 186 Germans who lived in New Netherland during that same period.[23] The Scandinavian settlers were practically all Lutherans, and the majority of the German settlers were Lutherans of the seventeenth century type.[24] Colonial records show that Germans and Scandinavians played a proportionately important role in the development of New York.[25] In

[20] The commerce between Norway and Holland was large, and Holland taught Norway that her future was on the sea.

[21] It was quite common in the seventeenth century that sons and daughters from Scandinavia would go to Holland for a shorter or longer stay. Erik Pontoppidan, a Bishop of Norway who had lived for some time in Holland, states in his anonymous work *Menoza*, that about 8000 to 9000 Norwegian, Danish and Holstein sailors would gather at the Dutch sea ports every fall. And Robert Molesworth in *An Account of Denmark as It was in the Year 1692*, states that many Scandinavians had settled in Holland. A Danish-Norwegian Lutheran congregation was organized at Amsterdam, Holland, in 1663. As for Hollanders living in Norway, see Evjen, *Scandinavian Immigrants in New York, 1630-1674*, page 14.

[22] Ibid., pp. 19-346.

[23] Ibid., pp. 390-436.

[24] The biographies just referred to indicate that the early Scandinavian and German settlers in New York represented the nobleman as well as the peasant. They were engaged in various types of work, representing the farmer, the miller, the wood-sawyer, the tobacco planter, the carpenter, the smith, the mason, the trader, the merchant, the soldier, the mariner, the boatbuilder, the shoemaker, the gauger, the tapster, the brewer, the surgeon, the fisher, the firewarden, the drayman, the land owner, the council member, the capitalist, the policeman, the judge, etc. Cf. Evjen, ibid., p. xiii. These Scandinavians had not left Scandinavia or Holland because of religious or political discontent, or for lack of industrial opportunity. They came voluntarily, seeking such opportunities as the New Netherland colony might offer.

[25] Scandinavian and German settlers served in various public offices, though the Germans soon overshadowed the Scandinavians in political influence. Cf. Evjen, ibid., p. 360. And a number of Lutheran colonists

fact, German and Scandinavian Lutherans seem to have been much more in evidence in New Amsterdam than Dutch Lutherans. The Lutheran petition of 1657, requesting that the Reverend John Ernestus Gutwasser be permitted to remain in New Amsterdam, appears to have been signed by sixteen Germans, five Scandinavians and three Hollanders.[26] The Reformed preachers in New Amsterdam, Megapolensis and Drisius, explicitly referred to Paul Schrick of Nuremberg as the leader of the Lutherans in New Amsterdam.[27] It appears, therefore, that the dominant element in the oldest Lutheran church in New Netherland was German-Scandinavian rather than Dutch.[28]

The early Lutheran centers in New Netherland were at Fort Orange (Albany) and at New Amsterdam (New York). But as Lutheran residents moved away from these centers and into new localities, the Lutheran pastors, like faithful shepherds, followed them into the wilderness. These new settlements marked the beginning of Lutheran congregations which were later organized at Loonenburgh (Athens), Hackensack (Teaneck),

---

were business partners with the Dutch. Jonas Bronck, the son of a Danish Lutheran clergyman, residing for some time at the Faroe Islands, has his name immortalized in Bronx Borough of Greater New York, in Bronx River, Bronxville, etc. Paul Schrick, a German Lutheran, had business connections far beyond the boundaries of the New Amsterdam colony. Another Lutheran, Volckart Jansen, was judge in Fort Orange (Albany). Matthew Capito, the secretary to Governor Stuyvesant, was also the secretary of the Lutheran congregation in New York City. Later he became the acting mayor of Esopus, now Kingston, New York. Ensign Niessen, a Lutheran, was in charge of the Kingston garrison during the Indian massacre of 1663, when he was commended by Governor Stuyvesant.

[26] Cf. Evjen, ibid., p. 394. It was Laurence Noorman, a Norwegian, who concealed Rev. Gutwasser on his farm for a whole winter, the Lutherans giving Noorman six guilders a week for the minister's support. Cf. Megapolensis and Drisius to Director General and Council, August 23, 1658, in *Ecclesiastical Records, New York*, p. 430.

[27] *Eccl. Recs. N. Y.*, p. 429.

[28] Colonial records tell nothing about squabbles between Dutch Reformed preachers and *Dutch* Lutheran laymen, but they do tell about disputes between Dutch Reformed preachers and German Lutheran laymen. Cf. Eccl. Recs., N. Y., i, p. 429; Evjen, ibid., p. 394.

LUTHERANS IN COLONIAL DAYS, 1492-1763   129

Esopus (Kingston), Bergen (Jersey City) and other places which will be mentioned in connection with the work of Justus Falckner.

At Fort Orange (Albany) the Lutherans grew steadily in number. By 1644 they were numerous enough to form a distinct group, and by 1656 they seem to have organized themselves into a congregation, for in that year they were forbidden by Vice-Governor de Decker to hold services. By 1657 they were aggressive enough to collect one hundred beaver skins, valued at eight hundred guilders, for the support of the new Lutheran minister they had sent for.[29] The first Lutheran minister to visit Albany was Jacob Fabritius, in 1669. During the ministry of Bernhard Arensius, and before 1674, a Lutheran church was erected near Fort Orange. Albany was a *filiale* of New York until 1731. It was then served for some time by W. C. Berkenmeyer from Loonenburgh, and later by Peter Sommer from Schoharie.

In New Amsterdam the Lutheran group grew steadily and became very cosmopolitan in its make-up, for it included Germans, Norwegians, Swedes, Danes and Dutch.[30] By 1643 they were numerous enough to form a distinct group, and by 1648 they had organized a congregation of "The Unaltered Augsburg Confession of Faith."[31] That same year the members of the congregation appealed to the Lutheran consistory of Amsterdam to request the Directors of the Dutch West India Company to

[29] Megapolensis and Drisius to Classis of Amsterdam, October 25, 1657, in Eccl. Recs., N. Y., i, p. 409.

[30] According to colonial records, a number of Scandinavian Lutherans lived in New Amsterdam as early as in 1630-31. Cf. Evjen, ibid., pp. 54, 56, 89, 101, 105, 108, 120, 138. The Borough of Bronx is named after Jonas Bronck, the son of a Danish Lutheran clergyman who had resided for some time at Thorshavn, Faroe Islands. Father Jogues, a Jesuit missionary, makes mention of Lutherans in New Amsterdam in 1643.

[31] The minutes of 1649 of the Lutheran consistory of Amsterdam refer to the Lutherans in New Amsterdam as a "congregation." Cf. Nicum, in *Lutheran Church Review*, Vol. XII, p. 182.

130   THE LUTHERAN CHURCH IN AMERICA

concede the privilege of the public exercise of their religion in New Netherland.[32] The request was not granted.

Undaunted by this apparent defeat, the Lutherans continued to send petitions to the Dutch authorities. Letters were sent to the States of Holland, to the Directors of the Dutch West India Company,[33] and on October 4, 1653, they petitioned the Director General for official sanction of their congregation and for permission to call a Lutheran minister from Holland. In that same year, in October, 1653, the Lutherans on Manhattan Island (New York) numbered fifty families.

The Dutch Reformed ministers of New Amsterdam brought the matter to the attention of the Classis of Amsterdam, and they also addressed themselves directly to the Dutch West India Company. The ministers well knew that the Classis of Amsterdam was even less tolerant of ecclesiastical differences in New Amsterdam than they were. The Dutch West India Company, with the moral support of the Classis of Amsterdam and the States of Holland, pronounced its decision on February 23, 1654, stating that no Lutheran pastor would be tolerated in New Amsterdam, nor would the authorities permit of any other public worship than the true Reformed.[34]

The Lutheran issue entered a new phase when New Sweden was conquered in 1655. Here a group of Swedish Lutheran settlers, under the authority of the Dutch West India Company, were permitted to continue their divine services "according to the Unaltered Augsburg Confession, the Council of Upsala, and

[32] The letter, recorded in the minutes of 1649 of the Lutheran consistory of Amsterdam, also includes an appeal for a Lutheran minister. Cf. Nicum, in *Lutheran Church Review*, XII, p. 182.

[33] Letters of Megapolensis and Drisius to Classis of Amsterdam, October 6, 1653, in *Eccl. Recs. N. Y.*, I, pp. 317-18.

[34] Governor General Kieft, in his patents to Mespath, March 28, 1642, and to Hempstead, November 16, 1644, assured the colonists the "exercise of Reformed Christian Religion and church discipline which they profess," because these colonists were English Presbyterians who were in accord with the Dutch Reformation in doctrine and in polity. Cf. *Book of Patents G.G.*, p. 49, and Thompson, *Hist. of Long Island*, II, pp. 5-6.

LUTHERANS IN COLONIAL DAYS, 1492-1763 131

the ceremonies of the Swedish Church," and also to have their own minister. But this concession was dictated by policy and not by principle.[35] This concession to New Sweden was not enjoyed by Lutherans in other parts of New Netherland. Lutherans in New Amsterdam met in private conventicles where they held divine services with prayer, reading and singing. On February 1, 1656, the Director General and the Council regarded it as their duty to decree that all such conventicles, both public and private, should be strictly prohibited. Leaders of such conventicles would be subject to a fine of one hundred pounds Flemish; and any man or woman attending such conventicle would be subject to a fine of twenty-five pounds Flemish.[36]

This decision did not please the Directors in Holland. In "a full meeting" these Directors of the Dutch West India Company resolved that the doctrines of the Unaltered Augsburg Confession should be tolerated in New Netherland "under their jurisdiction, in the same manner as in the Fatherland, under its excellent government." On October 24, 1656, the Lutherans of New Amsterdam informed the Governor General and the Council of this decision, and petitioned "that henceforth we may not be hindered in our services. These with God's blessing we intend to celebrate, with prayer, reading and singing, until, as we hope and expect, a qualified person shall come next spring from the Fatherland to be our minister and teacher, and remain here as such." Meanwhile the Classis of Amsterdam protested against this free exercise of dissenting worship, and the Directors were finally influenced to abide by the resolution of the preceding year.[37] On the basis of this decision, the Governor General and

[35] The outbreak of Indian hostilities in New Amsterdam at this time, made it impossible for the Dutch colonial authorities to abolish entirely the Lutheran worship in New Sweden.

[36] According to a letter of June that year, from the Directors to the colonial authorities in New Amsterdam, some Lutherans were actually imprisoned. Cf. *Documents Relating to the State of New York*, Vol. XIV, p. 351.

[37] Classis of Amsterdam. *Act of Deputies*, VI, pp. 45 and 375. April 10, 1657.

the Council gave the Lutherans in New Amsterdam permission "quietly to have their exercises at their own houses," but not in private conventicles.[38]

In July, 1657, the first regular minister to the Lutherans in New Amsterdam arrived from Holland. His name was John Ernestus Gutwasser.[39] The colonial authorities forbade his holding services or performing any ministerial acts,[40] and the Dutch Reformed ministers of New Amsterdam demanded his immediate deportation. The Lutherans responded by sending in their well known Petition of October 10, 1657,[41] in which they earnestly requested the Director General and the Council to revoke the order of deportation. Their petition was followed by a letter from Rev. Gutwasser to the same authorities; but all pleading was in vain. Rev. Gutwasser was again commanded to leave the country. He managed to remain till June, 1659, when he was arrested and deported. A Lutheran student, Abelius Zetskorn, who came to New Amsterdam in 1662, did not fare any better. He was deported to the Dutch settlement of New Amstel on the Delaware, where he was ordained in the spring of 1663 by Rev. Lars Lock, according to a letter of Rev. Andrew Rudman, dated October 4, 1703. Since Rev. Lock had no official authority from the Church of Sweden to perform this ordination, it can not be considered valid. Meanwhile Governor Stuyvesant did his utmost to make Lutheran preaching in New Amsterdam an utter impossibility. In 1662 he published a new proclamation

---

[38] *Col. Docs. N. Y.*, XIV, pp. 386-88.

[39] The archives of the Lutheran consistory at Amsterdam give his name as Goetwater. Documents at Albany, New York, give the name variously as Gutwater and Gutwasser.

[40] Lutherans in New Netherland were not only obliged to attend the Reformed services, but also to have their children baptised and instructed by Reformed pastors and in the Reformed faith. The Reformed Dutch Order of Baptism of 1591 stipulated that the child should be brought up in the doctrines of the Old and New Testaments and in the Creed. But the Synod of Dort of 1619 narrowed this formula to the doctrines of the Reformed Church. While the use of this revised formula was very limited in Holland, it was rigidly adhered to in New Netherland.

[41] Petition of Lutherans, October 10, 1657. *Eccl. Recs. N. Y.*, I, p. 405.

LUTHERANS IN COLONIAL DAYS, 1492-1763   133

against the preaching of any other than the Reformed doctrine, "either in houses, barns, ships or yachts, in the woods or fields."

Liberty of worship came for the Lutherans with the conquest by the British in 1664 and the transformation of New Amsterdam into New York. The charter of December 6, 1664, signed by Governor Richard Nicolls, granted the Lutherans the right of free and public exercise of divine worship according to their conscience.[42] St. Matthew's Lutheran Church, organized in 1648 and chartered in 1664, regards this "charter" document of 1664 as one of the treasures of its archives.[43]

Governor Nicolls granted a request from the Lutherans that they be permitted to call a minister. A call was extended to a young minister in Holland, and he waited three years before answering and then he declined. They called another minister and he also declined. Finally a third minister, Jacob Fabritius, a Lutheran pastor from Grosglogan, Selecia, accepted and arrived in February, 1669. He served the New York-Albany parish for a short time and proved to be a keen disappointment to his parishioners because he was too despotic and hot-headed.[44] He left the parish in August, 1671, and was succeeded by Rev. Bernhard Arensius who served the New York-Albany parish from 1671 to 1691, spending part of the winters in Albany and the rest of the year in New York. After a vacancy of more than ten years, the New York-Albany parish was served by Rev. Andrew Rudman, a Swedish minister on the Delaware, for one year, 1702-03, and then he entrusted the parish to Rev. Justus Falckner.

The first Lutheran church in New York City was built on the exact site where the spire of the Trinity (Episcopal) Church now stands, directly opposite Wall Street. During the Dutch

---

[42] This charter did not imply complete parity, however, nor did it mean autonomy.

[43] The congregation has been known as St. Matthew's since 1826.

[44] After Fabritius was transferred to Swedish congregations in Delaware and Pennsylvania, he lived like a different man, and gained the respect and esteem of his parishioners and the Swedish provost, Acrelius.

re-occupation in 1673, the military defense of the city made it necessary for the Dutch to abandon the western end of the old wall built by Stuyvesant in 1653, which ran along the north side of the Lutheran church property. The new wall built in

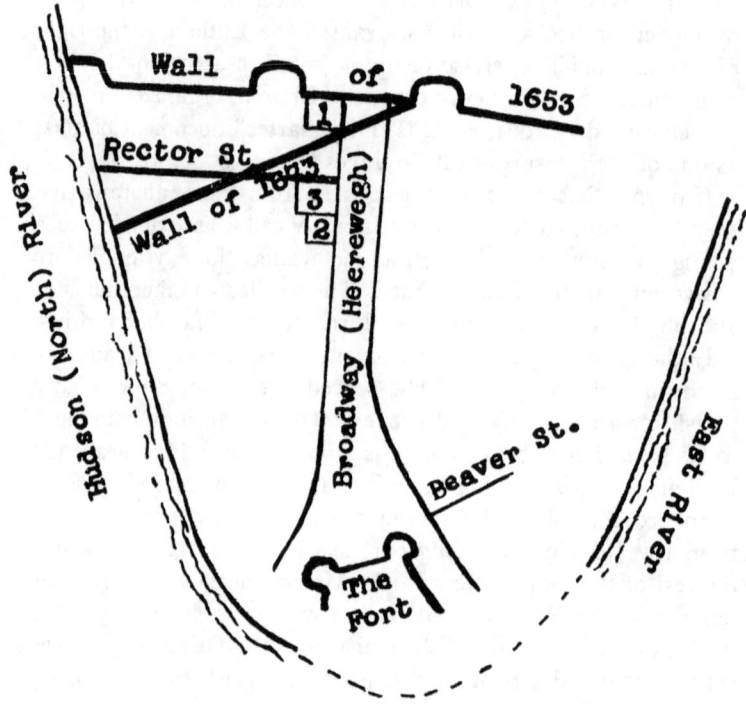

DIAGRAM SHOWING LOCATION OF LUTHERAN
CHURCH IN OLD NEW YORK

1673 left the Lutheran church building outside the wall, where in case of siege it might offer shelter to the enemy. It was consequently ordered demolished, together with other buildings left outside the new wall. The Lutheran congregation was granted a new piece of property, west of Broadway near Rector Street, and 415 gulden in cash. On this property, now valued at millions of dollars, a small wooden church was erected in 1674. It was replaced by a stone church, built in 1729 on the corner of Broadway and Rector Street.

9. REVIEW QUESTIONS

1. Of what significance was the American colonization?
2. What characterized the Spanish settlements in America?
3. Who were the first Lutheran settlers in South America? In North America?
4. Why did French colonization in America fail?
5. Why did the English colonists succeed?
6. Why were practically all the early permanent settlers Protestants?
7. How was this spread of Protestantism similar to the spread of Christianity from ancient Judea?
8. Why is the church history of Colonial America largely a chapter from European church history?
9. Why was the Anglican Church the first established Protestant church in America?
10. Which denomination, in point of time, was the second to be established by law in the American colonies? When? Where?
11. What was the background of early Congregationalism in New England?
12. How was Lutheranism first established in America?

TOPICS FOR SPECIAL STUDY

1. The "fullness of time" for America.
2. Motives for exploration and colonization.
3. Lutherans in New York in the seventeenth century.
4. Religious groups in New York prior to 1700.
5. The German Lutheran element in New York prior to 1700.
6. Early Scandinavian settlers in New York and their contribution.
7. Forerunners of universal religious liberty.

5. Swedish-Finnish Lutherans on the Delaware, 1638.—It has been said that America has three birthplaces, namely Jamestown, Virginia; Plymouth Rock, Massachusetts; and Tinicum Island on the Delaware. Jamestown owed its origin largely to a spirit of adventure; Plymouth owed its origin to a wish to escape religious persecution; New Amsterdam started as a commercial enterprise; and New Sweden on the Delaware resulted from a combined desire for commercial enterprise and the propagation of the Protestant faith "among all kinds of nations and many thousands of souls who hitherto have lived and are still living in terrible pagan idolatry and great godlessness."

Gustavus Adolphus, King of Sweden, shared the interests of his age in trade and colonization. On December 21, 1624, he commissioned William Usselinx, the founder of the Dutch West India Company, to assist in the establishment of a Swedish trading company to do business in Asia, Africa, America and Magellica.[45] Usselinx prepared a charter which, after several revisions, was signed by Gustavus Adolphus in June 1626.[46] Meanwhile Usselinx travelled through Sweden, Finland and the Baltic states, soliciting subscriptions to the new commercial project.[47] As time went on he conceived of the idea of enlarging the scope of the company so as to form a great international Protestant association. In 1629 he went to France, Spain, Portugal and Holland, seeking to enlist the interest of crowned heads, governments and influential men in his commercial scheme, but the result was meagre. In 1632 he went to the headquarters of the Swedish armies in Germany and secured the approval of Gustavus Adolphus for an extension of the old charter. The amended charter, drawn up on October 16, 1632, was not signed, however, by Gustavus Adolphus. Three weeks later, on November 6, 1632, he fell in the battle of Lützen.

In the spring of 1633, during a convention of the Protestant League at Heilbronn, Germany, Usselinx presented his project to the assembled nobles of Protestant Germany.[48] In the convention of the Protestant League at Frankfort in 1634, Usselinx had a charter sanctioned, and it appeared as if his plan should materialize; but a sudden defeat of the Protestant armies absorbed the immediate attention of the members of the Protestant

[45] *Col. Docs. N. Y.*, XII, 1-2.
[46] *Col. Docs. N. Y.*, XII, 7.
[47] Louhi, *The Delaware Finns*, p. 24.
[48] In June, 1633, Usselinx published a general summary of his plans for a Protestant commercial company, in two volumes, the *Argonautica Gustaviana*, and the *Mercurius Germanica*.

LUTHERANS IN COLONIAL DAYS, 1492-1763

League, and Usselinx was relegated to oblivion. His subsequent effort to enlist the interest of Louis XIII of France failed, and his proposal to the States General that the Swedish-Dutch project unite with the Dutch West India Company, was flatly rejected.

Meanwhile several influential men, like Samuel Blommaert, a director of the Dutch West India Company, and Joachim Stumpff of Hamburg, Germany, and Peter Spiring, a Dutchman in the service of Sweden, and Peter Minuit, former Director General of New Netherland, became interested in the New South Company. They could not establish a company on the Dutch pattern because the charter of the Dutch West India Company prevented all competition in that country. A Swedish-Dutch company was formed which intended to trade and colonize on a part of the North American coast which had not yet been occupied by either English or Dutch. In preparing for the first expedition, there was frequent mention of "a voyage to Florida,"[49] while Peter Minuit seems to have had his mind set on a trading expedition to the Delaware under the Swedish flag. He planned for a colony on the west side of the Delaware river, and his plan was apparently sanctioned by Axel Oxentierna, Chancellor of State of Sweden.[50] Two ships, the Kalmar Nyckel and the Fogel Grip, were prepared, and the expedition, in command of Peter Minuit, left Gothenburg in November, 1637. All but one officer, and most of the sailors, soldiers and servants were

[49] Correspondence between Blommaert and the Swedish Chancellor and the Swedish Admiral Fleming, as from January 14, 1637 to September 9, 1637, in Kernkamp, *Bijdragen en Mededeelingen van Het Historisch Genottschap*, 29 Deel, pp. 106-132.

[50] Minuit communicated his plan to Oxentierna at Stralsund, Germany, in June, 1636; and in the meeting of the Council of State at Stockholm, September 27, 1636, this plan was discussed. A charter of privileges was granted to the company, including the sole right in Sweden to trade in America from Florida to Newfoundland. Admiral Klaus Fleming and Peter Minuit were left in charge of the preparations for an expedition to the Delaware River, and Samuel Blommaert was to manage the company's affairs in Holland.

138   THE LUTHERAN CHURCH IN AMERICA

Dutch.[51] This is possibly the reason why no Swedish Lutheran clergyman accompanied the first expedition. Another reason may be that this first expedition was a feeler whether Swedish colonization would be possible because of Dutch and English claims.

After a successful journey over the Atlantic, the ships sailed up the Delaware River about the middle of March, 1638.[52] Peter Minuit, the Director of New Sweden, bought some land from the Indians on the west side of the river, and settled on the present site of Wilmington, where he built Fort Christina and some houses. Later the company bought additional land from the Indians, so that New Sweden extended "from the borders of the Sea to Cape Henlopen in returning southwest towards Godyn's Bay; thence towards the great South River, as far as the Minquaaskil, where Fort Christina is constructed; and thence again towards South River, and the whole to a place which the savages call Sankikah."[53]

The second expedition, 1639-1640, brought a number of Swedish colonists[54] and a Swedish Lutheran clergyman, Reorus Torkillus, who ministered to the spiritual needs of the colonists until his death, on September 7, 1643.[55] He was the first regular Lutheran minister in America.[56] Services were at first conducted in one of the houses built by Peter Minuit, but when this became too small, a chapel was erected. This chapel must have been built in 1641 or 1642, because when Governor Printz

---

[51] Lieutenant Mans Kling is the only Swede expressly mentioned among the first colonists. He was left in charge of the forty-three men at Fort Christina when Minuit sailed in the fall to the West Indies.

[52] The place where they landed was named "Paradise Point."

[53] *Col. Docs. N. Y.*, XII, 28 note.

[54] The Swedish government had captured Swedish soldiers who had evaded service, or were guilty of some offense, and ordered them and their families to be deported to New Sweden, under promise that they could return in two years. A number of these came with the second expedition.

[55] He is buried under the southern end of the Old Swede's Church at Wilmington.

[56] The first Lutheran minister to conduct a regular Lutheran service in North America was Rev. Rasmus Jensen, chaplain to the Jens Munk expedition which came to Hudson Bay in 1619.

LUTHERANS IN COLONIAL DAYS, 1492-1763   139

came in 1643, he came with instructions to decorate this little church according to the Swedish custom.[57]

Meanwhile the Dutch stockholders had become dissatisfied with the commercial venture of New Sweden and desired to withdraw from the company. The Swedish government, desiring to continue the enterprise, decided in February, 1641, to buy out the Dutch partners. A new company was formed, known as New Sweden Company, with John Printz as the new Governor.[58] He arrived at Fort Christina on February 15, 1643, and with him came another Lutheran clergyman, John Campanius Holm. He was charged by the Swedish government to conduct divine services in the colony "according to the Unaltered Augsburg Confession, the Council of Upsala, and the ceremonies of the Swedish Church."

In January, 1640, the Swedish government issued a charter to Henrik Hooghkamer, permitting a number of families from Utrecht, Holland, to settle in New Sweden, with freedom to exercise the Reformed religion, and with their own government, but under the suzerainty of the Swedish crown. This was the first edict of religious toleration issued to the "New World." Full religious liberty was practiced in the Rhode Island colony from its beginning in 1638, but the royal charter of the colony dates from 1647. The Maryland Assembly proclaimed religious liberty in that colony in 1649. A company of about twenty families and fifty souls in all, came from Holland to New Sweden in November, 1640. Two years later, when Governor Printz came, he had instructions from the Swedish government to grant these Dutch settlers "the exercise of the Reformed religion

[57] Johnson, *The Swedish Settlements on the Delaware, 1638 to 1664*, p. 366.
[58] This marks the beginning of the second period of New Sweden. Governor Printz was invested with practically unlimited power to rule New Sweden in the name of the Queen of Sweden. Besides being governor, he was also appointed judge and prosecutor. The colonists could not trade with the Dutch or the English or with the Indians. They had to sell their products to the New Sweden Company at the company's price, and likewise buy their necessities from the company.

according to the aforesaid Royal Charter." The new governor was also charged to treat the Indians "with much humanity and kindness."

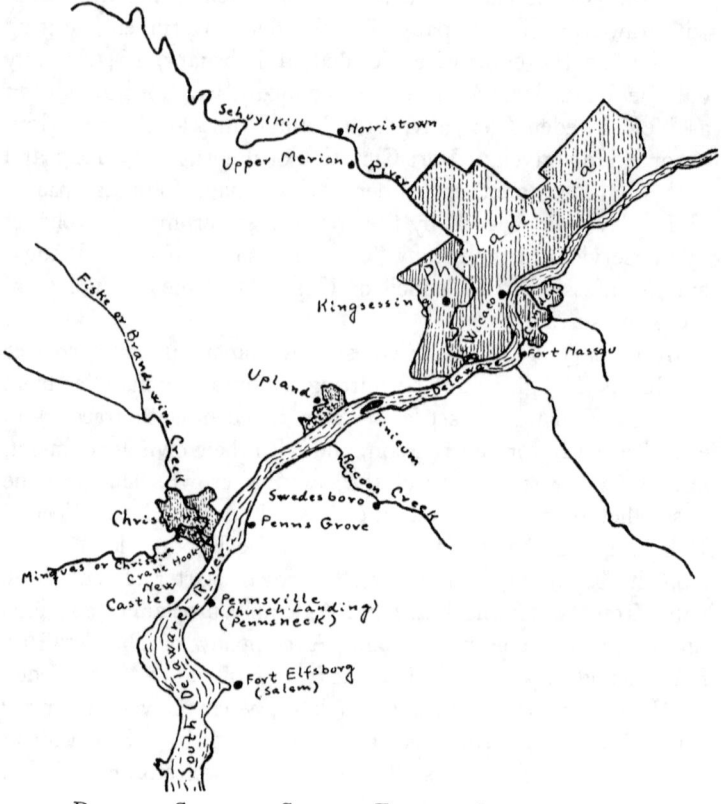

DIAGRAM SHOWING SWEDISH-FINNISH SETTLEMENTS IN NEW SWEDEN

John Campanius Holm had his chief station at the Island of Tinicum, where Governor Printz had his headquarters.[59] Here

[59] The Tinicum Island, located nine miles southwest of Philadelphia, had been given to Governor Printz as a gift from Queen Christina of Sweden. On this island the Governor built a palace for himself called Printz Hall.

LUTHERANS IN COLONIAL DAYS, 1492-1763

he built the first Lutheran church in the "New World" in 1643. The church burned down in 1645, but it was rebuilt and consecrated, together with the adjoining burying ground, on September 4, 1646. At this time there were about five hundred people in New Sweden, including a goodly number of Lutheran Finns.[60] John Campanius Holm began mission work among the Indians, and translated the Catechism into their language.[61] Rev. Israel Fluviander Holgh, the son of Governor Printz's sister, came to the colony in 1644 but stayed only three months. Rev. Lars Carlson Lock,[62] a native of Finland, came in 1647. The following year Rev. John Campanius Holm left for Sweden, and for several years Rev. Lock was the only clergyman residing in New Sweden.

Meanwhile the Dutch continued to claim the Delaware Valley as their territory. They were actually the *first* to explore the region and to attempt any settlements there.[63] Cornelius

---

[60] Between 1600 and 1650 there were many Finnish settlements in Sweden. These Finnish communities the Swedes called "Finmarker" or Finlands. The Finnish settlers retained their language and usually also maintained their own churches. During the Thirty Years' War much copper and iron were needed, and those metals were mostly found in the mountainous forests where the Finns had settled. Men of influence sought means to have these Finnish settlements vacated, and their strongest weapon was found in the Finnish method of cultivating land by burn-beating. By this method the forest was cut down in the fall, and all timber suitable for building material or for firewood would be taken away. In spring the remaining branches were burned, and grains were sown into the ashes. This gave a good crop for about three years. Swedish authorities claimed that this method was destructive to the forests and had it prohibited by law. In consequence there was, for some time, considerable friction between the Finnish settlers and the Swedish authorities. Many Finns welcomed the opportunity to migrate to New Sweden.

[61] The printing of the translation was delayed until 1696, when it was undertaken at the personal expense of Charles XI. Eliot's Indian translation of the New Testament appeared in 1661, and the Old Testament translation appeared in 1664.

[62] Rev. Lock preached in the colony for about forty years. In a letter to Governor Stuyvesant, dated April 30, 1662, he signed his name as Laurentius Carolus Lokenius.

[63] When Fort Nassau was built, four couples and eight sailors were

Hendricksen of Holland explored and mapped the Delaware country in the spring of 1616. In 1620 another Dutchman, Cornelius Mey of Hoorn, sailed up the Delaware River. In 1621 the Dutch West India Company sent a ship from Holland to trade at the "South River," as the Dutch called the Delaware as distinguished from the "North River," the Hudson. In 1623 the Dutch built Fort Nassau on the Big Timber Creek at Gloucester Point. When Peter Minuit and his expedition arrived in 1638 under the Swedish flag, the Dutch assistant commissary at Fort Nassau, Peter Mey,[64] protested against the landing and settling of Minuit's expedition. His protests were vigorously seconded by Governor Kieft in a letter of May 6, 1638, in which the Governor told Minuit that the whole South River had for many years been in Dutch possession. Minuit, however, answered that the Swedish Queen had as much right on the Delaware as the Dutch, and he went right on with his settlement.[65]

In 1652 the Dutch West India Company ordered Governor Stuyvesant to build Fort Casimir on the site of the present town of New Castle. Governor Printz, who had orders from the Swedish government to keep out the Dutch, made vigorous but futile protests against the erection of this fort on Swedish soil. When Governor Johan Rising came to New Sweden in 1654, he immediately took Fort Casimir and changed the name

---

left to settle there. On July 16, 1630, Samuel Godyn and Samuel Blommaert were granted a patent for land on the south side of the Delaware Bay, extending northward about thirty miles from Cape Henlopen to the mouth of the Delaware River, and inland about two miles. Twenty-eight colonists settled there in April, 1631, but they were all killed by the Indians, save one who escaped and left the settlement. Another group of settlers arrived in December, 1632.

[64] The Dutch commissary at Fort Nassau, Jan Jansen, was at that time visiting in New Amsterdam.

[65] England made similar claims on the Delaware River district. On the basis of the John Cabot expedition of 1497, and the Sir Walter Raleigh expedition of 1584, and other alleged discoveries, the English based their claim to the American coast from Labrador to Florida.

LUTHERANS IN COLONIAL DAYS, 1492-1763   143

to Fort Trinity.[66] The Dutch retaliated the next year. In September, 1655, New Sweden became subject to the rule of Governor Stuyvesant. The seventh article of the capitulation stipulated that "those who will then remain here and earn their living in the country, shall enjoy the freedom of the Augsburg Confession, and one person to instruct them."[67] The one allowed to remain was Rev. Lars Carlson Lock, who ministered to the Swedes and the Finns in the colony. Two Swedish Lutheran ministers, Peter Hjort and Matthias Nertunius, were returned to Sweden. Governor Rising and thirty-seven who refused to take oath of allegiance to the Dutch, likewise returned to Sweden.[68] This marked the close of the *second period* of New Sweden.

New Sweden as a political unit came to an end in 1655. The colony was unable to resist the Dutch demand for surrender. Sweden, being engaged in various wars in Europe, gave the colony neither adequate support nor valid defense. Furthermore, neither Sweden nor Holland had at this time much show of maintaining their holdings in America. In 1664 New Netherland had but 10,000 colonists, while the English had 50,000 in New England, and another 50,000 in Maryland and Virginia. So even if New Sweden could have resisted the Dutch successfully in 1655, it could only have been a matter of time before they would have to yield to the English.

The expenses incurred for the recovery of South River put the Dutch West India Company deeply in debt to the City of Amsterdam. To liquidate this debt, the company surrendered Fort Casimir and the land about it to the City of Amsterdam, in December, 1656. Fort Casimir now received the name of New Amstel, and about six hundred people were sent from Amsterdam to settle in the colony. On September 11, 1663,[69]

---

[66] The fort was captured on Trinity Sunday. Hence the name.
[67] *Col. Docs. N. Y.*, I, p. 608.
[68] Louhi, *The Delaware Finns*, p. 79.
[69] In a report by the Commissioners in Amsterdam, on August 10, 1663,

the entire South River district was ceded to the City of Amsterdam.[70] The next year the colony was taken by Great Britain.

During the period of Dutch rule, it appears that the majority of settlers in New Sweden were Lutheran Finns.[71] A number of Swedish settlers refused to take oath of allegiance to the Dutch and left, some for Sweden and some for other settlements. In the same period, several Finnish expeditions came to the colony. Accordingly, there appears to have been good reason why the Finnish born Rev. Lock should be retained as minister to the colonists. Governor Stuyvesant arranged the South River colony into two administrative and court districts, the Fort Casimir and the Swedish-Finnish Colony. Captain Dirck Smidt was appointed as Dutch commander, while the Swedish-Finnish colonists were allowed to form an autonomous government under Dutch rule.[72] They elected Peter Cock, Peter Rambo, Olof Stille and Matts Hansson as their magistrates. These were all Finns. The Swedish Lieutenant Sven Schute was elected Captain of their militia, and the Dutch Gregory van Dyck was elected commissary or sheriff. In a letter of February 13, 1659, the Directors of the Dutch West India Company objected to this arrangement with the Swedish-Finnish colonists, and Governor Stuyvesant accordingly followed a policy of ridding the Swedish-Finnish colonists of their own officers. By 1661 there was very little left of their autonomous government. For a short time, in 1662, Rev. Lock was assisted

---

the South River colony is said to have had 110 good farms, which were stocked with about 2,000 cows and oxen, 20 horses, 80 sheep and several thousand swine.

[70] By doing this the Dutch West India Company hoped to hold the South River Colony from the aggression of the English, with the powerful aid of the City of New Amsterdam.

[71] Cf. Louhi, *The Delaware Finns*, pp. 35-122.

[72] Knowing something about the friction in Sweden with the Finns, Governor Stuyvesant's policy was to win the Finnish settlers out of the Swedish influence. One of the Finnish colonists, Israel Helme, went to Sweden to induce the Finns in Sweden to come to the colony.

LUTHERANS IN COLONIAL DAYS, 1492-1763   145

in his work by a Lutheran student, Abelius Zetskoorn.[73] Rev. Lock continued his work alone until Rev. Jacob Fabritius came in 1671.

6. *The establishment of other Protestant groups in America in colonial times.*—English Catholics began to settle in Maryland in 1634 under the direction of Leonard Calvert.[74] The most important feature of the early Maryland history was the practice of religious toleration. Wishing Maryland to be a place where English Catholics might find refuge from persecution, the Calverts could not, however, establish Catholicism as a state religion; and they would not permit an established church of any other faith. Furthermore, a Catholic majority could not be maintained in the Assembly of Freemen because the majority of the settlers were Protestants. Calvert proposed, therefore, a law which would provide for religious toleration, which led to the adoption of the famous "Toleration Act of 1649." Maryland, however, became a royal colony in 1692, and the Church of England was established as the state church.

The Baptist denomination was transplanted to Providence, Rhode Island, in 1639, through the efforts of a learned Anglican clergyman, Roger Williams. Other early Baptist leaders were John Clark and Henry Dunster, first president of Harvard College, who resigned his office in 1654 because of his Baptist views. Brown University, founded in 1765, was the earliest Baptist institution of learning in Colonial America. The Bap-

[73] Governor Stuyvesant sent Zetskoorn to the colony with "a recommendation to the vestry of the Augsburg Confession to ordain him to the ministerial office." Acrolius, *History of New Sweden*, p. 101.

[74] George Calvert, first Lord of Baltimore and founder of Maryland, obtained from Charles I a tract of land which had its northern boundary from the Delaware River towards the west "the fortieth degree of north latitude, where New England is terminated." This included the present Maryland and parts of Pennsylvania, West Virginia and Delaware. Over this domain he was to exercise almost regal powers. He died before the charter was granted, and his eldest son, Cecelius, became the proprietor of Maryland. Actual settlement was started by his brother, Leonard Calvert.

146 THE LUTHERAN CHURCH IN AMERICA

tists held to the congregational principle and recognized no higher office than pastor. They strongly advocated the separation of Church and State.

Scotch-Irish Presbyterians were quick to find their way to the new world. Reverend Alexander Whitaker, a man of Presbyterian views, settled in Virginia in 1611 as pastor of a Puritan congregation. Persecution soon drove these Virginian Puritans out of the colony and many settled in Maryland and North Carolina between 1642 and 1649. Reverend Richard Denton, who also held Presbyterian views, located with a congregation in the Massachusetts colony in 1630, but the unfriendly attitude of the colonial authorities caused him and his friends to move to New Amsterdam. The first permanent Presbyterian church of English origin was the noted Southold church, established on Long Island in 1640. Reverend Francis Makemie, who came in 1683, became the apostle of American Presbyterianism. He organized the first presbytery at Philadelphia in 1705, and the first synod in 1716.

Quakers arrived in 1656 in Massachusetts, Virginia and New York. Severe laws were immediately enacted against them. They were finally banished from Massachusetts and Virginia, and a death penalty was fixed for those who returned. Massachusetts executed four Quakers in 1659. Governor Stuyvesant persecuted the Quakers in New York (New Netherland). At the end of two decades the laws against the Quakers were suspended. Meanwhile Monthly Meetings had been organized at Scituate and Sandwich, Massachusetts, before 1660. A Yearly Meeting was established in New England in 1661. These Monthly and Yearly Quaker Meetings are the oldest of their kind in America. New Jersey, Delaware and Pennsylvania also became early centers of Quaker activity in America.

Dutch Mennonites appeared in America as early as in 1638. By 1644 a number of them lived in the New Amsterdam colony, but they did not organize any congregation. In 1683, shortly

LUTHERANS IN COLONIAL DAYS, 1492-1763   147

after the founding of Pennsylvania colony, thirteen Mennonite families from Crefeld, Germany, settled in Germantown, ten miles north of Philadelphia. Some of these settlers joined the Quaker church, but a Mennonite congregation was organized in 1688, after a number of co-religionists had arrived from the Palatinate and from Crefeld. The first Mennonite church was erected in 1708. It is estimated that about 2,000 Mennonite families were living in America at the end of the Colonial Period.

Moravian settlers began to arrive in 1735. They established permanent Moravian settlements in 1740 at Bethlehem, Nazareth and Lititz, Pennsylvania, and subsequently at Salem, North Carolina. Wesleyan immigrants came to Virginia in the early 'thirties of the eighteenth century. George Whitefield visited the colonies and preached in 1739-40. Robert Strawbridge, a Methodist preacher, began to preach in Maryland in 1664 and founded a Methodist Society near Pipe Creek. The first American Methodist "Conference" was held in 1773.

Many additional Protestant groups were established in the colonial period. German Baptist Brethren, or Dunkers, settled in Germantown, Pennsylvania, 1719-23. A group of Schwenkfeldians settled near Philadelphia in 1734. Swiss immigrants transplanted the Brethren in Christ denomination to Lancaster, Pennsylvania, in 1752. This denomination was later called the River Brethren because they lived by and baptized in a river. The Society of Believers, commonly called Shakers, was established by a small group of English immigrants in New York in 1774. John Murray and his fellow laborers built the first Universalist church at Gloucester, Massachusetts, in 1779. In 1785 the first Episcopal church in New England was re-organized as the first Unitarian church in America, under the leadership of James Freeman. The Society of Universal Baptists was organized in 1785 by Elhanan Winchester, a Calvinist Baptist minister, in Philadelphia. In 1789, when George Washington was inaugurated, twenty-eight distinct Protestant denominations existed in the new republic.

V. Lutheranism in America, 1664-1700.—No other *group* of Lutheran settlers came to America till after the turn of the century. There were sporadic cases of German and Scandinavian settlers, explorers and adventurers who found their way to various parts of the colonies,[75] but they formed no definite groups and they organized no churches of their own. With the loss of New Sweden, the Swedish immigration practically ceased, though there was a small influx of Finnish settlers.[76] The great waves of German immigration to the American colonies did not appear until the eighteenth century. Advance movements were heralded, however, by the first permanent settlement of Germans at Germantown, Pennsylvania, during the last quarter of the seventeenth century, but practically all of these settlers were Mennonites, Schwenkfeldians and Quakers.

1. *James Island, South Carolina, 1674.*—In 1674 a number of Dutch and German Lutheran colonists from New York settled on James Island, South Carolina.[77] Besides Lutherans, the population of the colony was composed of Scotch Presbyterians, French Calvinists, Irish Catholics, English Churchmen, Quakers and Dissenters, immigrants from Bermuda and the West Indies.[78] Though the Lutherans on James Island formed a distinct group, there is no evidence of their building any church of their own, or of having their own pastor.[79] When the Church of England was established by law in 1704 as the Church of the Colony, to be supported by the public treasury, the Lutherans became discontented. Many of them moved away, and others lost

---

[75] According to the list of names recorded by Captain John Smith, there were several Germans among the first settlers at Jamestown in 1607.

[76] Finland was a Swedish dependency until 1809, when it was ceded to Russia.

[77] Bernheim, *German Settlements and the Lutheran Church in the Carolinas*, p. 56.

[78] Martin, *History of North Carolina*, I, p. 218.

[79] They likely conducted their divine services in their homes, as they were accustomed to do in New Amsterdam under Governor Stuyvesant.

LUTHERANS IN COLONIAL DAYS, 1492-1763

their Lutheran identity through marriage with non-Lutheran settlers.[80]

2. *New York*.—In this same period a Dutch Lutheran settlement was formed at Loonenburgh, now Athens, New York. The first Dutch Lutheran settler there was likely Nicolaus Van Hoesen who came in 1662. In 1665 Jan Van Loon bought 17,500 acres of land from the Indians, and the settlement was named after him. By 1669 a considerable number of families had moved in and settled at Loonenburgh. This flourishing community formed the nucleus of the Evangelical Lutheran Zion's Church of Loonenburgh which is now the second oldest church of the United Lutheran Synod of New York. The earliest authentic ministerial records of this congregation date back to 1703, to the ministry of Andrew Rudman, but the congregation is older than that. Bernard Arensius preached at Loonenburgh, and it is generally believed that this congregation united in the call, on the basis of which Justus Falckner was ordained. He served the Loonenburgh church until his death in 1723. From 1726 to 1731 the Loonenburgh and the Newburgh churches were served by the same pastor, William Christopher Berkenmeyer, who was as fluent in Dutch as in German and English.

Another Lutheran group settled at Esopus, near Kingston. Matthew Capito, Christian Niessen and Martin Hoofman had settled there during the Dutch regime, or before 1664. Lutherans in the Esopus settlement held services in the house of Martin Hoofman, the man who helped collect funds for the first Lutheran church building in New York City in 1671.

Farther down the river the sheltered cove around Newburgh Bay and vicinity attracted a number of Lutheran settlers in this same period. On the east side of the Hudson, about 1685, Nikolaus Emig from Mecklenburg and Peter Lassing, staunch Lutherans, had settled. On the other side of the river, and a little south of where Kocherthal later established the Lutheran

[80] Hewatt, *History of South Carolina*, I, p. 73.

settlement of Newburgh, another staunch Lutheran, Patrick McGregorie, settled in 1686. The settlers at Newburgh and at Esopus likely enjoyed the spiritual care of the Lutheran pastor who made his regular tours up and down the Hudson between Albany and New York City.

3. *New Jersey.*—A number of Lutherans from New York City moved across the Hudson and settled in Northern New Jersey. Laurens Andriessen Van Boskerk, Hermann Schneemann and Caspar Steinmetz, members of the Lutheran Church on Manhattan, bought property in 1662 in Bergen, now Jersey City. Later Laurens Andriessen Van Boskerk added large land holdings in the Greenville section of Jersey City and in the Constable's Hook section of Bayonne, and in 1682 he received a grant of 1,076 acres on the east side of the Hackensack River, near New Bridge. Lee in his *History of New Jersey* states that there was a Lutheran church on the Hackensack River before 1690. Lutheran services were also held at the Van Boskerk Homestead on Constable's Hook prior to 1700. Lutherans, like the Zabriskies, who settled in the Saddle River Valley before 1700, attended the Hackensack Church.

4. *New Sweden.*—In the course of time it was found that the old settlement at Christina was somewhat removed from the main travelled highway of that region, the Delaware River. Consequently a new log church was built in 1667 on a projection of land called Tranhook or Cranhook, near the confluence of the Christina Creek and the Delaware River. This church became the center of the lower part of the New Sweden settlement, while the upper part of the settlement was served by the church on Tinicum Island, erected in 1646. In order to meet the spiritual needs of the settlers, another church was erected at New Castle, and in 1669 a combination of fort and church was erected at Wicaco, now a portion of southern Philadelphia.

In a session of the General Court at New Castle, on May 13, 1675, it was decided to divide the New Sweden region into

LUTHERANS IN COLONIAL DAYS, 1492-1763   151

parishes.[81] On the following day the location of the Swedish-Finnish churches was taken up. The Swedish-Finnish settlers were to have the existing churches, one at Cranhook and one at New Castle for the lower parish, and one at Tinicum Island and one at Wicaco for the upper parish. These churches were served by two ministers, Rev. Lock who had been in the colony since 1647, and Rev. Jacob Fabritius, who came to New Castle on the Delaware on December 10, 1672.[82] In compliance with the order of the General Court of 1675, the Swedish-Finnish settlers constructed or re-constructed a church at Wicaco by converting an old blockhouse, built in 1669, into a church. Rev. Fabritius preached his first sermon in the Wicaco church on Trinity Sunday, 1677. From that time he preached at Wicaco and at Tinicum Island on alternate Sundays.

After the Delaware Colony had been under English rule for about seventeen years, it came under the direct control of William Penn, the founder of Pennsylvania. In 1682 he brought more than a thousand immigrants to the colony, and others kept on coming so that by the end of 1683, the old settlers and native inhabitants of Pennsylvania were far outnumbered by English and German immigrants. This great influx did not cause any immediate change in the set-up of the Swedish-Finnish parishes. What did cause these churches concern, however, was the fact that Rev. Fabritius became totally blind in 1683, and Rev. Lock died in 1688. Rev. Fabritius continued to serve the congregations as best he could, but the infirmities of old age rendered his work difficult and inefficient. For some time the Swedish-Finnish congregations on the Delaware were in a rather sad and greatly neglected condition.

The Swedish-Finnish settlers were in dire need of ministers

[81] The colony had been under Dutch rule for a brief period, 1672-73, under Governor Colve. This General Court was held under Governor Andros.
[82] When Rev. Fabritius came to New Castle on the Delaware in 1672, the people were at their own consent, divided into two parishes, between Rev. Lock and Rev. Fabritius.

of their own faith, but they were difficult to secure because the bond that had united the colony with Sweden had been entirely severed. William Penn, during his visit to England in 1684, informed the Swedish Ambassador in London of the desire of the Swedish-Finnish colonists for a minister and some books, but Sweden did not act upon the request. A Swedish traveller, Charles Springer, who visited the colony, was asked to secure a Lutheran minister. He wrote to the authorities in Sweden, but there was no reply. He wrote to the Lutheran Consistory in Amsterdam, but there was no reply. Another Swedish visitor to the colony, Andrew Printz, nephew of former Governor Printz, tried to stimulate interest in Sweden for the spiritual needs of the colonists. A letter was sent from Sweden to the colony for additional information, and the letter was answered on May 31, 1693, by Charles Springer. He asked for two ministers and some books. In the letter was enclosed a list of the Swedish-Finnish colonists, comprising 188 families and 942 souls. This did not include, however, the Swedes and the Finns who had intermarried with the Dutch and the English.

No action was taken, however, till in 1696, when King Charles XI arranged to send two ministers, Andrew Rudman and Erick Bjork. On second thought the King added a third minister, Jonas Auren, who was to study the conditions in the colony and then report to him. The party left Sweden in August, 1696, and arrived in the colony in June, 1697, after some delay in London and in Maryland and Virginia.

Finding the old churches in a ruinous condition and outgrown for the increased population, the new pastors soon addressed themselves to the task of building new churches. The Christina congregation laid the cornerstone of *Holy Trinity Church*[83] on May 28, 1698, to replace the Crane Hook church. The inside of the new church was sixty feet in length, thirty feet in breadth, and twenty feet in height. It was built of granite, the foundation being six feet thick, the walls three and a half feet

---

[83] Better known as "Old Swedes' Church."

up to the windows, and above that two feet thick. It was dedicated on Trinity Sunday, July 4, 1699.

The Philadelphia congregation decided, after much discussion, to build their church at Wicaco. The inside dimensions were the same as those of Holy Trinity Church at Christina. The foundation was of stone and the walls were of brick, every other one glaced black. On July 2, 1700, the church was dedicated, receiving the name of *Gloria Dei*. The three Swedish ministers officiated in the ceremonies, while members of the German Rosicrucian Brotherhood, a group that came to the colony in 1694, assisted in the ceremonies with instrumental music and singing.[84] These two churches were for many years the landmarks of the country.

Rev. Jonas Auren did not return to Sweden. After some mission work among the Indians, he settled in the Swedish-Finnish colony at Elk River, Maryland. In 1707 he moved to the Racoon settlement, where there had been Swedish and Finnish colonists since 1661. He served this parish until his death in 1713.[85]

There was a steady influx of Swedish Lutheran ministers for some time after the turn of the century. Their work will be discussed in a subsequent section.

5. *German Lutherans in Pennsylvania before 1700.*—In June, 1694, a famous band of about forty German Mystics, known as Rosicrucians,[86] settled on the Wissahickon, near Philadelphia. Johann Valentine Andreae (1586-1654), a Lutheran court preacher was the founder of this secret brotherhood.[87] The name Rosicrucian signifies the union of science and Christianity, as symbolized by the rose and the cross (*rosa*: rose + *crux*: cross). Besides nourishing certain mystical speculations, the Rosicru-

[84] The German Theosophic Society had settled in some kind of a cloister at the Wissahickon, and in its membership were a number of scholars.

[85] Rev. Auren, after his acquaintance with the Keithians in Philadelphia, became a Sabbatarian and advocated Saturday as the real sabbath. He was forbidden, however, by the other Swedish pastors to urge his sabbatarian views upon the congregation.

[86] Cf. Stapleton, *Memorials of the Huguenots in America*, p. 34.

[87] Cf. Holmquist, *Kirkehistorie*, II, p. 348.

cians aimed to combat alchemy and Roman Catholicism. The movement has since undergone a recrudescence in connection with freemasonry.[88]

The chapter which settled on the Wissahickon had been organized by Johann Jacob Zimmermann, one of the leading European mathematicians and astronomers of his day. He died at Rotterdam on the eve of his embarkation for America. The chapter came under the leadership of Baron Johannis Kelpius. Other members of the chapter included Henry Bernhard Koester, Conrad Matthai, Seelig, Daniel Falckner and later Justus Flackner. Kelpius made several attempts to unite the various religious groups in the settlement under one church roof. He had several conferences with the Swedish pastors, Rudman and Auren, but his union efforts were not crowned with success.

Henry Bernhard Koester, who had been the chaplain of the chapter during the voyage, continued in that capacity in the Wissahickon colony. This learned brotherhood started to conduct Lutheran meetings in a little log-house which belonged to a Mennonite named Van Bebber.[89] These services soon attracted so many English speaking people that arrangements had to be made for English services in a private house in Philadelphia. This group of English worshippers started to build a church in 1696. This was the *Christ Church*, the first Episcopal church in Pennsylvania; and the church in which George Washington frequently worshipped. In 1698 the Bishop of London sent Rev. Thomas Clayton to take care of these English Churchmen, as they were named in distinction to the Quakers. Koester assisted the Anglican clergyman in gathering members who refuted the Quaker doctrine. Thus the first Anglican church

---

[88] The popular name for this brotherhood in the colony was "The Woman in the Wilderness," Rev. 12:14; but the members themselves never acknowledged this name. A successor to this brotherhood was the Ephrata Community on the banks of the Cocalico, Lancaster County.

[89] Koester preached in German and used the German liturgy. He conducted the first German Lutheran service in Germantown in 1694.

LUTHERANS IN COLONIAL DAYS, 1492-1763

became established on the Delaware. The Rosicrucian Brotherhood did not establish any congregation of their own. Koester returned to Germany in 1700. The Falckner brothers entered the Lutheran ministry.

6. *Other Lutheran Settlements before 1700.*—There were several German and Dutch Lutheran settlements prior to 1700 where there were no organized congregations or regular church buildings, but when Lutheran services were conducted more or less regularly in private homes. Such settlements included James Island, South Carolina; Elk River, Maryland; Racoon Creek, where Swedesboro now stands; the Constable's Hook section of Bayonne, New Jersey; the Greenville section of Jersey City; the Saddle River Valley where the settlers worshipped for some time together with the Hackensack congregation near New Bridge; and the Lutheran settlements at Newburgh, Kingston and Athens, New York, have been mentioned in a previous section. The Raritan Valley attracted Lutheran settlers after the turn of the century.

7. *Retrospect.*—By 1700 the Lutheran colonists in America had a number of churches and preaching places. In these early churches the Dutch Lutherans were more influential than historians have generally been willing to admit. The pioneers in New York City, Albany, Loonenburgh, Kingston and Newburgh were Dutch. Furthermore, the pioneers of the Hackensack congregation and in Saddle River Valley and in Bayonne and in Jersey City were Dutch. The same is true of Mahwah (Remmerspach or Ramapo) and of at least two of the early Raritan Lutheran churches. There was also a heavy infiltration of Dutch Lutherans into Palatine churches of later years. It is also significant that the first synodical constitution for New York and New Jersey churches, prepared in 1734, was distributed in four Dutch and only one German copy. The Dutch copies were known respectively as the New York, the Loonenburgh, the Hackensack and the Raritan copy. The German copy was for

Wolff's parish in the upper reaches of the Raritan River, New Jersey.

The Swedish-Finnish Lutherans in New Sweden had four churches and several preaching places by 1700. Though these churches were in frequent correspondence with the Lutheran authorities in Holland and Sweden respectively, they had, nevertheless, no synodical organization. Besides these organized churches, there were several Lutheran settlements, mentioned in the preceding section, which had no churches prior to 1700. However, it is not always easy to draw the line between organized churches and mere settlements, as church organization in the seventeenth century was very different from that of the twentieth in America. There were also numerous Lutheran individuals scattered in the various colonies at this time.

Naturally, Lutheran orthodoxy of the seventeenth century type[89a] dominated Lutheranism in the American colonies up to the turn of the century. This was particularly true of the German, the Swedish and the Finnish settlers. The Dutch assumed a more moderate attitude.[90] In the stormy and distressing seventeenth century—in Europe and in the American colonies—orthodoxy formed a hard but necessary bulwark or shell within which Lutheranism could preserve its best heritage.

While the Lutheran colonists were one in faith, they had no uniformity of worship and of church government. Being of various nationalities, each national group tended to perpetuate its own separate church constitution and peculiar church regulations. The principal types were the Dutch and the Swedish.

The Dutch element contributed comparatively little to American Lutheranism as far as membership, churches and pastors are concerned. But the Dutch made important and permanent contributions to congregational and synodical organization of

---

[89a] Cf. pp. 94-96.

[90] The Lutheran Church in Holland was at this period practically like the Reformed, except in doctrine and in one or two features of public worship. The Lutherans used the Gospel and Epistle texts for the church year, and they used Luther's Catechism in the instruction of the young.

LUTHERANS IN COLONIAL DAYS, 1492-1763

a considerable portion of present day American Lutheranism. This Dutch influence was transmitted largely through Muhlenberg, who held a temporary pastorate of the Dutch Lutheran Church in New York, and who also came in vital contact with Dutch Lutheran influences through the German Lutheran churches in London, England.[91]

According to the Ecclesiastical Laws of 1577, published by William of Orange and the States General, the Protestant churches of Holland—Reformed and Lutheran—were to recognize four classes of officers, namely pastors, professors of theology, elders[92] and deacons. The churches were to be served by duly called and ordained ministers only. The ministers of every city or section were to hold a pastoral conference every two weeks. The duties of elders and deacons were carefully prescribed and other regulations were given. On the basis of these laws, the Dutch Lutheran church constitution of 1597 was prepared. This constitution, as revised in 1614, 1644 and 1681, bound pastors to teach and preach the Word of God as found in the Old and New Testaments and as expressed in the Unaltered Augsburg Confession, its Apology, the Schmalkald Articles, the Formula of Concord, and Luther's two Catechisms. Each congregation was to be governed by a *consistorium*, composed of the pastor or pastors and lay elders. The elders and the deacons were to be elected on the first Sunday in May. The elders, usually five in number, were held responsible for the pure preaching of the Word of God, the right administration of the Sacraments, the godly life and observance of the church regulations by the pastor. Hence at least one elder had to be present at each service. The deacons, usually six in number, were to collect and distribute alms and to urge the negligent to come to church. There was also a parish clerk who, besides keeping the records of the congrega-

[91] These German Lutheran churches in London were greatly influenced by Dutch Lutheranism through their frequent communications with Amsterdam.

[92] This provision for lay elders has been adopted, with certain modifications, by certain groups of Lutherans in America.

tion also was to act as "comforter of the sick," or "Ziekentrooster" as they called it.[93]

The Church of Sweden adhered to the Council of Upsala of March 20, 1593 and the "Church Order" of 1572. The Decree or Council of Upsala affirmed the Bible as the only standard for life and doctrine, and accepted the Apostle's, the Nicene and the Athanasian Creeds and the Unaltered Augsburg Confession as the symbols of the Swedish Church. The Church Order of 1572, with later modifications, provided for careful instruction of the young and impressive divine services with much ceremonial beauty. The Swedish church government was thoroughly organized with a happy balance between centralizing and decentralizing forces.

However, the Swedish-Finnish churches on the Delaware made their contribution to American life, not so much along the lines of church organization or form of public worship, but rather in the zealous, powerful preaching and the resulting Christian morality; and also in the thorough instruction of the young and in Bible lectures, all of which, in their total results, produced strong Christian personalities. They built Christian character, which again asserted its influence in various ways, during the troubled years of the American Revolution and the formative years of the American Nation.

While Lutheran orthodoxy of the seventeenth century type dominated Lutheranism in America up to about 1700, several other strands were also woven into the general fabric. The cosmopolitan atmosphere of New York coupled with the unconventional atmosphere of the New World, promoted a more tolerant and cooperative attitude. The initial religious interest was soon subordinated to the all absorbing task of subjugating a new continent. This rough and ready frontier life promoted an intensely practical, business-like way of doing church work. The Rosicrucian settlers on the Wissahickon near Philadelphia

[93] The Dutch Reformed had a similar office. It was transplanted to the American colonies.

LUTHERANS IN COLONIAL DAYS, 1492-1763

ushered in the problem of secret societies which later caused so much discussion within the Lutheran Church. Through the ministry of the Falckner brothers, Pietistic influences were introduced.

Towards the close of the century the severe friction and hard feeling between Lutherans and Reformed began to disappear in the consciousness of the common people. Furthermore, the proprietor of the New Netherland territory, the Duke of York, turned Roman Catholic five years after the conquest of New York. When he ascended the throne of England as James II in 1685, there was considerable fear that Catholicism would become a power in the American colonies, and this common danger drew the contending Protestants closer together.

Up to the year 1688, the French Catholic colonization in America had been left fairly undisturbed. In that year it is estimated that France owned 80 per cent, Spain 16 per cent, and England only 4 per cent of the North American Continent. The Roman Catholic Church dominated North America, and there was a real danger that the English colonies along the Atlantic sea border might be cut off from territorial expansion. But in 1688 the war started between the English Puritans and their Indian allies on the one hand, and the French Jesuits and their Indian allies on the other, the war lasting, intermittently, for almost a hundred years, and ending in victory for the English and for Protestantism. The accession of William and Mary as King and Queen of England in 1689, also saved Protestantism in Western Europe.

10. REVIEW QUESTIONS

1. What motivated the Swedish expeditions to the Delaware?
2. What general territory did New Sweden cover?
3. Did New Sweden conflict with other territorial rights? Explain.
4. How was religious liberty practiced in New Sweden?
5. What attitude did New Sweden take toward the Indians?
6. What was the status of New Sweden under Dutch rule? Under English rule?

160 THE LUTHERAN CHURCH IN AMERICA

7. What other Protestant denominations were transplanted to America in colonial times?
8. How were the Swedish-Finnish churches located after 1675? How were they served?
9. What new impetus did these congregations receive in 1697?
10. What was the status of Lutheranism in America about the year 1700?
11. What contributions did Dutch Lutheranism make to colonial America?
12. What contributions did Swedish-Finnish Lutheranism make to colonial America.

TOPICS FOR SPECIAL STUDY

1. The projects of William Usselinx.
2. Conflicting territorial rights in New Sweden.
3. Forerunners of universal religious liberty.
4. The St. James Island colony.
5. The Racoon Creek settlement.
6. The Elk River settlement.
7. The Swedish-Finnish self-government, 1655-81.
8. Swedish efforts to regain New Sweden.
9. Types of Lutheran pastors in early colonial America.
10. The founding of Pennsylvania and its effects upon New Sweden.
11. The George Keith Schism of 1692.
12. The Rosicrucian Brotherhood of 1694.
13. Paul Bryzelius and the Moravians.

VI. Lutheranism in America, 1700-1742.—There was a great tide of German immigration to the American colonies during the first decades of the eighteenth century, while during that same period immigration from Scandinavia was practically at a standstill. A large number of the German immigrants were Lutherans. As the German element increased, the colonial congregations which in their origin were basically Dutch Lutheran, were gradually changed into German Lutheran congregations. Steps were taken toward the close of these decades to gather the scattered congregations into organic unity. The Swedish-Finnish congregations also continued to prosper for some time, but after 1735 their "Golden Age" had practically ceased, and largely because the authorities in Sweden insisted on the use of the Swedish language in these churches. As the Swedish-Finnish settlers of the second and third generation did not, in the

LUTHERANS IN COLONIAL DAYS, 1492-1763

majority of cases, understand Swedish, they preferred the English language for their church, and many united with English churches.

1. *Eclipse of the Swedish-Finnish Churches.*—For several decades there was a considerable influx of Swedish Lutheran pastors to New Sweden. Some of these were highly gifted men, such as John Dylander,[94] Israel Acrelius[95] and Charles Magnus Wrangel.[96] New preaching places were established, annex congregations were organized and churches were built.

The Racoon or Swedesboro Church was built in 1703-04 and dedicated by Rev. Lars Tolstadius. The Racoon parish is known today as "Trinity Parish." During the years 1715-17 the St. George's Church was built by the Pennsneck settlers at a place known today as Church Landing. The St. James Church was built in Kingsessing[97] in 1762-63 and dedicated by Dr. Wrangel. This church, which stands on Darby Road between 68th and 69th Streets in Philadelphia, was built as an annex to the Wicaco Church. Another annex church was built at Upper Merion in 1763 and named Christ Church. It stands on the bank of the Schuylkill, below Norristown, about sixteen miles from the Wicaco Church. These three churches at Wicaco, Kingsessing and Upper Merion were incorporated[98] under the name of "United Swedish Lutheran Churches," and a charter was granted them by Governor John Penn, on September 25,

[94] John Dylander was pastor at Wicaco from 1737 to 1741. He cultivated friendly relations with the English and the Germans, and was widely known as an eloquent speaker.

[95] Israel Acrelius wrote the valuable *History of New Sweden.*

[96] Charles Magnus Wrangel was one of the Swedish branch of nobility, of the illustrious Esthonian family of Wrangels. He worked with distinction in New Sweden from 1759 till 1768. He was a man of marked linguistic ability.

[97] Kingsessing, an old Swedish-Finnish town, was later included in the city of Philadelphia.

[98] The purpose of incorporation was to preserve the Lutheran faith by keeping these churches in the hands of the descendants of the people who built them.

162   THE LUTHERAN CHURCH IN AMERICA

1765. Some of the preaching places established were among the Swedish-Finnish settlers on Maurice River, Egg Harbor and Pennypack Creek.

But in spite of this geographic expansion, the life of these congregations was greatly hampered by the following factors: (1) Insistence by the authorities in Sweden that their ministers in New Sweden should use Swedish exclusively in all their preaching, teaching and soul-care, in spite of the fact that only a few of the parishioners of the second and third generations understood this language.[99] Because of this short-sighted policy the descendants even lost their forefather's religion, as they joined with English speaking, and mostly Episcopalian,[100] churches. (2) New Sweden was treated as a perpetual missionary outpost, where pastors came as temporary missionaries, to be recalled at the will of the authorities in Sweden, and with no regard for the wishes of the parishioners. The recall of a man like Dr. Wrangel caused bitter resentment among the congregations. (3) The Swedish crown did not favor the training and use of native Americans for the mission in New Sweden,[101] and the laymen were rarely called upon to assume any responsibility. (4) The official relation between the Swedish crown and the Swedish-Finnish Lutheran churches on the Delaware was severed in 1789. The Swedish archbishop recalled his missionaries, and thus a number of parishes were left vacant. The

---

[99] Dr. Wrangel found that not one-fourth of the members of his congregation understood Swedish sermons. On November 3, 1759, he wrote to the Consistory of Upsala, "A minister who will satisfy his conscience can not altogether refuse preaching in English."

[100] The Episcopal liturgy was followed by the Swedish ministers in their English services, and the Swedish-Finnish Lutherans could see little difference between these two churches.

[101] An exception was made, however, in the case of Daniel Kuhn, a descendant of the early colonists, who went to Sweden in 1771 to study at the University of Upsala. He was ordained in September, 1775 and commissioned as pastor for the Wilmington congregation. But he never got back to his native land. He died in London, on October 7, 1776.

LUTHERANS IN COLONIAL DAYS, 1492-1763   163

congregations concerned united, one after another, with the Episcopalians. The Lutheran name disappeared from the last charter in 1846.[102]

2. *The Falckner Brothers.*—Daniel and Justus Falckner were the sons of a Lutheran clergyman in Saxony, Germany. Daniel, born in 1666, studied theology at the University of Erfurt, where he also joined a group of Pietists. He was ordained in Germany, either before his coming to America in 1694, or during a visit in 1698-1700. His brother, Justus, born in 1672, studied theology at the University of Halle under Christian Thomasius and August Hermann Francke. Daniel was a member of the Rosicrucian Brotherhood which came in 1694 under the leadership of Baron Johannis Kelpius to settle in Germantown, Pennsylvania. Justus Falckner also appears to have been a member of the same organization.

The relation between the German Rosicrucian Brotherhood, the new English Episcopal congregations and the Swedish-Finnish congregations became very friendly, and together they greatly strengthened the morale of the Anti-Quaker party in Pennsylvania and the Delaware. They also had common interests in the purchase of land. In 1698 the Rosicrucian Brotherhood, partly at the suggestion of the Swedish pastors, sent Daniel Falckner to Germany to report conditions in the Germantown settlement. He returned in 1700 accompanied by his brother, Justus, and several theological students. He also came back commissioned to replace Francis Daniel Pastorius as the

---

[102] These churches were much in the center of conflict during the American Revolution. The old church bell of the Wicaco church was carried to safety by the American forces. English and American naval forces engaged in a naval battle opposite the Pennsneck church in 1776. Two companies of the American forces encamped in and around the Wilmington church in 1777. In 1778 the English broke the pews in the Wicaco church to convert the building into a hospital for soldiers. The Racoon church was used for some time as barrack by the American forces, and during this occupation, the school house built by the parish near by, was destroyed by fire.

164   THE LUTHERAN CHURCH IN AMERICA

official land agent of the Frankfort Land Company.[103] Justus Falckner was granted the power of attorney by the same company. Business interests brought Justus Falckner in contact with the Swedish pastor, Andrew Rudman, who was interested in land along the Manatawny. Rev. Rudman in turn influenced Justus Falckner to accept the pastorate for the New York and Albany Lutheran churches. He was ordained on November 24, 1703, in the Gloria Dei Church in Wicaco. The officiating ministers were Andrew Rudman, Erick Bjork and Andrew Sandel.

This ceremony had a manifest historical significance, as it was the first Lutheran ordination of a minister in the New or Western World.[104] The Swedish pastors had no authority of their own to ordain a minister. They had to be duly authorized to do so by the Archbishop of Sweden. Rev. Rudman is said to have received such authority from his archbishop.[105] A similar occasion occurred in 1739 when the Archbishop of Sweden and the Consistory of Upsala commissioned two Swedish pastors in America, John Dylander and Peter Tranberg to ordain to the ministry William Malander. The ordination was not performed, however, because Rev. Dylander died, and Rev. Tranberg was without authority to administer ordination alone.

Justus Falckner worked for twenty years as pastor of a parish that extended about two hundred miles, from Albany to Long Island; and from the Raritan Valley in New Jersey to the Schoharie and Mohawk Valleys in upper New York. Using New York City and Albany as terminals, he made regular visits to Hackensack, now Teaneck; to Constable's Hook, now

---

[103] The Frankford Land Company was formed in 1683, and at that time the company bought 25,000 acres of land from William Penn. Germantown, Pennsylvania, was the first settlement of the company.

[104] This was not, however, the first Protestant ordination in America. Twenty-four years earlier, on October 9, 1679, Peter Tesschenmacher was ordained in New York City to the ministry of the Dutch Reformed Church with the approval of the Classis of Amsterdam. Abelius Zetskoorn was ordained by Rev. Lock in 1663, but without proper credentials. Cf. p. 132.

[105] *Hallesche Nachrichten*, New Edition, p. 478.

LUTHERANS IN COLONIAL DAYS, 1492-1763   165

Bayonne; to Elizabethtown, now Elizabeth; to Amboy and Remmerspach, Ramapo, now Mahwah; to Piscataway and to various settlements in the Raritan Valley; and along the Hudson, in Philipse Manor, now Yonkers; in Philipsburg, now Tarrytown; in de Lange Rack, Fishkill, now Beacon; on the Quassaick, now Newburgh; at Loonenburgh, now Athens; at Claverack, Coxsackie, Klinckenberg, Kinderhook; in Kingston, Roosendaal and Shawangunk; he also made trips to New Rochelle. Appointed "Readers" conducted services while he visited other congregations and preaching places.

In order to serve his flock better, Justus Falckner prepared and published a catechism called *Thorough Instruction*, in the Dutch language. This is the first orthodox Lutheran textbook published in America. It issued from the famous Bradford printing-press. In 1696 Henrich Bernhard Koester made use of the same press in issuing his *History of the Protestation*, and in 1697 when he published his *Ein Bericht an alle Bekenner und Schriftsteller*. These two books by Koester were issued as propaganda material against Franz Daniel Pastorius and the Quakers in general. In his Lutheran catechism, Falckner stressed his loyalty to the confessional books of the Lutheran Church.

His labors were crowned with much success. He was a man with a winning personality, thorough culture and fine theological training. He died in 1723. There is no known record of the time of his death, nor of the place of his burial.[106]

Daniel Falckner continued for some time as land agent of the Frankfort Land Company. But Pastorius also continued, stubbornly, in office with the support of the Quaker Council. The controversies finally ended in the failure of the Frankfort Land Company. Falckner himself was intrigued by his own business partners. He lost all his property, and for some time he was

---

[106] Justus Falckner was a man of thorough education and deep spirituality. He was an intense missionary, searching out the lost sheep of the Lutheran fold in many parts of New Jersey and New York. He exerted a strong Pietistic influence on his parishioners.

even imprisoned. Toward the close of his life, and broken in spirit, he became pastor of Lutheran congregations in New Jersey. After the death of his brother, he also served for some time as pastor of the New York-Albany parish.[107]

3. *Early Palatine Immigration.*—For about twenty-five years after the founding of Germantown, Pennsylvania, in 1683, no large group of Germans sought homes in the New World. Intermittently, individuals with their families came, but there were no large movements of immigrants. By 1707, however, an advance band of immigrants from Wolfenbüttel and Haberstadt, Germany, settled in German Valley, New Jersey. In 1708 a group of fifty-five Palatines came under the leadership of Reverend Joshua Kocherthal, and this was the prelude to the immense Palatine immigration, and to the later heavy German immigration of the eighteenth century. The religious background of these Palatines is most interesting.

Palatinate was the name of two small countries in the old German Empire, namely, Upper Palatinate with Amberg as its capital, and Lower or Rhenish Palatinate with Heidelberg, and for a time Mannheim, as its capital. About 1620 these countries were separated, the Upper Palatinate and the electoral vote passing to Bavaria. By the Peace of Westphalia in 1648, the Lower Palatinate became a separate electorate, and from this time it was generally known as the *Palatinate.* It covered an area of about 3,150 square miles, and was composed of an irregular and disjoined territory on both sides of the Rhine, included roughly within the space marked off by the cities of Mainz, Worms, Heilbronn, Landau and Zweibrucken. It included the Electoral Palatinate with Heidelberg as its capital, the principality of Simmern, the Duchy of Zweibrucken, and the principalities of Veldenz and Lautern. Within its borders were also the episcopal sees of Worms and Speyer. During the

---

[107] Daniel Falckner is said to have organized a Lutheran congregation in Falckner's Swamp, now New Hanover, Pennsylvania, in 1703. He served as pastor of this congregation for some years.

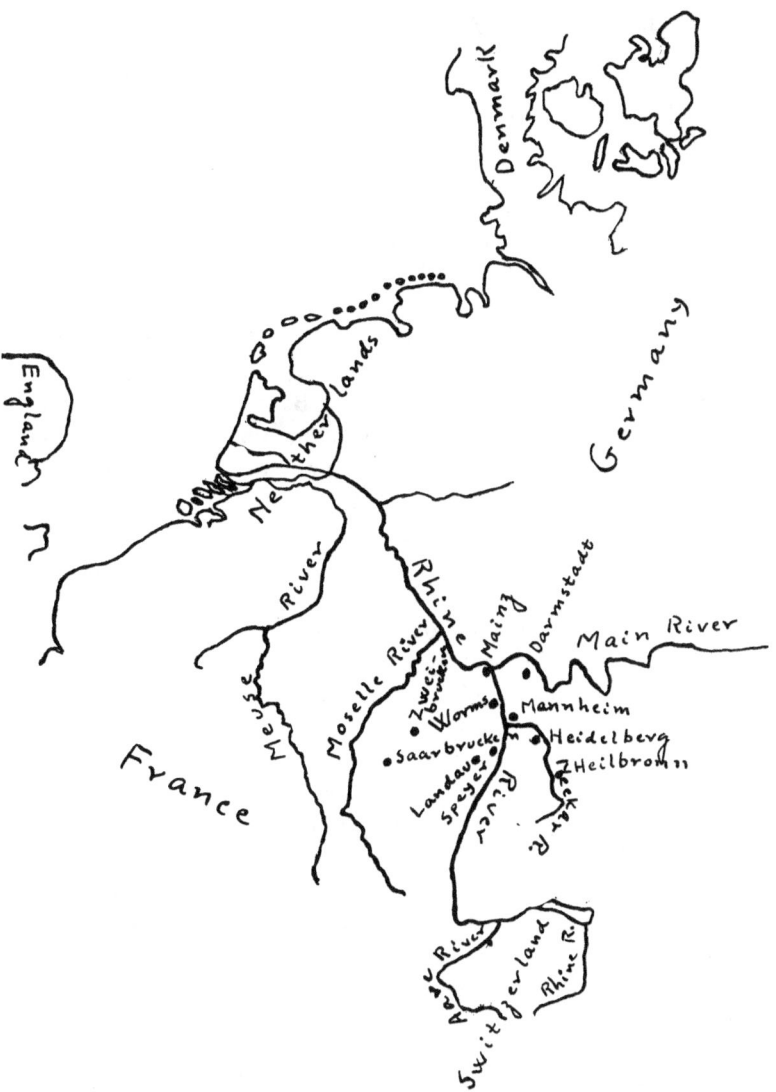

THE HOMELAND OF THE PALATINES

reign of Louis XIV of France (1661-1715), the Palatinate was one of the richest and most fertile lands in Germany.

Although the great majority of immigrants concerned came from the Rhenish or Lower Palatinate, yet a number of "Palatines" came from the neighboring territories as well.[108] The area from which the emigration poured, extended along both sides of the Rhine River and its tributaries, the Main and the Neckar Rivers. It extended from the junction of the Moselle and the Rhine, south to Basle, Switzerland; and from Zweibrucken, alongside Lorraine, as far west along the Main River as Baireuth, bordering the Upper or Bavarian Palatinate. In 1709-10 large numbers of Palatine immigrants started out in search of new homes in America. A few settled in England, and some crossed over to Ireland, but the great majority found their way to the New World. Several causes may be given for this unprecedented size of immigration, but the essential cause was the religious situation in the Palatinate.

The Protestant Reformation had made rapid progress in the Palatinate and, influenced by the teachings of Melanchthon,[109] the Elector Frederick II embraced the Evangelical faith in 1544, two years before the death of Luther. During the strong Catholic counter-movement, ushered in by the Schmalkald War, 1546-47, Calvinism rather than Lutheranism appealed to the aggressive Protestants, because Calvinism was much more extreme in its anti-Romanism. Under Frederick III (1559-76), Calvinism was made the established religion of the Palatinate, and the *Heidelberg Catechism* was drawn up in 1563. The Palatinate became a haven of refuge for persecuted Protestants

---

[108] The home principalities of Palatine immigrants, as mentioned in a contemporary pamphlet, are as follows: the Palatinate; the districts of Darmstadt and Hanau; Franconia, including the area around the cities of Nuremburg, Baireuth and Wurzburg; the Archbishopric of Mayence and the Archbishopric of Treves; the districts of Spires, Worms, Hesse-Darmstadt, Zweibrucken, Nassau, Alsac and Baden. To this list Wurtemberg must be added, since a number of Palatines, including John Conrad Weiser, are known to have migrated thence.

[109] See pp. 89-90.

LUTHERANS IN COLONIAL DAYS, 1492-1763   169

in France, and also for many Lutherans. It must be remembered that during the controversies[110] within the German Lutheran Churches, 1555-80, the Gnesio-Lutherans or Genuine Lutherans denied the Philippists or Melanchthonians, after 1557, the right to adhere to the Augsburg Confession, thereby excluding them from the benefits of the Religious Peace of Augsburg, secured in 1555. Opposition was so violent that many Philippists were driven over to the ranks of the Calvinists, while others sought refuge in the Calvinistic Palatinate. This moving together of various shades of Evangelicals produced a *Middle Type*[111] of Protestantism which, after 1580, gave rise to the name *Reformed Church*. Later this name was applied to all the followers of Zwingli and Calvin.

This religious background should be kept clearly in mind while Palatine immigration is the focus of attention, in order that a proper evaluation may be made of the contribution made by Palatine Lutherans to Lutheranism in America. It was through the Palatine Lutherans that the Melanchthonian or Philippist emphasis first exerted its influence on American life and thought.

In 1685 the Simmern line of Palatine Electors died out and was succeeded by the collateral line of Neuberg, whose members were of the Catholic faith. In that same year, Louis XIV of France revoked the Edict of Nantes which had guaranteed religious freedom to the French Protestants. The Protestant nations retaliated by supporting William of Orange in organizing a formidable Protestant confederacy known as the League of Augsburg, 1686. Louis XIV struck back by invading the Palatinate, 1688-89, reducing it to ruins. Among the places ruined were the historic towns of Heidelberg, Spires and Worms. Even fruit trees, vines, and crops were destroyed, and upward of a

[110] See pp. 90-94.
[111] Among other characteristics, this modified form of Calvinism lacked the doctrine of Predestination. Moderate Calvinists also favored the Erastian or State-Church form, while traditional Calvinism favored the Theocratic form of church government.

hundred thousand peasants were rendered homeless. Another and more formidable coalition, known as the Grand Alliance, was formed against Louis XIV in 1689, including England, Holland, Sweden, Spain, Savoy, the Emperor, the Elector Palatine, and the Electors of Bavaria and Saxony. For ten years almost all of Europe was a great battlefield, and the Palatinate was repeatedly the stamping ground of Louis XIV's armies.

During the War of the Spanish Succession, 1701-14, Marshal Villars crossed the Rhine unexpectedly in May, 1707, terrorizing southwestern Germany, and plundering and requisitioning freely on the Palatinate, Wurtemberg, Baden and Swabia. This was the immediate cause of the immense Palatine emigration of 1709-10. Between May and November, 1709, shiploads of Palatines, variously estimated from thirteen thousand to thirty-two thousand, arrived in London on their way to the New World in search of new homes.

To the curse of devastation was added the unusually severe winter of 1708-09, cruel beyond the precedent of a century. The cold was tense even in October. By November, it was said that firewood would not burn in the open air. In January of 1709, wine and spirits froze into solid blocks of ice; birds on the wing fell dead; and, it is said, saliva congealed in its fall from the mouth to the ground. Most of Western Europe froze tight. The rivers were ice-bound, and, what had never been seen before, the sea froze sufficiently all along the coasts to bear carts, even heavily laden. Fruit trees were killed and the vines were destroyed. The loss fell heavily on the husbandmen and vine-dressers, who in consequence made up more than half of the emigrants of 1709.

The large Palatine emigration of the second decade of the eighteenth century was due in a general way to these causes: (1) Religious oppression; (2) An extraordinarily severe winter; (3) Heavy taxation[112] resulting from wars; (4) Devastations

---

[112] Petty princes tried to imitate the "Sun Monarch" Louis XIV, and the expenses of their lavish and arrogant living had to be met by heavy taxes on their subjects.

LUTHERANS IN COLONIAL DAYS, 1492-1763

of war; (5) Desire for new homes on the part of the elderly and desire of adventure on the part of the young; (6) Liberal advertising by colonial proprietors;[113] and (7) Benevolent and active cooperation of the British government.[114]

A brief survey of conditions in England at this time, may help the student to understand better the early eighteenth century immigration to America. The period between 1688 and 1815 was marked by a gigantic rivalry between England and France for supremacy in the commercial and colonial world, with England emerging the victor. The reign of William and Mary, 1689-1702, was a triumph for Protestantism in Western Europe. Queen Anne, 1702-14, was friendly disposed toward distressed Protestants on the European continent. Her consort, Prince George of Denmark, died in 1708, "to the unspeakable grief of the Queen." Prince George was of German stock and a Lutheran. It probably softened the Queen's grief to act as the gracious benefactor of the oppressed co-religionists of her departed husband. In 1709 the British Parliament adopted a bill providing for the naturalizing of foreign Protestants.[115] The law

---

[113] English proprietors of the colonies in America carried on an enticing and extensive advertising in the Rhine Valley. Pamphlets were distributed, extolling the climate and life of the New World. English land agents, or "Neuländer," were sent out to the Palatinate to induce immigration, much in the same way as did the western railroad companies in America of a later date. Correspondence was carried on between proprietors and prospective settlers. These activities were mostly in the interests of the Carolinas and Pennsylvania.

[114] England at this time assumed the position as the protector of the Protestant cause in Europe. William of Orange with his wife, Mary, took the English throne from his father-in-law, James II, in 1688, to secure intervention by England and support for the Protestant cause on the Continent against the encroachments of Catholic France. As early as 1689, when William declared war on France, he published a "Proclamation for encouraging French Protestants to transport themselves into this Kingdom." Seventeenth century British mercantilism attached a high value to a dense population. An English law of 1709 has this statement in the preamble, "the increase of people is a means of advancing the wealth and strength of a nation." *Statutes of the Realm,* IX, 63.

[115] William Penn was the author of this general naturalization bill for the colonies. The act of naturalization of 1709 was repealed in February,

172 THE LUTHERAN CHURCH IN AMERICA

is said to have been made with a particular view to the Protestant Palatines brought to England that year. The English government, under Queen Anne, began to embark upon a mercantilist policy of colonial development, in which its population was to be increased by stimulating immigration both from England and from foreign lands.

Queen Anne died in 1714, leaving no heirs. She was succeeded on the Throne of England by George I, 1714-27, who became the founder of a new line of English sovereigns, the House of Hanover, or Brunswick, the family in whose hands the royal scepter still remains. George I was a Lutheran who, besides being King of England, also was Head of the Lutheran Church in Hanover, Germany. He was a German in heart and in language. The same was true of George II, 1727-60; but George III, 1760-1820, being born and educated in England, was thoroughly British in heart and language. This royal connection with Lutheranism throws interesting light on the prosperous condition of the six German Lutheran churches in London at this time.[116] It also throws interesting light on the life and work of Henry Melchior Muhlenberg, who was a native of Hanover. The court chaplain of George II, 1727-60, Dr. Ziegenhagen, was a Lutheran pastor, and a close friend of Gotthelf August Francke of the University of Halle, who sponsored the sending of Muhlenberg to America in 1742.

1712, when it was discovered that up to April 14, 1711, more than 100,000 pounds had been expended upon the Palatines in various ways.

[116] These included (1) The Royal Chapel in St. James Palace, established in 1700 through the influence of Prince George, consort of Queen Anne. The Rev. Anton Wilhelm Böhme was pastor of this church during the early Palatine emigration; and he was also an influential friend of the Palatines at court. (2) Trinity Lutheran Church, in Trinity Lane; originally Swedish Lutheran, but in German possession since 1618. (3) St. Mary's Church in the Savoy, popularly known as Savoy Chapel from the name of the district in which it stood. This was the spiritual home of some of the best families in London. (4) St. George's Church in Goodmansfield. (5) Zion Church in Brown's Lane. (6) The Philadelphia Church in Whitechapel.

LUTHERANS IN COLONIAL DAYS, 1492-1763   173

Turning now to the actual record of the early Palatine emigration, the attention will be centered on the small Palatine emigration of 1708, and the large Palatine emigration of 1709. Of this large 1709 emigration, a small portion was settled in Limerick County, Ireland, and another group was sent to North Carolina. But the great majority, constituting the largest single immigration to America in the colonial period, was sent to New York.

a. *The Small Palatine Immigration of 1708.*—In 1708 a group of forty-one war refugees from the neighborhood of Landau in the Rhenish Palatinate, arrived in London under the leadership of Reverend Joshua Kocherthal.[117] The religious beliefs of the members of this group were given as fifteen Lutherans and twenty-six Calvinists.[118] Before their departure from London for New York, fourteen more Germans, two of them from Holstein, arrived unexpectedly and were permitted to join the group. After some consideration[119] it was finally decided to send these Palatines to settle on the Hudson in New York, as a frontier against the Indians, and for the production of naval stores.[120]

In October, 1708, the Palatines, fifty-five in all, sailed for New York. The winter was spent in New York City, but in the spring of 1709, Governor Lovelace settled them, forty-seven in all,[121] on the west side of the Hudson River, about fifty-five miles north of New York City. This settlement, at the mouth of

[117] Kocherthal had visited London two years earlier and canvassed the possibilities for Palatine emigration. He was the author of a book, published in 1706, with a promising description of Carolina.

[118] *Board of Trade Journal, 1704-1708,* page 483.

[119] The Board of Trade first suggested that these Palatines be sent to Jamaica, where large tracts of land and a great need of white people existed, but fear that the hot climate would adversely affect them, led to the selection of New York.

[120] Naval stores as a general term includes masts, ship timber of all kinds, tar, pitch, rosin, hemp, and even iron in some of its manufacture.

[121] Knittle, *Early Palatine Emigration,* p. 42.

the Quassaick Creek, was the beginning of Newburgh, New York.[122]

These pioneer settlers were at first well taken care of, but soon after the death of Governor Lovelace, May 6, 1709, they were in actual want of provisions. At the same time there was some religious dissension.[123] Nineteen of the settlers were accused of turning "Pietists" and of withdrawing from communion with the pastor, Rev. Kocherthal, and the others. Toward the end of June, Kocherthal started out on a trip to London, England, to see what he could do to improve the condition of the settlers, including himself. He did not return to London in order to lead the 1710 immigrants. But his presence in London late in 1709, naturally brought him in contact with the large number of Palatines encamped at that time in and about London. He did receive some help from funds voted by Parliament, but he got no support for his proposed plan of a large plantation of vineyards. Upon his return to New York, the history of the Newburgh Palatines is merged with that of the large 1709 Palatine emigration to New York.

b. *The Large Palatine Immigration of 1709.*—Reference has already been made to the many thousand Protestant Palatines who came to England in 1709.[124] Among these were also thousands of Roman Catholic Palatines, of whom 2,257 were sent back to Rotterdam in September of that year. The others were allowed to continue their migration.

[122] Lots of from one hundred to three hundred acres were divided among the settlers. Each person was allowed fifty acres. Governor Lovelace also allowed nine pence per day for each person for food and other necessities.

[123] On June 21, 1709, a committee of the Council investigating these charges, found "that nothing of the aligations suggested against those called 'Pietists' have been proved before them." Consequently, their subsistence allowance, which had been withheld on account of the charge, was restored to them.

[124] In the official correspondence there is a mention of 13,146, but the actual number was considerably larger, since quite a few Palatines were sent by the packet boat or by regular shipping at their own expense or by charity funds, after the official transportation ceased, on July 18.

LUTHERANS IN COLONIAL DAYS, 1492-1763

For some time London had between 10,000 and 11,000 alien people in need of food and shelter. The Board of Trade and the English Whigs deserve much credit for their generous treatment of these aliens. Queen Anne's attitude has already been explained. But the British government was not prepared for this great influx of Palatines, and it took some time before the final plans could be worked out. Numerous proposals were discussed,[125] but the final plans were to send some to Ireland, some to Carolina, and some to New York.

In August, 1709, about 794 families were sent to Limerick County, Ireland, to strengthen the Protestant cause there. Some of these soon returned to England. The great majority of those remaining turned staunch Methodists, after a visit by John Wesley in 1745.[126]

As Pennsylvania was by far the best advertised colony in America, one might expect that William Penn would have taken some of the 1709 Palatines off the hands of the British government. But unfortunately, Penn was not in a financial position to send any settlers to his colony in 1709. He had just been released from a nine month's imprisonment for a 10,500 pound debt dishonestly claimed by former friends. Hence Penn could take but a small part in disposing of the Palatines in London in 1709.

On July 16, 1709, the Lord Proprietors of North Carolina offered the Board of Trade to take all the Palatines in London, from 15 to 45 years old, to their Carolina plantations, provided the British government would pay the expense of their transportation. Before this proposal could be duly considered, two Swiss promoters, Franz Louis Michel and Christopher von Graffenried, joined the Proprietors of Carolina in the project. Extensive preparations were made. Graffenried and Michel

[125] The proposed places included settlement on Rio de la Plata, South America; on Canary Islands; and at least a dozen other places.

[126] These Palatine descendants kept their national identity for a long time, but the last three generations consider themselves Irish, in evidence that they have been thoroughly assimilated.

were permitted to pick out 600 Palatines, and later about 50 more were added. By January, 1710, these 650 Palatines were sent to Carolina. Another group of Swiss Protestants sailed a few months later. These Palatine and Swiss colonists were settled on the Neuse River, and from a combination of the River name and Bern, the home city of the Swiss, the settlement was called New Bern. Through the efforts of Graffenried, a group of German and Swiss miners came to Virginia in 1714, where they founded the settlement of Germanna on the Rapidan River, a branch of the Rappahannock.

The pioneer Palatine settlers of New Bern adhered, some to the Lutheran and some to the Reformed Church, while nearly all the early Swiss settlers were Mennonites or Anabaptists.[127] Graffenreid, in a letter to the Bishop of London, petitioned that all these settlers might become members of the Church of England. The Bishop of London answered that as soon as the proper arrangements could be made, he would send them a clergyman of the Church of England, who could minister to this German and Swiss colony in their native language. Graffenreid considered this arrangement a matter of expediency, as the Church of England was the established religion in the Carolinas.

But London still had the great bulk of Palatines to care for. The London populace began to assume an ugly attitude toward these aliens, though they had been naturalized. The poorer classes of the English people claimed the Palatines had come to eat the bread of the Englishmen and to reduce the scale of wages. The "better" people of England were in great fear of contamination by prevalent contagious diseases, due to the crowded quarters and meager sustenance of the Palatines. Furthermore, these immigrants proved a heavy expense to the

---

[127] A religious schism had split the city of Bern, Switzerland, and the party of Mennonites, or Anabaptists as they were called in England, were forced to emigrate. A number of the group had been imprisoned for their Anabaptist beliefs.

LUTHERANS IN COLONIAL DAYS, 1492-1763   177

British government. Something had to be done to get them settled permanently. The final outcome was that the Palatines were placed under contract to settle in New York for the production of naval stores. The contract was in the nature of an indenture, making the Palatines indentured servants until they had repaid the British government.[128]

The expedition was equipped with 600 tents, 600 firearms and bayonets and a proportionate quantity of powder and shot, a quantity of hemp seed and other supplies, and ten ships were hired to take the Palatines to New York. The ships left London December, 1709, but they did not leave Plymouth until April 10, 1710.[129] The first ship, the *Lyon*, arrived in New York on June 13, 1710. One ship, the *Herbert*, was wrecked on the east coast of Long Island. The last ship arrived on August 2, 1710. Of the 2,814 who started out from London, 446 died before the end of July, and thirty children were born during the journey. The immigrants, nearly 2,500, were landed and encamped on Governor's Island. Many of the immigrants, weakened by the journey, were ravaged by typhus.[130]

What problems these 2,500 Palatines caused the authorities of New York City may be understood in part from a census taken on June 5, 1712, which showed that the city had at that time only 4,846 free inhabitants and 970 slaves.[131] These Palatines had to be lodged and cared for. It was also felt that the presence of these immigrants within the city might endanger the health of the inhabitants and also cause extortionate prices

---

[128] No time limit was set for the required service, and the government was to direct the work of repayment. By the terms of the contract it appeared that the Palatines might be kept in a perpetual serfdom, simply by charging more for expenses than the naval store profits could produce.

[129] The ships moved along the coast of England, touching Portsmouth and Plymouth during the early months of 1710, and then finally sailed on April 10.

[130] Peter Willemse Romers, a coffin-maker, asked payment for 250 coffins used for burial of Palatines during the summer of 1710. *N. Y. Col. Docs.*, III, p. 568.

[131] *N. Y. Col. MSS.*, LVII, p. 180.

178 THE LUTHERAN CHURCH IN AMERICA

on bread and other provisions. A number of Palatine orphans were apprenticed,[132] and Governor Hunter even apprenticed children whose parents were still living.[133] In the attempt to locate a suitable tract for settlement of the Palatines, four places were considered.[134] The tract chosen consisted of 6,300 acres on the west side of the Hudson River, about ninety-two miles from New York City. In addition, 6,000 acres were purchased from Robert Livingston on the east side of the Hudson. These locations gave rise to the names West Camp and East Camp. The land was surveyed, and early in October, 1710, the Palatines began to move into these settlements. In June, 1711, the total number of Palatines on the Hudson was 1,874.[135] The rest were still in New York City, though some moved in later. At least seven of the original families moved to Pennsylvania, New Jersey and Upper Hudson Valley.

The spiritual needs of these Palatines were taken care of by two German ministers, Joshua Kocherthal for the Lutherans, and John Frederick Haeger for the Reformed. Haeger had been employed by the London Society for the Propagation of the Gospel, after he had taken Anglican ordination from the Bishop of London, and his mission was to win these settlers for the Church of England. A school house was built in the settlement in 1711. In 1717 a licence was obtained for the building of an Anglican church, but it took several years before the church was actually built. Kocherthal preached in private homes. The first Lutheran church, a small log church 20 by 20 feet, was built on the corner of Kings Highway and Liberty Street, Newburgh, about the year 1730. In this church was a small 113 pound

---

[132] Among these were John Peter Zenger, famous in American history for his fight for the freedom of the press.

[133] George Frederick Weiser, a son of John Conrad Weiser, was separated from his family and apprenticed.

[134] One was on the Mohawk River, around Herkimer and the German Flats. Another was on the Schoharie River, and this was evidently the site favored by Queen Anne. The others were on the Hudson River.

[135] *Doc. Hist.*, III, p. 668.

LUTHERANS IN COLONIAL DAYS, 1492-1763   179

bell, given to Kocherthal and his congregation by Queen Anne as they sailed from England.

After the death of Kocherthal in 1719, these Lutherans were served more or less regularly by Justus Falckner, 1719-23; Daniel Falckner, 1723-26; William Christopher Berkenmeyer, 1726-31; and Michael Christian Knoll, 1733-49. By 1751, practically all the Palatines had moved away, and the original settlement was partially made up of other immigrants. On November 4, 1751, the Evangelical Lutheran Church in Newburgh was turned over to the Anglicans.[136] The present Evangelical Lutheran Church of Newburgh was organized on June 9, 1876, by Rev. Gustav Borchard.[137]

The Palatine settlement on the Hudson enjoyed a fair degree of success during the first years of its existence.[138] But the Ministerial Revolution in England in 1711, and the subsequent search for political campaign material to win the next election for the Tories and to keep them in office, had a disastrous effect upon the naval stores project on the Hudson.[139] The Tories found it politically necessary to condemn this and other Whig projects. They even claimed that the Palatine immigration had been a design against the Church of England.[140] A parliamentary investigation conducted in 1711 revealed that the English government had expended more than 100,000 pounds sterling on the

---

[136] *Doc. Hist.*, III, pp. 598-606. Margaret Ward was then the only surviving member of the original Palatine congregation living on the grant of Queen Anne.

[137] After the Palatines had been dispossessed by the Anglicans, November 4, 1751, the Evangelical Lutheran Church in Newburgh passed into Babylonian Captivity for 125 years.

[138] Kocherthal *Record MSS.* show 35 baptisms and 100 marriages from 1710-1712; during the same years, Haeger had 61 baptisms and 101 marriages. Cf. *Library of Congress*, Washington, D. C., A-8, 31, 158.

[139] The Palatine immigration had been particularly distasteful to the native English poor.

[140] The purpose, they claimed, was to increase the number and strength of the Dissenters and to strengthen the Low Church or Protestant party. This probably gained Queen Anne's sympathy for the opposition, as she strongly favored the High Church party, as did the Tories generally.

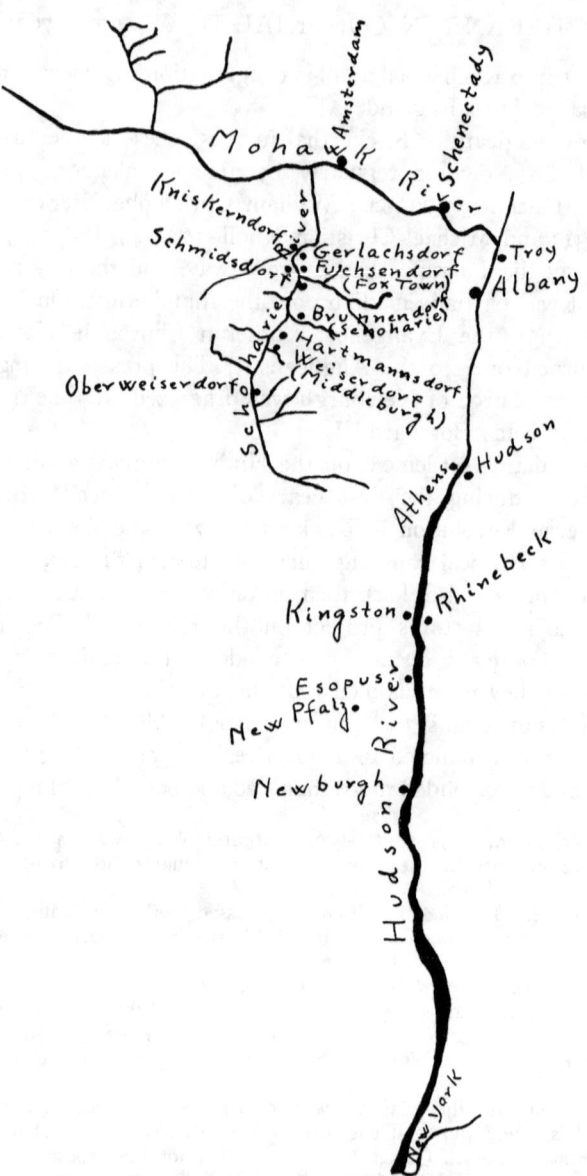

Early Palatine Settlements in New York

Palatines in various ways.[141] The House of Commons passed resolutions condemning the Palatine immigration project, and the act of naturalization of 1709 was repealed in 1712.[142] Hence the failure to give continued financial support to the naval stores project on the Hudson was purely political.

On September 6, 1712, the Palatines on the Hudson were informed that the naval stores project had been halted, and that they would have to subsist themselves until further orders were given.[143] The last day of government subsistence for the Palatines was September 12, 1712.[144] A few helpless widows and orphans were cared for until September 23, 1712, and then all support ceased. The people were permitted to hire themselves out if they could, anywhere in New York and New Jersey, as both regions were under the jurisdiction of Governor Hunter, but any one leaving without official permission was threatened with imprisonment.[145] It should be kept in mind that during the political disturbances in England, mentioned above, governmental support of the Palatines had not been regular. Meanwhile Governor Hunter had extended personal credit to the Palatine account to the extent of 20,769 pounds sterling.[146] He naturally expected reimbursement by the English government, but his claim was apparently not satisfied.[147] This large indebtedness, coupled with Governor Hunter's financial difficulties at this time and the political animosity of the Tories, may in

---

[141] *Journal of House of Commons*, XVI, p. 598.
[142] *Journal of House of Commons*, XVI, p. 472.
[143] John Conrad Weiser in his *Diary* gives 1713 as the year when government subsistence was stopped, but this is an error. Cf. *N. Y. Col. Docs.*, V, 347.
[144] *Public Record Office*, London, C. O., 5/1085, 67.
[145] *Doc. Hist.*, III, 683. John Conrad Weiser was even threatened with hanging.
[146] *Public Record Office*, London, C. O., 5/1085, 67. Cf. *N. Y. Col. Docs.*, V, 462.
[147] *Public Record Office*, London, *Gifts and Deposits*, 8/73; also *Acts Privy Council Col.* 1680-1720, p. 775.

part explain the harsh treatment of the Palatines after 1712.[148]

Within the next five years many Palatines moved elsewhere, to Pennsylvania; to Hackensack, New Jersey; to Rhinebeck, New York; to Livingston Manor itself; to New York City; and to Schoharie. The Palatines who intended to settle in Schoharie sent deputies to make arrangements with the Indians there.[149] Upon the return of these deputies, about 150 families moved in the autumn of 1712 to Albany and Schenectady where they stayed during the winter, with intention to move into Schoharie early in the spring. It appears that about fifty families did not wait till spring, but cut a road from Schenectady to Schoharie in two weeks, and then settled in Schoharie for the winter.[150] By March, 1713, the remainder of the 150 families joined them.[151] They settled in seven villages which were named, it is claimed, after the deputies who had made arrangements with the Indians.[152]

---

[148] The sufferings of the Palatines that first winter, without government aid, can only partly be imagined.

[149] Governor Hunter wrote to the Board of Trade, on October 31, 1712, that "some hundreds" of the Palatines had decided to go to Schoharie; that they had already started the march; and that some were busy cutting a road from Schenectady to Schoharie. *N. Y. Col. Docs.*, V, 347.

[150] *N. Y. Col. Docs.*, V, 347. John Conrad Weiser, in his *Diary*, gives 1713 as the beginning of the migration to Schoharie; and, staying in Albany and Schenectady over winter, they moved into Schoharie in 1714. But this is one year late, according to other documentary evidence here presented. Furthermore, Justus Falckner records a communion "at Schoharie" February 7, 1714.

[151] According to *Calendar of State Papers, Colonial, America and West Indies,* 1712-1714, p. 263, there were, on October 26, 1713, 1,008 Palatines in the Hudson River settlements; 500 in Schoharie Valley; and about 500 among various planters. In 1718 the two Palatine pastors, Kocherthal and Haeger, reported 224 families of 1,021 persons along the Hudson River and scattered areas, and 170 families of 580 persons in the Schoharie Valley. See *Doc. Hist.*, I, 693.

[152] These seven villages were: (1) Kniskerndorf, or New Heidelberg, located opposite the present village of Central Bridge, and nearly opposite the point where Cobleskill Creek empties into Schoharie River. (2) Gerlachsdorf, or New Cassel, of which there are no remains. (3) Fuchsendorf,

Being bitterly opposed to their settlement in Schoharie,[153] Governor Hunter in a spirit of revenge deeded away the land the Palatines had settled on.[154] The basic factors involved in this transaction appear to be: (1) In 1698 Governor Fletcher, just before he was replaced, had issued several extravagant land grants in the Mohawk, Schoharie and Hudson Valleys to Nicholas Bayard, Godfrey Dellius, Captain Evans and Caleb Heathcote.[155] (2) But Lord Bellomont, the next Governor of New York, favored another faction of the landowning class. Consequently he induced the New York Assembly, on March 2, 1699, to vacate, break and annul Extravagant Grants of land made by Governor Fletcher.[156] This act was confirmed by the London Authorities on June 26, 1708.[157] (3) Governor Hunter sent men to "survey the land on the Mohaques River, particularly the Skohare, to which the Indians have no pretence, being Colonel Bayard's Grant."[158] (4) The Indians refused to allow the men to survey the land which they claimed for themselves.[159] As Governor Hunter investigated their claims, he found at Albany instructions to restore to the Indians their right and

---

or New Hayesbury, later called Fox Town, where the Old Fort Museum of Schoharie now stands. (4) Schmidsdorf, or New Queensbury, later called Smith's Town, marked at present by a small railroad station. (5) Brunnendorf, or Fountaindorf, named from a large spring which furnished drinking water, near the site now occupied by St. Paul's Lutheran Church in Schoharie. (6) Hartmannsdorf, or New Annesbury, the site of which is indicated by an iron marker. (7) Weiserdorf, or New Stuttgart, on the edge of the present site of Middleburgh. Oberweiserdorf was settled later.

[153] *Eccles. Rec.*, III, 2146 and 2170; *Calendar of State Papers, Colonial, America and West Indies,* 1712-1714, p. 82.
[154] The recipients were the Five Partners referred to later.
[155] *N. Y. Col. Docs.*, V, 117; *Eccles. Rec.*, III, 1685.
[156] *Calendar of State Papers, Colonial, America and West Indies,* 1698, p. 914; *Eccles. Rec.*, III, 1812; *N. Y. Col. Docs.*, V, 117.
[157] *N. Y. Col. Docs.*, V, 25, 48.
[158] *N. Y. Col. Docs.*, V, 167.
[159] *Doc. Hist.*, III, 560; *N. Y. Col. Docs.*, V, 117.

title to the land in question.[160] Hunter consequently acknowledged their claim. (5) In a conference at Albany on August 22, 1710, the Indian Hendrick told Governor Hunter that he had heard of the decision of Queen Anne to settle a large number of people upon their land, which was a surprise to the Indians, as the land rightly belonged to them. However, he and his people were willing to surrender the land to the Queen for Christian settlements, referring apparently to the Palatines. This Indian gift was made at Fort Albany, on August 22, 1710.[161] Hunter accepted the land in the Queen's name, and promised the Indians a suitable reward. (6) On November 3, 1714, Governor Hunter granted the land upon which the Palatines had settled, being a part of the original Nicholas Bayard grant, to five citizens of Albany, namely Myndert Schuyler, Peter van Brugh, Robert Livingston, Jr., John Schuyler and Peter Wileman.[162] Lewis Morris, Jr. and Andrus Coeman surveyed the land and found that the flats of Fox Creek and a large part of Kniskerndorf had been omitted. The surveyors secured this land for themselves, so the Five Partners became the Seven Partners.[163]

In 1715 the Palatines were called upon to purchase, lease or vacate their land. This naturally led to friction and violence.[164] In a conference with John Conrad Weiser in 1717, Governor

[160] *Calendar of State Papers, Colonial, America and West Indies,* 1710-1711, p. 223.
[161] *Calendar of State Papers, Colonial, America and West Indies,* 1710-1711, pp. 834, 223.
[162] *N. Y. Patent Books,* VIII, 74; *N. Y. Council Minutes,* XI, 245. About this time a grandson of Nicholas Bayard, and of the same name, visited the Palatines at Schoharie and promised to issue a deed to their land in the name of Queen Anne. The Palatines did not accept his deeds because they regarded him as an imposter. Bayard belonged to the colonial opposition to Governor Hunter, and his intentions as to the Palatines are not clear. He was taken as a representative of Hunter, and the Palatines drove him out. According to Palatine tradition, Bayard then sold the Schoharie title to the Five Partners.
[163] Simms, *History of Schoharie County,* p. 60.
[164] *Doc. Hist.,* III, 687, 688, 713; *Eccles. Rec.,* III, 2171.

Hunter promised to send twelve men to estimate the value of the improvement of the land the Palatines had settled, but he failed to carry out his promise. In 1718 the Palatines selected three men, John Conrad Weiser, William Scheff and Gerhart Walrath, to go to London to ask for justice.[165] Weiser stayed in London for five years and then had to return without help.[166] The Palatines who chose to remain in Schoharie had to agree to lease or buy their land from the supposed legal owners.

By 1723 the Palatines in the Schoharie were somewhat divided. About three hundred of them chose to remain on their farms in Schoharie.[167] About sixty families, under the leadership of John Christopher Gerlach, settled in the Mohawk Valley, between Fort Hunter and Canada.[168] On October 19, 1723, the Stone Arabia patent was issued, and a number of Palatines settled at Palatine Bridge.[169] A third group, at the invitation of Governor Keith, moved to Tulpehocken, east of the Swatara Creek in Pennsylvania.[170]

The first recorded Lutheran service in Schoharie is given as February 7, 1714. Hence this may be taken as the birthday of St. Paul's Lutheran Church of Schoharie, though the provisional organization was not perfected till after the coming of Reverend Peter Nicholas Sommer in 1743. At first they met for services in private homes. Their first church building, combining chapel and parsonage, was dedicated on September 12, 1743. The second church, built of stone, was dedicated on May 6, 1751. Their third church, built of brick and stone, was dedicated in 1796.

---

[165] *Calendar of State Papers, Colonial, America and West Indies,* 1720-1721, p. 102.
[166] Walrath soon returned, but died on his way back to New York. Scheff returned in 1721.
[167] *N. Y. Col. Docs.,* V, 634.
[168] *Eccles. Rec.,* III, 2196.
[169] *N. Y. Land Papers,* VI, 138.
[170] Some of the Palatines from New York had settled in Pennsylvania as early as 1717; see *Pennsylvania Archives,* 2nd series, VII, 78, 94; *N. Y. Col. Docs.,* V, 677. But the 1717 group apparently did not settle in the same locality as the 1723 group; see Weiser *Diary,* 45.

186 THE LUTHERAN CHURCH IN AMERICA

The pastors serving this church in the Colonial Era include Joshua Kocherthal, 1714-19; Justus Falckner, 1720-23; Johann Bernard Von Dieren, 1723-23; Christopher William Berkenmeyer, 1724-42; Peter Nicholas Sommer, 1743-87. For more than a century, the Lutherans of the Upper Valley looked to the pastors of this church for their spiritual care.[171]

Lutheran Palatines who settled in Mohawk Valley[172] were frequently visited by Rev. Peter Nicholas Sommer who conducted worship in their private homes. He did not consider it necessary to organize a church. The congregation was finally organized by George A. Lintner of the mother church in Schoharie, with fifty members, on May 17, 1824. The congregation was incorporated on July 28, 1896 under the title, "St. Mark's Evangelical Lutheran Church of Middleburgh, New York." Its first church building was dedicated on October 30, 1824. For some years St. Mark's and St. Paul's of Schoharie and Zion of Cobleskill formed one parish.

The Palatine settlement at Tulpehocken in Pennsylvania was augmented by thirty-three families which moved in 1725.[173] Fifty more families arrived in 1729.[174] Among them was the family of Conrad Weiser, who served Pennsylvania and other colonies as a valuable intermediary with the Indians.[175] The father, John Conrad Weiser, joined the settlement a few years later, after he had failed to secure an Indian deed for land on

[171] In 1918, after the throes of the World War, the 158 communicants of St. Paul's Lutheran Church united with the local Methodist Episcopal Church and the Reformed Church, to form a community church. This union robbed the Lutherans of their proud distinction of being the mother church of Schoharie County.

[172] For about thirty miles, the Mohawk became a Palatine river. Present Palatine names in the Mohawk region include Palatine Bridge, Oppenheim, Newkirk, Herkimer and German Flats.

[173] *Col. Rec. of Pa.*, III, 352. Appendix G.

[174] Häberle, *Auswanderung und Koloniegründungen der Pfälzer in 18ten Jahrhundert*, p. 94.

[175] As a young boy, Conrad Weiser, with the consent of his father, had been taken by the Indian chief Quaynant to live with him. Weiser lived among the Indians for several years, learning their language and customs.

LUTHERANS IN COLONIAL DAYS, 1492-1763

the west side of the Delaware River.[176] The elder Weiser, a former magistrate in old Würtemberg in Germany, was the most eminent as well as the most fiery leader among the early Palatine settlers in America. In 1711 he served as a captain in the expedition of the English against the French and their Indian allies. Because of his participation, numerous Lutheran Palatines took part in the same expedition.

4. *Later German Immigration.*—For more than four decades the doors of the Palatinate seemed wide open, and an almost continuous stream of emigrants found their way to America. For numbers and steadiness of inflow, there was nothing quite like it in the history of colonial America. When the tide finally subsided, more than 30,000 Palatines had settled in the various American colonies. The stream was augmented by emigrants from other sections of Germany. The high tide of German immigration came between 1735 and 1745. By the middle of the century more than 60,000 Lutherans had settled in Pennsylvania alone. Counting the Reformed, the Mennonites and other groups, it is reasonable to infer that in the sixth decade of the eighteenth century, something like 80,000 Germans had settled in America.

The Palatine immigrations of 1709 and 1710 to New York proved to be diversions from the normal course of German immigration; for after 1717 the German colonists, with few exceptions, established themselves in Pennsylvania. A colonial writer[177] states in part, "It sometimes happened that they were forced to go on board such ships as were bound to New York; but they were scarce got on shore, when they hastened on to *Pennsylvania* in sight of all the inhabitants of New York." No other English province had such magnetic attraction for the Germans in the eighteenth century as Pennsylvania. In consequence, colonial New York ranked only fourth in population;

---
[176] *Cal. N. Y. Hist. MSS.*, II, 497.
[177] Peter Kalm, *Travels in America*, I, 271.

Massachusetts ranking first, Pennsylvania second and Virginia third.

Various reasons may be given for this flow of German migration to Pennsylvania rather than to New York. (1) Pennsylvania was the most widely advertised of the American colonies. It was the "promised land" to the Germans of the eighteenth century. New York lacked such publicity as to its land terms and opportunities. (2) Prospective settlers were offered more liberal land terms in Pennsylvania. In New York large land grants were given to the Lords of Manors, who in turn generally insisted on leases or shares, rather than outright sale.[178] (3) William Penn and others made much of the promise of religious toleration in Pennsylvania. (4) The Indian barrier presented by the Six Nations may in part account for the sparseness of European settlers in colonial New York; but it must be remembered that the Palatines were in friendly relations with the Indians of the Six Nations, in sharp contrast to the general hostility of the Scotch-Irish settlers, who invariably had trouble with the Indians.

a. *Pennsylvania.*—The stream of German immigration ran steadily toward Pennsylvania, and the majority of these immigrants were Lutherans. The first German Lutheran congregation in Pennsylvania was organized at Falckner's Swamp or New Hanover in 1703 of immigrants who came with Daniel Falckner in 1700. A Lutheran congregation was formed by the Palatines who settled at Tulpehocken in 1723 and 1729. The Lutheran congregation at Philadelphia was organized about 1728. One year later the largest and strongest of these early Lutheran congregations was organized at Lancaster. Another (the Trappe) was organized at Providence. Soon the counties of York, Lebanon, Lancaster, Berks, Lehigh, Bucks, Adams and Montgomery were dotted by Lutheran preaching places and congregations. Pennsylvania became the center of the Lutheran popula-

---

[178] *Calendar of State Papers, Colonial, America and West Indies,* 1700, p. 678; *N. Y. Col. Docs.,* V, 480.

LUTHERANS IN COLONIAL DAYS, 1492-1763

tion in colonial America. Lutheran pastors who served these congregations in the pioneer days included Daniel Falckner, Anthony Jacob Henkel, John Caspar Stoever, Sr., John Caspar Stoever, Jr., and John Christian Schultz. But these were far too few to minister to the spiritual needs of the widespread Lutheran settlements, and new immigrants who kept on coming failed to bring pastors and teachers with them. Consequently, the settlers often fell a prey to unscrupulous sectarian and heretical tramps. A delegation was sent to England and Germany in 1733, but it took nine years before there was any specific result. In 1742 Henry Melchior Muhlenberg came, and this marked a new era in the history of Lutheranism in America.

b. *New York and New Jersey.*—Prior to 1742, New York had Lutheran congregations in New York City; in Albany; on the Hudson at East Camp, Rhinebeck, Loonenburg and West Camp; at Newburgh; at Middleburgh; and some preaching places. Pastors who served these congregations in this period, 1700-1742, were Andreas Rudman, Justus Falckner, Joshua Kockerthal, Johann Bernard Von Dieren, William Christopher Berkenmeyer and Michael Christian Knoll.

In this same period, 1700-1742, Lutheran congregations and preaching places existed in New Jersey at Raccoon Creek or the present Swedesboro; at Pennsneck, now Pennsville; the Cohansey Church near Friesburg, about ten miles east of Salem; at Fort Elfsborg; at Hackensack, Teaneck Township; at Constable Hook or Bayonne; at Ramapo in the Saddle River Valley; at Potterstown in the upper Raritan Valley, behind the Watchung Mountains; at Pluckemin in the Raritan; at Fox Hill and at Lesly's Land, both in the Raritan; and in the German Valley, named Long Valley since the World War of 1914-17. These congregations and preaching places were served in the period 1700-1742, some by the Swedish pastors Lars Tolstadius, Jonas Auren, Abraham Lidenius, Peter Tranberg, Olaf Malander and John Sandin; and some by the German pastors Justus Falckner,

William Christopher Berkenmeyer, Michael Christian Knoll and Johann Augustus Wolf.

c. *New England.*—In 1739 Samuel Waldo established a small colony of German immigrants at Waldoborough, on the left bank of the little Muscongus River, near Broad Bay, Maine. In 1740 the colony was augmented by forty Lutheran families from Brunswick and Saxony, Germany. In this company was an ordained minister, Tobias Wagner of Wurtemberg. He ministered to their spiritual needs until 1743 when he moved to Tulpehocken. Meanwhile the spiritual work at Waldoborough was entrusted to a layman, Johann Ulmer, and under his leadership, the first Lutheran church was constructed. In 1762 Rev. John M. Schaeffer, who had been a pastor in New York City, came to serve these Lutherans.

d. *Maryland and Virginia.*—The Swedish-Finnish settlement at Elk River, Maryland, has been mentioned in a previous section. This settlement enjoyed the occasional spiritual services of Swedish Lutheran pastors. In this same period, 1700-1742, small groups of German settlers had scattered throughout the Maryland and Virginia territory. In the fourth decade of the eighteenth century these settlements were greatly augmented, and new ones were formed, by immigrants who pressed across the Susquehanna and into this territory. Some of these settlements may have had preaching places, but as far as is known, none of them had any organized churches prior to 1742.

e. *North and South Carolina.*—The Lutheran settlement of 1674 at St. James Island, South Carolina, and the German-Swiss settlement of 1710 at New Bern, North Carolina have been mentioned in previous sections. Some time between 1710 and 1734 a number of Germans settled in Charleston, South Carolina. When the Lutheran pastors, Bolzius and Gronau, passed through Charleston in 1734 on their way to Ebenezer, Georgia, they found a number of Germans in that city, some of them having come from the Palatinate. The Lutheran element enjoyed occasional visits by the pastors of the Salzburg colony in Georgia, and Henry Melchior Muhlenberg visited them in 1742.

A Swiss colony was established at Purysburg, South Carolina, in 1732. A few Lutheran families lived in this colony, according to the *Journal* of Rev. Bolzius, but no Lutheran church was established by them. Another German-Swiss colony was established at Orangeburg, South Carolina, in 1735. Here the first congregation in South Carolina was established. It was first served by John Ulrich Giessendanner. Two contemporary and neighboring pastors, Bolzius and Gronau, said that he was a Lutheran, and that many Lutherans lived in and about Orangeburg at this time. From Orangeburg, a number of people moved further inland and formed the Saxe-Gotha settlement, later known as Lexington County. These early settlers were Reformed, and were served by a Reformed minister, Christian Theus.

f. *Georgia.*—In 1734 a shipload of Lutheran refugees from Salzburg, Austria, came to Georgia and settled at Ebenezer, twenty-five miles north of Savannah. The colony was soon augmented by additional immigrants, and by 1741 the settlement had a total population of twelve hundred. They built four churches, Jerusalem, Zion, Bethany and Goshen; and they also built schools and an orphanage. They were served by two very able pastors, John Martin Bolzius and Israel Christian Gronau, who had been trained at the University of Halle. Whitefield and the Wesleys, who visited the colony, were deeply impressed by these thrifty and God-fearing colonists. No secular authority was needed to settle disputes and maintain order. All disputes were settled by their spiritual leaders. The colony suffered severely during the War of Independence. Many of the settlers were scattered to other German Lutheran settlements toward the north.

5. *Palatine Contributions.*—Their influence on the future development of the United States of America and its institutions was not equal to the formative power exerted by other groups, such as the Puritans of New England. Having suffered a great deal in a war-torn Europe, they loved peace and seclusion, and

assumed the general attitude: *leave alone and let alone*. But they fought successfully, through John Peter Zenger, for the freedom of the Press. Their broad religious background promoted tolerance and an easygoing cosmopolitanism. They were sturdy, freedom-loving, but orderly people who promoted a frontier individualism which was tempered by much community cooperation among themselves. They pushed the New York frontier westward into the Mohawk Valley, and the Pennsylvania frontier into the Great Appalachian Valley. They served as a barrier against the French, but cultivated friendly relations with the Indians of the Six Nations allied with the English. This was in sharp contrast to the Scotch-Irish who, because of their hostile attitude, invariably had trouble with the Indians. The Palatines participated in the English and colonial expeditions against Canada in 1711. In 1732 John Conrad Weiser, Jr. became the Head of the Indian Bureau of English Government. Having spent some years of his youth with an Indian chief, and being an adopted son of an Indian tribe, he wielded a great influence in Indian circles. It was mainly through his efforts that the Iroquois Indians were kept from joining the French; and thus he helped to save the English colonies in America. Furthermore, the early settlers of the Middle Atlantic States typified, more than in Virginia or in New England, the present day complexion of the population of the United States of America.

11. REVIEW QUESTIONS

1. What geographic and numeric expansion did the Swedish-Finnish Lutheran churches on the Delaware enjoy during this period?
2. What happened to these churches? Why?
3. What did the Falckner brothers contribute to Lutheran progress?
4. What conditions in Continental Europe contributed to the early Palatine emigration?
5. What conditions in England and America favored the Palatine exodus?
6. Why were the early Palatines settled in Ireland, in North Carolina and in New York, while only a few came to Pennsylvania?
7. Under what conditions did the Palatines live in the Hudson settlement?

LUTHERANS IN COLONIAL DAYS, 1492-1763

8. In what ways did the Ministerial Revolution in England in 1711 effect the Palatines on the Hudson?
9. Why did the Palatines encounter so many difficulties in Schoharie?
10. Why did not New York come first, but *fourth*, in size of population in colonial times?
11. Why the trek to Pennsylvania after 1717?
12. How were the Lutheran settlements distributed in the American colonies by 1742?
13. What did the Palatines contribute to colonial America?

TOPICS FOR SPECIAL STUDY

1. New Sweden and Anglicanism.
2. The land system in colonial New York.
3. Individualism and the colonial frontier.
4. The redemptioner system.
5. Joshua Kockerthal.
6. John Frederick Haeger.
7. John Conrad Weiser.
8. Conrad Weiser and the Indians.
9. Government operation of industry in competition with private business.
10. Governor Hunter and the Palatines.
11. The manorial system of the Palatines.
12. The Schoharie land grant and the Palatines.

6. *The First Lutheran Synod in America, 1735.*—After the death of Justus Falckner in 1723, his large parish was served temporarily by his brother, Daniel, except that Joshua Kockerthal served the Palatine churches on the Hudson until his death in 1719. The New York Church petitioned the Lutheran Consistory of Amsterdam to provide a new pastor for them. As a result, William Christopher Berkenmeyer came in 1725. He was a man of thorough culture, strict Lutheran convictions and a pleasing personality. In him the organizing talent of the North Germans was fully developed.[179]

Berkenmeyer's first task was to allay the confusion caused by Johann Bernhard von Dieren, who had served some of the churches of his parish after a fashion during the vacancy.[180] He

[179] Berkenmeyer was a man of mature age when he came to America. He was born on April 14, 1687, in Bodenteich, in the Duchy of Lueneburg. He received his theological training at Altdorf, under Dr. Sontag.

[180] Von Dieren made such persistent efforts to establish himself as pastor in New York, that Berkenmeyer found it necessary to publish a

then devoted his energies chiefly to securing new church buildings for the congregations in New York and Loonenburgh. The New York Church was dedicated on June 29, 1729, and named Trinity Church.[181] He then addressed himself to the task of dividing his large parish. The northern portion of his parish had grown to such proportions that he considered it best to devote all his time to it. Accordingly, he retained for himself Loonenburgh and the German churches in the Hudson Valley, vacated by the death of Joshua Kocherthal; while Newburgh and other preaching places south of it were to be served by a pastor from the New York congregation. This division occurred in 1732. In that same year Michael Christian Knoll came as pastor of the New York parish.[182]

Meanwhile Daniel Falckner continued to serve a group of German churches which had come into existence along the upper reaches of the Raritan River in New Jersey. They included the "Rariton Church" near the present Pluckemin; the church at Racheway, now Potterstown, and founded by a Lutheran negro, Are van Guinea; and a settlement on the Uylekill or Owl Creek, now called Whippany River, near Hanover, New Jersey. By 1734 he had become so incapacitated for the ministry by old age, that he was replaced by Johann August Wolff. Accordingly, toward the end of 1734, the New York and New Jersey Lutheran churches had three active ministers, Berkenmeyer, Knoll and Wolff.

In this little circle of ministers, Berkenmeyer was the most talented. He felt the need of a closer union of these churches into

---

pamphlet, exposing his pretention and citing statements of four Swedish pastors on the Delaware concerning him and his petition for ordination.

[181] This church stood on the southwest corner of Broadway and Rector Street. It was a substantial stone edifice, thirty-six by forty-six feet, with a spire fifty-eight feet high and furnished with the bell Queen Anne had given to the Palatines of Newburgh in 1709. The Lutherans of New York worshipped in this church until it burned down in the great fire of 1776.

[182] Knoll was a native of Holstein. He was ordained by Lutheran pastors in London.

LUTHERANS IN COLONIAL DAYS, 1492-1763   195

a more efficient organization. His original plan was to organize not only the Dutch and the German, but also the Swedish-Finnish churches in New Sweden into an ecclesiastical unit. Since the Swedish Church Laws of 1686 closely resembled those of the Dutch Church, he desired to have the proposed American Lutheran consistorium or synod under the care of the King of Sweden. All ministers were to be legitimated by the Swedish Church authorities, and all who failed in this test were to be barred, by a special decree of the King of England, from serving as pastors in the Lutheran churches in America. This plan failed because it was impracticable.

His next concern was to unite the Lutheran churches in the Hudson Valley into a fraternity in 1734. He prepared a constitution, written in Dutch on forty-nine pages of folio, as a bond between the Lutheran congregations in the Hudson Valley and in New Jersey. This constitution conformed to a strict confessional standard. The translation, as found in *Appendix I* of this volume, is based on a copy found in 1910 in the archives of Ulster County, New York. This constitution was evidently an adoption to American needs of the Amsterdam Church Order of 1686.

The first synodical meeting of the New York and New Jersey churches was held on August 20-21, 1735, at the "Rariton Church" near what is now Pluckemin, New Jersey. The immediate occasion for this meeting was the general desire to adjust grave dissensions between parishioners and pastor in the Raritan parish.[183] But Berkenmeyer also used this occasion to cement the friendship between the sister churches. There seem to have been four Dutch copies of the above named constitution, known respectively as the New York, the Loonenburgh, the Hackensack and the Raritan copy. There was also a German

[183] Wolff was dissatisfied with his salary, the "ministerials" and the parsonage. The congregation claimed that he neglected the instruction of children, failed to use the forms prescribed in the agenda and did not preach his sermons from memory, etc.

copy for the German churches in Raritan, New Jersey. This constitution was made the basis of the bond of union between the churches concerned, and pastors and delegates agreed as to its contents. The roll and organization of this synodical meeting were as follows: pastors, Berkenmeyer, Knoll and Wolff. Lay delegates: New York: Charles Bekman and Jacob Bos; Hackensack; Jan van Norden and Abraham van Boskerk; Uylekill; Pieter Friederich; Rareton; Daniel Schumacker and Henry Schmid; Racheway; Balthasar Bichel and Lawrence Rulofsen. The total was three pastors and nine lay delegates. Berkenmeyer was chosen *praeses et scriba*.

Although there is no known record of more than this one meeting, held at Pluckemin, New Jersey, in 1735, Michael Christian Knoll states in a letter of 1774 that this Lutheran Brotherhood continued to exist till about the time of the Revolution. Records of this earliest Lutheran Synod in America may still come to light. This New York and New Jersey synod represented the orthodox school of Lutheranism. Muhlenberg and his associates, on the other hand, represented Lutheran Pietism as emanating from the University of Halle.

Berkenmeyer continued his pastoral work until he entered into his rest on August 25, 1751, at the age of sixty-five. He preached in three languages, Dutch, German and English, and was held in high esteem by his people. He kept aloof from Muhlenberg because of his aversion to Pietism. By 1742 his parish had become so extensive that he gave the northern portion—including Schoharie, Stone Arabia, Palatine Bridge and Cobleskill—to his son-in-law, Rev. Peter Nicolas Sommer.

7. *The First Great Awakening, 1734-44.*—The Great Awakening in America was somewhat analogous to, and practically contemporaneous with, the Pietist movement in Germany and the Methodist revival in England. This far-reaching movement is not to be confused with the *Great Revival* from 1796 to 1805.

There was a large number of unchurched people in the American colonies. Religion played, of course, a very prominent part

LUTHERANS IN COLONIAL DAYS, 1492-1763

in the American settlement, but the initial religious interest was soon subordinated to the all absorbing issue of subjugating a new continent. Lack of organized churches and schools, shortage of worthy pastors, the rough frontier life, and constant border warfare,[184] had a demoralizing influence on colonial society. Something had to be done to make the colonists more interested in religion. The new technique evolved for this purpose was frontier revivalism, with its camp-meetings.[185]

The Great Awakening movement was first noticed among German Mennonites, Dunkers and Moravians in Pennsylvania. Next came the revivalist preaching of Theodore J. Frelinghuysen, a German Pietist minister to the Dutch Reformed in northern New Jersey (the Raritan Valley). By 1726 his preaching had resulted in numerous conversions and in the ingathering of many new members. The revival movement spread, about 1728, to the English and the Scotch Presbyterians through the medium of Gilbert Tennent, a young Presbyterian minister of New Brunswick, New Jersey. Tennent had been influenced, not only by Frelinghuysen, but also by his training in the Log College built by his father, William Tennent, for the education of evangelical ministers.

In 1734 a great awakening started among the people of Northampton, Massachusetts, under the ministry of Jonathan Edwards. Being alarmed by the growing tendency toward Arminianism, Edwards preached a series of sermons on justifica-

---

[184] The hundred years' struggle between France and England for the Mississippi Valley included King William's War (1689-97), Queen Anne's War (1702-13), King George's War (1740-48), and the French and Indian War (1755-63). Disputes concerning the boundary line between Maryland and Pennsylvania during the years 1730-40 caused bloody conflicts and legal difficulties. The boundary line was finally settled in 1763 by the royal engineers Mason and Dixon, whose names it still bears.

[185] The camp meetings originated during the *Great Revival* of 1796-1805, in Kentucky and Tennessee. These camp meetings were peculiarly well adapted to the circumstances, though often attended by extravagances. Something strong was needed to stir the frontiersman.

198 THE LUTHERAN CHURCH IN AMERICA

tion by faith alone.[186] The result was an absorbing interest in personal religion, by young and old, in the Northampton community. Within a year more than three hundred persons, nearly all the people in town above sixteen years of age, professed conversion. From Northampton the revival spread down the river and along the coast, thence to the Middle and Southern Colonies. In Virginia it had greatest progress among the Baptists, through the activities of two Baptist preachers, Shubal Stearns and Daniel Marshall. From the Baptists it spread to the Wesleyans (Methodists). The Swedish Lutherans on the Delaware, adhering to the official attitude of the Church of Sweden toward Pietism,[187] took a rather conservative attitude toward the *Great Awakening*, while German Lutherans on the other hand, were strongly influenced through the *Halle* controlled churches in Pennsylvania and the South. The Anglican Church (Episcopal) took an attitude of opposition.

The high tide of the *Great Awakening* came in 1740-41 during George Whitefield's second visit. His incomparable eloquence drew thousands of people to his meetings, and many were truly converted. His itinerant preaching and his visits to Gilbert Tennent, Frelinghuysen, Edwards and other revival speakers, brought in a sense the movements in the various colonies together. Edwards and other New England ministers joined for a time the itinerant evangelistic campaign. The great appeal was to *fear*. This motive was particularly prominent in Edward's famous sermon, *Sinners in the Hand of an Angry God*, preached at Enfield, Connecticut, in July, 1741. After this date the revival lost much of its force and popularity because of extravagances of action and speech, including groans, outcries, convulsions, fainting, visions, ecstasies, and an unbridled denunciation of all who did not agree with the revivalists.

[186] Jacob Arminius opposed five points in Calvinism: (1) Conditional election; (2) Limited atonement; (3) Total depravity; (4) Irresistible grace; and (5) Eternal security.

[187] The Pietistic movement in Sweden was suppressed by royal decree in 1706.

LUTHERANS IN COLONIAL DAYS, 1492-1763   199

But many important results may be registered. There was a general quickening of the religious life, a revival of personal religion, a large increase in church membership, and a higher general standing of morality. The awakening promoted missionary work and benevolent enterprises in the colonies, such as the

THE FRONTIER LINE OF THE ENGLISH COLONIES IN 1740
(The ...... line indicates the western edge of the fully settled areas.)

Indian Christianization and the Bethesda Orphan House which Whitefield built in Georgia. The educational influence was particularly significant. Many denominational colleges and religious schools were founded. While the revival deepened church divisions, it also aroused a general consciousness of a national religious unity. In this way it prepared for the birth of the

American nation. Whitefield impressed the character of Methodism upon American church life for more than a century.

8. *Forerunners of Muhlenberg.*—Meanwhile a continuous influx of German immigrants continued to press farther and farther toward the western frontier. The Governor of Pennsylvania, in 1748, estimated their number as three-fifths of the population of the entire province. In 1752 Pennsylvania had 90,000 Germans, out of a total of 190,000 white inhabitants. Three years later the white population in the province had increased to 220,000, and about one half of this number were Germans.[188] The German element was strongest in south-eastern Pennsylvania, and certain individuals of English stock were much concerned about this large percentage of German settlers. Numerically, the Lutherans were the strongest.

For some time these Lutherans lived in great spiritual destitution. Their supply of pastors and teachers was entirely inadequate for the large and widely scattered population. Preaching places and congregations came into existence in various localities, and these were cared for in many instances by school teachers who could read sermons to the people, but who also often assumed to act as though they were ordained ministers of the Gospel. These Lutheran groups were also frequently exposed to fake pastors and wandering religious fanatics.

Several devoted pastors, however, were active among them. The first of these was Daniel Falckner who organized the congregation at New Hanover (Falckner's Swamp) about 1703 and who ministered to this congregation till about 1708. He was the first regular pastor of the first German Lutheran congregation in Pennsylvania. Another pastor, Anthony Jacob Henkel, came in 1717 and made Falckner's Swamp his residence. He served as pastor of the New Hanover congregation till his death in 1728. He also visited all German settlements within reach, going even to distant Virginia; and it is likely that he was the founder of the Lutheran congregations at Phil-

[188] Mann, *Life and Times of Henry Melchior Muhlenberg*, p. 93.

adelphia and Germantown, though the Philadelphia congregation was not fully organized till some years later.

In 1728, the same year Henkel died, John Caspar Stoever, Sr., and his son, John Caspar Jr., arrived in Philadelphia. The father settled at Spottsville, Virginia and was ordained by John Christian Schulz in 1733. The next year Stoever went on a fundraising trip to Germany. He returned in 1738 but died during the voyage and was buried at sea. The son made his first home at Trappe (New Providence) and became an important forerunner of Muhlenberg. After Daniel Falckner had refused to ordain him in 1731, he was finally ordained by Schulz in 1733. Schulz had arrived in September, 1733 and had ministered to the Philadelphia congregation. It was Schulz who had united the congregations at Philadelphia, Trappe (New Providence) and New Hanover (Falckner's Swamp) into one parish, and had persuaded these congregations to send him and two delegates to London and to Germany to secure funds and a pastor. Stoever was to have charge of his ministerial work while Schulz was on this journey. Schulz never returned to America.

John Caspar Stoever, Jr. severed his connection with the Philadelphia and Trappe congregations in 1735 and made his new home, first at New Holland and later in Lebanon County. For fifty-one years, until his death in 1779, he travelled as a missionary from place to place in Eastern Pennsylvania and in Maryland and Virginia. He was not always an exemplary pastor, and seemingly lacked in deep devotion and passion for souls, elements which are so essential to a successful missionary. He was not on friendly terms with Muhlenberg and he waited twenty years before he joined the synod Muhlenberg and his adherents had organized.[189]

After Stoever had left Philadelphia in 1735, a layman named J. A. Langerfeld of Halberstadt, who had studied at Halle but was not ordained, promised to conduct services for the Phila-

---

[189] Count Zinzendorf, acting as a self-appointed judge, deposed Stoever; but Stoever and his many friends cared little for this decision.

delphia congregation every two weeks. It is not definitely known how long he continued these services. From 1737-41 Rev. Dylander of the Swedish Church held German services in the *Gloria Dei* church every Sunday. But the German congregations longed for a regular German pastor who could devote all his time to their spiritual needs. The congregations at Philadelphia, New Hanover and New Providence each numbered five hundred families.[190] In 1734 these fifteen hundred families sent two delegates, Daniel Weissiger and John Daniel Schöner, together with Rev. Schulz, to Europe to secure a Lutheran pastor through Ziegenhagen or through Halle. The congregations waited until 1739 without any apparent result,[191] and as many of the settlers had come from Hesse-Darmstadt, they then petitioned the Lutheran consistory of the Church of Hesse-Darmstadt to send them a pastor. In response, an old preacher, Valentin Kraft, came and his services were evidently accepted at Philadelphia, Germantown and Trappe. Kraft, however, brought no credentials; and yet he soon claimed to be superintendent of the Lutheran churches in Pennsylvania, and to be the head of a consistorium he had organized. After Zinzendorf's arrival, Kraft continued to serve the minority group of the Philadelphia congregation. Meanwhile the Lutherans at Falckner's Swamp had secured N. Schmidt as their preacher. His profession was that of a quack doctor and a dentist.

The coming of Count Zinzendorf in 1741 caused considerable confusion among the Lutherans in Pennsylvania. Acting under an assumed name,[192] he posed as "Evangelical Lutheran Inspector

[190] Stated in a letter published by Daniel Weissiger in May, 1734.

[191] This long delay was due to mutual misunderstanding. The appeal from the congregations for a pastor was laid before Ziegenhagen in London and Francke at Halle; but these authorities insisted on advance arrangements for support of the pastor; and such arrangements the congregations, numbering fifteen hundred families, firmly refused.

[192] He used the name Count von Thürnstein, and also Herr von Thürnstein. In a letter of 1742 to an official of Philadelphia, he signed his name "Lodewyk of Thürnstein."

LUTHERANS IN COLONIAL DAYS, 1492-1763

and Pastor at Philadelphia," though he was really a Moravian.[198] He offered his services free to the Lutheran congregation in Philadelphia and began to build a new church which was completed in 1742. He took possession of the Lutheran church record, the sacred vessels and the keys to the money-box of the congregation. As he discontinued his services in the old meeting-house in order to devote his time to Indian missions, he put Rev. John Christopher Pyrelaeus, a Moravian missionary, in his place; but the Reformed, who had used the same meeting-house, and who were much embittered against Count Zinzendorf, forcibly drove Pyrelaeus from the pulpit.[194] When the new church building was completed, Zinzendorf's adherents worshipped in it, while Kraft served the minority. Meanwhile Count Zinzendorf retained the Lutheran church record, sacred vessels and money-box until it was ordered returned by decree of court. Such was the general condition when Muhlenberg arrived, on November 25, 1742.

12. REVIEW QUESTIONS

1. What was the immediate occasion for Berkenmeyer's coming to America?
2. What contributions did Berkenmeyer make to Lutheranism in the colonies?
3. Why the Lutheran synod of 1735?
4. What was the *First Great Awakening* in America?
5. In what ways did this movement affect the Lutherans?

[198] Zinzendorf had been ordained as Bishop of the Moravians in 1737. His indifference toward doctrinal formulas and confessions of faith brought him into discredit with the Lutheran Church and the Government of Saxony. He was exiled from Saxony for more than ten years, 1736-47. It was during this exile he visited America. He schemed to form an international association of true Christians with membership in all Christian churches, including the Roman and the Greek Catholic communions, and with Herrnhut, Germany, as the general headquarters. His most formidable opponents came from the Pietistic center, the University of Halle.

[194] The Reformed disliked Zinzendorf because he had said he would no longer allow the Lutherans to worship in the same building with the Reformed.

6. What was the proportionate Lutheran population in Pennsylvania in 1748? In 1752?
7. Who ministered to these Lutherans before the coming of Muhlenberg?
8. What particular problems confronted these men and the congregations they served?
9. How do you account for the scarcity of pastors and teachers at this particular period?
10. What was Count Zinzendorf's mission to America?
11. How did his visit affect the Lutherans in Pennsylvania?
12. What was the general situation of the Lutherans in Pennsylvania and vicinity immediately before the coming of Muhlenberg?

TOPICS FOR SPECIAL STUDY

1. The first Lutheran synod in America.
2. The synodical constitution of 1735.
3. Results of Count Zinzendorf's visit to America.
4. Count Zinzendorf versus Halle.
5. Count Zinzendorf versus Muhlenberg, Philadelphia, 1742.

VII. From the Coming of Muhlenberg to the American Revolution.—The coming of Henry Melchior Muhlenberg marked a new epoch in the history of the Lutheran Church in America. He came as pastor of the Lutheran congregations at Philadelphia, New Providence and New Hanover, but his influence soon extended to all Lutherans in America. He saw it as his task, not merely to serve these congregations, but to bring order into the chaotic condition of the scattered Lutherans and to lay the foundation for organized Lutheranism. For this great task he was admirably well qualified. He was strong in body and richly endowed in heart and mind. Dignified and magnetic in his personal appearance, endowed with unusual tact and adaptability, pleasant and cordial in his relations with men, capable of speaking Latin, Dutch and English fluently besides his native German, trained in the German School of Pietism in its best days, a scholarly theologian and a firm Lutheran, and possessed with remarkable powers of organization and administration—these characteristics made Muhlenberg the *Patriarch of the Lutheran Church in America*. He brought the pioneer congregations into order, secured worthy pastors, founded

LUTHERANS IN COLONIAL DAYS, 1492-1763

schools for the education of the young, and organized Lutheran congregations into a permanent synod.[195]

1. *Years of Preparation.*—Henry Melchior Muhlenberg was born on September 6, 1711, at Eimbeck, a town of Hanover, Germany. He hailed from an ancient noble family. One of his ancestors lived near the present Mühlberg on the right hand on the Elbe River in the Merseburg district of Prussian Saxony. The mills (mühlen) erected in the vicinity gave name to the town and also to the reigning family of that town and vicinity.

He studied at one of the classical schools at Eimbeck and later at the classical school of Zellerfeld. In 1735 he entered the newly opened University of Goettingen, where he graduated in 1738. He then accepted a call to teach at the charitable institutions connected with the University of Halle. At that time these institutions had between two and three thousand scholars. Before entering upon his active duties as a regularly installed teacher of these institutions, he spent some time at the University of Jena.

The ultimate design was to send him to East India as a missionary to a newly opened field in Bengal. Meanwhile a pressing call came in 1739 that he should accept a pastorate at Grosshennersdorf in Upper Lusatia, in the eastern part of Saxony. This parish was not far from the Bohemian border, and only a few miles south of Herrnhut, the center of Moravianism and the headquarters of Count Zinzendorf. Muhlenberg accepted this call and was ordained in 1739 at Leipzig, the University of Saxony, under the sovereignty of which Grosshennersdorf stood.

For two years he labored with much success as pastor of his large parish, also acting as superintendent of an Orphan House which Baroness von Gersdorf, the sister of Count Zinzendorf's mother, had founded at Grosshennersdorf. In 1741 he paid a

---

[195] With Muhlenberg, the Falckner brothers, and Boltzius and Gronau, the errors of Pietism, cf. Chapter I, Section 6e, also crept into the fabric of Lutheranism in America.

visit to his childhood community,[196] and on his way he stopped at Halle. During this visit, Gotthelf August Francke offered him a call to "the dispersed Lutherans in Pennsylvania." After careful consideration he accepted the call, and preached his farewell sermon to the congregation at Grosshennersdorf on December 9, 1741.

On his way to America, Muhlenberg visited Rev. Frederick Michael Ziegenhagen, D.D., court-preacher at the German St. James Chapel in London. During his years in this office, 1722-76, Ziegenhagen did much to promote the best interests of Lutheranism in America. It should be kept in mind that his first English sovereign, George I (1714-27), was also the Head of the Lutheran Church in Hanover, Germany; and that George II (1727-60), was also a German in heart and language. These circumstances, coupled with his warm personal interest, made him a staunch friend of the Lutheran settlers in America. During this visit, on May 24, 1742, Ziegenhagen handed Muhlenberg the formal, official call to the Evangelical Lutheran congregations of Philadelphia, New Providence and New Hanover in Pennsylvania. Meanwhile Muhlenberg secured a clerical gown like the gowns of the clergy of the Anglican Church. This gown, which differed considerably from the official robes of the Lutheran clergy of Germany, was used by Muhlenberg during his pastorate in America.

It was arranged that on his way to his parish, he should first visit the Salzburg Lutherans in Georgia; then Boltzius was to accompany him to Pennsylvania to assist him in the beginning of his pastoral work there. He spent one hundred and two days on the packet ship which took him to Georgia. After a delightful visit with the Salzburg Lutherans in Georgia, he was accompanied by Boltzius to as far as Charleston. While waiting for a

[196] His support had been reduced considerably because of financial reverses suffered by one of his strongest backers, Baroness von Gersdorf. He went home to receive a portion of his paternal inheritance, in order that he might be able to continue his pastoral work at Grosshennersdorf. Before this, he had declined a call to another parish.

ship at Charleston, two pamphlets fell into his hands, one giving an account of some conferences Count Zinzendorf had held in Pennsylvania, and the other relating a disturbance of July 18, 1742, between Moravians, German Reformed and Lutherans in Philadelphia. Somehow, he keenly sensed the nature of some of the difficulties he might have to contend with in his new field of labor. After some waiting, he was finally able to book passage on a small sloop; and after a very stormy voyage, he arrived in Philadelphia on November 25, 1742, just as he completed the thirty-first year of his age.

2. *Early Pastoral Work in Pennsylvania.*—There was no one to welcome Muhlenberg upon his arrival at Philadelphia. Finding himself a total stranger, he settled temporarily in an English inn. He soon discovered that the majority of his congregation had joined with Count Zinzendorf, and that the minority was served by John Valentin Kraft. On his way to New Hanover (Falckner Swamp) he overheard a conversation of some Germans that Kraft had been accepted at Philadelphia, Germantown and Trappe (New Providence). He also learned that his third congregation, at New Hanover, had hired a preacher by name N. Schmidt. Such news was not encouraging to Muhlenberg.

He found the congregation at New Hanover in a confused and dismembered condition. Some adhered to Schmidt and others to Zinzendorf, while a goodly number had lost interest in the affairs of the congregation. By tact and patience, Muhlenberg soon established himself as the rightful pastor, not only in New Hanover, but also at New Providence. The situation in Philadelphia was more difficult, but Muhlenberg took his time, and soon the officers of the Philadelphia congregation also accepted him as their rightful pastor. He was kindly received by Governor Thomas and Rev. Robert Jenney, the Commissary of the Anglican Church in Pennsylvania.

Muhlenberg's greatest obstacle to early activity and usefulness was Count Zinzendorf. He exerted a peculiar influence on Lutherans in Pennsylvania, and in Philadelphia he had persuaded a number of them to follow his leadership, although there was no official relation whatever between him and the Lutheran congregation in Philadelphia. When Muhlenberg arrived, Zinzendorf sent a representative to inquire about his intentions. He sent others to invite him to a conversation with the Count. Muhlenberg responded, but instead of having a private interview as he expected, he was[197] led into a large hall where Zinzendorf had assembled a large number of his followers. Before this audience Zinzendorf, in a haughty and superior manner, examined Muhlenberg. The conversation between the two men is enclosed in *Appendix II*, in order that it may make its own impression upon the reader. After this affair, Zinzendorf left for Europe. His threats against Muhlenberg were never carried out.

Muhlenberg now launched upon a most self-sacrificing and far-reaching activity. He took as his motto: *Ecclesia Plantanda,* the Church must be planted. He began this work of planting by opening a school in each of his congregations.[198] The congregations grew, and new churches were built, and a fourth church, the congregation at Germantown, was added to his charge. But he did not confine his work to these four congregations only. Calls for help reached him from various quarters to open new fields, settle controversies, and reconcile contending parties; and he responded whenever possible. His presence inspired new life in all directions. His salary, to begin with, was pitifully meager. In his second year of service he found himself sixty pounds sterling in debt, and his clothes worn out. But he did not complain, and matters adjusted themselves. In 1745 he served notice that he was going to stay in America, for he married Anna Mary Weiser, daughter of Conrad Weiser, the famous Indian agent.

In order to keep the authorities in Germany informed as to

[197] If Muhlenberg had known Zinzendorf's intentions, he would have taken two of his church officers with him.

[198] Some of Muhlenberg's most valuable work was his careful instruction of the young. For this he was admirably well qualified by natural ability and by training.

the rapidly expanding work in America, Muhlenberg sent periodical reports to Halle. Published extracts of these reports in Germany had the calculated effect of keeping up the interest in the Fatherland for the spiritual needs of the brethren in America. A number of teachers and pastors responded to the call, "Come over and help us." Among early teachers who came to help Muhlenberg, mention may be made of J. F. Vigera, J. J. Loeser, John Nicolas Kurtz, and John H. Schaum. Among the early pastors who came to assist Muhlenberg were Peter Brunnholtz, John Frederick Handschuh and John Christopher Hartwig.[199]

3. *Organization of the Second Lutheran Synod in America, 1748.*—A most significant event in the public career of Muhlenberg was the organization of a Lutheran synod in 1748. This synod gradually gathered the scattered congregations in Pennsylvania and vicinity, and also in time absorbed the Dutch and German congregations that had been under Berkenmeyer's supervision.

Plans for a Lutheran synod comprising German and Swedish Lutherans in Pennsylvania and vicinity had been proposed in 1744 by two laymen, Peter Kock and Henry Schleydorn. But a Swedish pastor, Lawrence Thorstonsen Nyberg insisted that the synod should also include the followers of Zinzendorf, and to this Muhlenberg was definitely opposed; in consequence, the proposed synod could not be organized.

By 1748 the situation, however, was somewhat different. There was an increasingly felt need among the rapidly growing congregations for a uniform liturgy. There was also a keenly felt need for a synodical organization which could check and get rid of unworthy pastors. Furthermore, there was a request from the Tulpehocken congregation that Nicolas Kurtz be ordained and become their pastor. Finally, in August of that

[199] Among the men coming later were J. S. Gerock, J. Geo. Bager, J. D. M. Heintzelmann, Chr. Em. Schultze, J. H. Chr. Helmuth, J. Fr. Schmidt, J. L. Voigt, J. A. Krug, J. A. Weygand, etc.

year, the new St. Michael's Church in Philadelphia was to be dedicated. The general situation seemed to favor the organization of a Lutheran synod, and Muhlenberg was ready to take advantage of this opportunity.

On August 25, 1748, Kurtz was ordained[200] and the church was dedicated.[201] On the day following the synod was organized. It consisted of six pastors and twenty-four lay delegates, together with the entire council of the Philadelphia congregation. The pastors were Muhlenberg, Brunnholtz, Handschuh and Kurtz, with Hartwig of New York and Provost Sandin of the Swedish Church as advisory members.[202] The lay delegates represented ten congregations. Muhlenberg was elected president of the synod.

The chief business of this first synodical meeting was to examine and adopt a common liturgy which Muhlenberg, Brunnholtz and Handschuh had prepared in April of that same year. Using a liturgy of the Savoy Church of London as a foundation, they had also drawn from a number of Saxon and North German liturgies familiar to Muhlenberg. The product was essentially the "Common Service" of the present day. The liturgy was ratified by the synod, but it was not printed; each

---

[200] At this ordination Kurtz had to obligate himself to teach in his congregation "nothing, whether publicly or privately, but what harmonizes with the Word of God and the Confessions of the Evangelical Lutheran Church."

[201] At the dedication of St. Michael's Church, the speaker called to mind "that the foundation stones of this church had been laid with the intention that in it the Evangelical Lutheran doctrine, according to the foundations of the Prophets and Apostles, and the unaltered Augsburg Confession and all the other Symbolical Books should be taught."

[202] Men like John Caspar Stoever, Jr., Tobias Wagner, Christian Streiter and J. C. Andreae were not invited because of their antagonistic spirit. The record of the synod has the following explanation: "1. They, without reason, decry us (the members of the synod) as Pietists; 2. Are not sent and have neither an internal nor an external call; 3. Are unwilling to observe a uniform order of service with us, each following the ceremonies of his country; 4. An experience of six years had taught Muhlenberg that their object was nothing but bread; 5. They were subject to no consistory and gave no account of their office."

pastor making a copy for himself. After several years of use, this liturgy was sent to Halle in 1754 for approval.[203] This common liturgy was important because it promoted the proper character of the public services, the administration of the sacraments, and the unification of the congregations. Cf. *Appendix III*.

The synodical organizaton was known at first as the "United Pastors," and their parishes as the "United Congregations." Today it is called the Ministerium of Pennsylvania. The synod held regular conferences up to the year 1754 and then there was an apparent lull, for the next recorded convention was held in 1760. Muhlenberg was at this time exceedingly busy, responding to calls from far and near to come and help, and this may in part account for the temporary inactivity of the synod. At the instigation of Provost Wrangel of the Swedish Church, synodical activity was resumed in 1760.

No formulated constitution was at first adopted by the synod. The *Synodical Constitution* was developed gradually in unwritten form. Later being committed to writing, it was formally adopted in 1781. This constitution, which became the prototype of many later synodical organizations, contained the following confessional obligation, that "every minister professes that he holds the Word of God and our Symbolical Books in doctrine and life." A copy of this constitution is enclosed in the present volume as *Appendix V*. In 1738 the synod granted license "for preaching and the baptism of children" to candidates who made the signed promise "to preach the Word of God in its purity, according to Law and Gospel, as it is explained in its chief points in the Augsburg Confession and the other Symbolical Books."[204]

[203] They could not adopt the Swedish liturgy because so many of the people concerned considered singing of collects as papal. They could not very well favor any particular German liturgy, since practically every city had one of its own. The liturgy of the Savoy Church in London, used as a basis, was a translation of the order in use among Lutherans in Amsterdam.

[204] The revised constitution of 1792 made no allusion to any Lutheran symbolical book. Candidates at their ordination were required "to preach the Word of God in its purity according to the Law and the Gospel."

212   THE LUTHERAN CHURCH IN AMERICA

Adopting the synodical representative government of the Church was the best thing that could happen under existing circumstances. Each congregation concerned was made to feel that it was an organic part of the Church body. Through its lay delegates, each congregation concerned had a voice in the welfare of the Church as a whole and of its constituent parts. Synodical organization, properly used, would help to preserve the Church from dangerous disintegrating influences from without, and disturbing forces from within.[205]

4. *Constitution for St. Michael's Lutheran Church, Philadelphia, 1762.*—The Lutheran congregation in Philadelphia had increased considerably in membership, due largely to recent immigration. The nature of this membership is vividly pictured by Muhlenberg in these words, "Before the second generation grew up the congregation consisted of all imaginable varieties of Germans, from Hesse-Darmstadt, Hamburg, Dantzig, Mecklenburg, Holstein, Denmark, Hanover, Würtemberg, Zweibrücken, Durlach, Baireuth, Saxony, Brandenburg, Frankfort, Palatinate, Alsace, Frankia, Westphalia, etc., etc. And since every province, town and village in the German empire has something of its own and special variations and turns in the church melodies, and as some sing slowly, while others rapidly, each one thought that his manner and custom was the most proper, and made most strenuous efforts to carry through his melody and to teach the others to keep time."

This condition prevailed, not only in public worship, but in church government as well. This led to a most unfortunate friction in the congregation, and Rev. J. Fr. Handschuh, the pastor, was unable to iron out the difficulties. An urgent appeal was made to Muhlenberg to return and become the pastor of the congregation, in order that peace and order might be restored. He came in 1761, and due to his influence, the con-

[205] As will be seen in the next section, the synodical form of church government exerted some influence upon those who prepared the Constitution of the United States of America.

LUTHERANS IN COLONIAL DAYS, 1492-1763

gregation unanimously resolved to introduce a new congregational order or constitution. In consequence Muhlenberg, with the advice and cooperation of Dr. Wrangel, entered upon one of the most important works of his life. He was fully aware that it would become the model of similar constitutions for Lutheran churches in America. In the framing of this constitution, Muhlenberg incorporated much of his own personal experience and observation in church work, and he also benefited by the experiences of the Swedish and the Dutch Lutherans, and he also paid careful attention to the organization of the Lutheran churches in London.

This model church constitution was ratified by the congregation on October 18, 1762, under the title *Fundamental Articles*. It became the basic model for a vast number of German Lutheran congregations, including those of the General Synod. This document and the *Articles of Accord* which the "United Pastors" had agreed to when the Ministerium of Pennsylvania was organized in 1748, were evidently examined by Thomas Jefferson. It is known that Jefferson visited Dr. J. F. Schmidt, pastor of St. Michael's Lutheran church in Philadelphia, some time in May, 1776, and that he stayed with the Lutheran pastor from 4 o'clock in the afternoon of one day till noon of the next day. He spent most of this time in Dr. Schmidt's study. It is, of course, impossible to tell whether or not this visit had any influence upon the drafting of the Declaration of Independence. A copy of the constitution of the St. Michael's Lutheran Church of Philadelphia is enclosed in the present volume as *Appendix IV*.

The following principles were embodied in this constitution: (1) The pastor was pledged to "declare the Word of God publicly, in a pure, plain, solid and edifying manner, according to the foundation of the Apostles and Prophets, and the unaltered Augsburg Confession." (2) The local congregation was invested with the perpetual right to elect its own pastor and officers. (3) The government of the local congregation was not direct, but through the *council*, which consisted of the elected pastor and officers. (4) Synodical advice was provided for in case a pastor was to be called or deposed.

5. *A Native Lutheran Clergy.*—Muhlenberg and others sensed the need of a well trained native Lutheran clergy. He responded to this need by securing in 1749 forty-nine acres of land in Philadelphia as a campus for a school, a seminary and a home for the aged. But the urgent demand upon his services elsewhere forced the seminary project, temporarily, out of the focus of attention; and later war interfered, so the project could not be completed in the life time of Muhlenberg. Meanwhile Muhlenberg, Provost Wrangel, J. C. Kunze and J. H. Ch. Helmuth trained theological candidates in their respective parsonages.

Jacob van Buskirk of the Hackensack congregation in New Jersey was the first Lutheran born in America to devote himself to theological study. He studied first under Rev. J. A. Weygand in New York and later under Muhlenberg. William Graaf and William Kurtz also studied under Muhlenberg. Provost Wrangel trained Peter Muhlenberg, a son of the Patriarch, and also Daniel Kuhn and Christian Streit. Two other sons of Muhlenberg trained in Halle and were ordained in 1770.

This small beginning was very significant. The colonial period was soon to pass, and the people were soon to be moulded into a new, organic unity from which the ties to Europe were more or less to be severed. In such times it was essential for the Lutheran Church to have a clergy that saw America with American eyes, and spoke of America in terms understood by the American people.

6. *Muhlenberg's Views and Contributions.*—Muhlenberg was trained at Halle, the very center of German Pietism. For a discussion of historic pietism, see Chapter I, Section 6 of the present volume. He gave his hearty consent to the views and principles pronounced at Halle, and yet he differed somewhat from the traditional Pietists. His stress on infant baptism and catechetical instruction was similar to that of Lutheran Orthodoxy,

while his emphasis on personal religion was that of Lutheran Pietism. He minimized the theoretical and the polemical and stressed the practical, warm-hearted and devout in Christianity.

At his ordination on August 24, 1739, he had to pledge himself before the theological faculty of the University of Leipzig that he would assume the responsibility of "teaching the Gospel and administering the Sacraments according to the rule given in the writings of the Prophets and Apostles, the sum of which is contained in these three symbols, the Apostolic, Nicene and Athanasian, in the Augsburg Confession laid before Charles V, A.D. 1530, in the Apology of the same, in Dr. Luther's Large and Small Catechisms, in the Articles subscribed to in the Schmalkald Convention, and in the Formula of Concord."[206]

In response to certain accusers, Muhlenberg replied, "I defy Satan and every lying spirit to lay at my door anything which contradicts the teaching of our Apostles or the Symbolical Books. I have often said and written that I have found neither error, nor mistake, nor any defect in our Evangelical doctrine, based as it is, on the Apostles and the Prophets, and exhibited in our Symbolical Books." He accepted the standards of the Lutheran Church of the sixteenth century without reservation, though it is difficult to reconcile this with the fact that he also subscribed to the principles of Pietism.[207] He perpetuated a traditional Lutheranism in worship, in observance of the church-year and its festivals, in the use of the Gospel and Epistle Lessons, in the

[206] Translation of his certificate of ordination by W. J. Mann in *Lutheran Church Review*, Vol. VI, p. 28.

[207] "Pietism was indeed the form under which in those years warm-hearted godliness almost exclusively existed in Germany. Those who were animated by it knew its strong points by experience, and, as may be expected, were rather shortsighted as to its weak ones. It was the living source from which then proceeded most works of Christian charity, missionary enterprises, care of the orphans, the spreading of the Bible among the masses of the people, and instruction of the neglected. To this school, if we may so call it, Muhlenberg belonged. He could not absolutely escape the influence of its weaker points; its strong ones never found a worthier or a more energetic and successful representative." Mann in *Life and Times of Muhlenberg*, p. 393.

rite of Baptism and Confirmation, in the preparatory service for the Lord's Supper connected with the confession of sins and absolution. He introduced a warm-hearted, devout, practical Lutheranism with a tendency toward unionism.[208] He cultivated fraternal intercourse and intimate fellowship with other Lutherans, and even with the Episcopalians and the Reformed. On several occasions he exchanged pulpits with non-Lutheran pastors, and George Whitefield preached in his church. Muhlenberg and Provost Wrangel even considered a union of Lutherans with Anglicans. These considerations were likely influenced by the close relation at that time between the Lutheran and the Anglican churches in London.[209]

Muhlenberg's great contributions to Lutheranism in America were in the gathering of the scattered congregations into an organic unity; in formulating a common liturgy; in preparing a model constitution for a Lutheran congregation in America; in preparing a model synodical constitution; and also, in 1782, supervising the preparation of an American Lutheran Hymn Book. He also infused a warm Evangelical spirit among Lutherans.

13. REVIEW QUESTIONS

1. What qualifications did Muhlenberg have for leadership?
2. What training and experience did he have before coming to America?
3. What circumstances led to his coming to America?
4. What immediate problems faced him in his parish in Pennsylvania?
5. In what ways did he maintain contact with the mother-church?
6. Why was Count Zinzendorf such a formidable opponent?
7. Why the Lutheran synod of 1748?
8. What did this synod contribute to Lutheranism?
9. What particular contribution did Muhlenberg make to the local congregation?

---

[208] He carefully avoided, however, to build so-called union churches with the Reformed. Neither Muhlenberg nor his co-laborers wished a general union of the various denominations.

[209] Lutheran ministers frequently went to London to receive Episcopal ordination, as did Muhlenberg's oldest son, Peter. This was done, however, because the candidates concerned were to work in Southern Colonies where only Episcopal ordination was recognized by law.

LUTHERANS IN COLONIAL DAYS, 1492-1763

10. Why a native Lutheran clergy?
11. What contributions did Muhlenberg make to Lutheranism in America?
12. What was the status of Lutheranism in America at the close of the colonial era?

TOPICS FOR SPECIAL STUDY

1. The Lutheran synod of 1748.
2. Origin of "Common Service."
3. Constitution of the Pennsylvania Ministerium.
4. Constitution for St. Michael's Church, Philadelphia, 1762.
5. A native Lutheran clergy.
6. Muhlenberg's religious views.
7. Muhlenberg's contributions to America.
8. What the Lutheran Church had at the close of the colonial era.

VIII. Early Lutheran Education.—The Lutheran Church has always been a teaching Church. Luther's new theory of individual judgment and individual responsibility called for an active individual participation in and responsibility for the conduct of government and church, and this again involved a general education. Lutheran pastors, school-teachers and churches in colonial America tried, despite depressing circumstances, to perpetuate Luther's ideal; in fact, they did more than their share in helping to mould an intelligent citizenship based on sound morality and religion. In order to appreciate this important contribution properly, early Lutheran education must be studied as a phase of colonial education in general.

The school everywhere in colonial America arose as a child of the Church. European educational ideas, schools and types of instruction were transplanted by the various groups of immigrants. Gradually three types of educational practice prevailed. New England developed a system of state-supported common schools, English Latin grammar schools and several colleges for both religious and civic ends. The Middle Colonies developed a parochial school system which placed the schools under the direct church control of each denomination. Such schools were dominated by church purposes. A third type was introduced by the well-to-do planters of Virginia and other Southern Colonies. Children of the upper and middle classes attended small private pay-schools, or, they were sent to England to get their education. Colonial society of these colonies felt no obligation to provide an education for children of the poorer classes. Elementary education for them was left to philanthropic and religious effort.

Massachusetts founded Harvard College in 1636, and Connecticut founded Yale College in 1702 to perpetuate learning and to insure an educated ministry for the Congregational Church. William and Mary College was founded in Virginia in 1693 for the purpose of educating Anglican ministers. Several Latin grammar schools were established to prepare students for entrance requirements to college, but the attendance in all these schools was small in colonial days. Under the hard pioneer conditions, many communities even neglected the proper religious education of the children. Interest in religion frequently declined almost to the vanishing point. But the Great Awakening furnished a new stimulus. Six additional colleges were founded: Princeton as a Presbyterian institution in 1746, the Academy and College (University) of Pennsylvania in 1753-55 on a nondenominational basis, King's College (Columbia University) in 1754 as an Anglican institution, Rhode Island College (Brown University) by the Baptists in 1764, Rutgers College, New Jersey, by the Dutch Reformed in 1766, and Dartmouth College, New Hampshire, by the Congregationalists in 1769. Numerous parochial schools were established, the common school was put on a working basis, and the English Latin grammar school was gradually replaced by the American Academy with its more practical studies. What contribution did the Lutherans make?

Luther set forth his ideas on education in his *Letter to the Mayors of all the Cities of Germany in behalf of Christian Schools* (1524), and in his *Sermon on the Duty of Sending Children to School* (1530). In the first of these he states, "Were there neither soul, heaven, nor hell, it would still be necessary to have schools for the sake of affairs here below. The world has need of educated men and women to the end that men may govern the country properly; and women may properly bring up their children, care for their domestics, and direct the affairs of the household." He maintained, as did the other Protestant Reformers, that the child belongs first to God, then to the parents, and then to the State; and that the chief responsibility of their education rested on Church and parents. He summoned three agencies to aid in this general educational reform, namely the family, the Church, and the State.

A summary of Luther's general program of education may be of interest in connection with this study. He maintained that education must be based on the Bible which is the standard for faith and conduct. Parents or the home are responsible for the initial instruction of the young as based on the *Catechism*. The common school education is to be for boys as well as for girls, and with compulsory attendance. Instruction must be adopted to suit the need of the child, and the teacher must be well trained for his work. Education is to be supported by the State. The elementary course of study shall include singing, reading, writing, arithmetic, physical education, nature study and history. Arrangements shall be made for the establishment of secondary schools where provisions are made for the study of Latin, Hebrew, Greek, rhetoric, dialectic, history, science, mathematics, music and gymnastics. University training shall be provided for the higher service in Church and State. It may be needless to add that Luther's progressive proposals were entirely too advanced for his time. The ideal of supplying an education for all could not be generally realized until the nineteenth and the twentieth centuries.

The schools of Germany, Holland and Scandinavia were largely influenced by the Reformation. Lutherans regarded it as a Christian duty to build and maintain schools where the young might be taught to read and to understand the basic facts in the Bible. Lutheran congregations saw it as their duty to engage a teacher as well as a minister, and to provide both with a stated salary and a home. When the Lutherans came to America, they tried to follow the same plan, as far as conditions permitted. Wherever conditions permitted, a Lutheran congregation would usually build and maintain a school with an approved and duly elected teacher.

When Governor John Printz came to New Sweden in 1643, he had specific instructions from his government to see to it that "all men, and especially the youths, be well instructed in all the parts of Christianity." To begin with, the Swedish pastors also acted as teachers to the colonists, but as the colony became more established, the records indicate that schoolmasters were employed. Mention may be made of such men as Hans Stahl, Swen Colsbert, Arvid Herboom, John Goding and Charles Christopher Springer. In their official correspondence, the colonists of New Sweden frequently petitioned the home government to send them Bibles, Catechisms, primers and hymn books. These colonists were hardy folk, inured to labor, active, skilled in many homely arts and crafts, intensely patriotic and deeply and sincerely religious. The Swedish-Finnish colony dominated the Delaware Valley until the coming of William Penn in 1682.

It must be admitted that the early educational efforts in New Sweden were comparatively weak. The congregations were widely scattered, and there was a want of suitable text books. Some of the Swedish pastors, of high-church attitude and from aristocratic families, did not care to teach and did not want to remain long in a colonial congregation. But by 1700 there was marked progress in the matter of education.

Dutch and German Lutheran settlers also had a high respect for general and higher education. The majority of the male settlers could read and write,[210] and the large number of books

[210] Considering the prevailing illiteracy in Europe at that time, the literary of the Germans was relatively high. Seventy-five per cent of the males above sixteen could write; cf. *Pennsylvania German Magazine*, VIII, p. 306. Furthermore, seventy-four per cent of the male immigrants in the first half of the eighteenth century were able to sign the ship reg-

imported indicates their fondness of reading. While their education was neither broad nor deep, they took pride in having a pastor whom they could consider a learned man. The learned Rosicrucian Society on the Wissahickon was held in very high esteem by the people who knew of them, and many of the children in the community came to the Tabernacle where they were taught to pray, sing, and read the Bible. Daniel Falckner, one of the members of this society, established the Lutheran School at Manatawny in 1705. Another member, Justus Falckner, published the first Lutheran text book in America in 1708 entitled, "Fundamental Instruction upon certain Chief Prominent Articles of the Veritable, Undefiled, Beautiful Christian Doctrine, founded upon the basis of the Apostles and Prophets of which Jesus Christ is the cornerstone, expounded in plain but edifying questions and answers."

Both Lutheran and Reformed German colonists were deeply interested in a general education of the young. From Germany they had a well developed school system of elementary education, but it was extremely difficult for them to make practical application of this system in the new environment. Some of the difficulties may be enumerated as follows: (1) There was a dire need of suitable teachers. (2) General poverty among the settlers made it difficult, and at times impossible, to erect and maintain parochial schools. (3) The various religious groups in the community frequently refused to cooperate in the building and maintaining of schools; the "sects" refused to be with the "church people," and vice versa. (4) Since the poor German immigrants usually had to buy the less expensive land, far out toward the frontier, the distance to school was too far for younger children. (5) As there was no compulsory school attendance, children were often kept home to help with the planting and the harvesting of the crops. (6) The task of subjugating

---

isters, while for the period from 1751 to 1774, eighty-five per cent of the male immigrants were able to write. Cf. Maurer, *Early Lutheran Education in Pennsylvania*, pp. 40-41.

a continent was so intensely absorbing that religious and educational interests at times almost passed entirely out of the focus of attention.

The Lutheran congregation in New York City did not open a Lutheran school for more than a century. This was partly due to the opposition of the Dutch who compelled Lutheran children by law to attend Reformed church-schools. Even by 1730 the school teachers were prohibited from teaching children the Lutheran catechism. The first permanent Lutheran school was opened in 1753, during the pastorate of John A. Weygand.

Palatine immigrants established schools and churches at the same time. West Camp had a school house in 1710, with Johan Melchior Dauzweber as teacher. Newburgh had a school in 1708. Constant uncertainty and interference, due to wars with the Indians and the French, together with a lack of pastors and teachers, seriously arrested the progress of schools during the middle of the century.

A number of Lutheran parochial schools existed in the American Colonies prior to 1742,[211] but it was the merit of Henry Melchior Muhlenberg to become the patriarch, not only of the colonial Lutheran churches, but also of the colonial Lutheran schools. He established a number of parochial schools and instigated the establishment of many more; he established a uniform system for these schools; he secured suitable teachers; he urged the people to support these schools; he made frequent visitations, examining the pupils and encouraging the teachers; and he gave

[211] Besides the schools established by Swedish and Dutch Lutherans, there were at least twenty-seven Lutheran congregations in existence in Pennsylvania by 1740. They are enumerated and located on a map published in 1898 at the Sesquicentennial of the Lutheran Ministerium of Pennsylvania.

Dr. Schmucker says, "Each congregation formed in Pennsylvania, established a congregational school alongside the Church at the earliest possible period after its formation. This is a rule so absolute as to scarcely have exception. Even before a pastor could be obtained, a school was built, and the schoolmaster conducted Sunday services and read a sermon." Winston, *The Old Eagle School, Tredyfrin*, p. 22.

LUTHERANS IN COLONIAL DAYS, 1492-1763

general direction to the entire educational program of the congregations with which he came in contact. The German Lutheran school at Philadelphia became the largest Lutheran parochial school in colonial America. Other flourishing Lutheran school centers were at New Hanover, New Providence, Germantown, Lancaster, York, and an English school started by the Swedish pastor, Dr. Charles M. Wrangel, in one of his congregations.

In communities where Lutheran or Reformed schools had not been established, or where the existing schools were unable to accommodate all the pupils who applied for admission, the Society for the Propagation of the Gospel in Foreign Parts[212] frequently established so-called charity-schools. The charity-school idea originated in England, where the first school of this type was founded in London in 1680. From England the charity-school idea was transmitted to the Anglican Colonies in America where it became a fixed institution in New Jersey, Delaware, Pennsylvania, Maryland, and to a lesser degree in some of the regions further south. Seeing that neither the Lutheran nor the Reformed churches were able to erect and maintain enough schools to take care of the great tide of immigrants, men like Henry Melchior Muhlenberg and Michael Schlatter were for some time kindly disposed toward these charity-schools. However, opposition soon developed both among the leaders and the German populace. They objected to the selfish propaganda motives which apparently actuated the promoters; they revolted against the seeming reproach to the Germans that they were considered unable to educate their own children; and the German populace disliked the use of English as the medium of instruction, as this, they felt, involved the integrity of their own language and nationality.[213]

[212] This Society was founded in England in 1701 for the purpose of extending the work of the Anglican Church abroad, supply ministers, schools and schoolmasters; train the children to read, write and know the Catechism; make them loyal Church members and train them for good citizenship.

[213] About twelve charity-schools were established in Pennsylvania dur-

There was an urgent demand for a well-trained native Lutheran clergy. Sensing this need, Muhlenberg secured in 1749 forty-nine acres of land in Philadelphia as a campus for a school, a seminary and a home for aged. Shortly before the outbreak of the War of the Revolution, Muhlenberg and Wrangel planned a seminary to train ministers for German and Swedish Lutheran churches. But war interfered and the project was dropped. By 1765 Muhlenberg had a considerable sum of money at his disposal for a "Hoher Schule," but he did not consider the sum large enough for the establishment of a worthy institution. In 1775 John Christopher Kunze, with the aid of Muhlenberg, tried to establish a seminary in Philadelphia, but the project seemed premature.

Meanwhile Muhlenberg, Provost Wrangel, and two Lutheran professors at the University of Pennsylvania, John Christopher Kunze and Justus H. Chr. Helmuth, prepared young men for the ministry. A number of students attended seminaries of other denominations, with a special preference for Princeton. Franklin College, Lancaster, Pennsylvania, furnished a few candidates for the Lutheran ministry, including H. A. Muhlenberg and Benjamin Keller. But it was evident that the way to secure spiritual leaders from the native ranks was to establish Lutheran seminaries.

A small beginning was made in 1797 when Hartwick Seminary was founded. This seminary was named after Rev. John Christopher Hartwig, who left his estate valued at $16,000, to found an institution for the training of missionaries to the Indians and ministers of the Gospel. This institution consisted for a number of years of a preparatory department located near Cooperstown, Otsego County, New York, a college department

---

ing the years 1753-63, but general opposition in the communities where these schools were located caused a lack of attendance, and these particular charity-schools came to an end in 1763. However, the charity-school idea was revived later, and the Pennsylvania constitution of 1790 made special provision for a state charity-school system.

at Albany, New York, and an embryo seminary in New York City. Each department had but one teacher. Rev. J. F. Ernst was the teacher in the preparatory department; Rev. A. T. Braun, a former Roman Catholic missionary to the Indians, was in charge of the classical instruction at Albany; and Dr. John Christopher Kunze was the constituted theological professor. These three departments were later consolidated, and the first seminary building was erected in 1815 near Cooperstown, the school being formally opened in 1816.

It may seem surprising that the Lutherans, with their high regard for education and learning, should not establish a single Lutheran institution of higher learning in colonial America. Hartwick Seminary, of course, belongs to the National Era. The reasons, however, are quite obvious. (1) After New Sweden had been taken by the British in 1664, the settlers lost some of their initiative, and a number of them returned to Sweden. Those who remained used Swedish exclusively in their instruction and also at their services, and this drove many over to the Episcopalians. (2) The Dutch Lutherans were not only quite scattered, but they were rapidly eclipsed by the tides of incoming German immigrants. (3) Since the majority of the early German settlers came from the war-torn sections of Germany, they were generally poor. It took time before they could acquire material prosperity in America, and by the time they were ready to build and maintain institutions of higher learning, the country was thrown into the convulsions of a revolution.

Meanwhile, the Lutherans in colonial America did more than their proportionate share to educate their young for intelligent church membership and citizenship. When the time came that the American Colonies were drawn into the Revolutionary War, the Lutherans took an extensive and honorable part in the great struggle for independence, as will be seen in the next chapter.

IX. Lutherans in Canada.—Lutheran immigration and the establishment of a Lutheran Church in Canada should not be studied as isolated movements, but rather as an integral part of the general colonization and establishment of Canada. In consequence, some space will be given to the early history of Canada.

The Dominion of Canada has one of the largest areas, and at the same time one of the lowest densities of population of any country in the world. The area is divided into nine provinces and several territories which together form a federation under the British Crown. Canada is the only country in the world to recognize by law two official languages: English and French. How Lutheran immigrants in the Colonial Era came to this vast portion of the "New World" and established themselves, will be briefly considered in this section.

1. *The French-Canadian Era, 1534-1759.*—Scandinavian adventurers discovered North America about the year 1000 A.D., but they founded no permanent settlements. In 1497 John Cabot made an expedition in search of the North-West Passage and discovered Labrador and Newfoundland. The following year his brother, Sebastian Cabot, sailed up Davis Strait. Fisheries were formed along the coast of Newfoundland, and an effort was made in 1610 to establish a regular settlement, but the attempt failed, and the center of interest shifted to the St. Lawrence Valley.

In 1534 the Frenchman Jacques Cartier explored the St. Lawrence with a view of reaching the Pacific. He took possession of Labrador in the name of his sovereign, Francis I, and in 1535-36 he ascended the St. Lawrence as far as Montreal. The first permanent settlement in Canada was established 1608 in Quebec under the lead of Samuel Champlain, the "father of French colonization in Canada." The increase in French colonists was slow, however, and the stream of immigrants flowed westward toward the Mississippi. The plan of a French colonial empire in North America and why it did not materialize has been discussed on pages 118-119.

French colonists were usually followed by Roman Catholic priests who established mission stations and built convents and schools. Three Recollect (Franciscan) priests settled in 1615 in

LUTHERANS IN COLONIAL DAYS, 1492-1763

Quebec and formed the first regular establishment in Canada. These priests laid a splendid foundation for successful missionary activity among Indians. Jesuit priests arrived in 1625. They not only usurped the place held so worthily by the Recollect priests, but brought pressure to bear in France to prevent further emigration of Recollects to Canada. In consequence, Quebec was but a little more than a Jesuit mission by the middle of the seventeenth century.

Meanwhile Jens Eriksen Munck, in service of King Christian IV of Denmark, headed an expedition of 1619-20 which tried to find the coveted Northwest Passage to the gold and spices of India. Passing through the Hudson Strait, they entered the bay where Henry Hudson died nine years previous. Captain Munck landed at the mouth of the Churchill River, in the present Province of Keewatin, Canada, and took possession of the land in the name of his king, and called the land *Nova Dania*. The expedition settled there for the winter. Their spiritual needs were taken care of by Rev. Rasmus Jensen, who very likely was the first Lutheran clergyman to conduct a Lutheran divine service in North America. Gloom soon settled down on this happy expedition. All but the captain and two companions succumbed to the dreadful disease of scurvy. These three returned to Denmark in the smaller of the two vessels of the expedition, and *Nova Dania* was never claimed by Denmark.

The French settlements in Canada were generally closed against all save Roman Catholic immigrants. Admiral Coligny, wishing to establish a Protestant French empire in North America, procured a concession from Charles IX, and in 1564 planted a colony of Huguenots in Florida, on the banks of the May River, near St. John's Bluff. But in Canada the Huguenots were not allowed to settle after 1627. The Edict of Nantes, published in 1598 and revoked in 1685, gave the Huguenots of France freedom of conscience and practical freedom of worship, but Huguenots in *New France* derived no benefit from this religious toleration in the homeland, after 1627.

Jesuit leaders promoted a strong ecclesiastical control which, during the French regime, reached its zenith about 1672. Jesuit influence was increased by the policy of appointing government officials for the colony who were acceptable to the Society of Jesus. But the struggle in France between the Gallican or National party and the Ultramontane or Papal party also affected the affairs of Quebec. Gallican influence gradually limited the ecclesiastical control so that the colonial government, instead of being a handmaid of the Church, gradually became the master. Transfer to British control in 1763 was, therefore, not altogether unwelcome by certain French-Canadian church leaders.

François Xavier de Laval-Montmorency was appointed vicar apostolic of New France in 1657. His nomination by the pope, and not by the king, was a triumph for papacy. Protests from the Archbishop of Rouen and from the parliaments of Rouen and Paris at this exclusion of Canada from the Concordat, proved ineffective. Upon his arrival in Canada, Laval succeeded in ousting the Sulpician Vicar-general, Queylus, appointee of the Archbishop of Rouen.

Laval was determined to uphold papacy at the expense of the Gallican church. He turned his attention to the establishment of a bishopric at Quebec, and he influenced Louis XIV to send the proper petition to the pope. The king sent the petition in 1664, but he insisted that the new diocese should be dependent upon the Archbishop of Rouen, while the Propaganda insisted it should be an immediate dependency of Rome. A compromise was finally reached, and on October 1, 1674, the Papal Court established the See of Quebec. The right of nomination was vested in the king, and the bishopric became directly dependent upon Rome.

Canada was conquered by England in 1759. At that time the total population in New France was about 65,000, or about one-twentieth of the estimated population of the thirteen British colonies. In the Treaty of Paris in 1763, France ceded to Great

Britain all of Canada and all of her claims in North America east of the Mississippi River. This defeat of the French proved to be a great victory for Roman Catholicism. The Quebec Act of 1774,[214] and the Constitutional Act of 1791,[215] vested in the Roman Catholic Church in Canada a control which is without a parallel in Roman Catholicism.

Joseph Octave Plessis, Bishop of Quebec from 1806, became the first Canadian archbishop in 1819. An Apostolic Delegation was established in Canada in 1889, and from 1910 the title has been the Apostolic Delegation for Canada and Newfoundland.

The French Canadian is of a traditionalistic and conservative type of mind. The French language, controlled by the Church, has proved an effective weapon of isolation, and a warding off of modernism in every form. French literature has been carefully censored so that only ideas in complete harmony with the Church have been allowed to come to the reading French-Canadian public. The use of two official languages, English and French, has proved a barrier to spiritual understanding and sympathy and has given rise to a difficult educational problem in communities where instruction is desired in both languages.

2. *The British Era, 1759 to Present.*—The conquest by the British in 1759, and the Treaty of Paris of 1763, opened up Canada for Protestant immigration. The nature of this immigration was somewhat different, however, from that of the earlier immigration to the Thirteen Colonies. Puritan immigration to New England was prompted by religious motives, or by the desire for freedom to worship God according to the dictates of conscience, while the early immigration to Canada was largely

[214] The Quebec Act of 1774 has been called "the Magna Charta of the French-Canadian race." It stipulated "free exercise of Religion of the Church of Rome, subject to the King's Supremacy."

[215] The Constitutional Act of 1791 recognized the fact that there were two separate races or nations in Canada which could not at first unite. Provisions were consequently made for a division of Canada into Upper and Lower Canada, each with a separate government. Lower Canada became subject to French-Canadian rule.

economic and political. The 60,000 Loyalists, who migrated to Canada after the Revolutionary War, came because they preferred to remain under British rule; and other early Protestant settlers came to Canada rather than to the United States, because they preferred the British connection and Monarchical government. As a general consequence, Protestant Canadian character became rooted in traditionalism and conservatism, while American character became more rooted in idealism and progressivism.

Sir Humphrey Gilbert paved the way for British colonization of Canada in 1583 when he took formal possession of Newfoundland in the name of the King of England. All during the French-Canadian era, Newfoundland remained nominally under British control. Nova Scotia, or Acadia, "with all its ancient boundaries," was ceded to England by the Treaty of Utrecht in 1713, but little provision was made for an early Protestant settlement of either Newfoundland or Nova Scotia. The first permanent Protestant settlement in Canada was made when Lord Cornwallis founded Halifax in 1749. Four years later Halifax had a population of approximately 5000 people.

3. *First Permanent Lutheran Settlement.*—German Lutherans who came to Halifax about the year 1750 formed the first permanent Lutheran settlement in British North America. A Lutheran congregation existed in Halifax by 1752, for it was so recognized in a will. In 1761 St. George's Lutheran Church was built in Halifax.

Meanwhile a group of these Lutherans moved from Halifax to Lunenberg, beginning in 1753, and a Lutheran congregation was soon organized. Already in 1755, Henry Melchior Muhlenberg had a call from these Lutheran congregations at Halifax and Lunenberg to come and serve them as pastor. Muhlenberg considered the call seriously, but finally declined. Meanwhile Rev. Daniel Schumacher served the parish for a brief period. Later it was served by Rev. Bernard Michael Hausihl, after he left New York during the Revolutionary War. Descendants of

LUTHERANS IN COLONIAL DAYS, 1492-1763

these early pioneers form the nucleus of the present Lutheran Synod of Nova Scotia. Their subsequent history belongs to another chapter.

X. Retrospect.—In order to get a fairly correct perspective of the status of the Lutheran Church in Colonial America about the year 1763, it is necessary to know something of the national backgrounds of its membership.

In the fifteenth and sixteenth centuries, the chief political trend in Western Europe was toward the formation of nations with strong, centralized governments. Feudalism broke down, and the royal power tended to become absolute. New national languages and literatures were also coming into being. At the beginning of the sixteenth century the four great European powers were England, France and Spain with strong national governments, and Germany where a tendency toward national unity was evident. In the seventeenth century Holland and Sweden were added to the great powers of Europe.

England was the first country to become a compact nationality. The feudal lords were ruined and the king was free to rule as he pleased, under parliamentary forms. The English king had been supreme head of the English Church ever since William the Conqueror in 1066. A new estate, the commons, had had a voice in the English government ever since 1265 when the House of Commons was formed. The middle class constituted the main prop of the English throne.

In France the feudal lords were forced to yield to a strong royal government, supported by the commons who had had representatives in the National Assembly ever since 1302.

Germany had a political organization similar to the American union under the Articles of Confederation. By the close of the Hohenstaufen period (1138-1254), Germany was divided into about three hundred virtually independent states, but seven of the leading princes had usurped the power to elect king. These seven electors, four of whom were secular and three of whom were prince-bishops, exercised a strong influence over Germany until the Holy Roman Empire was dissolved by Napoleon in 1806.

The Netherlands renounced their allegiance to the Spanish crown on July 26, 1581. Their independence was finally acknowledged at the Peace of Westphalia in 1648. The establishment of the Dutch Republic had great political significance, because Holland was in the seventeenth century the foremost champion of the cause of political freedom against Bourbon despotism. It was William, Prince of Orange and Stadtholder of Holland, and his wife, Mary, the daughter of King James of England, who ascended the throne of England in 1688.

Sweden in the first half of the seventeenth century had a territory almost twice as extensive as now. It included all of present Sweden, and Finland, Esthonia and Ingria. During the reign of Gustavus Adolphus, 1611-32, Sweden was, perhaps, the most feared and courted single power in Europe.

Norway and Denmark were united kingdoms under one sovereign, the King of Denmark, but each country retained its own constitution and made its own laws. This union involved Iceland and Greenland. Sweden had broken away under Gustaf Vasa in 1523.

What contributions did immigrants of these various nationalities make to America? The Scandinavians and the Dutch did not come to America because of political discontent or for lack of industrial opportunity. They came voluntarily in the service of the West India Company. They were not aliens; they were not refugees; they came here to be Americans. The Scandinavians were individualists with a marked cooperative instinct. They were splendid sailors, skilled artisans and farmers, loyal, law-abiding, hardy and deeply religious. They were generally educated and promoted the education of the young.

The Dutch were above all cosmopolitans. They were champions of political freedom, and they made laws consistent with their political views. These laws were honestly and fearlessly enforced. They were also ready, in time of need, to fight for that which they considered right. Protestantism in Holland was predominantly of the Reformed type, and the Dutch Lutherans were strongly influenced by their Reformed brethren, especially in church government.

The early German immigrants were somewhat different from the later Palatines. A number of Germans in New Netherland came from the commercial centers of the "Kayserreich," and some acquired considerable political influence, especially in New Amsterdam. Nicholas de Meyer from Hamburg was mayor of New York City in 1676; and Jacob Leisler became lieutenant-governor of the New York Province.

Palatine immigrants and later German settlers were somewhat different. They came in great poverty from a troubled and war-torn Europe where they were constantly molested. As they settled on the frontier and elsewhere, their great desire was to be left alone and to leave others alone. Hence they made no vital impress upon colonial society; and they asserted themselves but modestly in business and in politics.

Before 1648 the term "Dutch" applied to all members of the German Empire. Later the term was narrowed to inhabitants of Holland. The Germans, in their own language, called themselves "Deutsch." This caused their English neighbors in Pennsylvania to call them "Pennsylvania Dutch."

The Germans clung to their native language. They were deliberate and calm. Unlike the English, they could not be moved in masses for the accomplishment of any general task. In New England the clergy was frequently looked to also for civic leadership, but not so among the Germans. Though they respected their pastors, they very rarely permitted them to become their secular leaders. They were not easily led; they refused to be driven.

Furthermore, the Lutheran Church in Colonial America was strongly influenced by the Reformed Church. In New York City there was no Lutheran school house for nearly a hundred years after Lutheranism had been established there. The Lutheran children attended Reformed schools. Several "union" churches were also in existence. Reformed influence exerted itself in the Lutheran form of church government. And last but not least, through the *First Great Awakening*, 1734-44, George Whitefield impressed the character of Methodism upon American church life for more than a century.

What was the status of Lutheranism in America at the beginning of the era of the American Revolution? Lutheran congregations and preaching places dotted the entire Atlantic seaboard, from Maine to Louisiana, and in many instances, Lutheran settlers had pressed far inland. The Dutch Lutheran element was still strong in some of the Lutheran congregations in New York and New Jersey; and Berkenmeyer, a representative of firm Lutheran Orthodoxy, exerted a controlling influence over these congregations until his death in 1751. The Palatines, coming from the region in Europe where the "Reformed" originated, injected the element of tolerance and an easy-going cosmopolitanism. The Salzburgers in the South represented a warm, pious Lutheranism somewhat akin to Pietism. Their outstanding leader, John Martin Boltzius, came from Halle. The Falckner brothers introduced the element of secret societies, which later became such a troublesome problem in the Lutheran Church. The organizing and unifying genius of Muhlenberg has just been discussed. Living in the most densely populated Lutheran section of colonial America, he gave to the Lutherans of Pennsylvania and adjacent territory a synodical organization, a uniform liturgy, a model constitution for a local congregation, a common hymn book, and he also infused a warm, Evangelical spirit into the Lutheran fold under his care. It was well that the Lutheran Church in America was thus prepared, for the War of Independence cut the ties with the mother-church in Europe. The Lutheran Church in America was prepared to enter upon a more independent existence, analogous to that of the American nation.

Furthermore, it should be remembered that the Lutheran

churches never stood as entities apart from secular life. Like other settlers, the Lutherans came to America to seek half a dozen objects at once. They wanted freedom to worship according to their own ideas; but they also wanted greater economic well-being, wider social equality and fuller political liberty. Most of the settlers hoped to win all these benefits together. They blended the religious and economic and political motives. In consequence, the rank and file of Lutherans became an integral part of the great struggle for American independence.

14. REVIEW QUESTIONS

1. Why is the Lutheran Church a teaching Church?
2. In what writings did Luther express most extensively his ideas of education?
3. What was Luther's program of education?
4. How did Luther's followers carry out this program?
5. In what ways did it influence education in colonial America?
6. What provisions did Dutch and Swedish Lutherans make for the education of the young?
7. Why is Henry Melchior Muhlenberg considered the patriarch of colonial Lutheran schools?
8. Why did the Lutherans fail to establish institutions of higher learning in colonial America?
9. What are some of the conditions peculiar to Canada?
10. What are some of the Canadian Protestant characteristics?
11. What efforts and events paved the way for Protestant settlements in Canada?
12. When and where did the Lutherans form the first permanent settlement in British North America?

TOPICS FOR SPECIAL STUDY

1. Early Lutheran education in America.
2. The parochial school system: Protestant and Catholic.
3. The unique ecclesiastical control in Quebec.
4. Early Lutheran settlers in Halifax and Lunenberg.

A SELECTED BIBLIOGRAPHY FOR CHAPTER II

1. *Documentary History of the State of New York*, edited by E. B. O'Callaghan.
2. *Ecclesiastical Records of the State of New York*, edited by Hugh Hastings.

3. *Documents Relative to the Colonial History of New York*, by John Romeyn Broadhead. Edited by E. B. O'Callaghan.
4. Calendar of Council Minutes of New York, 1668-1683 (Albany).
5. *Colonial Records of North Carolina, 1662-1790.*
6. *Pennsylvania Archives, 1664-1698.*
7. *Minutes of the Provincial Assembly of Pennsylvania.*
8. *Hallesche Nachrichten.*
9. Andrews, Charles M., *The Colonial Period in American History.*
10. Bernheim, G. D., *History of the German Settlements and of the Lutheran Church in North and South Carolina.*
11. Evjen, John O., *Scandinavian Immigrants in New York, 1630-1674.*
12. Johnson, Amandus, *The Swedish Settlements on the Delaware, 1638-1664.*
13. Louhi, *The Delaware Finns.*
14. Chambers, T. F., *Early Germans in New Jersey.*
15. Cobb, S. H., *The Story of the Palatines.*
16. Knittle, W. A., *Early Eighteenth Century Palatine Emigration.*
17. Weiser, Conrad, *Diary.*
18. Simms, J. R., *History of Schoharie County.*
19. Jacobs, H. E., *The German Emigration to America, 1709-1740.* (In Pennsylvania-German Society Proceedings, Vol. VIII).
20. Sachse, J. F., *The German Pietists of Provincial Pennsylvania.*
21. Sachse, J. F., *The German Sectarians of Pennsylvania, 1708-1800.*
22. Scharf, J. T., *History of Maryland.*
23. Semmes, Raphael, *Captains and Mariners of Early Maryland.*
24. Lawson, John, *History of North Carolina.*
25. Faust, A. B., *The German Element in the United States.*
26. Mann, W. J., *Life and Times of Henry Melchior Muhlenberg.*
27. Proud, Robert, *History of Pennsylvania, 1681-1742.*
28. Smith, Samuel, *The History of the Colony of Nova-Caesaria, or New Jersey, to the Year 1721.*
29. Kalm, Peter, *Travels in North America.*
30. Morris, H. C., *The History of Colonization.*
31. Kretzmann, Karl, in *Concordia Historical Institute Quarterly.*
32. Maurer, C. L., *Early Lutheran Education in Pennsylvania.*
33. Beck, Walter H., *Lutheran Elementary Schools in the United States.*

CHAPTER III

LUTHERANS AND THE ESTABLISHMENT OF THE AMERICAN NATION, 1763-89

In order to understand and evaluate this formative period in American history, it is necessary to have an intimate knowledge of the divergent aims of mother country and colonies; for there are always two sides to a revolution. What were the forces which caused mother country and colonies—for more than a hundred years—to move in exactly opposite directions, one toward empire and the other toward intensive self-government? Why did colonial America, like an original stock transplanted to new soil, advance politically, socially, and morally at a much more rapid pace than the mother country? If this general development is properly understood, and the lesser causes are seen in their proper relation to the entire situation, it will become quite evident why a final rupture between England and the colonies was inevitable.

I. General Development in England.—The reign of James I (1603-25) marked the commencement of the colonial expansion of England in the New World and in Asia.[1] This expansion movement brought England in sharp rivalry, first with Spain and then with the Dutch Netherlands. By the end of the seventeenth century, England had practically triumphed over these commercial rivals. France was the next great competitor, and from 1688 to 1815 there was a gigantic struggle between England and France for commercial and colonial supremacy, with England emerging the victor. The French and Indian

[1] Jamestown, Virginia, was founded in 1607; English colonies were established in East India; and the Plantation of Ulster in Ireland was settled by English and Scotch Protestants.

War, 1756-63, gave England supremacy over North America and mastery of the sea. France retaliated by giving aid to the American Colonies during the War of Independence. In the Peace of Paris in 1783, England had to acknowledge the independence of the Thirteen Colonies.

Throughout the seventeenth and eighteenth centuries there was a widely held theory of government which exerted a great influence upon the historical development of Europe. This theory was known as the *Divine Right of Kings*. According to this theory, the nation is a great family with the king as its divinely appointed head. The duty of the king is to govern like a father; the duty of the people is to obey their king as children obey their parents. The king can neither be corrected nor deposed by his subjects. The king is responsible to God alone; and to God the people, quietly submissive, must leave the avenging of all their wrongs. This theory, held by the Stuart kings, caused considerable trouble, for in it lay the germs of the Civil War and all that grew out of it—the Commonwealth, the Protectorate, and the Revolution of 1689.

A successful challenge of the Divine Right of the King was made by Parliament, especially the House of Commons, which asserted in the *Great Protestation* of 1621 that "the liberties, franchises, privileges, and jurisdictions of Parliament are the ancient and undoubted birthright and inheritance of the subjects of England, and that the arduous and urgent affairs concerning the king, state, and defense of the realm and the Church of England . . . are proper subjects and matter of council and debate in Parliament." After a long struggle, the *Bill of Rights* of 1689 settled the dispute in favor of Parliament. Furthermore, by deposing James II and giving the royal crown to William and Mary, it was clearly demonstrated that Parliament may depose any king, exclude his heirs from the throne, and settle the crown anew in another family.[2]

---

[2] The union of the Parliaments of England and Scotland in 1707 marked another important step in the political, commercial and colonial expansion of Great Britain.

During the reign of the early Hanoverian kings, George I (1714-27) and George II (1727-60), the crown lost much of its former influence because these kings, ignorant of English affairs, had to trust their ministers with the practical administration of the government. George III (1760-1820), who reigned during the American Revolution, tried with but little success to regain some of the lost royal prestige. The power lost by his predecessors passed into the hands of the chief minister, or Prime Minister. The first English Prime Minister in the modern sense was Sir Robert Walpole (1721-42). During his administration, the Cabinet assumed substantially the form it has at present. It is interesting to note that Parliament up to 1750, wishing to prevent any increase in the royal authority, protected the chartered rights of the American colonies; while after 1763, when it was determined to uphold its own authority, refused to recognise any claims the colonists made on behalf of their liberties.

In order to understand England's attitude toward the Thirteen Colonies, it is well to remember that English colonial policies were predicated on the postulates of mercantilism accepted by seventeenth century Europe. This mercantilism was a materialistic, self-protective philosophy of a growing state that was striving to win for itself a place of superiority among the nations. Being self-sufficient and exclusive, it opposed cosmopolitan cooperation and every form of international control.[3] The English mercantilist wished to shape governmental activity to material ends. Art, science, culture and intellect must be subordinated to the selfish gains of trade and commerce. The trade monopoly was to be limited to England only, that is, to the realm defined by "England, Wales, and Berwick-on-Tweed."[4] The lesser dependencies, such as Ireland, Scotland and the American colonies must supplement, but not compete with the

[3] It has its counterpart in modern nationalistic and self-protective policies, the chief characteristics of which are isolation, high protective tariffs, and the subordination of dependencies.

[4] The mother country consisted of England, Wales, and the town of Berwick-on-Tweed. After 1707 it included Scotland.

mother country. Hence, to give these dependencies an independent life was, according to the mercantilist, to counteract all the advantages that arose from the colonial relationship. The mercantilist doctrines also attached a high value to a dense population, as an element of national strength. In consequence, the mercantilist took great interest in the settlement of foreign Protestants in the American colonies.[5]

After 1763, England had to face a new issue, that of territorial imperialism. By the conquest of North America, a British territorial empire had come visibly into existence; and with this new status came the problems of adequate territorial administration and support. The system of colonial administration, inaugurated after 1763, was expensive, and the colonies were no longer self-supporting, as they had been under the mercantilist control.

Mercantilism and imperialism had nothing in common. Mercantilism with its "pay as you go" policy, promoted only such undertakings as had prospects of immediate financial returns. Imperialism, on the other hand, accepted this opening up of new territory as an investment in deferred values, which in turn would bring substantial gains through an expanding population and the consequent market for British goods. Meanwhile the extra expenses involved in this imperialistic policy had to be met, and the British statesmen concerned resorted to taxation of the colonists in various ways. From this it will be seen that it was imperialism, rather than mercantilism, which caused a final rupture with England.

In the quarrel that followed during the next decade, the relation between England and the Thirteen Colonies entered its *third* and final stage. The problem no longer centered in the old mercantile trade question, the *first* stage; nor did it center in the imperial question of revenue, the *second* stage; but it centered

---

[5] Archdale, the Carolina proprietor, stated that 2,000 white people in Carolina were worth 100,000 at home, because of their use of English goods and the products they exchanged so favorably for England.

in the fundamental issue of *status* of the colonies and their political and legal relations to England. During these crucial years the ministerial leaders of England were, with few exceptions,[6] statesmen of second-rate ability, who showed complete ignorance of colonial business methods and colonial conditions in general. With different men at the helm during these years, the outcome of the struggle might have been quite different from what it actually turned out to be. As it was, England knew but one remedy for radicalism, and that was coercion. Much responsibility for the revolt must be attributed to the obstinacy, prejudice and personal government of George III. Of still graver consequence was the inability of British officials and lawyers to depart in any essential from the traditional interpretation of the law and the constitution. For England alone was the world made. Law, education, religion, and also the colonies existed for her benefit. The crown lawyers would permit no encroachment upon the royal prerogative, nor would they allow any reflection upon the authority of Parliament. They insisted on the *status quo*.

II. Developments in the Thirteen Colonies.—In the colonial era the Thirteen Colonies along the Atlantic sea border had a western frontier which extended from Lake Champlain to South Carolina, notably along the Susquehanna, in western Maryland, and in the Shenandoah Valley of Virginia.[7] These colonies represented a miniature New World where a great variety of religious, political, social, economic and racial interests furnished excellent ground for experimentation. The thirteen colonies were in reality not colonies but settlements and private estates, under private control and under management of local

[6] One of these notable exceptions was the elder William Pitt, later Earl of Chatham, known as "the Great Commoner." Frederick the Great expressed his estimate of him in these words, "England has at last brought forth a man."

[7] The Northwest Territory, ceded to England in 1763, was not generally settled by white people during the colonial era. This territory included what was later to become the states of Ohio, Indiana, Illinois, Michigan, and parts of Wisconsin and Minnesota.

governments, under the terms of the charters granted them by the king. Consider the feudal seigniories of New York and the Carolinas; the similar seigniories of Maryland and Pennsylvania, where a holy experiment and a religious refugee problem were brought into being and partly carried out and solved under the legal protection of feudal lordships; and the separatist communities of New England where the Puritans established religious commonwealths.

In nature and purpose these colonies were at first *religious* and *commercial*, rather than political and administrative. England looked upon these colonies, not so much as political organizations and centers of population, but rather as farming areas, outposts of trade, and sources of wealth. In her dealings with the colonies, England had at this time but little concern for the finer aspects of art, literature and religion. The colonies were desirable only as far as they were profitable to England, and they were profitable to England only as far as they procured for England new advantages and means of extending English commerce.

Theoretically, the colonies belonged to the king. He alone had the right to grant and revoke charters. In the early history of the colonies various efforts were made to bring the loosely controlled and privately managed colonies into a closer unity under the crown; and by the middle of the eighteenth century all of the Thirteen Colonies, except Maryland, Pennsylvania, Connecticut and Rhode Island, were in the king's hands. Colonial agents and proprietors quickly sounded the alarm against this extension of royal power, and Parliament, wishing to prevent any increase in the royal authority, protected the chartered rights in America, that is, prior to 1763. These rights included the exercise of self-government, but within certain defined limits.[8]

---

[8] The Plymouth colony began as a self-governing civil and religious community; and Massachusetts and Connecticut started as Puritan commonwealths.

And this leads to the second great feature of colonial history, the growth of colonial self-government.

Up to 1763 the Thirteen Colonies manifested no general and self-conscious desire for a union among themselves. Because of isolation, local environment, religious differences and admixture of racial stocks, they looked on each other as "foreigners" in the medieval sense of the word; so that, whatever misfortune happened in one colony, the rest remained more or less unconcerned.[9] The only bond that held these colonies together was their legal subordination to the authority of the British crown. However, as these colonies gradually grew, they used similar methods of increasing their self-governing powers.

At the beginning of the eighteenth century, every British colony in America had a representative assembly elected under a limited popular suffrage. As time went on, these representative assemblies increased the number and sphere of their powers. This frequently caused severe friction, as in Maryland, between the proprietor and the popular element. The proprietor tried to invoke the divine right of the proprietors, and this was worse than the divine right of kings. However, the popular element gained steadily, and the feudal privilege, as a feature of government, gradually passed away in America. In every colony there came into existence a miniature House of Commons which was exercising full powers over legislation, membership, and finance, and claiming legislative equality with the highest legislative body in the realm. Madison wrote in 1800, that "the fundamental principle of the Revolution was that the colonies were coördinate members with each other and with Great Britain of an empire united by a common executive sovereign, and that the legislative power was maintained to be as complete in each American parliament as in the British parliament."

The British Parliament had, as previously stated, successfully increased its own power at the expense of the crown; but in the

---

[9] There were some notable exceptions, but they were *exceptions* to the general spirit of early colonial America.

crucial decade, 1763-73, Parliament refused to grant similar powers to the colonial assemblies. Parliament failed to understand and to successfully solve the issue of coördinate legislatures and a common king, a doctrine which became so firmly rooted in later decades. This again involved the fundamental issue of the *status* of the colonies, in religion, in government, in trade and commerce.

Prior to 1763, the colonists made no serious opposition to the extension of English law to the colonies, nor did they make any serious denial of Parliament's right to legislate for them. The right of Parliament to legislate for the colonies was not expressly denied by the colonists before 1765. The issue of parliamentary sovereignty was not raised until the events of the pre-Revolutionary years made it necessary for the colonists to discover some constitutional argument that would serve as a pretext for revolt.

Meanwhile the colonies had grown to manhood, a fact which England took no account of in her official relations with them. The American colonies were advancing politically, socially and morally at a much more rapid pace than did the mother country. England and the colonies were moving in exactly opposite directions, each in obedience to historical tendencies that could not be resisted. As for the colonists, they were fast becoming impatient of too strict an exercise of the royal prerogative and the claims of Parliament.

III. Conditions Leading to Revolution.—The American Revolution centered in one fundamental issue, that of the *status* of the colonies in their relation to the mother country. This status involved the religious, political, economic and social life of the colonies. The issue is partly expressed in these words of the *Declaration of Independence*, "We hold these truths to be self-evident: That all men are created equal; that they are endowed by their Creator with certain inalienable rights; that among these are life, liberty and the pursuit of happiness; that, to secure these rights, governments are instituted among men, deriving their just powers from the consent of the governed;

that, whenever any form of government becomes destructive to these ends, it is the right of the people to alter or abolish it, and to institute a new government, laying its foundation on such principles, and organizing its powers in such form, as to them shall seem most likely to effect their safety and happiness."

1. *General Trends.*—Colonial America experienced a change in religious thinking and a gradual estrangement from England almost immediately after the Great Awakening, 1734-44. These changes were caused by rude frontier conditions, the decline of the old religious fervor and intolerance, the rising interest in shipping and trade, the gradual breakdown of aristocratic traditions and customs, the rising tide of individualism, the displacement of the old religious town government and the original religious town school by a civil town government and the secular district school, and the new state theory of education which embodied the idea that schools were essentially for the promotion of the everyday interests of society and the welfare of the state. Public interest centered in political discussion rather than in religious controversy. Colonial newspapers frequently attacked both Church and State. The old religious solidarity was broken, and the life of Colonial America was rapidly secularized.

Practically all the early settlers in the Thirteen Colonies were Protestants, many of whom came in search of religious freedom. These settlers were imbued with the Protestant idea of an active participation of all citizens in government and religion. It asserted the divine right of the common people as over against the divine right of kings. English traditions of representative government and liberty formed the foundations on which the limited self-government in each colony was built.

But the colonists soon displayed a love of religious and political liberty and independence to which even Englishmen were scarcely accustomed. Just as an original stock transplanted to new soil perpetuates the best qualities of the old, and yet develops faster than the mother plant, so the colonies in America were more advanced politically, socially and morally than the mother country. The spirit of independence in the colonies became very pronounced, and colonial recognition of the supremacy of the British Parliament became increasingly difficult. It was evident that the colonists and the English were rapidly drifting apart.

2. *The Religious Problem.*—Serious opposition was first caused by agitation for the establishment of an Anglican bishop in America. This came at a most inopportune time, for the colonists would no longer endure British domination. They knew that the appointment of an Anglican bishop would involve British supremacy in ecclesiastical affairs in the colonies, and the exercise of vast political power. Opposition was especially strong among Congregationalists and Presbyterians in New England and the Middle Colonies. John Adams said, "The objection was not only to the office of bishop, though that was dreaded, but to the authority of Parliament on which it must be founded. The reasoning was this: There is no power less than Parliament which can create bishops in America. But if Parliament can erect dioceses and appoint bishops, they may introduce the whole hierarchy, establish tithes, establish religion, forbid dissenters, make schism heresy, impose penalties extending to life and limb as well as to liberty and property."

Van Tyne[10] and others have pointed out that the more the evidences for the remote and the immediate causes of the American Revolution are brought to light and studied, the more does the religious, sectarian, or ecclesiastical cause force itself to the front. Charles Evans[11] states that in its controversial phases, "the struggle for civil liberty in the American Colonies assumes something of the nature of religious warfare, in which the dissenting churches are opposed by the Established Church of England." Evans also points out that from 1700-50, two-thirds

---

[10] Van Tyne, *Influence of the Clergy and of Religious and Sectarian Forces on the American Revolution,* in the *American Historical Review,* Vol. XIX, p. 44.

[11] Charles Evans, *American Bibliography,* Vol. V, p. 9.

of the books and pamphlets published in the colonies were on the religious questions, and from 1750-75, at least one half of the colonial literature dealt with the religious aspect of the Revolution.

3. *The Economic Problem.*—Adhering strictly to the seventeenth century mercantilist policy, England barred the Thirteen Colonies from trade with rivals of Great Britain. Furthermore, as early as 1699, England started the policy of restricting manufactures in the colonies, on the ground that the colonies should not have the same economic interests as England, and should not be allowed to make the same things that England was making. The English merchants declared that should the colonists be allowed to cultivate the same products and have liberty to carry them to the same markets, they would destroy the commerce of England by selling at a lower price.[12]

Meanwhile it was well known that New England furnished the Newfoundland fishermen with provisions at a cheaper rate than England herself could supply them; that New England even challenged England's supremacy in the fish markets of Europe; that merchants and sea captains of Pennsylvania, New York and New England carried their surplus products to the West Indian islands, frequently glutting the markets and selling cheaper than the English; and that the colonists carried on a profitable trade with the French. In consequence, the colonists were accused of transferring to foreigners the benefits of a trade which belonged to England, and that by continuing this illicit trade, the colonists enriched themselves at the expense of England. Several measures were taken to stop this traffic. Consider the Molasses Act of 1733, the Sugar Act of 1764, and the Townshend Act of 1767.

[12] The most useful colonies to England were the British West Indies with their sugar, and the Southern Colonies with their tobacco, rice, indigo and naval stores. New England and the Middle Colonies had a much lower rating because they furnished but little that could not well be supplied by Ireland and England. However, the Northern Colonies were looked upon as offering a more favorable market for British manufactures.

Before 1750 the Thirteen Colonies exported more than they imported and received cash in return. After 1755 their imports from England began to exceed their exports, and this unfavorable balance increased tremendously with the years. To make the situation even more precarious, the English insisted on cash transactions. In consequence, there was soon a tremendous scarcity of cash in the colonies, and there was even a scarcity of other medium of exchange. The year 1770 ushered in a brief period of inflation. Meanwhile the colonists were fast becoming impatient of the unfair control of trade, and they also became aware of the need of united action against this common evil.

4. *The Political Problem.*—The real struggle between England and America started when the English government tried to make the colonists pay some of the expenses of the Seven Years' War, 1755-63, and some of the expenses of colonial administration. In order to increase the colonial revenue, the English government undertook, in 1764, to enforce the Molasses Act of 1733. For similar purposes the Stamp Act of 1765 and the Townshend Act of 1767 were passed by Parliament. These acts raised the question whether or not there should be taxation without representation, or, to state it more positively, should there not be coördinate legislatures and a common king?

The mass of colonial population did not focus attention on the more technical problems involved. But the legislative acts just mentioned touched intimately the daily conditions of their lives, and they made serious objections to these laws which seemed contrary to the fundamental laws of reason and justice. They realized that these laws, if successfully enforced, would drain the colonies of their silver, and would consequently prevent the colonial merchants and planters from using this money to meet their trade balances. Everywhere the colonists denounced these acts as an imperialistic attack on colonial resources, and the logical place to seek redress appeared to be the respective colonial assemblies. As this was done, the colonists gradually brushed aside the issue of mercantilism and the issue of imperialism and centered in the issue of status.

5. *The Problem of Unification.*—Up to the decade preceding the Revolution, certain religious, social, economic and educational barriers had separated the Thirteen Colonies. They dreaded unification and resisted consolidation even more than did their mother country. Franklin's Plan of Union, the Albany Plan of 1754, was not ratified by the colonial assemblies. Nevertheless, the general trend in colonial life was toward greater unity.

The Great Awakening, 1734-44, aroused a general consciousness of a national religious unity and in this way prepared for the birth of the American nation. Furthermore, soldiers from the different colonies fought for a common cause in the French and Indian War, 1755-63; they began to know one another much better; and they were beginning to see a common interest, that of a closer union.

As the issue of taxation without representation was raised, it caused a division of sentiment among the colonists, and by 1770 two parties were in the process of formation. The Loyalist or Tory party took the side of England in the taxation controversy, while the American or Patriot party cared little for England and was intensely loyal to America. The Tory party included many wealthy men and the more important colonial officials. The Patriot party included chiefly the middle and lower classes, but also a few men of wealth, such as George Washington, Thomas Jefferson, Benjamin Franklin, Alexander Hamilton, John Dickinson and John Adams.

The Patriot party asserted that taxation without representation was tyranny, and refused to pay the taxes assessed. The Boston Massacre of 1770; the burning of the *Gaspee*, a British revenue vessel, in 1772; the organization of the Committees of Correspondences in 1773; the Boston Tea Party of 1773; the passing of four intolerable acts by Parliament in 1774 against Massachusetts; the Quebec Act of 1774; the Declaration of Rights adopted by the colonies in 1765 and in 1774 and forwarded to the king; the formation of a Union of Colonies by the First Continental Congress in 1774; all these acts indicate how the colonists and the British thought and felt towards each other. Great Britain resorted to the policy of coercion, meeting blow with blow. The colonists were determined to uphold their rights. War was inevitable.

15. REVIEW QUESTIONS

1. Why study both the English and the American side of the Revolution?
2. How did the doctrine of divine rights of kings assert itself in the colonial situation?
3. How is this related to the assumed divine rights of Parliament?
4. What did seventeenth century mercantilism stand for, and how did it influence the history of the American Colonies?
5. In what ways did imperialism clash with mercantilism, and how did imperialism influence the course of development in the colonies?
6. What was the fundamental issue in the Revolution, and why?
7. What territory did the Thirteen Colonies cover?
8. What was the nature and purpose of these colonies?
9. What conditions promoted the growth of colonial self-government?
10. Why was there so little sense of unity among the colonies?
11. Why was the religious problem of prime importance in the struggle for independence?
12. What specific factors were involved in the economic and political problems?
13. What general situation rallied the American forces to war?
14. Was America unified at the beginning of the Revolution? Explain.

TOPICS FOR SPECIAL STUDY

1. Fundamental constitutional rights.
2. Coordinate legislatures and a common political head.
3. Mercantilism versus imperialism.
4. Protestantism and democracy.
5. The right of armed resistance.
6. American leaders in the cause of liberty.
7. Frontier individualism and the Revolution.

IV. The American Churches and the War.—The churches in Colonial America must not be considered as foreign or imported. They became charter members of the American Republic by right of creation. The American Revolution was not only a political but also a religious revolution. Churches were active in arousing and in forming public opinion, in stirring the people to united action; and when the war actually started, the churches willingly gave of their lifeblood and of their means in order to help in the rearing of the Temple of Liberty.

1. *The Established Church* was handicapped because the colonists looked upon it as the Church which oppressed their fathers. Furthermore, its ministry had come from England and its congregations were largely sympathetic with the mother country. This was particularly true of the Anglicans in New England. In the Middle Colonies the lay sentiment was more divided, while in the Southern Colonies it was largely pro-American. George Washington, James Madison, John Marshall, Patrick Henry and Alexander Hamilton were members of the Established Church; and Bishop Perry claims that two-thirds of the signers of the Declaration of Independence were members.

This Church had been too closely identified with aristocratic society to be a notable factor in the spiritual uplift of colonial life. In Virginia three-fourths of the people were outside the Established Church. Its failure to adopt itself to the new Evangelical Christianity, rather than to its political connections, caused this Church to approach extinction toward the close of the war. A drastic readjustment was essential. This was done under the able leadership of William White and Samuel Seabury, Jr., and by 1789 the Established Church had been completely re-organized, independent of state and of English church control, and with representative bodies composed of both clergy and laymen. This new organization is known as the Protestant Episcopal Church.

2. *The Congregational Church* was more influential than any other denomination in the struggle for independence. This was partly due to the fact that the Puritan clergy, Congregational and Presbyterian, had been entrusted with political leadership as well as with moral and spiritual guidance. The pulpit reached the masses, informing and influencing public opinion, more than any other single agency in colonial times. Numerous Puritan

sermons were published in pamphlet form by act of legislature, and distributed through the colonies.[13]

After 1750 Puritan sermons were used for political instruction. Standing squarely on their rights as Englishmen, the Puritan ministers defended the rights of resistance, urging their flocks to refuse submission to royal power when arbitrarily exerted. Following the doctrines of Sidney, Milton, Locke and Hoadley, the Puritan clergy developed the whole political philosophy of the American Revolution, as set forth in the preamble to the Declaration of Independence.[14]

Due credit must be given to the dominant influence of Jonathan Edwards on public opinion regarding the questions of religious liberty and the separation of church and state. Imbued with Augustine's ideal of the *City of God*, he asserted that the church was greater than the state, and in an entirely different sphere. State control over religion was impossible. Edwards, more than any other man, paved the way for the complete separation of church and state. His influence, exerted indirectly, induced the colonists to oppose the encroachments of the Church of England upon their religious rights. Jonathan Mayhew, another Congregational leader, exerted a similar but lesser influence.

When war broke out, many Congregational ministers became "fighting parsons." Others enlisted volunteers and pecuniary and material support. The Congregationalists proved staunch friends of the cause of the colonists.

3. *The Presbyterian Church* deserves a similar testimony. This Church included all colonists of Presbyterian descent, the Huguenots, the Dutch Reformed and the Scotch-Irish. The Presbyterians in New York, Virginia, and South Carolina had

---

[13] It must be kept in mind that the Puritan commonwealths of New England were modelled on Calvin's church-state of Geneva. This explains the dominant political influence of the Puritan clergy in America.

[14] In this, however, they were not alone. German and Scandinavian Lutherans also exerted a dominant influence, as will be seen later in this chapter.

carried on a determined struggle with the Church of England and the Tory governors. It was really a continuation of the Presbyterian-Episcopalian conflict carried on in the mother country since the days of Oliver Cromwell. The Scotch-Irish Presbyterians of Virginia and North Carolina formulated a declaration of independence as early as in January, 1775. Walpole made this characteristic statement in English Parliament, "Cousin America has run off with a Presbyterian parson."

The most influential leader was John Witherspoon, 1722-94, a well-known Scotch preacher who became the president of the College of New Jersey in 1768. He early won recognition as an educational and religious leader and as a man of public affairs. In 1776 he was elected a member of the Continental Congress and was one of the signers of the Declaration of Independence. He also signed the Articles of Confederation. William Livingston, the distinguished lawyer in New Jersey, also was a Presbyterian.

Presbyterian ministers and elders took an active part in the War of Independence. George Duffield, John Rodgers, James Caldwell, Alexander McWhorter, James F. Armstrong, Adam Boyd and Daniel McCall were chaplains in the American army. Jacob Green, Henry Patillo, William Tennent and John Murray were members of Congress from New Jersey, North Carolina, South Carolina and Massachusetts respectively. Prominent Presbyterian elders were General Morgan, General Pickens, Colonel Campbell, Colonel James Williams, Colonel Cleaveland, Colonel Shelby, Colonel Sevier, Colonel Bratton, Colonel Sumpter and Major Dickson.

A slight pro-British sentiment was evidenced only among the German Reformed. Two ministers, John Michael Kern and John Joachim Zubly, and a few of their followers, were prominent Tories or Loyalists.

4. *The Roman Catholic Church* took a worthy part in the War of Independence, with the majority of its members ranging themselves on the side of the colonists. Wholehearted Catholic aid

was given by the comparatively small body of Catholics residing in the colonies, by the Catholic Indians of Maine and of the old Northwest, by the Catholic Canadian volunteers, and by the French and Spanish allies.[15]

Numerous Catholic volunteers joined the army and the navy. Pennsylvania sent Colonel Moylan and Captain Barry of the Navy, and Colonel Doyle and Captain Michael McGuire. Maryland contributed Neales, Boarmans, Brents, Semmers, Mattinglys, Brookes, and Kiltys.[16] Among the signers of the Declaration of Independence and the Articles of Confederation were three Catholics, Thomas Fitzsimmons, Daniel Carroll and Charles Carroll.

But there were also, as the Catholic historian Peter Guilday has pointed out,[17] a number of Catholic Tories. "The Roman Catholic Regiment, recruited in Philadelphia in 1777-78, while General Howe and his officers occupied that city, was in command of Lieutenant Colonel Alfred Clinton, then a member of St. Mary's parish."[18] The Catholics were divided, as some of the Protestant groups were divided.

The French Alliance of 1778 and the friendly attitude of Spain brought numerous Catholic officers from Europe. "Catholic army officers like Lafayette, Kosciusko, du Portail, Gimat, Mottin de la Balme, Pulaski, Tronson du Coudray, navy officers like Dourville and Pierre Landais, were already in America aiding by their skill and experience the brave but untrained levies of the Continental Congress."[19]

5. *The Baptists* were strong supporters of the cause of the colonists because they felt that failure would mean the failure of the struggle for religious freedom and separation of church and state. Numerous Baptist volunteers joined the army, while

[15] Guilday, *The Life and Times of John Carroll*, p. 73.
[16] McSherry, *History of Maryland*, p. 379 f.
[17] Guilday, *The Life and Times of John Carroll*, p. 81.
[18] Shea, *Life and Times of the Most Rev. John Carroll*, Vol. II, p. 165.
[19] Guilday, *The Life and Times of John Carroll*, p. 83.

prominent Baptist leaders at home kept up a continual fight for the American cause. The Warren Association, made up of Baptist churches in New England, was organized by Isaac Backus, President Manning of Rhode Island College, John Gano, Morgan Edwards and other Baptist leaders. This organization presented the Baptist grievances to the First Continental Congress at Philadelphia, and to the Provincial Congress of Massachusetts. Prominent Baptist leaders in Virginia, John Leland, David Barrow, Lewis Connor and others, organized a General Committee of Baptists in 1784 which was made up of not more than four delegates from each district association. This Committee exerted a powerful influence, and was partly responsible for the abolishment of religious inequalities. It was through this Committee that the Baptists sent an address to the newly elected President Washington, and his reply was an address to all Baptists in the United States.

6. *The Methodists* or Wesleyans were under constant suspicion during the early years of the War of Independence because they were still a part of the Church of England, and consequently they were identified with the Tory cause. John Wesley stirred up a lot of hard feeling by issuing a *Calm Address to the American Colonies*, counselling the submission to the king. But when war was begun, he instructed the Wesleyan preachers in America to observe strict neutrality. All of his English-born preachers returned to England, save Francis Asbury who believed that America would become a free and independent nation. All the native preachers, including Philip Gatch, Freeborn Garrettson and William Watters, were in sympathy with the cause of liberty, although non-combatants from principle. Methodism recovered rapidly on the close of the war, and was one of the first religious groups to form a national organization.

7. *Quakers, Mennonites and Moravians* were conscientious objectors or non-combatants from principle. These groups were much misunderstood because they were not only against war,

but seemingly also against the new government. In consequence, these non-resistant groups suffered heavily. Opposition to a defensive war was not, however, unanimous among Quakers and Mennonites. Many Quakers and Mennonites were at least willing to pay the war tax, while a considerable number of Quakers actually joined the army. In consequence, all who had performed military duties were expelled from the regular Quaker Society. These "disowned" members organized a society known as Free Quakers.

8. *The Lutheran Church* gave almost unanimous support to the cause of the colonists. It is true that immediately *after* the Revolutionary War, a number of German Lutherans from the frontiers of Pennsylvania, Mohawk and Schoharie migrated to Welland, Waterloo and York counties in Canada; but they moved, not so much because of Loyalist sentiment as for other apparent causes to be mentioned. *First,* the majority of these settlers had come from a war-torn Europe. They had left the mother country for the express purpose of finding peace and prosperity in the New World. With the repetition of the ravages of war, their first reaction was to move to more peaceful settlements. *Secondly,* these particular colonists were content to settle on the frontier and elsewhere, wishing to be let alone and to leave others alone. They were content to live by themselves and made no vital impress on society. They asserted themselves but modestly in business and politics. *Thirdly,* it was the wealthy merchants and the landed proprietors who laid the basis for the American Revolution by limiting the power of the Crown's representatives, the colonial governors. The frontier had but little influence upon these privileged classes. In consequence, it would be difficult for the rank and file of colonists on the isolated frontier to see the issue clearly and choose the right side. *Fourthly,* Lutherans are everywhere a law-abiding people and are not easily subject to revolt or revolution. They are willing to obey the powers that be, because they believe the state

LUTHERANS, 1763-89 257

is a divine institution. In view of these facts, the migration to Canada may be easily understood.[20]

In the pre-Revolutionary years the Lutherans kept themselves somewhat in the background, not because they lacked zeal for the American cause, but because they had been taught to obey. But after the colonies had declared themselves independent, the rank and file of Lutherans became some of the most determined supporters of the cause of liberty. The German settlements were among the first to organize companies and to send troops to the front.[21]

Lutheran ministers sounded privately the notes of freedom and fired their audiences to political and patriotic excitement. John Peter Gabriel Muhlenberg, a son of Henry Melchior Muhlenberg, is typical of the general attitude of the Lutheran clergy. Reverend Muhlenberg, who formed a close friendship with George Washington, Richard Henry Lee and Patrick Henry, was appointed colonel of the Eighth Virginia Regiment in December, 1775. In the middle of January, 1776, he preached his farewell sermon, concluding, "In the language of Holy Writ, there is a time for all things. There is a time to preach and a time to fight; and now is the time to fight." He pronounced the benediction and then, throwing back his clerical robe, he stood before them in the uniform of a continental officer. He then ordered the drums to beat at the church door for recruits. The next day he was off for war with three hundred of his frontier parishioners.

Muhlenberg's association with the dragoons during his three

---

[20] It must be kept clearly in mind that sentiment was divided in all denominations and among all colonists. Not a single denomination, and no single nationalistic group could boast a hundred per cent loyalty to the American cause. However, the proportion of Patriots among Lutherans compares most favorably with that of Congregationalists and Presbyterians.

[21] Lutherans had already rendered invaluable service to the Thirteen Colonies. During the French and Indian War, 1755-63, it was Conrad Weiser who swung the Thirteen Colonies from French Catholic to English Protestant control.

258   THE LUTHERAN CHURCH IN AMERICA

years study in Germany had aroused in him a militaristic spirit inherited from his grandfather, John Conrad Weiser.[22] He showed military talent. General Lee said of his troops, "Muhlenberg's regiment was not only the most complete in the province, but, I believe, of the whole continent. It was not only the most complete in numbers, but the best armed, clothed and equipped for immediate service. His soldiers were alert, zealous, and spirited." And Calvin Coolidge said in 1924, "Muhlenberg and his men from Pennsylvania and the Lutheran soldiers from Western Maryland, the Shenandoah Valley of Virginia, western North Carolina and South Carolina made glorious history for the patriotic cause during the Revolutionary War."[23]

In recognition for his services, he was elevated to the rank of Brigadier General in 1777, and in 1783 he was made a Major General. He never returned to the ministrations of the altar. At the close of the war he took up statesmanship, serving in several positions of honor.

His brother, Frederick Augustus Conrad Muhlenberg, also left the pulpit for the service of the halls of legislation. He was forced to leave his congregation in New York when the British came. He took a prominent part in the affairs of state and nation, and had the distinction of being the first speaker of the lower house in the National Congress.

John Adams said of these brothers, "These two Germans who had been long in public affairs and in high office, were the great leaders and oracles of the whole German interests in Pennsylvania and the neighboring states. The Muhlenbergs turned the whole body of Germans, great bodies of the Irish and many English, and in this manner introduced the total change that

---

[22] As a young man he had been sent to Halle, Germany, for his education. He ran away and enlisted in a dragoon regiment. A British officer recognized him and got him out with much difficulty, because enlistments in the German army were then for life.

[23] He fought at Sullivan's Island, Brandywine, Germantown, Monmouth, Stony Point, and led the assault at Yorktown.

followed in both houses of the legislature and in all the executive departments of national government."

Among the officers under George Washington were the Lutherans, Lutterloh, the quarter-master; Dr. Bodo Otto, from old Trinity, Reading, the sergeant-general; Christopher Ludwig, from Old Zion, Philadelphia, the baker general; and Henry Venderslice, wagon-master of all teamsters and wagons of the continental army. Other Lutheran officers included Kichlein, Shimer, Kiefer, Edelman, Righter, Eckert, Hain, Young, Wenrich, Spyker, Miller, Ernst, Lechner, Lesher, Weiser, Livingood, Zerbe, Seltzer, Brown, Knopp, and Boyer. The German Fusiliers of Charleston and the German regiment of the Valley of Virginia were mainly Lutherans. The Lutheran Salzburgers organized three companies for active service. Christian Streit was one of several Lutheran pastors who served as chaplain. One of the prominent Lutheran laymen was John Adams Treutlen, elected Governor of Georgia in 1777. As governor he successfully thwarted the encroachments of the British and the approaches of the Loyalists in that region.

Only two Lutheran clergymen, Bernard Michael Hausihl (Hauseal), pastor of the Raritan congregations in New Jersey, and Christopher F. Triebner, pastor to the Salzburgers in Georgia, are known to have lined up with the Loyalists. The only two regions where there was a slight pro-British sentiment were among Lutherans in Georgia and in a small Lutheran settlement in Maine.

V. Two Prominent Lutheran Leaders.—The outcome of the Revolutionary War and the history of the United States of America might have taken an entirely different turn, had it not been for the vision and leadership of two prominent Lutherans, one representing the religious and the other the civic interests of the Thirteen Colonies. These leaders were Henry Melchior Muhlenberg and John Hanson. The first is so well known that little needs to be said about him here. The other, because he has been almost entirely ignored, will be given the proportionate prominence he deserves.

1. *Henry Melchior Muhlenberg*, the great representative of German Lutherans in colonial America, did much to shape the views of his sons, and to enlist the general support of German Lutherans in the struggle for liberty. Muhlenberg knew Luther's view on armed resistance, as it had been shaped when Luther gave his consent to the formation of the Schmalkald League.[24] He saw that the relation between England and the colonial governments was a relation similar to that of the emperor and the princes and the free cities in the time of Luther. Hence, when these governments had found it necessary to declare their independence, it was the duty of Christian colonists to support these colonial governments, even to the point of war.

Furthermore, *The Augsburg Confession, Article XVI,* states in part, "Of Civil Affairs, they teach, that lawful civil ordinances are good works of God, and that it is right for Christians to bear civil office, to sit as judges, to determine matters by the Imperial and other existing laws, to award just punishments, to engage in just wars, to serve as soldiers, to make legal contracts, to hold property, to make oath when required by the magistrates, to marry, to be given in marriage."

The Declaration of Independence is in such fundamental agreement with Luther's views that Daniel Webster could say that the origin of American liberty dated from the Reformation. The Lutherans did not have to change their thinking in the matters of constitutional and individual rights; they already looked upon such rights as their precious inheritance. In con-

---

[24] In consenting to the formation of the Schmalkald League, Luther reasoned that the princes and the free cities constituted the government to which the Christians concerned owed their allegiance. The emperor was elected by the princes, not by God; and the princes had a right to depose the emperor if he violated their rights. The relation between the princes and the emperor was a political question which the jurists, not the theologians, should decide. The Christians were in duty bound to take up arms in defense of their princes, when these were unlawfully assaulted.

sequence, Muhlenberg could use his tremendous influence to enlist the entire Lutheran constituency in the colonies in support of the cause of freedom.[25]

Knowing the attitude of their beloved leader, the vestries of the German Lutheran churches in Philadelphia sent a pamphlet of forty pages to Germans in New York, North Carolina and other colonies, stating that the Germans in Philadelphia and throughout Pennsylvania had formed militia companies and a select corps of sharpshooters that were ready to march wherever required. Those who could not join the militia tried to contribute of their means according to ability. A German newspaper, *Staatsbote,* published jointly by Lutherans and Reformed, made strong appeals to the Germans to support the cause of the colonists.

2. *John Hanson* of Maryland, the distinguished representative of Swedish Lutherans in colonial America, and the first *President of the United States in Congress Assembled,* was one of that illustrious company of leaders and statesmen who contributed so worthily to the stupendous task of rearing the Temple of Liberty in America.

John Hanson's forefathers were Lutherans who came from Sweden. His great grandfather, Colonel John Hanson, was a distinguished military leader under Gustavus Adolphus during the Thirty Years War. His grandfather came to New Sweden with Governor Printz, but settled later in Charles County, Maryland, where he took a prominent part in the struggle for religious and civic liberty. His father, Samuel Hanson, served for several terms as a member of the General Assembly of Maryland. He also served as County Sheriff, Commissary, Clerk, and as a member of the board of visitors to the County School. He was a man of learning, good judgment, wide experience and

---

[25] It is interesting to notice that the minutes of the Ministerium of Pennsylvania for the years 1773-1790 contain but three references to the great struggle for independence, namely for the years 1775, 1776 and 1777. There is not a single official resolution in connection with the War of Independence.

strict Lutheran convictions. His home had an aristocratic atmosphere mingled with Christian simplicity. John Hanson grew up in such home environment.

He was born on April 3, 1721, at the Mulberry Grove plantation, the home of Assemblyman Samuel Hanson. He enjoyed a training that was thorough in all essentials. By the age of twelve, he knew the Prayers in the Catechism, the Commandments, the Creed, many hymns and long passages in Scriptures by heart. His ambition was to master statecraft and to follow in the footsteps of his father. His ambition was realized in 1757 when he was elected a member of the General Assembly of Maryland, a position he held until 1773. During these years he gained fame as a statesman. He took a definite stand in opposition to the English Stamp Act of 1765, and urged the holding of a general convention, where delegates from various colonies could come together and plan a united action of the Thirteen Colonies. The proposed convention was held in New York in October, 1765.[26] John Hanson was a member of the legislative committee which drew up instructions for the Maryland delegates to this convention. These instructions, together with similar statements from other colonies, formed the basis of the document known as the Declaration of Rights, adopted by the New York Convention and sent to British Parliament and to the king. In June, 1769, John Hanson signed the Non-importation Act as adopted; and in October of that same year, when a cargo of British goods had been landed at Tobacco Creek, Charles County, Maryland, John Hanson led a group of colonists who in broad daylight compelled the captain of the ship to take the goods back to England. This was four years prior to the Boston Tea Party.

In 1773 John Hanson moved to Frederick, Maryland, and

[26] This was the second convention held in America for the purpose of promoting united action of the Thirteen Colonies. The first convention was held at Albany in 1754, when Benjamin Franklin proposed a Plan of Union which was designed to draw the colonies closer together.

that same year he was chosen Assemblyman from Frederick County. This was the year of the Boston Tea Party. Maryland and Virginia contributed liberally to the distressed people of Boston. John Hanson personally supervised the collection of two hundred pounds sterling, and this gift was gratefully acknowledged by Samuel Adams in a letter to him. In June, 1774, John Hanson was chosen chairman of a meeting of patriotic citizens of Frederick County, and this meeting adopted a resolution prepared by him against the Boston Port Bill. This resolution, with slight changes, was later incorporated in the Articles of the American Association, and adopted by the First Continental Congress in October, 1774. The resolution denounced slave trade; the colonies were not to trade with nations engaged in slave trade; they were not to use British goods; and they were not to trade with any colony that refused to join this association. "Minute Men" were organized to enforce this resolution.

When the British heard that the Minute Men had collected ammunition and military stores at Concord, they ordered these destroyed. The warning of Paul Revere and William Dawes, on the night of April 18, 1775, and the fatal skirmishes at Concord and Lexington, have become outstanding incidents in the annals of American history. When news came of the approaching conflict at Bunker Hill, June 15, 1775, John Hanson led the organization of two companies of riflemen, and these were ready to leave on the third day. They marched 550 miles to Cambridge, Massachusetts, in 22 days, and joined Washington's army on August 9th. These were the first Southern troops to join Washington's army.

During the eventful years that followed, John Hanson exerted a remarkable influence which was felt in ever widening circles. He became one of the leading men, not only in Maryland, but also in the colonies, as will be seen in the events that followed. He was Treasurer of Frederick County, and chairman of two important committees from Frederick County, namely the Committee of Observation and the Committee of Correspondence; and he was also a member of the Maryland Convention. He used his influence to promote the Maryland Bill of Rights and the new Constitution of Maryland, adopted on November 10, 1776. And when the Revolutionary War started in earnest, the task of organizing an army in Maryland was largely the task of John Hanson. Besides the two companies already mentioned, Maryland sent forty companies of Minute Men to the front. John Hanson was also chosen by the Maryland Convention to establish a gun-lock factory at Frederick. John Hancock, President of the Continental Congress, considered John Hanson one of the most trustworthy men in the colonies.

One of the most important contributions John Hanson made to the American Union was his successful fight to have all "backlands" become the property of the Union. It will be remembered that on July 4, 1778, Virginia troops headed by General Clark, crossed the Ohio River, conquered the British troops, and took possession of the Northwest Territory. By virtue of this conquest, Virginia claimed not only the Northwest Territory but also considerable adjoining land. Furthermore, Massachusetts, Connecticut, New York, the Carolinas and Georgia claimed extensive backlands in addition to the territory within the regular boundary of each colony. As the Articles of Confederation were prepared, this perplexing land question had to be settled, one way or the other. John Hanson led the Maryland fight for the settlement of this momentous question. One by one the other colonies dropped their claims to backlands, but Virginia persisted. Finally, when it became evident that the Maryland delegates, of which John Hanson was one, would refuse to sign the Articles of Confederation until the backlands became the property of the Union, Virginia finally yielded, and the Union became a reality. John Hanson, as a delegate from Maryland, became one of the signers of the Articles of Confederation. Senator Louis E. McComas of Williamsport, Maryland, said on the occasion of the dedication of the statues of John Hanson and Charles Carroll, on behalf of Maryland, in the Congress of

LUTHERANS, 1763-89   265

the United States on January 31, 1903, that "For his share in this pregnant service, John Hanson's name will be forever associated with the laying of the cornerstone of our great nation."[27]

But John Hanson's contributions to the cause of liberty did not end with his personal services. Like Muhlenberg, he wielded a large influence on his family. His brother, Walter Hanson, served as Commissary for Charles County. Another brother, Samuel Hanson, gave George Washington eight hundred pounds sterling to buy shoes for his soldiers at Valley Forge. John Hanson's oldest son, Alexander Contee Hanson, served for some time as private secretary to George Washington in the field; he was finally compelled to resign because of ill health. A second son, Samuel Hanson, served in the field as surgeon in Washington's Life Guards. A third son, Peter Contee Hanson, was made first lieutenant by the Continental Congress in September, 1776. He died shortly after as a British prisoner of war.

After the ratification of the Articles of Confederation, the election of the first president took place, on November 5, 1781. John Hanson was chosen "President of the United States in Congress Assembled." From that illustrious company of leaders and statesmen assembled, John Hanson was selected as the foremost person in the United States of America.[28] George Washington sent him a letter of congratulation. During his residence in Philadelphia, John Hanson worshiped in the Gloria Dei Church, built by Swedish Lutherans nearly a century before; the church in which Betsy Ross was married, and the church to which the women belonged who helped her make the American flag.

On November 28, 1781, George Washington made a visit

[27] *Senate Document No. 13*, Fifty-eighth Congress, special session.
[28] This election was held by delegates from the Thirteen States, and in accordance with the newly adopted Articles of Confederation. The Federal Constitution was not adopted until 1787. John Hanson was the first President under the Articles of Confederation; George Washington was the first President under the Federal Constitution of 1787.

to Congress at Philadelphia. On that occasion President John Hanson made a brief, eloquent address, and George Washington responded. As President of the United States in Congress Assembled, it became the lot of John Hanson to guide the nation through one of the most crucial and formative years. Among the notable things accomplished were the organization of a strong cabinet, the creation of a National Seal, the same as is used today, and proclamation of a Thanksgiving Day on the last Thursday in November.[29]

His services as National President were brief. Declining health caused him to seek voluntary retirement. Anticipating the trends of the election of November 4, 1782, he stated in a letter of September 4, 1782, "I think the public has no further claim to my services. I have performed my term of duty, and they must give me a discharge." His wish was respected. About a year later, on November 15, 1783, he passed away.

The method of governing the Union was changed in 1787, when the Federal Constitution was adopted, and three branches of government were created, the executive, the legislative and the judicial. On April 30, 1789, George Washington became President under the new Federal Constitution. Thus, John Hanson was the first President of America under the Articles of Confederation, and George Washington was the first President of America under the Federal Constitution.

VI. Other Lutheran Contributors.—About the year 1770, a prominent member of the Lutheran Church of Denmark, Captain Abram Markoe of the distinguished Markoe family, moved from the Danish island of St. Croix to Philadelphia. Being a man of wealth, he purchased an entire city block in Philadelphia, where he built a mansion on the model of a Danish manor house, with stables and other outbuildings. Being also a man of high qualities of leadership, he organized, on September 17, 1774, the Philadelphia Troop of Light Horse, the First City Troop, in

---

[29] This date, suggested by President John Hanson, has been followed almost invariably as National Thanksgiving Day until Nov., 1939.

anticipation of the coming conflict. This is the oldest military organization in America.

The next year, in 1775, Captain Markoe presented his troop with a very beautiful silk flag which is of great historic importance. In the center of this flag was a knot tied with thirteen cords, and in the canton thirteen horizontal stripes, alternating blue and silver. It is claimed that this is the first flag on which the union of the colonies was represented by thirteen horizontal stripes. This flag was carried during all the campaigns in which the troop was engaged throughout the Revolution. It was also carried while Captain Markoe and his troop escorted George Washington through Pennsylvania, New Jersey and New York to the Connecticut line, just after his election as Commander-in-Chief of the Army. The idea of thirteen stripes in the union became very popular. It appears certain that the idea originated with the flag designed by Captain Markoe. Rhode Island is said to have produced the first flag on which the thirteen colonies were represented by thirteen stars.

From the membership of the Lutheran congregation at Charleston, South Carolina, came the second oldest military organization in the United States of America, the German *Fusileers*, organized in 1775. The Fusileers, who originally numbered 137 men, were called into service immediately upon the outbreak of the Revolutionary War. Another 100 men from this same congregation, knowing that they were unable to endure the hardships of active military service, organized themselves into the *Friendly Society,* and voted 2000 pounds for defense against the Crown. The pastor, John Nicholas Martin, who was a strong supporter of the colonists, refused to pray for the King of England. In retaliation, the Tories refused him permission to enter his church, and his property was confiscated.

John Adam Treutlen was the greatest Lutheran layman produced by the Salzburgers of Georgia. He helped to form the state of Georgia, and was elected first Provincial Governor of Georgia in 1777. Through one of his appointees, Colonel Elbert, and his brilliant victory at the Fortress of Frederica in April, 1778, he successfully upset the British plan to subjugate Georgia and South Carolina and make them the basis of operations against the other colonies. This achievement was of vital importance to the cause of American independence. Being betrayed by an enemy Tory, Treutlen had to flee for his life. He joined the army of General Wayne where he served as Quartermaster-general until the end of the war.

Doctor Bodo Otto, senior surgeon in charge of hospitals in the Continental Army from 1776 to 1782, was a staunch Lutheran. He was born of Lutheran parents in Hanover, Germany and soon gained fame as an army surgeon in Germany. In 1755 he migrated to America and settled in Pennsylvania. At the outbreak of the Revolutionary War he was chosen delegate to the Provincial Congress of June 18, 1776. Although 67 years of age, he offered his services to the army, and his two sons, also surgeons, likewise offered their services. Their offers were gratefully and promptly accepted.

It is a well known fact that after 1778, Washington's body-guard was composed almost exclusively of Germans. In his former body-guard were suspected Tories who had made plots to take his life. Washington's body-guard of Germans, known as *The Independent Troop Horse*, was under the command and direction of Major Bartholomew Van Heer. He recruited most of his men from the German counties of Berks and Lancaster, where the Lutheran population was large. Among the prominent members of this body-guard were Captain Ignatius Von Effinger and Ludwig Boyer (Beyer), and these were staunch Lutherans.

Christopher Ludwig, a member of Zion Lutheran Church, Philadelphia, and also a member of the Continental Congress, deserves honorable mention. As Baker General he furnished the armies with good, wholesome bread; and he furnished more loaves of bread per 100 pounds of flour than any other baker seemed capable of doing, or was willing to do. Ludwig performed an important service to the men in service by his good bread, and also to the colonial authorities by his great honesty.

On several occasions, George Washington attended services at Zion Lutheran Church, Philadelphia. He was much impressed by the dignity of the service, the symmetry and spaciousness of the building, and the deep-toned harmony of the Tannenberger organ.

The late President Hibben of Princeton University said, "The Lutheran Church has stood for both religious and civil freedom at the great crises of the world's history, and our American institutions have drawn much of their vitality and strength from the spirit which has animated its followers."

Adolph Wertmuller, a Swedish Lutheran artist, made a painting of George Washington in 1794 which has received much favorable comment. It was among the number selected to be reproduced in the Centennial edition of Irving's *Life of George Washington*.

VII. Conclusion.—From the general facts mentioned above it will be seen that Lutherans in colonial America took a most active and worthy part in the great struggle for independence. The Lutherans were less conspicuous than the Congregationalists and the Presbyterians, but they played a role fully as important as that of the descendants of the Pilgrim Fathers.

Is the Lutheran Church an imported church? No, it is here by virtue of birthright. Lutherans are not foreigners in America. They were among the early settlers; they took a worthy part in the subjugation of the great American Continent; and they took a worthy part in the rearing of the Temple of Liberty in America.

16. REVIEW QUESTIONS

1. What position did the Established Church in the colonies take in the War of Independence?
2. What contributions did the Congregational and the Presbyterian Churches make to the cause of liberty?

270 THE LUTHERAN CHURCH IN AMERICA

3. In what ways did the Roman Catholic Church help the Thirteen Colonies?
4. Why did the Baptists give whole-hearted support to the colonies?
5. What handicapped the Methodists, the Quakers, the Mennonites and the Moravians?
6. Why did the Lutherans support the colonies in their struggle for liberty?
7. What attitude did Luther take toward armed resistance?
8. Why did not the Ministerium of Pennsylvania as such make official resolutions regarding the war; why did the Lutheran pastors sound the notes of freedom privately?
9. What part did the Muhlenberg brothers take in the Revolutionary War?
10. What attitude did the Patriarch, Henry Melchior Muhlenberg, take toward the war? Why?
11. What part did John Hanson and his family play in the struggle for American independence?
12. Why has this man and his family been almost entirely ignored in popular histories?

TOPICS FOR SPECIAL STUDY

1. German Lutheran contributions to American liberty.
2. Swedish Lutheran contributions to American liberty.
3. Fundamental characteristics of the young American nation.

A SELECTED BIBLIOGRAPHY FOR CHAPTER III

1. *Hallesche Nachrichten.*
2. *Journal of the House of Commons.*
3. *Pennsylvania Archives.*
4. *Archives of Maryland,* Maryland Historical Society, Council of Safety.
5. *Maryland Senate and House Journals, 1757-1784.*
6. *American Archives,* Vol. I-V.
7. *United States Documents, Formation of the Union* (Congressional Library).
8. *United States Journals of Continental Congress* (Vol. XIX-XXIII).
9. *United States Journals of Congress, 1781-82.*
10. *Dictionary of American Biography.*
11. Wharton, *United States Revolutionary Diplomatic Correspondence,* Vol. V-VI.
12. Fiske, *Critical Period of American History.*
13. Williams, *History of Frederick County, Md.*
14. Thomas, *Chronicles of Colonial Maryland.*
15. *Senate Document No. 13,* Fifty-eighth Congress, special session.
16. Danes, *Maryland in the Campaign.*
17. Knott, *Contribution of Maryland to the Formation of the Federal Union.*

LUTHERANS, 1763-89

18. Burns, *Controversies between Royal Governors and their Assemblies in the Northern American Colonies.*
19. Heckscher, *Mercantilism.*
20. Bittinger, *The Germans in Colonial Times.*
21. Faust, *The German Element in the United States.*
22. Mann, *Life and Times of Henry Melchior Muhlenberg.*
23. Bernheim, *History of the German Settlements and the Lutheran Church in North and South Carolina.*
24. Baldwin, *The New England Clergy and the American Revolution.*
25. Breed, *Presbyterians and the Revolution.*
26. Cathcart, *The Baptists and the American Revolution.*
27. Thornton, *The Pulpit and the American Revolution.*
28. Van Tyne, *The Causes of the War of Independence.*
29. Jameson, *The American Revolution Considered as a Social Movement.*
30. Cobb, *Rise of Religious Liberty in America.*
31. Nelson, *John Hanson and the Inseparable Union.*
32. Andrews, *The Colonial Background of the American Revolution.*

APPENDIX I

CONSTITUTION OF THE FIRST LUTHERAN SYNOD IN AMERICA[1]

TITLE PAGE

GENERAL CHURCH ORDER for the Congregations Adhering to the Unaltered Augsburg (Confession) after Previous Comparison with THE GENERAL CHURCH ORDER by The Very Venerable Lutheran Consistory at Amsterdam Transmitted to Us and also by the Very Venerable Consistory Recommended to Us for Our Christian Congregations in the Province of New York and New Jersey, made Applicable.

". . . each and every member of the classis, for example, preachers, elders, deacons, and all other consistorial (Members) representing a congregation, who now are or hereafter shall come, shall before the beginning of their functioning have signed this order without reservation and shall punctually conduct themselves according to it, so that under the aforesaid Amsterdam Consistory our congregations, being one in the pure doctrine, may by means of this church order establish good harmony, . . . according as it was printed in 1686 and reprinted in 1725."

PART I

CHAPTER I. CONCERNING DOCTRINE

ARTICLE I

"All called preachers of the congregations shall regulate their teaching and preaching according to the rule of the divine Word, the Biblical, prophetical and apostolical writings, also according to our Symbolical Books, the Unaltered Confession of Augsburg, its Apology, the Schmalkald Articles, both Catechisms of Luther, and the Formula of Concord;

[1] This constitution was found in 1910 in the archives of Ulster County, New York, by Dr. Karl Kretzmann of Orange, New Jersey. There seem to have been five copies of this constitution, four in Dutch and one in German. The Dutch copies were known respectively as the New York, the Loonenburgh, the Hackensack and the Raritan copies. The German copy was for the Raritan churches in New Jersey. The text from which this translation is made is evidently from the Loonenburgh copy. This translation is by Dr. Kretzmann, as printed in the *Concordia Historical Institute Quarterly*, Vol. IX, No. 1 and No. 3.

neither should they teach or preach, privately or publicly, anything against these [Confessions] nor even use any other new phrases which would contradict the same."

ARTICLE II

This article treats of the manner of preaching to be done in the churches, and of brotherly admonition in case of failure to preach the pure doctrine and of leading an irreproachable life.

ARTICLE III

It deals with public rebuke of sins on the part of the preachers.

ARTICLE IV

This obligates the preachers to use the Amsterdam Church Order of 1689.

ARTICLE V

This article prescribes the order of the funeral services. This is not contained in the Amsterdam Church Order. The article is rather lengthy and detailed.

CHAPTER II. CONCERNING TIME AND PLACE FOR WORSHIP

ARTICLE I

On Sundays and festival days, at 10 o'clock in the morning, the Gospels and at 3 o'clock in the afternoon the Epistles shall be explained; on the second holiday (Christmas, Easter, Pentecost) and Ascension there shall be only one sermon; in Loonenburgh on Maundy Thursday. During May, June and July only the Epistles shall be explained. The time of the services depends on the "wind and weather" (many of the parishioners had to cross from the east side of the Hudson); but the catechization should begin at 10 o'clock.

ARTICLE II

Order of service on Sunday morning: Prayer; reading of the Gospel; the first hymn; one or two chapters from the Bible, with a summary in Low-Dutch and a short direction for use in doctrine and life (on Dom. X, p. Trin. the history of the destruction of Jerusalem should be read); the second hymn; the sermon, preceded by a prayer and the hymn *Herr Jesu Christ, dich zu uns wend,* or, *Nun bitten wir den Heiligen Geist* and followed by the absolution and the common morning prayer; a hymn; the benediction (on festival days the festival prayer shall take the place of the morning prayer). In the afternoon, after the first prayer, Bible-reading, hymn, sermon, *Liebster Jesu, wir sind hier,* prayer, hymn, examination of the youth in the Six Chief Parts of the Christian doctrine, with explanations.

ARTICLE III

All conventicles and secret meetings shall be forbidden as being liable to cause offense.

ARTICLE IV

But in the absence of the domine the "voorlezer" shall observe the same order, except that he shall omit: 1) the prayer before the sermon, 2) the application of the reading of the Bible, 3) the absolution after the sermon; and that he shall use in the place of the benediction the words: "The peace of God, which is higher than all understanding, keep our hearts and minds unto eternal life. Amen. Depart, then, in the peace of the Lord. Amen."

CHAPTER III. ADMINISTRATION OF HOLY BAPTISM

ARTICLE I

Baptism shall be performed in conformity with the agenda, so that even in *adiaphoris* there may be, as far as possible, conformity; water should be used "met de volle hand," and the sign of the cross should be made upon the child's breast and face at the prayer, "The almighty God and Father of our Lord Jesus Christ," etc.

ARTICLE II

Baptisms in the homes should take place only in the case of bodily illness of the child. As a rule, the children should be brought to the services of the church for baptism.

ARTICLE III

Adult Baptism. If it is found that adults have not been baptized correctly, they shall be instructed in our Catechism and make their baptismal vow, according to the agenda. "In regard to the Negroes the preacher should be careful that they promise not to abuse their Christianity or break the bond of submission."

ARTICLE IV

Baptisms should be entered with the names of the parents and witnesses and the dates in a special church record.

ARTICLE V

Fathers should be present at the baptism of their children and be intent on taking pious witnesses and adherents of our religion.

ARTICLE VI

Our Christians should beware of being witnesses at baptisms in other denominations or of bringing the children to baptism in other denominations, since it is more advisable to commend them in prayer to God and to rest on the infinite mercy of Christ than to burden the conscience of the parents.

CHAPTER IV. PENITENTIAL SERMON AND ABSOLUTION BEFORE LORD'S SUPPER

ARTICLE I

The Holy Supper shall ordinarily be given in New York at the stated time, namely, on Pentecost and on the Ninth and the Twenty-first post Trinity; in other congregations as time and circumstances will permit; in Loonenburgh, on Easter and the second or third Sunday in August and Christmas, or on the Festival of the Circumcision; in Hackensack, on First Christmas Day, First Easter Day, and Eleventh Sunday after Trinity.

ARTICLE II

The preachers shall admonish the Christians four weeks in advance to prepare themselves for the Lord's Table and that those who intend to commune should examine themselves well and not receive the Holy Sacrament without sincere repentance and turning to God, but after Christian and brotherly reconciliation with their neighbor.

ARTICLE III

The young people who have not yet gone to the Lord's Table or have not been sufficiently instructed in the Christian doctrine, and likewise such as have been burdens of conscience should be earnestly admonished that they should come to the preacher during the week to be examined in the Catechism and the chief parts of the Christian doctrine and to be instructed in, and comforted from, the Word of God; and private absolution shall not be denied them who desire it.

ARTICLE IV

It shall be the custom to have a sermon on Saturday, at a certain time in the afternoon, which, together with the prayers and the singing, should not last much over an hour, after which the regular questions according to the agenda should be asked of the Christians who intend to go to the Lord's Supper. In the country churches, as in Loonenburgh, and in itinerary, as in the Highlands [of the Hudson], this preparatory sermon may be held the same day when the Lord's Supper is celebrated.

ARTICLE V

In order that no one may be admitted to the Lord's Supper who has not been duly instructed, the congregation shall be properly requested to have their names written down either after the [confessional] sermon in the church or in the house of the domine. In Loonenburgh the communicants announce themselves to the domine before the confessional sermon begins, or the house-father his family.

Chapter V. Administration of the Lord's Supper

Article I

The Christians who have prepared themselves for the Lord's Supper should come on Saturday morning to the sermon. The sermon being ended, the deacons shall prepare the table, furnish it with bread and wine and whatever else is necessary of plates and cups, if this has not been done before the sermon.

Articles II and III

The admonition, consecration, and distribution shall take place as is customary in our Low-Dutch congregations in this country. In *externis*: At the words "He took bread" and "He took the cup" the vessels with the bread and wine shall be touched, and at the words "This is My body," "This is My blood," the hand shall be extended *"quasi monstrando"* over the bread and wine until the words of consecration have been fully uttered; and thereupon the communicants shall receive the Lord's Supper with reverence and "Eerbiedigheid."

Article IV

During these actions proper psalms and hymns should be sung, and also fitting prayers shall be read; and after the administration of the Sacrament the preacher shall close with prayer and thanksgiving, with a spiritual hymn of praise, and finally with the benediction. The remaining bread and wine shall be given to the preacher in the presence of the deacons and the "voorlezer."

Chapter VI. Christian Discipline. Excommunication

Article I

No one living in manifest sins, such as adultery, unchastity, drunkenness, blasphemy, witchcraft, shall be admitted to the Sacrament. Those who sin should be admonished privately; if this is in vain, the preacher or some one delegated by the consistory shall be called in, and the admonition should be repeated. If he will not hear them or make amends, he shall be admonished once more; and if this does not help, he shall be bidden with the consent of the preacher and those delegated [by the consistory] on a Sunday after the sermon to appear before them; and if that does not help, it is recommended that each consistory act in the matter according to conscience and the circumstances of the congregation.

Chapter VII. Of the Solemnization of Marriage

Article I

The bans shall be published three times. Strangers should bring written testimony that they are free to marry, such as a licence from His Excellency the Governor or proof of proclamation.

ARTICLE II

Those intending to marry should first go to the Lord's Supper together and prepare to make their household truly Christian.

ARTICLE III

After public proclamation the marriage shall take place, if possible, in the church in the presence of parents and friends and with the knowledge of the consistory.

(Here is to be added what was resolved upon and decreed on November 11, 1740, that, if there is any suspicion of adultery, malicious desertion, or elopement, the domine should refuse to perform the ceremony.)

PART II

OF THE CALL AND OFFICE OF THE PREACHERS AND OF THE ELECTED ELDERS AND DEACONS

CHAPTER I. OF THE ORDER IN THE CONSISTORY

ARTICLE I

Because God is a God not of confusion, but of peace (1 Cor. 14), a church assembly shall be instituted, called the consistory, or church council, which shall ordinarily meet twice a year (in Hackensack on New Year's Day and Ascension; in the city [New York] no certain date can be set on account of the members of the church council living beyond the [Hudson] River; in Loonenburgh the time has been set for Maundy Thursday or the day after Easter and the day after New Year.)

ARTICLE II

At this consistory there shall appear the called ministers, the elected elders and deacons, and such other persons as the congregation are wont to call in. The preacher shall preside and shall record all churchly matters and consistorial resolutions and actions.

ARTICLE III

Order of meetings. After the invocation the presiding preacher or, in his absence, the president of the elders shall state what is necessary at the time to vote upon, to ask every one what he might wish to propose, and to transact nothing but what is necessary for the government of the churches.

ARTICLE IV

In the matters of doctrine, faith, and morals the preacher shall have power to decide with the elders; but in regard to the church funds the elders shall have power to act alone, according to the judgment of the majority.

ARTICLE V

In highly important matters, especially in the calling, nomination, or election of preachers or the choosing or engaging of other servants of the church, the elected and former elders, together with the governing and old deacons, according to the custom of each congregation, shall be called in, and their advice shall be solicited, after which the majority shall decide.

ARTICLE VI

If any dissension should occur in any church or between churches which cannot be settled among themselves, it shall be settled according to a resolution of the classis [synod] at the cost of those who wish such a decision. If the decision does not find favor, advice shall be sought from some consistory in Europe, wherewith all parishes shall be satisfied.

ARTICLE VII

In case of remissness in office or life on the part of preachers and other officers of the church they shall be reproved in a brotherly manner.

ARTICLE VIII

The transaction of the church council shall be kept secret and revealed to none except those whom they may concern.

ARTICLE IX

The most important transactions shall be recorded, together with the names of those present.

CHAPTER II. OF THE OFFICE, SALARY, AND RETIREMENT OF PREACHERS

ARTICLE I

Since God has gathered a church here, the Christians shall be admonished to call upon God to send faithful laborers into the harvest. The call, signed by the officers of the calling congregation, shall be sealed by the consistory of New York and be sent to one of the consistories in Europe, to wit, to Hamburg, London, or Amsterdam, at the expense of the calling congregation.

ARTICLE II

No person shall be admitted to our pulpits unless he can show proper credentials that he was admitted and ordained by one of the afore-mentioned consistories or other orthodox academies or *ministeria*. In the absence of proper testimonials such tramps (*currents*) shall immediately be rejected as men who do not seek to build the Church of God, but destroy it. In the case of one who never was in the ministry before, the calling congregation shall immediately give notice to the consistory of New York and to the nearest congregations and preachers. Before these such a person shall produce lawful attestations concerning his orthodoxy and life and shall preach a trial sermon in New York. Having done this and having been found capable, he may be permitted to do the ordinary preaching for one year. In the mean time the consistory of New York shall procure information from the consistories or the university where the *vocandus* has studied, and if he proves to be competent and no unfavorable advice is received, the officers of the church, with the consent of the nearest preachers, shall make out the call after he has been properly examined and ordained. This examination and ordination shall be done by the Swedish consistory in Pennsylvania (if there be but one preacher among us) or otherwise by the consistory of New York through three commissioned [preachers] of the nearest congregations. Those who were in the ministry before shall be obliged to produce from the place where they last officiated, together with documents of their former call and ordination, as well as a testimonial of their blameless life and conversation and a declaration that they have adhered to the pure doctrine of our Symbolical Books. Besides, if they wish to be called by our congregations and looked upon as colleagues (*Amtsbroederen*), they shall promise to obey and follow this Church Order according to form and content in all points and articles and therefore introduce and use no new form in Baptism, absolution, the Lord's Supper, and the blessing of marriage, but maintain uniformity even in regard to these ceremonies; also with their own hand and signature promise to be faithful and zealous in their office and ministry, to preach God's Word alone, purely and truly, and to lead a Christian and blameless life and thus be an example to the churches of Christ; and all this on pain of ecclesiastical censure, even unto suspension and removal, subject to appeal to the consistory in the fatherland (*salva appellatione ad Consistorium in patria*), named in Article I. And to this end shall this Church Order be entered into a book, sealed by the church seal, and attested and given into the custody of the consistory of New York, until occasion presents itself to print the same and the signatures of the teachers shall be affixed. However, a copy of the original shall be delivered to our churches, which is to be signed by the domine and the church council of each congregation.

ARTICLE III

In case the preachers give any offense in doctrine or life, the officers of the congregation shall take notice thereof and admonish them to desist and to promise to do better. In case they fail, the preacher shall be subject to churchly censure and, with the knowledge and consent of the consistory through which the preacher has been called, the three nearest congregations in this country, convened at the expense of the guilty party, shall be deposed from his office and ministry and shall expect no further salary without previous confession of his sin and sincere promise of amendment.

ARTICLE IV

No accusation shall be received against a preacher without two or three witnesses.

ARTICLE V

Differences between preachers should not be brought before the simple-minded congregations, but before the consistories or otherwise be as much as possible composed and decided in conformity with the resolution of the classis [synod] of 1676.

ARTICLE VI

The preacher shall also not seek a following among some rebellious members or schismatics and have nothing to do with them without the consent of the consistory, much less write or print anything without the consent of the preachers of our fraternity (*Maatschappye*).

ARTICLE VII

They [the preachers] shall be satisfied with the promised wages and shall not desire more than the congregation in the call has stipulated; however, free-will offerings and *honoraria* as well as testamentary gifts shall remain unforbidden.

ARTICLE VIII

At the demise of preachers the back salary shall be paid by the church council to the widow and children or their executors and administrators in this manner, that, whether death occurs at the beginning of the half of the year or at the end, a full half year's salary be paid. The other preacher of our fraternity shall admonish and induce the congregation of deceased preachers thereto. In case a preacher dies unmarried, the outstanding salary and other goods of the domine shall be delivered to his servants.

CHAPTER III. OF THE CALLING AND THE OFFICE OF THE ELECTED ELDERS

ARTICLE I

Since Paul, 1 Cor. 12, says that God wants governors and helpers in His Church, the preachers and church councils shall see to it, though our congregations be weak, that there is the proper change in the servants of the Church, and that such persons be chosen by the congregations as have the testimony of a blameless life and manifest a sincere love to our divine service.

ARTICLE II

This election shall take place at Pentecost or Christmas or at any stated time, according to the circumstances of each church, in this manner, that at least every two or three years there be a change. The chosen ones should be made known publicly to the congregation and inducted into office with the laying on of hands, according to the church agenda.

ARTICLES III AND IV

The office of the elected elders shall consist chiefly of the following points: 1) They shall show all diligence that God's Word be proclaimed purely and truly by pious preachers and teachers to the Christians in our congregations, that the holy Sacraments be administered according to the command and institution of Jesus Christ, in all points, and that the pure doctrine be transplanted to our descendants. To this end they should, if possible, be present at all sermons and listen to them. 2) They shall take care that the called preachers and other servants of the church receive their promised wages and salary according to the subscription of the congregation, semiannually or quarterly, and that all other things be done that are necessary. They shall request and receive the contributions from the Christians in person or through the deacons (and not without reason through others) and give account of their receipts to the church council. 3) Together with the preachers they shall have the oversight of the whole congregation, that all manner of sins, vices, and offenses be avoided or, on the other hand, properly reproved and done away with. 4) They shall keep an account of all the free-will promises toward the upkeep of the church, so that they can give an annual accounting and, whenever their office expires, liquidate; and the original of their accounting shall be deposited in the church chest (Kerkenkist); and they shall be given a receipt from the domine and the church council. 5) The annually elected [officers] shall be held to carry out resolutions of their predecessors made for the peace and welfare as well as for the benefit and profit of the congregations. 6) They shall at all festival, Sunday, and weekday services, according to old custom, gather and receive the donations and contributions of the congregation for the benefit of the church and the poor.

ARTICLE V

None of the church officers shall be permitted to keep more than ten pounds without a bond or without paying the ordinary interest thereon nor to loan out money without giving notice to the church council, or without security and interest as the law allows. If he acts otherwise, it shall be at his own expense.

CHAPTER IV. OF THE OFFICE, CALLING, AND SERVICE OF THE DEACONS

ARTICLE I

Since the deacons are to be elected according to apostolic example in the same manner as the elders, they shall receive the alms and contributions of the Christians and disburse them again in behalf of the poor and the church.

ARTICLE II

Their office shall consist chiefly in this, that, besides the elders, they receive the alms of the Christians, according to the custom of each congregation, and the recipient shall enter them immediately in a special book.

ARTICLE III

A yearly account shall be rendered, and the annual surplus shall be placed into the church treasury, and at the conclusion of his term the surplus shall be delivered to his successor.

ARTICLE IV

If new members are added to the church, they shall be asked by the deacons to contribute to the support of the ministry and the poor. If any Christian intends to go on a journey, he shall be admonished to give a donation or alms. Christians shall be admonished to remember the poor and the church in their testament.

ARTICLES V-VIII

Whenever alms are given to the poor, this shall be made known by the deacons to the church council.

ARTICLE IX

The church chest and church papers shall be kept thus: One deacon shall have the chest and the other the key in his house, that without the presence of both nothing can be taken therefrom nor put into it; and these church papers shall be inspected once a year. Thus also the church seal shall not be used except in the presence of two members of the church council.

CHAPTER V. OF THE READER'S [VOORLESER'S] INSTALLATION AND OFFICE

ARTICLE I

The *Voorleser* shall promise at his public installation: 1) to adhere with all his heart to our Christian doctrine as contained in the Sacred Scriptures and our Church Symbols; 2) to read nothing to the congregation but what is contained in the books given him by the domine or which belong to the church; 3) to lead an edifying and unoffensive life; 4) to conduct his office as of the strength which God gives.

ARTICLE II

His service consists: 1) in leading in the singing (voorsingen), whether the preacher is present or not; 2) in reading to the congregation (voorlesen) whenever the domine is absent, in the forenoon as well as in the afternoon; 3) he shall find out from the domine what is to be sung; 4) he should prepare the Lord's Table and what belongs thereto; 5) for some compensation he should walk beside the domine at funerals; 6) he should attend the meetings of the church council, so as to be able to serve the congregation with good counsel, having his pew in the church next to the domine's and his rank in Communion and in the church council next to the councilors.

ARTICLE III

Since his office does not take any of the time he needs to make a living and tends to edify his soul as well as that of others and to speed the honor of God, he shall show godliness with contentment and be satisfied with what a weak congregation can allow him for his services, remembering that God is a Rewarder in those things which are not compensated for by men, whereof the apostle says, Heb. 6:10: "God is not unrighteous to forget your work and labor of love."

ARTICLE IV

On the other hand, the congregation shall be earnestly admonished and urged by the church council to remember that the laborer is worthy of his hire, Luke 10:7, so that every one subscribe to the *voorleser's tractament* as well as to the domine's salary according to ability, since we are so situated that we can spare a *voorleser* as little as a domine for our public service. "If he has sown spiritual things, should he not also reap carnal things?" 1 Cor. 9:11.

CHAPTER VI. OF THE BELL-RINGER'S SERVICES AND WAGES

ARTICLE I

The bell-ringers service consists in this: 1) to ring the bell for every service, regulating himself for the first and second time after the other churches and getting his order from the domine for the third time (of ringing); 2) to sweep the church every four weeks and the pulpit (chancel) every Sunday, with a broom; 3) to have the baptismal water on hand whenever there is a child to be baptized; 4) during the services to watch the door, the gallery, and the church to prevent anything whereby the Christians might be disturbed in their devotions; 5) to open and lock the church and bolt the windows and not give up the key; however, when it is wanted, to go along, for which he shall be allowed to accept a tip (quaertje); 6) to offer his services in the meetings of the church council if he is needed as a messenger.

ARTICLE II

As grave-digger he shall ring the bell and dig the grave, and whenever he is asked to bid people to the funeral (aanspreeken) and to collect the money for the ringing and the burial; however, he is not permitted to accept a funeral unless he has informed the domine and the church council.

ARTICLE III

Concerning the wages he shall enjoy his share out of the church treasury; but as grave-digger he shall be paid by those who engage him according to the regulation of each church.

So done in consenting order and accepted with the approval of the church councils of the Low-Dutch congregations in New York and on the Hackensack as well as in the city and county of Albany, sealed in New York.

"We have given our consent to this Order and bind ourselves with one consent to regulate our congregations according to it and thus set our hand and seal hereto. So help us God!

"S<small>UBSCRIBIMUS</small>"[2]

[2] This copy, found in 1910, was signed with some reservations on November 17, 1735, at Loonenburgh, by "Willem Christop Berkenmeyer" and eleven members of his church council. It was also signed on May 2, 1743, by Rev. Peter Nicolas Sommer; and on the Fourth Sunday after Trinity, 1747, by "Johannes Christopheras Hartwig."

APPENDIX II

ZINZENDORF VERSUS MUHLENBERG

What transpired during the meeting of these two men in Philadelphia in 1742, has been carefully recorded by Muhlenberg. Note the change of style of the Count in addressing Muhlenberg during the course of the conversation. This translation is from Mann, *Life and Times of Henry Melchior Muhlenberg*, pages 117-24.

Zinzendorf. On what conditions are you here?

Muhlenberg. I have been called and sent here by the reverend the courtpreacher Ziegenhagen in accordance with the commission of the congregations.

Zinzendorf. What commission had Ziegenhagen?

Muhlenberg. The three congregations anxiously solicited him for a number of years to send a pastor. The copies are deposited in Providence, the letters in London; which, if deemed necessary, may at any time be printed.

Zinzendorf. When did the congregations petition the last time?

Muhlenberg. This I do not know; it can be found in the copies.

Zinzendorf. You [here the count changes the form of his address, using the term *"Er"* instead of *"Sie"*] must answer at once when the last letter to Ziegenhagen was written. (To this the brewer and some other friends of the count's people assented, but said the last letter may have been sent about 1739.)

Muhlenberg. I am not in condition to answer this question just now. Neither is it of any weight, for I am called, sent, and accepted. The deacons and elders of the three congregations gave their signature to a "recepisse."

Zinzendorf. Here in Philadelphia there are no officers of the Lutheran congregation to give signatures. For before me here in this place the officers of the Lutheran congregation are seated, and there is no other Lutheran congregation or church besides the one we have. Did you see the church which we lately erected?

Muhlenberg. I know nothing of it, since I am convinced that I preached to the Lutherans and was accepted by them.

Zinzendorf. Those are not Lutherans, but rebels, disturbers of the peace. And of such people you have become the head, and preached to them in the house from which they expelled by Pyrlaeus. The rebels must first come to us and beg pardon.

Muhlenberg. My opinion, count, is that your people must first come to us Lutherans and beg pardon for having broken the lock off of our church and commenced the tumult.

Zinzendorf. This is not true.

Muhlenberg. This is quite true, for this is the very reason that both parties are now involved in a lawsuit.

Zinzendorf. I know of no lawsuit.

Muhlenberg. Well, indeed, everybody does know what happened last summer, July 18th.

Zinzendorf. Let us stick to the subject. At my last meeting with Ziegenhagen I asked him about Pennsylvania. He answered that he could not send any preacher, since the congregations were not willing to determine the salary. As Ziegenhagen knew that I was coming here, why did he send you?

Muhlenberg. I am sent here to inquire into the condition of things and to see whether order can be established.

Zinzendorf. Herr Ziegenhagen is an arch-liar and a hypocrite. When I am in his presence he is quite humble and submissive; when I am gone he uses his tongue and scolds. This is another trick which he and Herr Francke are playing off on me. I shall tell him of it when I reach London.

Muhlenberg. It is a shame to speak of the absent in such terms. I have often heard in Germany that you are in the habit of calling people L.L.L. [liars]. Now, how can I avoid believing it?

Zinzendorf. I am informed that you read all of my writings. Did you not read that I had established a Lutheran consistory in Philadelphia?

Muhlenberg. I read in Charleston of seven conferences, and learned that a certain Herr von Thürnstein had occasioned disturbances in various places; I did not know the Herr Count had formed a Lutheran consistory.

Zinzendorf. Oh, these are jesuitical tricks!

Muhlenberg. I heard once in Germany that you were installed by a Reformed preacher, a Moravian bishop. How could you in this capacity form a Lutheran consistory?

Zinzendorf. I am inspector of all Lutheran congregations in Pennsylvania and a Lutheran pastor in Philadelphia. I held synodical meetings here in this city and in the country. I have ordered pastors to some places, and one, Caspar Stoever, I have deposed. [In this Zinzendorf acted with two of his adjuncts altogether as a self-appointed judge.]

Muhlenberg. Can a Reformed preacher give such authority to you?

Zinzendorf. Do you not understand the canonical law? Do you not know that in Wittenberg the highest dignitary of the Lutheran Church is ordained by a Catholic?

Muhlenberg. But how is this, that you are sometimes a Moravian bishop, sometimes an inspector and a Lutheran pastor?

Zinzendorf. In Holland in the presence of lords and princes I resigned my episcopal office.

Muhlenberg. You change frequently.

APPENDIX II

Zinzendorf. I have a call in writing from the Lutheran congregation here in Philadelphia, as also my adjunct Pyrlaeus has.

Muhlenberg. Had your call the proper signatures?

Zinzendorf. There is no need of this.

Muhlenberg. My call has them. I shall carry out my instructions. If you find fault with this, you can settle it with my superiors in Europe.

Zinzendorf. But is it not contrary to all fairness and decency that after I have been so long in this country you should not have come to visit me? If you were sent to inquire into the condition of things here, why did you not inquire into my affairs? Any one who hears that there is a consistory and an inspector in any place, even if the thing be illegal, should go and try to inform himself.

Muhlenberg. If I, as a stranger, had called on you, you would not have been present. I was told you had gone to the Indians. One meets here with a good many parties. To call on all of them would be impossible for me. To the Lutherans I am sent, and with them I have work enough.

Zinzendorf. I am a Lutheran pastor; why did you not come to me?

Muhlenberg. I was not advised to do so, and I am not now.

Zinzendorf. Did Herr Ziegenhagen say that you should pass by the inspector and Lutheran pastor?

Muhlenberg. No, sir. This thing was not mentioned at all. Herr Ziegenhagen did not know that there was an inspector and a Lutheran pastor.

Zinzendorf. Did Herr Ziegenhagen not know that I was in Pennsylvania?

Muhlenberg. Yes, sir.

Zinzendorf. Do you not see now, from this, my brethren, that this man contradicts himself and lies, since to the same thing he says both yes and no? (The whole brotherhood assented with submissive bows.)

Muhlenberg. Herr Ziegenhagen knew well enough that Count Zinzendorf had gone to Pennsylvania. He did not know that the count intended to be a Lutheran inspector and pastor.

Zinzendorf. Did you not know that I was inspector and pastor?

Muhlenberg. I heard in Germany that you went to Pennsylvania with a definite intention.

Zinzendorf. What was that intention?

Muhlenberg. You had certainly an intention.

Zinzendorf. Just speak out; what was it?

Muhlenberg. I do not know.

Zinzendorf. Do you hear, brethren? This man is insane.

Muhlenberg. Not so quick! In your answer to the publication of Ad. Gross you say at the conclusion, "Brethren, I am now going to Pennsylvania; pray the Savior to reveal to you my intention." Consequently, who can know what your purposed intention was?

Zinzendorf. As soon as I arrive in London I will go to the archbishop [at London there is only a bishop] and tell him that I established order among the Lutherans, and that when order was established Herr Ziegenhagen sent some one who spoiled all and made confusion.

Muhlenberg. You may do as you please. The fact is, that you have now put all in confusion. I hope, with the help of God, to establish some order.

Zinzendorf. Go on with your work. If you succeed, it must eventually serve for the increase of my Church. You have my good wishes. It is not to be denied that you were a Lutheran student in good standing, that you had a pastoral charge, as was reported to me nine months ago from Herrnhut. No more is expected of you than that you beg pardon, since you are an intruder here and passed me by.

Muhlenberg. It will come to pass that you will be compelled to beg pardon of the whole Lutheran Church.

Zinzendorf. How can you, a young person, a village preacher, talk thus?

Muhlenberg. You must not wax warm.

Zinzendorf. Make haste to consider and to acknowledge that you have done wrong; if not, on my return to Germany I will make it all public.

Muhlenberg. In case I sin against God, I will in the name of Christ beg forgiveness. But I do not see why I should beg your pardon. You may publish in Germany what you please; your affairs are well known there.

Zinzendorf. What is published there against me is nothing but pasquils, to which no one ventures to put his name. I am willing to give you time to beg pardon. You are ambitious, and that is the motive by which you are governed.

Muhlenberg. Your brain is very fertile of suggestions. Indeed, I find it as your aunt [Baroness von Gersdorf at Grosshennersdorf] told me.

Zinzendorf. Say not a word of her or I shall be compelled to expose her. I might speak very differently to you if I wanted.

Muhlenberg. I am willing to hear.

Zinzendorf. The Hallenses are Pietists. Were you not educated at Halle?

Muhlenberg. I was educated in Hanover, studied at Göttingen, and also at Halle. I am a Lutheran, and shall so remain.

Zinzendorf. Are you such a Lutheran as Herr Ziegenhagen?

Muhlenberg. I have had intercourse with him for some time, have become acquainted with his character, and hope to become more and more such a Lutheran.

Zinzendorf. It will not take a year, and I shall bring forward more than a hundred witnesses to prove that Herr Ziegenhagen is not a genuine Lutheran.

Muhlenberg. Herr Ziegenhagen is not afraid of it, and will not be disturbed. But it is strange that you wish to entrap me with your questions to find a charge against me.

Zinzendorf. Oh, I am casting a hook into your conscience.

Muhlenberg. Not at all. You do not touch my conscience. But this I gather from your questions, that your heart is not sincere. If you had a guileless spirit you would not put those questions.

Zinzendorf. You came here to speak about a church record-book and a cup?

Muhlenberg. Yes; I wanted to ask whether you would return them or not.

Zinzendorf. What should we return? Those things belong to our Lutheran church and congregation. But in case you stand in need of them we will present them to you, provided you give a receipt in writing.

Muhlenberg. I desire no present from you. I only claim what belongs to us. The book and the cup had been paid for out of our collections. (Here I rose up.)

Zinzendorf. Consider well the matter of begging our pardon. Otherwise you will regret it.

Muhlenberg. I need no consideration. I do not acknowledge you as a genuine Lutheran, much less as an inspector or Lutheran pastor.

Zinzendorf. Do you hear, brethren? Now there is revealed what the man has in his heart. (Now much murmuring arose among the brethren, and hearty assent to his words by nodding their heads.)

Muhlenberg. It is also revealed what is in your heart. If you are such a genuine Lutheran, why were you prevented from preaching in the Swedish church?

Zinzendorf. Only one man, Kock, the Swedish merchant, interfered.

Muhlenberg. Mr. Kock is an officer in the Swedish church. Certainly, he did not prevent you from preaching without the knowledge of the only Swedish pastor, Rev. Tranberg.

Zinzendorf. Can you say that Mr. Tranberg refused me permission?

Muhlenberg. I can not say it positively. Enough, you were refused.

Zinzendorf. There, brethren, you hear it again, that the man contradicts himself and lies! (The assent of the brethren became so strong and noisy that I could not reply.)

In conclusion, the count said: You will not preach in the Swedish church more than twice or thrice before they cast you out as they did my adjunct, Pyrlaeus, from the old meeting-house.

Muhlenberg. I am willing to wait. I wish you a happy voyage to Europe. Farewell!

APPENDIX III

The Liturgy of 1748[1]

[The Agenda of 1748 was never printed; but each pastor provided himself with a written copy for his own use. Two of these copies came into the hands of the late Rev. Dr. J. W. Richards of Reading, who himself was a descendant of the patriarch Muhlenberg. The oldest and most complete copy came down from the hands of Pastor Jacob van Buskerk, and is from the year 1763. It has the chapters and paragraphs numbered, while the ritual and liturgical appointments are complete. The other copy is from the hand of Pastor Peter Muhlenberg, who was in Dunmore County, Va., at the time when this copy was written, that is, in 1769. Here the chapters and paragraphs are not numbered. The directions for the several divisions are not given in full; but the liturgical material is complete.

What we here furnish in print is taken from the copy of Pastor van Buskerk, and varies from it only in certain unimportant parts, that have been somewhat confused, the correction being supplied from the copy of Peter Muhlenberg. Notice of these variations is always given.

All the contents of the Liturgy are given, in regular order; yet only the more important parts are printed in full.]

Chapter I. The Manner in Which Public Worship Shall be Conducted in All Our Congregations

§ 1

When the pastor enters the church the worship shall begin with the singing of the hymn, "Nun bitten wir den Heiligen Geist," either entire, or several verses of it; or a verse of the hymn "Komm Heiliger Geist, Herre Gott."

§ 2

After the singing of the hymn, or verse, the pastor goes to the altar, turns his face to the congregation, and says:
Beloved in the Lord!
Thus saith the High and Lofty One that inhabiteth eternity, whose name is Holy: I dwell in the high and holy place, with him also that is of a contrite and humble spirit, to revive the spirit of the humble, and

[1] From H. E. Jacobs, *A History of the Evangelical Lutheran Church in the United States*, pp. 269-75.

APPENDIX III

to revive the heart of the contrite ones: I will not always chide, neither will I keep anger forever: only acknowledge thine iniquity, that thou hast transgressed against the Lord thy God.

If we confess our sins, He is faithful and just to forgive us our sins, and to cleanse us from all unrighteousness.

Accompany me therefore in making confession of sins, saying:

I, a poor sinner, confess unto God, my heavenly Father, that I have grievously and in various ways sinned against Him; not only by outward and gross sins, but much more by inward blindness of heart, unbelief, doubt, despondency, impatience, pride, selfishness, carnal lusts, avarice, envy, hatred, and malice, and by other sinful passions which are naked and open in the sight of my Lord and God, but which I, alas! cannot so fully understand. But I do sincerely repent, in deep sorrow, for these my sins; and with my whole heart I cry for mercy from the Lord, through His dear Son Jesus Christ, being resolved, with the help of the Holy Ghost, to amend my sinful life. Amen.

Lord God the Father in heaven, have mercy upon us. Lord God the Son, Redeemer of the world, have mercy upon us. Lord Holy Ghost, have mercy upon us and grant us Thy peace. Amen.

§ 3

After the confession the hymn "Allein Gott in der Höh sei Ehr" shall be sung.

§ 4

During the singing of the last verse the pastor goes to the altar, turns his face to the congregation, and says:

The Lord be with you.

The congregation responds:

And with thy spirit.

The pastor says:

Let us pray.

Then he prays in the words of the Collect which is appointed for the Sunday or the festival, in the Marburg Hymn-book. After the Collect the Lesson from the Espistle shall be read, being introduced with the following words:

Let us devoutly listen to the reading of the Lesson for this day, from the, etc.

§ 5

Then shall be sung the principal hymn, selected by the pastor, from the hymns in the Marburg Hymn-book—one familiar to the whole congregation. The whole hymn, or only a part of it, shall be sung, as circumstances may decide.

§ 6

After the singing of the principal hymn the Gospel Lesson shall be read, being introduced with the same words as before the Epistle. After the Gospel the pastor repeats devoutly the Creed, in verse, "Wir glauben all." If children are present to be baptized, the Gospel and the Creed are omitted.

§ 7

Before the sermon the hymn "Liebster Jesu, wir sind hier," or "Herr Jesu Christ, dich zu uns wend," is sung, either entire or in part.

§ 8

Ordinarily, the sermon shall be limited to three quarters of an hour, or, at the utmost, to one hour. If the pastor is moved to have an exordium or a series of supplications before he begins the Lord's Prayer, he is at liberty to do so. After the Lord's Prayer, as usual, [the Gospel is read?] during which reading the congregation shall stand. The sermon being concluded, nothing else shall be read than the appointed church-prayer here following, or the litany instead of it, by way of change; and nothing but necessity shall occasion omission. . . .

After the general prayer petitions for the sick shall follow, in case request has been made to that effect; then shall follow the Lord's Prayer, and then whatever proclamation and notices may be required. When all is done, the pastor closes with the votum:

The peace of God, which passeth all understanding, keep your hearts and minds, through Christ Jesus, unto eternal life. Amen.

§ 9

[This paragraph is taken from the copy of Peter Muhlenberg.]

Then a hymn shall be sung. After the sermon and the closing hymn the pastor goes to the altar and says:

The Lord be with you.

Congregation Responds: And with thy spirit

Pastor: Let us pray

Hold us up, O Lord, Lord our God, that we may live; and let our hope never make us ashamed. Help us by Thy might, that we may wax strong; and so shall we ever delight ourselves in Thy statutes, through Jesus Christ Thy dear Son, our Lord. Amen.

After the sermon in the afternoon shall be sung the hymn "Ach, bleib bei uns, Herr Jesu Christ." Then shall follow

The Benediction

The Lord bless thee and keep thee, and give thee peace, in the name of the Father, and of the Son, and of the Holy Ghost. Amen.

CHAPTER II. OF BAPTISM AND WHAT IS TO BE OBSERVED AT ITS ADMINISTRATION

[This agrees, nearly word for word, with the printed Liturgy of 1786.]

CHAPTER III. OF PROCLAIMING THE BANS

APPENDIX III

Chapter IV. Of Confession and the Holy Communion

§ 1

Ordinarily, whenever circumstances admit of it, the Supper of the Lord shall be administered on Christmas, on Easter, on Pentecost. It may also be administered at other times, as the necessity of the congregation may demand.

§ 2

The pastor shall give notice from the pulpit of the administration of the Lord's Supper, one week or two weeks before the time of its celebration. To this notice he shall add a short exhortation, and at the same time he shall inform the people as to the day when they shall report themselves to him and have their names recorded.

§ 3

The pastor shall keep a register of the communicants, which is to continue in the care of the congregation.

§ 4

In case the pastor should know that, among those who call upon him to report their names for Holy Communion, there is one or more who are living in strife, or occasional public scandal, and his own influence should not be sufficient to remedy the evil, he may call the vestry of the congregation together, and direct such offenders to appear before them, with their plea and answer.

§ 5

On the day before the administration of the Lord's Supper, and at the hour appointed by the pastor, the communicants shall all assemble in the church, when the following order shall be observed:

1. A penitential hymn, or a hymn suited to the object of the meeting, shall be sung.
2. After the hymn the pastor, speaking from the pulpit, exhorts the people to repentance; and in the application makes use of what he may have observed and learned about their spiritual state at the time when they reported their names.
3. After the Lord's Prayer the pastor reads aloud the names of the communicants that have reported to him.
4. After the reading of the names a verse is sung, and the pastor goes before the altar and receives and writes the names of those persons who, for satisfactory reasons, could not report themselves before.
5. Then the pastor calls upon the male communicants first, to come before him, and addresses to them the following questions:

I now ask you, in the presence of the omniscient God, and upon the testimony of your own conscience:

(1) and (2) [The first two questions have been retained unchanged in all subsequent editions of the Pennsylvania Liturgy.]

(3) I ask you: Whether you are fully resolved, with the help of God, to yield yourselves entirely to the gracious direction of the Holy Spirit, by his word; in order that by the power, the help, and the grace of the same, sin may be subdued in you, the old man with his evil deeds and corrupt affections be weakened and overcome by daily sorrow and repentance, and that you may win a complete victory over the world and all its allurements?

If this be your serious purpose, confess it and answer, Yes.

(4) Finally, I ask you: Whether any one of you yet has, in his heart, any complaint against another?

6. After these questions are answered the pastor and all of them together kneel down, when one of the communicants leads in repeating the confession of sin aloud, the pastor himself adding a short ejaculation thereto.

[The copy of Van Buskerk has no form of confession for this act; but the Muhlenberg copy supplies the following.]

I, a poor sinner, confess unto God, my heavenly Father, that I have grievously and in various ways sinned against Him, not only by outward, etc; . . . with the help of the Holy Ghost to amend my sinful life. Amen. [The same as under § 2.]

7. The pastor pronounces the absolution in the following words:

Upon this confession of sin which you have now made, I, a minister of my Lord Jesus Christ, hereby declare, to all them who are truly penitent and heartily believe in the Lord Jesus Christ, and are sincerely resolved, in heart, to amend their lives and daily to grow in grace, to them I declare the forgiveness of all their sins; in the name of the Father, and of the Son, and of the Holy Ghost. Amen.

But, on the other hand, I declare to all who are impenitent, to the hypocritical as well as the openly ungodly, and I testify, by the Word of God, and in the name of Jesus, that so long as they continue their impenitent state, loving sin and hating righteousness, God will not forget their sins, but retains their sins against them, and will assuredly punish and condemn them for their iniquities, in the end, except they turn to Him, now, in this day of grace; except they sincerely forsake all their evil ways, and come to Christ in true repentance and faith; which we heartily pray they may do. Amen.

Then the service shall close with the singing of a verse, and the pastor pronouncing the benediction.

[Here a leaf is missing from the Van Buskerk copy, that contained all of the *Retention*, after the words "openly ungodly," and the beginning of the order for the Holy Communion. The missing portions are supplied from the Muhlenberg copy. The Van Buskerk copy, which is defective in sections 6 and 7, begins again in section 8.]

APPENDIX III

THE HOLY COMMUNION

The minister goes before the altar, places the bread and the wine in order, then turns to the congregation and says:
Minister: The Lord be with you,
Congregation: And with thy spirit.
Minister: Let us lift up our hearts,
Congregation: We lift them up unto the Lord.
Minister: Holy, holy, holy is the Lord of Sabaoth.
Congregation: The world is full of his glory.

§ 8

Before the communion the pastor addresses the communicants in the exhortation here following:
Beloved in the Lord!
[Here follows Luther's Paraphrase of the Lord's Prayer, and his exhortation to the sacrament, exactly as it occurs in his *Deutsche Messe* (German Communion) of 1526.]

§ 9

The pastor turns his face to the bread and wine, and repeats the Lord's Prayer, and the words of the institution.
Let us pray: Our Father, etc.
Our Lord Jesus Christ in the night . . . in remembrance of me.

§ 10

Then the pastor turns to the congregation and says:
Now let all those who are found to be prepared, by the experience of sincere repentance and faith, approach, in the name of the Lord, and receive the Holy Supper.

§ 11

In giving the bread the pastor shall say these words:
Take and eat: this is the true body of your Lord Jesus Christ, given unto death for you; may this strengthen you in the true faith unto everlasting life. Amen.
In giving the cup:
Take and drink: this is the true blood of your Lord Jesus Christ, of the New Testament, shed for the forgiveness of your sins, unto everlasting life. Amen.

§ 12

The communion being finished, the pastor shall say:
Oh give thanks unto the Lord, for he is good: Hallelujah.
The congregation responds:
And his mercy endureth forever: Hallelujah.
Then the pastor says the following collect:

We give thee thanks, O gracious God, our heavenly Father, because Thou hast refreshed us with these Thy salutary gifts; and we humbly beseech Thee to strengthen us, through the same, in faith toward Thee, and in fervent love toward one another, through Jesus Christ our Lord and Savior. Amen.
Receive the blessing of the Lord.
The Lord bless thee and keep thee, etc. Amen.
In the name of the Father, and of the Son, and of the Holy Ghost. Amen.

Chapter V. The Burial of the Dead

[This form is much more extended than what occurs in later editions.]

Note: Both copies, Jacob van Buskerk's and Peter Muhlenberg's, have forms for baptism and for the marriage ceremony taken from the *Prayer Book* of the Church of England. The Muhlenberg copy also has a German translation of the morning prayer and the form for marriage as found in the *Anglican Liturgy*.

APPENDIX IV

Constitution of St. Michael's Church, Philadelphia, 1762[1]

We, the subscribers, the lawfully called Pastors, Trustees, Elders, Vorsteher and communicant members of the German Evangelical Lutheran Congregation of St. Michael's Church, acknowledge and bind ourselves to the following Church and School Constitution.

Chapter I. Of the Pastors

1. The present living pastors, and their successors regularly called, shall preach the Word of God, as given by the Apostles and Prophets, and in accordance with the Unaltered Augsburg Confession, publicly, purely, briefly, clearly, thoroughly, and to edification. They shall also have liberty on weekdays, or in the evening to hold meetings in the church or school for edification, admonition and prayer, as their circumstances and strength allow; and in addition, in accordance with the command of Christ their Master, take most diligent care that the Word of God be freely sown, as living seed, and that the congregation be directed to true repentance of heart, living faith, and the power of godliness, unto their soul's salvation.

2. The regular Pastors, as faithful stewards of the mysteries of God, shall, at proper times, administer the Holy Sacraments to those who apply for them in the appointed way, and who are fit, worthy and well prepared to receive them, at least in so far as external evidence shows; but they shall also have liberty, to be exercised conscientiously, not by reason of sinful passion of whatever kind, but according to the rule of the divine Word, to exclude from the Holy Supper, and from standing as sponsors at Baptism those who spiritually live in grievous sin and transgression, contrary to the salutary doctrine of our Lord Jesus Christ, or who by undisputable evidence are convicted thereof, until they have amended.

3. They shall not hesitate, when possible, to visit the sick, as soon as they have information and it is requested of them; at which time they shall use the Word of God for instruction, admonition, awakening, edification and comforting; and when the sick have been thus prepared and

[1] The original German text is recorded in Hallesche Nachrichten, II, pp. 435-41. As far as is known, there is only one *summary* translation into English by Beale M. Schmucker in *Lutheran Church Review*, Vol. VI, pp. 219-24.

are found worthy, they shall be strengthened by receiving Holy Communion; and thus prepare them for a blessed departure from this life.

4. They shall especially have regard to the instruction of the young, have supervision of the regular School and the School Teacher as well as the Church Library; arrange for a sound program of instruction and examinations; and as far as possible, visit the schools diligently, encourage the young to become firmly grounded in the Word of God, the Catechism and the other approved text books, and in the knowledge of the Way of Salvation and the Christian Life, as well as in knowledge useful to good citizenship.

5. They shall preside at the annual *Kirchenrechnung*, and at all meetings of the church council, and at the election of officers, and see to it that the procedure and the decisions are in a Christian spirit, and that the elections of Trustees, Elders and Vorsteher are in the best interest of the congregation.

6. They shall not absent themselves from the annual general church meeting or convention of the regular ministers, without the most urgent necessity and the weightiest reasons, but willingly attend, and also assist as much as possible in serving vacant congregations connected with the meeting, until the vacancy in said congregations has been filled.

7. They shall themselves discharge the duties of their office in Church and School as faithful stewards, as God may give them health and strength, and not have any minister or student take their place, who has not been examined duly and called and ordained in accordance with our Evangelical Church government. If, however, a pastor is unable to serve his parish because of prolonged illness or because of other unavoidable circumstances known to the parish, the other pastors [of the United Congregations] shall be asked to help him as much as possible, without neglect to their own parishes. It is not in conflict with this rule that our regular ministers should invite another of rightfully called ministers connected with us, when visiting them, to preach for them, to the encouragement of fellowship, in conformity with the rule for a mutual life of pastor and congregation, as given by Christ in Matthew 7:12.

8. If a pastor of our congregation, should give occasion for serious offense, scandal or injury to the congregation, either in doctrine, or in life and conversation, or by violation of this church constitution; then the degrees of admonition shall be impartially followed, in the manner here described: (1) The Elders, or two-thirds of them, shall lay before such Pastor, with gentleness, the offense in doctrine or life which may have been evident, or which shall have been sustained by two or three indisputably credible witnesses, and if he prove to be guilty, admonish him to amendment. (2) Should this avail nothing, the whole Church Council shall invite the nearest Pastors of the United Congregations to meet at a convenient place, and in their presence renew the admonition. (3) Should this also fail of the desired end, the matter shall be considered at a special meeting of the United Ministerium, or at the Annual

APPENDIX IV 299

Meeting, if it admits of such delay, and there be thoroughly examined, and the Minister, if found to be guilty, and offending, shall be suspended from his office and the benefices, and a full account thereof be published. The vacant parish shall be taken care of by the other United Pastors until said vacancy has been filled.

9. The election of a Pastor shall be held in the following manner: The whole Church Council shall consult with the older Pastors of the United Congregations, and carefully deliberate on this important matter and take note of the grace, gifts and experience of the several pastors, and at successive sessions impartially consider which one would best suit the vacant congregation, and at the same time would be willing to accept the call. When they agree upon some one as suitable for the congregation, they then invite him to preach a trial sermon, or as a visitor, and several Sundays or other days afterward, they shall ask the communicant members of the congregation for their opinion, or their vote may be sent in writing to the Church Council, whether they desire to receive and acknowledge him as their pastor or not. Should two-thirds of the whole Church Council and two-thirds of the communicant members agree in approving the election, he shall be called. Should there be no one in the American Lutheran Ministerium who suits, and is willing to accept a call, the Church Council shall have full liberty, with the consent of the congregation, and of the United Ministerium, as they may deem best, to write to some godly Reverend Consistorium, or Ministerium, of the Evangelical Lutheran Church in Europe, interested in the extension of the Kingdom of Christ, and call one or more pastors, on condition that they be duly examined, rightfully ordained, pure in the Evangelical doctrine, and edifying in life and conversation, as becomes their doctrine.

10. Pastors and workers in Church and School, who perform their duties according to the grace of God and their several abilities, should according to the command of Christ and His Word, be supported by the congregations they serve. Such support enables them to give all the more diligence to the work of their calling, since they have no need of seeking financial support in some other way.

11. In the Public Worship, the administration of the Holy Sacraments as well as all other ministerial acts and ministrations, the Pastors shall conform to the Agenda and usage, which have been introduced, until such time as the United Ministerium and the congregation shall deem it necessary and profitable to make a better.

CHAPTER II. OF THE EXTERNAL GOVERNMENT OF THE CONGREGATION

From a very modest beginning in 1743, our congregation has grown rapidly from year to year, while at the same time the first pastors have solicited a number of loyal and cooperating members who have been constituted Trustees and Elders, and together they have promoted the best welfare of the congregation. As the years have passed and the membership has increased, there has been a repeated and growing demand for an external form of church government suitable to needs of this land. In consideration of this situation, and after mature deliberation, the following rules have been prepared for Pastors, Trustees, Elders and Vorsteher, in their governing the congregation.

1. The congregation shall, by virtue of this new constitution, have the perpetual right and liberty, to elect and confirm, in Christian order, by a majority of votes, the officers and ministrants necessary for the congregation.

2. The Church Council of the congregation shall hereafter consist of the Trustees,[2] six Elders and six Vorsteher, regularly elected or confirmed by the congregation.

3. Temporary provision for surviving Trustees. These shall hold office until this constitution is adopted and new Trustees have been elected and duly installed.

4. The method of election of Elders shall be as follows: (1) The whole Church Council shall assemble on the day before the election, shall select from the members who have subscribed to this constitution, according to their best judgment, impartially, without respect of persons, eighteen worthy Christian men of good repute, whose names shall be distinctly written down and be presented to the congregation at the election. (2) At the election the congregation present shall have the right and liberty to elect, by a majority of votes, six Elders out of the eighteen persons presented. These six Elders shall be presented to the congregation by the Pastors at the next public service, be reminded of their duties, and their names be entered in the Church Record. (3) The aforesaid six Elders continue in office for three years, God willing, if they demean themselves as becomes their office; but the congregation shall also have the liberty to re-elect them, if they consent to re-election.

5. As regards the office of the Vorsteher, it shall be as heretofore, except that there shall be six, instead of four, of whom one-half go out of office after serving two years, and new ones are to be elected in their place, in the same manner as is prescribed in § 4 for the election of Elders. The Vorsteher also shall be presented publicly to the congregation by the Pastors, be reminded of their duties, and thanks be returned to those who go out of office.

Should any person elected as Elder or Vorsteher, decline, without sufficient reason, to accept the weighty office, he shall not go free without paying a considerable donation into the treasury; and then the person who received the next highest number of votes shall be presented. If the vote for several persons be a tie, the Church Council shall decide the case.

6. In the above described manner the Church Council consists of Trustees, Elders and Vorsteher.

7. When any important and weighty matter arises in the congregation,

---

[2] The Pastors were Trustees. In 1791 the Church Council was made to consist of the Pastors, Elders and Vorsteher, the Trustees being omitted. Schmucker in *Lutheran Church Review*, VI, page 221.

APPENDIX IV

of whatsoever kind, whether within or without the church, whether it concerns the parsonage or the school house, the church yard or the burial place, it shall not be decided by the Pastors alone, nor by the other Trustees alone, nor by the Elders alone, nor by the Vorsteher alone; but it must be carefully and well considered by the whole Church Council, and be approved by at least two-thirds of their whole number, and after that be laid before the whole congregation, and be approved by two-thirds of the communicant members of the congregation, especially when it demands contribution from the members. For these purposes, in such weighty matters, the whole Church Council shall be publicly invited to meet, and no member shall absent himself without sufficient cause, and no decision shall be valid or dare be executed, which has not been approved and taken by two-thirds of the members, entered in the Record and subscribed by their signatures, to the end that all occasion for strife may, as far as possible, be avoided.

8. The duties of the ruling Elders are, among others, these: (1) They shall endeavor, by the grace of God, to set a good example, as well to their own households as to the congregations, by a Christian life and conversation. (2) Take care, with the Pastors, that the Evangelical doctrine and the Christian discipline be maintained and perpetuated in the congregation. (3) That the debts of the congregation, both principal and interest, be decreased and removed, by payments from the treasury and by generous gifts, in the most advantageous manner. (4) That the Ministers of the Word in the congregation be supported. (5) That the account of all receipts and expenditures be carefully kept, be submitted to the whole Church Council on the day before the annual congregational meeting, be examined, approved and subscribed to by the Trustees, and there be publicly laid in full before the congregation at the meeting, and be entered in the Record. (6) They shall attend the school examinations, and by several deputies, to be elected by the Church Council from their number, be present at the annual meeting of Synod, and in all other matters aid in promoting the welfare of the congregation.

9. The duties of the Vorsteher are, among others, these: (1) They shall set an honorable Christian example to the congregation. (2) They shall render all necessary aid at the public and special services of worship and in the administration of the Lord's Supper, especially at the Kinderlehre and in the visitation of the sick. (3) They shall gather the offerings, keep an account of the same, and pay them over to the Elders as often as they may deem necessary to the welfare of the congregation. (4) They shall maintain good order at the services of public worship. (5) Should they find disorder, discord, or occasion of offense in the congregation, they shall endeavor to remove them, or report them to the Church Council, that remedies may be applied in time. (6) They shall collect the pew rents, and the charges for burial places. (7) They shall give notice to the Elders of special meetings of the Church Council, attend all meetings of the Council and especially the annual meetings to prepare and present

the financial accounts, give in beforehand their own accounts, and help to decide when any important matter is to be determined or adopted.

10. And inasmuch as church offices and ministrations in the country, although before God weighty and important, are yet considered contemptible by the ignorant and evil-minded, and are therefore exposed to many unfavorable criticisms and suspicions, when administered as God's Word directs; therefore, no complaint against Pastors, Trustees, Elders or Vorsteher shall be entertained, unless sustained by two or three credible witnesses, 1 Tim. 5:19. If, however, real offenses and transgressions, as Gal. 5:19-21; 6:1, become evident in the case of one or other, which may God avert, the whole Church Council shall appoint an impartial committee, and through them examine the case, and pursue the grades of admonition, as Christ has commanded, without respect of persons.

Chapter III. Of the Members of the Congregation

1. Whoever would be a regular member of our Evangelical Lutheran congregation of St. Michael's Church, have a vote at elections, have part in the rights of membership and hold office therein; must, in accordance with Christ's command, so far as external evidence shows: (1) Be baptized. (2) Receive the Lord's Supper. (3) Not live in open works of the flesh, Gal. 5:19. (4) But lead a Christian life, and not be engaged in any disreputable occupation. (5) Contribute, according to ability, to the support of church and school, and of the laborers in the same, so long as there is need, be it little or much, though it were only a cup of cold water. (6) Be subject to Christian order and discipline, and allow himself to be corrected in brotherly love, when he does wrong. (7) And, next to God and the government, so conduct himself toward the faithful Pastors and elected officers of the congregation, that they may administer their office with joy and not with grief.

2. Whosoever fails in the aforesaid points, or in any of them, wilfully and of purpose, and will not by the grace and mercy of God correct his faults after the degrees of admonition have been observed, nor will be subject to Christian order, he cannot and shall not be a member of our Evangelical Lutheran congregation, and he shall have no right or share in its privileges, still less have right to vote or to hold office.

3. In case anyone of the communicant members of the congregation, should through the deceitfulness of sin and of Satan, fall into gross sin, or open works of the flesh, which may God avert, and should such offense be established by credible and incontestible evidence, then shall he: (1) Be privately admonished by the Pastor and be counselled to true repentance and reconciliation through faith. (2) Should this not avail, he shall again be admonished by the Pastor, in the presence of the Elders and the Vorsteher. (3) Should this fail, he shall be excluded from the congregation, in the presence of the Church Council or by its action, and he shall have neither part nor will, until by the goodness or the severity of God, he has been led to repentance and ask forgiveness of

the congregation for the offenses committed, which shall be done through the Pastor, without mention of the name. In such cases he shall be received again and acknowledged as a member, if his life and conversation prove the repentance and amendment to be sincere.

* * *

This constitution as a whole and in all its parts, shall be held inviolate in our Evangelical Lutheran congregation of St. Michael's Church and dependencies, and shall hold good and continue in force, until the whole Church Council and congregation, or at least two-thirds of both, to wit, of the Council and of the communing members, shall deem it necessary and useful to amend, or to add, or to exclude anything in the same; all of which is certified by our signatures; done at Philadelphia, October 18, 1762.[8]

[8] This constitution was widely used in Pennsylvania, Maryland and Virginia. It became the basis for constitutions used by congregations of the General Synod. It has some marks of Reformed influence, especially in the provision of Elders. A German version of this constitution is found in Chr. O. Kraushaar, *Verfassungsformen der Lutherischen Kirche Amerikas*.

APPENDIX V

CONSTITUTION OF THE MINISTERIUM OF THE EVANGELICAL LUTHERAN CHURCH OF NORTH AMERICA IN FORCE IN 1781[1]

CHAPTER FIRST
OF THE NAME AND THE FUNCTIONS OF THE FRATERNAL ASSOCIATION OF THE LUTHERAN MINISTERS OF NORTH AMERICA

We, Evangelical Lutheran Ministers of North America, who, by subscribing our names to this Constitution, do hereby declare ourselves an organized body, and, for the sake of establishing the Kingdom of Christ, whose we are and whom we serve, which can only be accomplished by unity (combined effort), and who never mean to consider ourselves otherwise, call this our Mutual Association, "An Evangelical Lutheran Ministerium in North America," and every meeting, "a Synodical Meeting."

CHAPTER SECOND
OF THE PRESIDENT OF THE SYNOD

§ 1. The Synod has (elects) a President who is to be respected and honored, by all its members, as one having the oversight, both during the meetings of the Synod and at other times.

§ 2. He is elected annually during the meeting of Synod by a majority of votes. The office can be filled by the same person who held it during the previous year, as often as Synod sees fit.

§ 3. The President announces the meeting of Synod, designating the time and the place, if these have not been determined beforehand by resolution of Synod, and presides during the meeting. In case the Synod have already determined the time and the place of the next meeting, the President still directs attention to it by a circular letter issued six or eight weeks in advance. Both the regular and the special meetings are included under the synodical meetings which he announces.

§ 4. If at the time of any meeting of Synod, the President should be sick, or absolutely prevented from being present, the Synod, immediately at the opening of the meeting, elects another President.

§ 5. In case of a tie, the President has the casting vote.

§ 6. Under the supervision of the President, and in accordance with his direction, the Secretary keeps the minutes and reads them publicly in the Convention. In like manner, the President has letters read, written, dis-

[1] This translation is from *Documentary History of the Evangelical Lutheran Ministerium of Pennsylvania and Adjacent States, 1748-1821.*

patched, and similar things done, by the Secretary; and, in case of necessity, he has them read also by others.

§ 7. The President, at each meeting of Synod, lays before it the most important matters transacted at special meetings, and reported to him concerning them.

§ 8. The President puts all motions presented to the meeting, or causes it to be done by the Secretary in accordance with his directions, signs them and hands them to the delegates of the congregations, records them carefully, or sees that it is done by the Secretary. When this has been done, he likewise puts his signature to the entire transactions of a Synodical meeting in the Protocol. To this signature the Secretary afterwards appends his.

§ 9. The President takes the vote on all matters to be decided, stating the motions offered so plainly that every one may know what the subject is on which he is to vote.

§ 10. The President appoints committees to carry out measures determined upon, but not for determining them.

§ 11. The President is required to receive the motions of each and every member, and submit them for consideration and decision.

§ 12. The President is not allowed to take the sense of the house until he perceives that there is no further speaking on the question to be decided.

§ 13. It is the duty of the President to see that the right of every one to express his views freely and fully, be maintained. He is also required to insist strictly upon good order, so that no one improperly interrupt another.

§ 14. The act of Ordination, in which he is assisted by other ministers, belongs to the President. It dare not be administered except in open convention, and to none other than a candidate received as one to be ordained by a majority of votes.

In a case of necessity, a special meeting may be called by the President for this purpose.

§ 15. That which applies to Ordinations applies also to the granting of a license. The President is allowed to do it only in open convention and by permission of the majority.

For further directions as to ordination and licensure, see further on.

§ 16. The President appoints the examiners of the candidates to be examined, or of the licentiates, but every member retains the privilege of examining afterwards in proper order.

§ 17. The President admonishes the brother who errs several times, privately. If this be without effect, he is reported to the Synodical meeting, which investigates and decides the matter.

CHAPTER THIRD
OF THE SECRETARY OF SYNOD

§ 1. The Secretary of Synod is elected annually from among its members, during the meeting of Synod, after the election of the President.

§ 2. The Synod must continually take care that the fittest and most learned persons are put into this office, since many of the documents which they have to prepare will be regarded as the work of the entire Synod, and, therefore, require thoroughly capable persons to frame them.

§ 3. If the Synod, perchance, should have found the one having held the office previously specially adapted to it, it is not necessary, on this account, to pass him over in the election.

§ 4. Upon request of the President, the Secretary writes letters, draws up agreements and fills out certificates of licensure, ordination, etc.

§ 5. The Secretary, in the name of the Synod, after the President has signed his name, attests all transactions recorded by his signature.

§ 6. The Secretary has charge of the Synodical seal and attaches it to such papers as require it. But in every instance the President's signature must be attached beforehand.

CHAPTER FOURTH
Of Reception Into the Ministerium

§ 1. All those who set their names to this Constitution, and to the agreement (pledge) to be mentioned further on, are members of this Ministerium. As a continued remembrancer, and for the glory of God in the Future, when a more imposing array of members of Synod may probably be presented, our present paucity is here at the same time freely acknowledged.

The following membership belong to our Synod:

Henry Melchoir Muhlenberg (†1786)
Nicholaus Kurtz (dec'd) (1794)
Ludwig Voigt (dec'd) (1800)
Wilhelm Kurtz (†1798)
Joh. Andr. Krug (dec'd) (1796)
George Bager (dec'd) (1791)
Emanl. Schulze (dec'd 1808)
Heinrich Helmut (dec'd) (1825)
Friedr. Schmidt (†1813)
Joh. C. Kunze (†1807)
Carl Fried Wildbahn (dec'd) (1804)
Jacob V. Buskirk (dec'd) (1800)
Christian Streit (dec'd) (1812)
Heinrich Moeller (†1830)
Joh. G. Jung (dec'd) (1793)
Heinrich Muhlenberg, Jr. (†1815)
Joh. Christian Lepps (dec'd)
Conrad Roeller (dec'd)
Samuel Schwerdfeger (dec'd) (1788)
Jacob Goering (†1808)
Daniel Lehman (†1810)

Daniel Schroefer (dec'd)
Friedr. Ernst (†1805)
Daniel Kurtz (†1856)
Friedr. Melsheimer (†1814)
David Schaeffer (†1836)
W. Frederici ———

§ 2. In those cases in which important questions of conscience and points of doctrine are to be investigated and decided, only ordained ministers have a vote, although licensed candidates, are, in other respects, regular and full members.

§ 3. The minister who desires the reception of a candidate, and consequently the granting of a license to him, is required to present him to the President, giving the same account of the educational advantages enjoyed by the candidate, and of his conduct as observed by him, appending some proof of his capacity, viz., a sermon or theological treatise, which he certainly knows the candidate to have prepared himself. In this he makes written application to the President to introduce and present such candidate to the next Synodical Convention.

§ 4. The candidate having been presented to the assembled Synod by the President, and the most important incidents in the candidate's career having been cited, he withdraws until called again. The President then asks whether any one objects to the reception of the candidate. If two-thirds of those present vote for him, he is received.

§ 5. Those who are sent by a religious establishment, as the Orphans' Home at Halle, or by any Evangelical Consistory of any locality in Europe whatever, upon request, are to be deemed unworthy of reception only if objections made to their reception be declared weighty and well-founded by a majority of the votes.

§ 6. Every member signs this article or agreement:
"I, the undersigned, called as a minister of the Gospel in North America, promise before God and my Chief Shepherd, Jesus Christ:

"1. That as long as I serve any congregation in North America, I will not declare myself independent of the Evangelical Ministerium, whose Constitution I have signed; and that I will obey its rules and regulations.

"2. That I will, as God gives me strength, faithfully obey the Constitution of the Ministerium subscribed by me, use the Liturgy to be introduced, and comply with the resolutions of the Synod as long as I exercise the office of a minister in North America; and that, as much as in me lies, I will promote the observance of the Constitution of the Ministerium by others.

"3. That I will not absent myself from any meeting of Synod without urgent necessity.

"4. That I will never consent to receive any minister whom I know to be unfit because of a lack of attainments, or of an immoral life, into our Synodical connection.

"5. That, unless for well-founded reasons, and impelled by conscience, I will never oppose the reception of any candidate or minister into the Ministerium.

"6. That I will not rudely refuse reproofs from the President, but even in case of an inward consciousness of innocence I will submit to them; and in case of an abiding consciousness of having been wrongly judged by the President, I will appeal to the judgment of the Synod, with whose decision I expect to be satisfied; and I will neither denounce the President nor treat him unkindly because of his censures.

"7. That in case two-thirds of the Synod should declare me no longer worthy to be a member of the Evangelical Ministerium of North America, and consequently to have a seat and vote in a Synod, I will then give up my congregations, and no longer exercise the functions of a minister in any of the United Evangelical Lutheran Congregations of North America."

To this the signature is to be attached.

§ 7. Every candidate and every minister about being received, after having entered into this compact, also attaches his name to this Constitution of the Ministerium. Provision is on this account to be made that every minister be furnished with a copy thereof, so that he may always know precisely to what he has obligated himself; and, further, that the President always have at hand, among the other documents of Synod, a copy for general use, to which every one received now or hereafter may attach his name.

§ 8. Whenever a candidate has received his training from one of the United Ministers, that one, and none other, must be the one to recommend him to the President for reception.

CHAPTER FIFTH
Of the Meetings of the Synod and the Business Transacted Thereat

§ 1. At least one meeting of the Synod must be held annually. If the Ministerium itself has not determined with reference to the time and place of its next meeting, that is left to the President.

§ 2. No one of the brethren associated together is allowed to absent himself without the most urgent necessity, and should a case of such urgent necessity occur, a written excuse must be sent in.

§ 3. Whoever does not appear personally, or else present a written excuse, is called to account therefor by the President at the next meeting of the Synod. This must be done publicly, in the presence of the entire Synod.

§ 4. Whoever does not appear personally, or else present a written excuse, for three successive meetings, shall be expelled from the Association, and shall be regarded as one who has violated his pledge, unless sickness should each time have prevented him from writing, and consequently he have caused himself to be excused verbally.

§ 5. The Pastor loci provides in advance lodgings for the ministers, and for the keeping of their horses. If there should be any for whom

APPENDIX V

he could not make arrangements, they are to be entertained at the expense of the common Treasury, or by contributions.

§ 6. The ministers are required, if possible, to be at the place of the meeting in good time on the day preceding, so that the President may be able to assign the sermons appropriately. No minister is justified in leaving before the actual closing of the Synod by the President, unless a case of great urgency should constitute it an exception.

§ 7. The ministers dine together in a body at the expense of the Treasury as long as the meeting continues. The President each day appoints two to offer at some length prayers in behalf of all the congregations, one before, and one after dinner. Such as do not preach are appointed to offer these prayers. In the morning and evening, the ministers take their meals at the place of lodging. This matter will be arranged as soon as the Synodical Treasury, which is to be provided for, will allow.

§ 8. The business sessions of Synod begin precisely at 9 A.M., and continue until 1 P.M.; and at 3 P.M. and continue until 6 P.M., unless when matters of special importance require an extension of time.

§ 9. At the place where the meeting of Synod is held, there shall be three services on Sunday and one on every week-day evening. In the country, the service is omitted on Sunday evening, and during the week it is held in the morning at 9 o'clock.

§ 10. The ministers open their business sessions with a hymn and prayer—in the afternoon with a prayer only. This opening prayer in the morning and in the afternoon is offered kneeling. The President appoints those offering these prayers. They are not to be the same persons to whom sermons have been assigned, or those who have already offered prayer. The last session of the second day is closed with prayer by the President.

§ 11. After the prayer, the President lays before the meeting a programme of all the matters to be acted upon. Every minister who has anything to add now announces it, so that it may be noted down.

§ 12. After completing the programme the Secretary, by direction of the President, reads the Minutes of the former meeting. After this reading some further time is given, both for the making of observations in regard to them, and also for the enlargement of the programme referred to in § 11.

§ 13. After the reading of the Minutes the next item is the presentation of the Annual Settlement, as soon as that matter has been properly arranged. At this point, receipts and expenditures are plainly set forth by the President, or, at his request, by the Secretary. After some incidental remarks have been made in regard to it, the principal items of expenditure for the coming year are determined as far as possible, and the account is signed by the President, Secretary, and some of the members of Synod present.

§ 14. After the rendering of the account, the Synod at once occupies itself with the business of the delegates of the congregations, those from the most distant points having precedence, and those living nearest waiting until the last.

§ 15. The President is required individually to grant the delegates of the congregations a separate hearing, but not decide what they present to them, for he is required to lay before the meeting all the items gathered from the delegates, having any bearing on their requests.

§ 16. The President is required to cause the Secretary to read all letters referring to congregational affairs received by him, either before or during the meeting of the Synod. It is self-evident that those communications are not here included, in which, perchance, certain congregations or church officers, regarding the President as a private individual, and as one of the most experienced ministers, ask special advice in doubtful matters.

§ 17. It is the President's duty to present publicly to the Synod those delegates desiring it, or even to have them called in at the request of the members.

§ 18. The President is required to see to it that every item be considered and discussed, and as soon as no further remarks are made concerning it, to select from the various comments and suggestions presented, that which seems to him most thoroughly adapted for its adjustment, and have it voted upon. If this be rejected by the majority, he takes the next best, or even that which now for the first time seems to himself the surest mode of adjustment, or what is now for the first time offered by some one else. While the vote is being taken, no further remarks are permitted, but for the expediting of the schemes proposed, a simple aye or no.

§ 19. In case the President and Secretary should have too much writing to do, in writing out and recording the transactions of Synod, it may, at their request, elect several assistant Secretaries, whose term of office continues only during the meeting. These must at all times be thorough scholars, except where mere copying of business transacted is to be done, when the best penmen are to be selected.

§ 20. In case a matter to be acted upon should seem too difficult to be decided at once, it can be postponed for further consideration, if the majority so decide, and the determining thereof deferred from the first day to the second, or to the third, or from one meeting to the next, one year hence, or from the regular meeting of Synod to the next special meeting, to the district to which it belongs, as the nature of the matter under consideration may seem to require.

§ 21. After finishing the business with the delegates, the remaining items of the programme are acted upon in the order in which they are recorded, whether they refer to congregational affairs, to matters of-conscience, for the decision of which the Synod generally appoints a committee of the oldest, most experienced and most learned ministers, who must sit during those remaining hours in which Synod is not in session, or in reference

APPENDIX V 311

to complaints on account of the doctrine and life of the brethren lodged with the President and presented by him.

The Synod always endeavors to so arrange the programme that congregational affairs may be considered first, then questions of conscience which may be presented, and finally the complaints entered.

That which is laid down in Chapter 4, § 2, and is there made of general application, holds with reference to decisions in respect to this latter point.

§ 22. In complaints brought against ministers the subject of investigation must refer to:

1. Positive errors opposed to the plain teachings of the Holy Scriptures and our Symbolical Books.
2. Works of flesh, Gal. 5:19 ff., and offense given thereby.
3. Faithlessness and slothfulness in the ministry, and, in case of a candidate, also in those matters which are known to be necessary for his further preparation.
4. Neglecting attendance upon the meetings of Synod.
5. Bitterness and strife of ministers among themselves.

§ 23. The process of investigation is this: The President distinctly presents the heads of charges to the Synod, hears the witnesses in its presence, then gives an opportunity for remarks pro and con, allowing every one to express his opinion as his final judgment in the matter. The President and the Secretary must be very careful to recognize that judgment which is heard most frequently, as the prevalent one.

§ 24. The effect resulting from the decision must be limited to the following points:

1. The accused person, against whom no two or three credible witnesses appear, and against whom there is no other evidence of probability, is acquitted, and regarded as one against whom no complaint was ever brought.
2. Whosoever is found guilty in matters not of too gross a character, either by evidence of strong probability or upon the declaration of two or three witnesses, is publicly reprimanded by the President in the presence of Synod, or if the one found guilty be not present, he is most earnestly admonished, by means of a written document, prepared in the name of the entire Synod. Others of the brethren also add a word of reproof verbally.
3. In matters of a graver nature, and which have occasioned offence, such as would be irrevocable in their nature, he who is found guilty in the manner above indicated, is excluded from the Ministerium.

The committee adjudicating the case renders its decision to that effect, but the decision cannot be carried into effect without the assent of two-thirds of all the members of Synod. But in case of the subsequent ratification by the above-named two-thirds of Synod—in which case those also who rendered the decision as a committee have a vote as well as ordained members of Synod, although the latter cannot serve on the committee—the sentence must be executed without fail.

The Synod cannot make the sentence pronounced by the committee severer, but it may be modified by the assent of two-thirds. To follow the intention in this instance closely, and to know in how far the sentence is to be modified, the President proceeds in this particular as has been indicated in this chapter, §18, with this difference, that that which the President submits to vote is not binding without having been endorsed by two-thirds. If none of the motions proposed and voted upon, should be able to secure the endorsement of two-thirds, the verdict of the committee stands.

§ 25. After the transaction of matters of the kind referred to in § 21, the assembled ministers confer with one another concerning the blessings attending their labors, or the difficulties met with in their sacred office, each one also giving a detailed report of baptisms, confirmations, burials, communicants. Absent members likewise transmit this information in their letters of excuse. At this point the diaries of the licensed candidates are likewise read.

§ 26. Whenever examinations, the granting of licenses, or ordinations of licensed candidates occur, these items of business are transacted immediately after the edifying conference as to official experiences and the reading of the diaries.

§ 27. Every candidate desiring to be received must first undergo a brief examination in the ancient languages and theology, and then only does he receive a license. Before the ordination, however, the licensed candidate submits himself to a stricter examination, in which written questions are answered also in writing. The former may be called a test; the latter, an examination.

§ 28. No license is allowed to remain in force longer than until the next convention of Synod. It can then be renewed, if deemed proper. "EXTENDED" will then be written underneath, with the day and date of the year, and, finally, the name of the President and the Secretary.

§ 29. Candidates who have received license are allowed to preach, to catechise, to administer the Holy Sacraments, but these acts dare not be performed in any congregations beyond those designated in the document named.

§ 30. That licensed candidate who is convinced that, by private application, he has advanced sufficiently to be able to undergo the examination referred to above in § 27 may, in a spirit of meekness, make known his desire to be ordained in open session, but never without the aforementioned conviction as to a knowledge of the ancient languages and theology. No one will in future be ordained without both these requirements, unless in a very extraordinary instance, or the most urgent necessity.

§ 31. Ordination is administered according to the circumstances of the case, either publicly in the Church or in Synodical Meeting, not outside

APPENDIX V 313

the Church, without the most weighty reasons; in fact, never in special conferences, unless it should have been committed to a committee by the entire Synod.

§ 32. The election of the President and the Secretary, together with the fixing of the time and place of the next meeting, all of which are decided by a majority of votes, constitute the close of the business.

§ 33. Last of all, the ministers dwelling close together in one county or district confer, in regard to special meetings or conferences to be appointed, concerning which the details may be determined in due time by resolutions of Synod. Whenever a special matter has been referred to a conference of that kind, such conference must be positively determined upon, and with the knowledge of all the others.

CHAPTER SIXTH
OF THE CONDUCT OF THE MINISTERS IN THEIR OFFICIAL AND OTHER RELATIONS

§ 1. Every minister must earnestly endeavor to introduce into his congregations a constitution which corresponds as nearly as possible with those already in use, and which must not conflict with the Constitution of this Ministerium in any point.

§ 2. Every minister professes that he holds the Word of God and our Symbolical Books in doctrine and life;[2] that he so exercises his office that he may stand before his Great Shepherd, rejoicing in the great Day of Judgment, as well as promises to remain forever worthy of the fellowship of the Evangelical Lutheran Ministerium of North America.

§ 3. Every minister uses the Liturgy which has been introduced.

§ 4. No minister is allowed to encroach upon another's office, under whatever pretext it may be, without the other's consent. In actually vacant congregations an ordained minister is allowed to preach and administer the Holy Sacraments as often as he pleases, provided this can be done without neglect of his own pastoral duties. So, too, every ordained minister is at liberty to give up his congregations at his discretion, and to move into other actually vacant congregations which purpose connecting with us: provided, he do not thereby interfere with any other connection, and, also, that the change, when made, be, in every instance, communicated to the President.

§ 5. No minister is allowed to conform himself to the world in his walk and conversation.

§ 6. Licensed candidates must carefully record their official acts in a diary, which is handed over at each meeting of Synod.

[2] In the revised Constitution of 1792 there is no allusion to any Lutheran symbolical book; and candidates are required, at their ordination, "to preach the Word of God in its purity according to the law and the gospel."

1.
2.
3. Nicolaus Kurz
4. Ludwig Voigt
5. John Andreas Krug
6. George Bager
7. Emanuel Schulze
8. Friedrich Schmidt
9. Heinrich Helmuth
10. Johann C. Kunze
11. Carl Friedrich Wildbahn
12. Jacob V. Buskirk
13. Christian Streit
14. Heinrich Moeller
15.
16. Johann Georg Jung
17. Heinrich Muhlenberg, Jun.
18. Johann Christian Leps
19. Conrad Roeller
20. Samuel Schwerdfeger
21. Jacob Goering
22. Daniel Lehman
23. Daniel Schroeter
24. Friedrich Ernst
25. Johann Michael Enterline
26. Danl. Kurz
27. Fr. Val. Melsheimer
28. F. David Schefer
29.
30.

INDEX

Abraham, 8, 9
Acrelius, Rev. Israel, 161
Acts, Book of, 24-29, 35, 38
Adiaphoristic controversy, 136
Adolphus, Gustavus, 136
Albany, 123, 155, 182
Andreae, Jacob, 2
Andreae, Johann Valentine, 97, 153
Anglican Church, 121
Anne, Queen of England, 171, 172, 175, 179
Antinomistic controversy, 91
Apostolate, 39
Arensius, Rev. Bernhard, 129, 133, 149
Argentine, 115
Aristotle, 90
Arnd, Johann, 96 (ftn.)
Athens, N. Y., 155
Aufklärung, 101
Augsburg Confession, 32, 129, 130, 131, 158
Augsburg Peace, 93, 95
Augustine, church father, 7 (ftn.), 88
Augustine, City of, 116
Auren, Rev. Jonas, 152, 189

Baptists, War of Independence, 254-255
Barth, Karl, 106
Bayonne, N. J. (Constable's Hook), 150, 155
Bergen, N. J., 128
Berkenmeyer, Rev. W. C., 129, 149, 179, 186, 189, 190, 195
Bethesda Orphans Home, Ga., 199
Bible, first cardinal principle, 8; private interpretation of, 72-73; supremacy of, 72-73
Birthplaces of America, 135
Bishops, in New Testament, 40-41
Bjork, Rev. Erick, 152, 164
Blommaert, Samuel, 137, 142 (ftn.)
Böhme, Jacob, 97
Bolzius, Rev. John Martin, 190, 191
Bordel, Jean du, 116
Bourdon, Pierre, 116
Brazil, 115
Brethren in Christ, 147
Brown University, 145, 218
Brunner, Emil, 106
Brunnholtz, Rev. Peter, 209
Buenos Aires, 115
Buskirk, Rev. Jacob van, 214

Cabot, John, 120, 142 (ftn.), 226
California, 117, 118
Calovius, Abraham, 96

Calvert, Cecelius, 145 (ftn.); George, 145 (ftn.); Leonard, 145
Calvinism, 168, 173
Calvin, John, 2 (ftn.), 168-169; attitude toward mysticism, 96 (ftn.); church-state, 80
Cameron, 10 (ftn.)
Canada, 117, 118, 185, 226-231
Canstein Bible Institute, 100
Capito, Matthew, 149
Caracas, 115
Carolina, North and South, 175, 190
Catholicism, essence of, 46-51
Champlain, 118
Charismatic persons, 43
Charleston, S. C., 190
Charles V, 115
Charles XI of Sweden, 152
Chartier, Guillaume, 116
Chile, 115
Christ Church, Philadelphia, 154
Christ Church, Upper Merion, Pa., 161
Christianity, essence of, 1; influence of, 1
Christiansen, Henrich, 123
Christina, Queen of Sweden, 141 (ftn.), 142
Christological controversy, 93
Church bell, gift of Queen Anne, 178-179
Church, Christian, 1-3; birthday of, 32; definition of, 32; doctrine, 37-39; false view of, 54-57; life of, 33-36; organization, 32, 39-45; visible, invisible, 15, 89; worship, 36-37
Church history, branches, 3-4; relation to interpretation, 7; relation to origins, 7; relation to personalities, 8; value of study, 4-6
Civilization, Oriental, 111; Western, 111
Clark, John, 145
Clayton, Rev. Thomas, 154
Clergy, versus laity, 48, 52-54
Cock, Peter, 144
Coligny, Admiral, 115, 116, 117, 227
Columbia University, 218
Columbus, Christopher, 113, 115
Comforters of the sick, 125, 158
Concord movement, 90-94
Confessional school, 105
Congregationalists, 121, 251-252
Connecticut, 122
Constable's Hook (Bayonne), N. J., 150, 155, 164, 189
Copernicus, 97
Council of Upsala, 130
Councils, General or Ecumenical, 52
Cranhook, Del., 150, 151

315

INDEX

Dartmouth College, 218
Deaconate, 40
Declaration of Independence, 244, 260
Delaware, 124, 133, 135, 138, 155, 162
Demarkation line, 114
Denton, Richard, 146
Dewey, John, 10, 11
Dibelius, Martin, 16 (ftn.)
Dieren, Rev. Johann Bernhard, 186, 189
Divine right of kings, 238
Document Q, 16-19
Dorcas, or Tabitha, 35
Dricius, Rev., 128
Dunster, Henry, 145
Dutch, contributions, 232-233; India Company, 123; Reformed, 123, 125; Reformed Church, 126; Reformed ministers, 132; West India Company, 123, 130, 131, 136, 137, 142
Dylander, Rev. John, 161, 164

East Camp, 178, 189
Eastman, Burton Scott, 16 (ftn.)
Ebenezer, Ga., 190
Eck, John, 2
Edict, religious toleration, New Sweden, 139
Education, colonial, 178; colonial Lutheran teachers, 209, 220; early Lutheran in America, 217-225; Orthodox emphasis, 96; Pietistic emphasis, 99
Edwards, Rev. Jonathan, 197, 198
Eliot, Rev. John, 122
Elizabeth, N. J., 165
Elk River, Maryland, 153, 155, 190
El Paso, 118
Emig, Nikolaus, 149
Enthusiasms, versus mysticism, 96 (ftn.)
Episcopalians, 120, 251
Episcopate, diocesan, 42-43; historic, 46-51; monarchical, 41
Ericksen, Leif, 112, 226
Ernesti, Johann, 102 (ftn.)
Esopus, N. Y., 128, 149
Eucharistic controversy, 92
European culture, 113
Evjen, John O., 127

Fabritius, Rev. Jacob, 129, 133, 151
Falckner, Rev. Daniel, 163, 165-166, 179, 186, 189, 200
Falckner, Rev. Justus, 129, 133, 154, 163-166, 179, 186, 189; contribution, 165 (ftn.); his catechism, 165; his parish, 164-165; personality, 165
Falckner's Swamp, 188, 200, 201
Federal Constitution, 113
Ferdinand, King, 113
Fine for preaching, 131
Finns, 148; method of burnbeating, 141 (ftn.); migration to America, 141-146; prominent leaders, 144; settled in Sweden, 141 (ftn.)
First Great Awakening, 196-200
First Lutheran ordination in America, 164
Five Albany Partners, 184
Fletcher, Governor, 183

Florida (Flowerland), 116, 120
Fogel Grip, 137
Form criticism, 16 (ftn.)
Fort Carolina, 117
Fort Casimir, 142, 143
Fort Christina, 138, 139
Fort Elfsborg, 189
Fort Hunter, 185
Fort Nassau, 141 (ftn.), 142
Fort Orange (Albany), 124, 128
Fort Trinity, 143
Fox, George, mystic, 96 (ftn.)
France, 113, 117
Francke, August Herman, 99-100
Francke, Gotthelf August, 172, 206
Frankfort Land Company, 164, 165
Freeman, Rev. James, 147
Frelinghuysen, Rev. Theodore J., 197
French in North America, 118-119

George I of England, 172, 239
George II of England, 172, 239
George III of England, 172, 239
George, Prince of Denmark, 171
Georgia, 121, 190
Gerhard, Johann, 96
Gerlach, John Christopher, 185
German Baptist Brethren, 147
German contributions, 233
Germanna settlement, 176
Germantown, Pa., 148
Giessendanner, Rev. John Ulrich, 191
Gloria Dei Church, Philadelphia, 153, 164
Godyn, Samuel, 142 (ftn.)
Graffenried, Christopher von, 175
Grant, F. C., 16 (ftn.)
Greenland, 112
Gronau, Rev. Israel Christian, 190, 191
Gutwasser, John Ernst, 128, 132

Hackensack, N. J., 128, 150, 155, 164, 182
Hacking, 11
Haeger, Rev. Frederick, 178
Halle, Institutions, 100; University, 100, 191, 198
Handschuh, Rev. John Frederick, 209, 210
Hanson, Alexander Conte, 265
Hanson, John, attitude toward Stamp Act, 262; birth and early education, 262; created National Seal, 266; first President, 265; first President of the United States in Congress Assembled, 261; in General Assembly of Maryland, 263-265; moved to Frederick, Maryland, 262-263; positions of trust and honor, 262-266; resolution of 1774, 263; settling the troubled land question, 264; Swedish Lutheran ancestry, 261; Thanksgiving Day proclaimed, 266; tribute paid by U. S. Congress, 265
Hanson, Peter Conte, 265
Hanson, Samuel, 265
Hanson, Walter, 265
Hansson, Matts, 144

INDEX 317

Harnack, Adolf, 16 (ftn.), 20, 21 (ftn.), 108
Hartwick Seminary, 224
Hartwig, Rev. John Christopher, 209, 210, 224-225
Harvard University, 115, 122, 218
Hausihl, Rev. Bernhard Michael, 230
Helmuth, Rev. J. H. Ch., 214, 224
Hendricksen, Cornelius, 142
Hendrick, the Indian, 184
Henkel, Rev. Anthony Jacob, 189, 200
Henry VII, 120
Heresies, 46
Herrmann, Wilhelm, 108
Higher or historical criticism, 106
Holgh, Rev. Israel Fluviander, 141
Holland, 126
Holm, Rev. John Campanius, 139, 140 (ftn.), 141
Holtzmann, Heinrich, 108
Holy Trinity Church, Wilmington, 152
Homer, 13 (ftn.)
Homo, 10-11
Hoofman, Martin, 149
Hooghkamer, Henrick, 139
House of Commons, 181
Hudson, Henry, 123
Hudson, N. Y., 173, 183
Huguenots, 115, 126
Humanism, 10
Hunter, Governor, 178, 181, 183, 184, 185
Hurons, 119

Iceland, 112
Incarnation of Jesus Christ, 12-13
Inner Missions, 100
Iroquois, 119

James, Epistle of, 35
James I of England, 121, 237
James Island, S. C., 148, 155, 190
James the Just, 33
Jamestown, Va., 121, 135
James, William, 11 (ftn.)
Jensen, Rev. Rasmus, 138 (ftn.), 227
Jersey City, N. J. (Bergen), 150, 155
Jesuit priests, 118
Jesus Christ, his resurrection, 19-25; Incarnate, 12-13; Messianic consciousness, 16-19; relation to the Word, 15; the Christ of history, 16-19
Jews, 126
Julicher, A., 108
Justification by faith, 8-9

Kaftan, Julius, 108
Kalmar Nyckel, 137
Kant, Immanuel, 14, 102 (ftn.), 103
Kattenbusch, Fr., 108
Keith, Governor, 185
Kelpius, Johannis, 154
Kepler, Johann, 96
Kieft, William, 124, 142
Kingston, N. Y., 155
Kling, Mans, 138 (ftn.)
Knoll, Rev. Michael Christian, 179, 189, 190, 194

Kocherthal, Rev. Joshua, 173, 174, 178, 179, 186, 189
Koester, Henry Bernhard, 154
Kraft, Rev. Valentin, 202
Krol, Sebastian Jansen, 124
Kunze, Rev. J. C., 214, 224
Kurtz, Nicolas, 209

Labrador, 120
Laity, versus clergy, 48
Lancaster, Pa., 188
Land grants, 183, 184
LaSalle, 118
Lassing, Peter, 149
Laudonniere, Rene de, 117
Leon, Ponce de, 116
Lessing, Gotthold Ephraim, 102 (ftn.)
Leuba, 10 (ftn.)
Lidenius, Rev. Abraham, 189
Lightfoot, Robert Henry, 16 (ftn.)
Lima, University of, 115
Livingston Manor, 182
Livingston, Robert, 178
Lock, Rev. Lars Carlson, 132, 141, 143, 144, 145, 151
Loofs, Fr., 108
Loonenburgh, N. Y., 128, 149, 155, 189
Louisiana, 118
Louis XIII, of France, 137
Lovelace, Governor, 173, 174
Ludwig, Christopher, 259, 268
Luther, Martin, 8, 9; attitude toward contemporary Humanists, 83-84; attitude toward mysticism, 81-82, 96 (ftn.); attitude toward radicals, 81-82; Augsburg Confession, 76-77; cause of divergent influences, 87; childhood and youth, 58-61; Christ-centered religion, 76; church named after him, 1-2; church visible and invisible, 84-86; dispute with Zwingli, 83; education, 60-70; on general education, 80-81; on marriage, 86-87; principles of reformation, 8-10, 72-75; relation to New Testament, 12-45; relation to Old Testament, 8, 9; religious convictions, 68-70; view on grace, 75-76; view on war, 84; views on church government, 79-80; views on education, 218-220; views on worship, 77-79
Lutheran, 126; ancestry, 111; churches in London, England, 172 (ftn.); confessional standards, 2, 94; contributions, 256-269; Gnesio-Lutherans, 91, 168, 169; "Heretics of Meaux, 2, 115; in Canada, 225-231; name of honor, 2; native Lutheran clergy, 214; nickname, 2; number of Lutherans in the world, 2; position in Protestant America, 2; preaching places, 189; War of Independence, 256 (ftn.); when term was first used, 1-2
Lutheranism, American, 1, 3, 111, 126; and tradition, 89-90; Canadian, 225-231; consistent Christianity, 1; contributions of, 158; Dutch, 126-127, 155-157, 160; English, 172; French,

115, 117; German, 148, 160, 233; Scandinavian, 126-127, 148; Swedish-Finnish, 135-145, 156-158, 160-163, 190, 220; the concord movement, 90-94; the mid-stream of Christianity, 1

Mahwah, N. J., 155, 165
Maine, 118, 190
Majoristic controversy, 91-92
Makemie, Rev. Francis, 146
Malander, Rev. Olaf, 189
Manhattan, 123, 124
Maracaibo, 115
Markoe, Abram, a man of marked ability for leadership, 266; a man of wealth, 266; Danish Lutheran, 266; forming the oldest U.S.A. military organization, 266-267; historic importance of his silk flag, 267; moved to Philadelphia about 1770, 266; originated idea of thirteen stripes in the American flag, 267
Maryland, 121, 152, 190
Massachusetts, 122
Massacre, Fort Carolina, 117
Matthai, Conrad, 154
May, Cornelius Jacobsen, 124
Mayflower, 122
May River, 117
McGregorie, Patrick, 150
Mediating school, 105
Megapolensis, Rev., 128
Melanchthon, Philip, 75 (ftn.), 96; on church tradition, 89-90; on education, 89-90; on Humanism, 90; on Scholasticism, 90
Melanchthonians, 91, 168-169
Menendez, Pedro, 117
Mennonites, 126, 146-147, 148, 154, 254
Mercantilism, 172, 239
Methodists, 255
Mexico, 114, 115; City of, 115; University of, 114
Mey of Hoorn, Cornelius, 142
Mey, Peter, 142
Michaelis, Johann, 102 (ftn.)
Michaelis, Jonas, 125
Michel, Franz Louis, 175
Middleburgh, N. Y., 189
Ministerial Revolution, England, 179
Minuit, Peter, 124, 137, 138, 142
Miquelon Island, 119
Mississippi, 119
Mohawk Valley, 183, 185
Moravians, 147, 254
Muhlenberg, Henry Melchior, 172, 189; attitude toward Revolutionary War, 260-261; birth and education, 204-205; call to America, 206; contributions, 214-216; dispute with Count Zinzendorf, 208; *ecclesia plantanda*, 208; first impressions and experiences, 207; forerunners in America, 200-203; influence, 214-216; ministry in Germany, 205; model constitution for a congregation, 212-213; on to Philadelphia, 207; organizing congregations, 208-213; preparing a Lutheran hymnary, 216; religious views, 214-216; synodical organization, 209-210; teaching in Germany, 205; trip to America, 206-207; visit to London, 206
Muhlenberg, Rev. Frederick Augustus Conrad, 258
Muhlenberg, Rev. John Peter Gabriel, 257
Munck, Jens Eriksen, expedition, 227
Murray, John, Universalists, 147
Mysticism, 96-98; deviation from Luther, 97-98; deviation from the Bible, 97-98; opposed to enthusiasm, 96 (ftn.)

Naturalism, 10, 101
Naval stores, term explained, 173 (ftn.), 181
Netherlands, 113
New Amsterdam, 124, 128, 135
New Bern, Va., 176, 190
Newburgh Lutheran Church, 179
Newburgh, N. Y., 149, 155, 174, 189
New Castle, 150, 151
New Haven, Conn., 122
New Jersey, 121, 178
New Mexico, 117
New Netherland, 123-135
New Plymouth, 121
New Providence, Pa., 188, 201
New South Sweden Company, 137
New Sweden, 124, 130, 131, 135, 143, 150
New Testament, 7
New World, 112
New York, 118, 121, 177, 182, 189
Nicolls, Richard, 133
Niessen, Christian, 149
Norse discovery, 112
North America, 112
North Carolina, 120
Numinous element, 7 (ftn.)
Nyberg, Rev. Lawrence Thorstonsen, 209

Old Testament, 7, 8, 9, 10, 12
Orange, William of, 169, 171
Ordination, first regular Lutheran in America, 164
Orthodoxy, 94-96
Osiandrian controversy, 92-93
Otto, Dr. Bodo, 259, 268
Otto, Rudolph, 7 (ftn.), 11
Oxentierna, Axel, 137

Palatinate, 166-171
Palatine Bridge, 185
Palatines, causes of emigration, 170-171; contributions, 169, 191-192, 233; homeland, 166-170; in Carolina, 175-176; in New York, 177-187; Large Immigration of 1709, 174-187; religious background, 166, 168-169; settlement in Ireland, 175; Small Immigration of 1708, 173-174; villages in Schoharie, 182 (ftn.)
Patroons, system of, 125
Paul, the apostle, 29, 34
Paulus, H. E. G., 102

INDEX

Pennsville, N. J., 189
Pennsylvania, 151, 178, 182, 188
Pennsylvania University, 218
Penn, William, 151, 152
Peru, 115
Peter, the apostle, 24-29, 33, 34
Philadelphia, Pa., 150, 161
Philippists, 91, 95 (ftn.), 168-169
Philipsburg, Tarrytown, 165
Philipse Manor, Yonkers, 165
Pietism, 98-100, 234
Pilgrim Fathers, 122
Piscatawny, 165
Plymouth, 122, 135
Pontoppidan, Erick, 127 (ftn.)
Port Royal, 117
Portugal, 113, 114
Pragmatism, 106
Presbyterate, 40
Presbyters in New Testament, 40-41
Presbyterians, 252-253
Priesthood of believers, 74
Princeton University, 218
Printz, Andrew, 152
Printz, John, 139-140, 142
Protestants, Alsatian, 117; first preachers in America, 116; French, 115; Hessian, 117
Puerto Cabello, 115
Puritans, 126
Purysburg, S. C., 191
Pyrelaus, Rev. John Christopher, 203

Quakers, 126, 146, 148, 154, 255
Quebec, 118
Quenstedt, Andreas, 96

Racoon, N. J. (Swedesboro), or "Trinity Parish," 153, 155, 161, 189
Raleigh, Sir Walter, 120, 142 (ftn.)
Ramapo, N. J., 189
Rambo, Peter, 144
Raritan Valley, 155, 165
Rationalism, 101-103
Redemption, 14
Reformed Church, origin, 169
Reimarius, Samuel, 102
Religion, never static, 88; revealed, 1
Resurrection theories, 20-25
Revolution, American, 237f.
Rhinebeck, N. Y., 182, 189
Ribault, Jean, 117
Richer, Pierre, 116
Riddle, Donald, 16 (ftn.)
Rio de Janeiro, 115
Rising, Johan, 142
Ritschl, Albert, 106-109
Ritschlian school, 106
Robinson, John, 121
Roman Catholic Church, 54-57, 253-254
Roman Catholicism, 115, 154
Roman-Dutch law, 124
Roman Empire, 113
Rosicrucians, 153, 155, 158
Rousseau, Jean Jacques, 102 (ftn.)
Rutgers University, 218

Sacraments, Baptism, 52; Lord's Supper, 52; Seven, 52
St. George's Church, Church Landing, 161
St. James' Church, Kingsessing, 161
St. Mark's Church, Middleburgh, 186
St. Matthew's Church, New York City, charter of 1664, 133; early location, 133-134
St. Michael's Church, Philadelphia, 212
St. Paul's Church, Schoharie, 185
St. Pierre Island, 119
Saddle River, N. J., 150, 155
Salvation, way of, 8, 9, 73-74
Salzburghers, 117, 206
Sandel, Rev. Andrew, 164
Sandin, Rev. John, 189
San Francisco, 118
San Juan, 118
Santiago de Cuba, 115
Santo Domingo, 114
Satisfaction, dogma on, 96
Scheff, William, 185
Schenectady, N. Y., 182
Schleiermacher, Friedrich Daniel Ernst, 11, 21 (ftn.), 96, 103-106
Schneemann, Hermann, 150
Schoharie Valley, 164, 182, 183, 185
Schrick, Paul, 128
Schultz, Rev. John Christian, 189, 201
Schute, Sven, 144
Schwenkfeldians, 147, 148
Scriptures, 1
Semler, Johann Salomo, 102
Seven Albany Partners, 184
Seven Years' War, 119
Society for Propagation of the Gospel in New England, 122
Society of Believers, 147
Society of Universal Baptists, 147
Socrates, 13 (ftn.)
Sommer, Rev. Peter Nicholas, 129, 185, 186
South America, 115
Southold Church, Long Island, 146
South River (Delaware), 123, 142, 143, 144
Spain, 113, 114, 117
Spanish Armada, 120
Spanish Missions, 114-119
Spanish settlements, 113-118
Speedwell, 122
Spener, Philip Jacob, 98-99
Spiring, Peter, 137
Springer, Charles, 152
States General, Holland, 124, 137
Steinmetz, Caspar, 150
Stille, Olof, 144
Stoever, Rev. John Caspar, Jr., 189, 201, 210 (ftn.)
Stoever, Rev. John Caspar, Sr., 189, 201
Stone Arabia, 185
Storr, Gottlob Christian, 102
Stumpff, Joachim, 137
Stuyvesant, Peter, 124, 132, 134
Swedes, 135-145, 148

INDEX

Swedish Church, 131, 139, 158
Synod of Dort, 132

Tarao, 115
Tennent, Rev. Gilbert, 197
Tennent, Rev. William, 197
Tinicum Island, 135, 140 (ftn.), 150
Tolstadius, Rev. Lars, 161, 189
Tories, 179
Torkillus, Rev. Reorus, 138
Toscanini, Arturo, on interpretation, 7 (ftn.)
Tranberg, Rev. Peter, 164, 189
Tranhook, Del., 150
Treutlen, John Adam, 267-268
Triebner, Christopher F., 259
Tübingen school, 102
Tulpehocken, Pa., 185, 188
Twiller, Wouter van, 124

Unitarian, 147
United New Netherland Company, 123
United States of America, 116, 118
United Swedish Lutheran Churches, 161
Universalist, 147
University of, Brown, 145, 218; Columbia, 218; Halle, 191, 198; Harvard, 115, 122, 218; Lima, 115; Mexico, 115; Pennsylvania, 218; Princeton, 218; Rutgers, 218; William and Mary, 121, 218
Upsala, Council of, 139, 158
Usselinx, William, 136, 137

Valencia, 115
Van Boskerk, Laurens Andriessen, 150
Van Hoesen, Nicolaus, 149
Van Loon, Jan, 149
Venezuela, 115
Verhulst, William, 124
Vermont, 118
Verneuil, 116
Verrazzano, Giovanni, 123 (ftn.)
Villeganon, 116

Vinland, 112
Virginia, 120, 121, 152, 190

Wagner, Rev. Tobias, 190, 210 (ftn.)
Waldoboro, Me., 190
Waldo, Samuel, 190
Walloons, 124
Wall Street, New York City, 125, 133
Walpole, Sir Robert, 239
Walrath, Gerhardt, 185
Washington, George, 147, 259, 269
Weigel, Valentine, 97
Weiser, John Conrad, Jr., 192
Weiser, John Conrad, Sr., 185, 186
Wellhausen, Julius, 108
Welserland, 115
Welsers of Augsburg, 115
West Camp, 178, 189
West Indies, 114, 115
Whigs, 175, 179
Whitefield, George, 198
Wicaco, 150, 151, 153, 161, 164
William and Mary, 159, 171
William and Mary College, 121, 218
Williams, Roger, 145
Wilmington, Del., 138
Winchester, Elhanan, 147
Wissahickon, Pa., 154, 158
Wolff, Christian, 102
Word of God, 15, 16
Wrangel, Rev. Charles Magnus, 161, 162

Yale University, 122, 218

Zabriskies, the, 150
Zetskoorn, Abelius, 132, 145 (ftn.)
Ziegenhagen, Rev. Frederick Michael, 172, 202, 206
Zimmermann, Johann Jacob, 154
Zinzendorf, Count Nicholas Ludwig von, disputation with Muhlenberg, 208; in Philadelphia, 202-203; relation to Muhlenberg, 207
Zion Lutheran Church, Loonenburgh, N. Y., 149
Zwingli, Ulrich, 169

www.ingramcontent.com/pod-product-compliance
Lightning Source LLC
Chambersburg PA
CBHW051628230426
43669CB00013B/2222

J'ai rencontré le pasteur Daniel Del Vecchio pour la première fois à la fin des années 1960. À cette époque, le Seigneur a utilisé le pasteur Daniel et sa femme, sœur Rhoda, pour commencer le travail d'implantation dans mon cœur du message du Seigneur, le message de la Grande Commission. Les toutes premières années ont établi le modèle et l'appel à la mission dans nos vies, et nous avons continué à former d'autres personnes pour saisir l'appel à la mission et à *aller* dans le monde entier avec le message de l'Évangile.

—Dr. Dennis Lindsay, Directeur et Président du Conseil d'Administration de Christ for the Nations, Inc., Dallas, Texas, qui a formé plus de cinquante mille étudiants à porter la Bonne Nouvelle du Christ à travers le monde.

Le pasteur Dan Del Vecchio et son ministère apostolique ont eu l'influence la plus profonde sur ma marche spirituelle. Il y a quarante ans, alors que j'errais à travers l'Espagne, le pasteur Dan est devenu un « père spirituel » pour moi, comme il l'a été pour des centaines d'autres de ma génération. Il m'a enseigné les valeurs véritables et éprouvées de la foi et du sacrifice, non seulement avec des paroles, mais en me les modelant au quotidien. Sa foi en action m'a, à son tour, inspiré à le faire pour les autres, et c'est pour cela que je suis devenu la personne de foi que je suis aujourd'hui.

—Dr. Daniel Lucero, Directeur Mondial Afrique et Nations Francophones pour l'Église Internationale de l'Évangile Foursquare et Président/Fondateur de l'Église Foursquare en France

En 1972, je faisais du stop à travers l'Europe. À Rotterdam, j'avais été invité à rejoindre un groupe d'amis hippies pour un voyage au Maroc. Après avoir passé quelques semaines à Marrakech, j'ai décidé de passer Noël en Espagne. Bien que croyant et enfant de prédicateur, j'avais beaucoup de questions. J'essayais vraiment de me trouver. Je suis venu à l'ECC pour le culte de la veille de Noël et, cette nuit-là, Dieu a bouleversé toute ma vie. Assis sur le banc du fond, j'ai reçu un appel clair pour consacrer le reste de ma vie au ministère à plein temps. Je suis profondément reconnaissant au pasteur Dan pour le rôle important qu'il a joué en influençant le cours de ma vie et de mon ministère.

—Dr. Wayne Hilsden et sa femme Ann se sont associés à un autre couple pour créer la plus grande communauté chrétienne de Jérusalem, King of Kings Community, et sont co-fondateurs de FIRM (Fellowship of Israel Related Ministries)